The Evolution of Business Knowledge

Edited by
Harry Scarbrough

OXFORD
UNIVERSITY PRESS

OXFORD

UNIVERSITY PRESS

Great Clarendon Street, Oxford OX2 6DP

Oxford University Press is a department of the University of Oxford.
It furthers the University's objective of excellence in research, scholarship,
and education by publishing worldwide in

Oxford New York

Auckland Cape Town Dar es Salaam Hong Kong Karachi
Kuala Lumpur Madrid Melbourne Mexico City Nairobi
New Delhi Shanghai Taipei Toronto

With offices in

Argentina Austria Brazil Chile Czech Republic France Greece
Guatemala Hungary Italy Japan Poland Portugal Singapore
South Korea Switzerland Thailand Turkey Ukraine Vietnam

Oxford is a registered trade mark of Oxford University Press
in the UK and in certain other countries

Published in the United States
by Oxford University Press Inc., New York

British Library Cataloguing in Publication Data
Data available

Library of Congress Cataloging in Publication Data
The evolution of business knowledge / edited by Harry Scarbrough.
    p. cm.
Includes bibliographical references and index.
ISBN 978-0-19-922960-4   ISBN 978-0-19-922959-8
1. Knowledge management. 2. Management information systems.
3. Information technology — Management. I. Scarbrough, Harry, 1955-
HD30.2.E946 2008
658.4'038—dc22   20077051457

Typeset by SPI Publisher Services, Pondicherry, India
Printed in Great Britain
on acid-free paper by
CPI Antony Rowe, Chippenham, Wiltshire

ISBN 978-0-19-922959-8 (hbk.)
     978-0-19-922960-4 (pbk.)

1 3 5 7 9 10 8 6 4 2

Contents

Contents

List of Figures

List of Tables

Notes on Contributors

Kenneth Amaeshi, Research Fellow at Warwick Business School, University of Warwick

Elena Antonacopoulou, Professor of Organizational Behaviour, Liverpool Management School

Charles Baden-Fuller, Professor of Strategy, Cass Business School, City University

Charles Booth, Principal Lecturer, Department of Strategy, University of the West of England

Mike Bresnen, Professor of Organizational Behaviour, Leicester University Business School

James Brown, Research Officer, Cass Business School, City University

David Citron, Professor of Accounting, Cass Business School, City University

Peter Clark, Professor of Organizational Theory, Queen Mary College, University of London

Timothy Clark, Professor of Organizational Behaviour, University of Durham

Nigel Courtney, Honorary Senior Visiting Fellow, Cass Business School, City University

Agnes Delahaye-Dado, Researcher, Queen Mary College, University of London

Mark Easterby-Smith, Professor of Management Learning, Lancaster University Management School

Boris Ewenstein, McKinsey and Company Inc., Berlin

Jason Ferdinand, Management School, University of Liverpool

Robin Fincham, Professor of Business Studies, Stirling University

Anna Goussevskaia, Fundacao Dom Cabral, Brazil

Manuel Graça, Lancaster University Management School and Assistant Professor, University of Porto

Christine Greenhalgh, Reader in Economics, St Peter's College, Oxford University

Mike Hales, Visiting Senior Research Fellow, Science and Technology Research Unit, University of Sussex

Karen Handley, Senior Lecturer, Learning and Teaching, Oxford Brookes University Business School

Gerard Hanlon, Professor of Organizational Sociology, Queen Mary College, University of London

Chris Hendry, Professor of Organizational Behaviour, Cass Business School, City University

Jo Holden, Researcher, Cass Business School, City University

Robin Holt, **Reader**, University of Liverpool Management School

Clive Holtham, Professor of Information Management, Cass Business School, City University

Richard Holti, Senior Lecturer in Human Resource Management, Open University Business School

Pushkar Jha, Lecturer in Strategy, Business School, University of Newcastle upon Tyne

Oswald Jones, Professor of Innovation and Entrepreneurship, Manchester Metropolitan University

David Knights, Professor of Management and Organizational Analysis, School of Management, Keele University

Hannah Knox, Research Fellow, ESRC Centre for Research on Socio-Cultural Change, Manchester Business School

Joseph Lampel, Professor of Strategy, Cass Business School, City University

Allan Macpherson, Senior Lecturer, University of Liverpool Management School

Sue Newell, Professor, Department of Management, Bentley College, Boston, USA, and University of Warwick

Ademola Obembe, Lecturer, Roehampton University, London

Damian O'Doherty, Senior Lecturer in Organizational Analysis, Manchester Business School, University of Manchester

Fatma Oehlcke, Researcher, Cass Business School, City University

Stephen Procter, Professor, School of Management, University of Newcastle upon Tyne

Maxine Robertson, Professor of Organizational Theory, Queen Mary College, University of London

Mark Rogers, Fellow, Harris Manchester College, Oxford University

Michael Rowlinson, Professor of Organization Studies, Queen Mary College, University of London

Graeme Salaman, Professor of Organization Studies, Open University Business School

Harry Scarbrough, Professor, Warwick Business School, University of Warwick

Georges Selim, Professor of Internal Auditing, Cass Business School, City University

John Storey, Professor of Human Resource Management, Open University Business School

Andrew Sturdy, Professor of Organizational Behaviour, Warwick Business School, University of Warwick

Jacky Swan, Professor of Organizational Behaviour, Warwick Business School, University of Warwick

Richard Thorpe, Professor of Management Development, Leeds University Business School

Joe Tidd, Professor of Technology and Innovation Management, Science and Technology Research Unit, University of Sussex

Theo Vurdubakis, Professor of Organization and Technology, Lancaster University Management School

Chris Westrup, Senior Lecturer, Manchester Business School, University of Manchester

Jennifer Whyte, Reader in Innovation and Design, School of Construction Management and Design, University of Reading

Joanne Jin Zhang, EPSRC Research Fellow, Cass Business School, City University

1

Introduction

This book provides an overview of the findings from an ESRC and DTI-funded[1] research programme investigating the 'Evolution of Business Knowledge' (EBK). The EBK programme brought together research teams from a number of UK universities in search of a better understanding of the role that knowledge and learning play in the evolution of business firms. In setting out on this research, EBK researchers were not claiming that the importance of knowledge and learning to business is a brand new discovery. From Frederick Taylor's attempt to develop a science of management through to the pioneering work of thinkers such as Penrose and Burns, it is evident that the knowledge-base of the firm could exert an enormous influence upon its strategic and structural development (Burns and Stalker 1961; Penrose 1959; Taylor 1998). Despite these important insights, however, the effort to understand and manage the contribution of knowledge to firm evolution has accelerated rapidly within the last decade or so, and the EBK research presented here can be seen as both building on and advancing this recent surge in interest.

It is possible to identify a number of different reasons for the growth in interest. From a management perspective, for example, the effects of the Internet and other globalizing forces are seen as sweeping away many of the traditional sources of competitive advantage, including firm location, superior technology, and access to capital. Equally, a policy maker might point to the development of the 'knowledge economy' and the macroeconomic shift in industrial activity and occupations that it brings. Both of these perspectives converge on the view that knowledge has become the most powerful engine of economic performance and competitiveness. The

[1] Economic and Social Research Council, Department for Trade and Industry, UK.

resulting consensus on the critical importance of knowledge and learning is reflected in a vast and still growing literature, which sprawls across a number of different academic fields.

The distinctive contribution that the studies presented here make to this literature comes from the way they cut across existing academic special-isms. Previous studies have tended to treat the domains of science and technology, management and organization, finance and accounting, as largely separate spheres. In contrast, the broader focus on business know-ledge adopted by the EBK programme shows how the explosion of work on knowledge and learning is intimately linked to growing competitive and policy pressures to break down the boundaries between science, business, civil society, and government (Etkowitz and Leyesdorff 2000; Lambert 2003). These changes demand new perspectives on the evolution of know-ledge that are not limited to particular domains, be it the diffusion of ideas or the management of R&D (Abrahamson 1996; Coombs 1996), but are able to embrace both the diversity and interdependency of the forms of knowledge developed and exploited by business.

Researching knowledge in a business context

This previous work provides an important backdrop for the studies pre-sented here. Its diversity represents both a resource, providing us with a rich vocabulary of types and constructs, and a problem, because it makes the comparison and consolidation of studies more difficult. This is espe-cially the case with the way researchers have developed different and competing interpretations of the concepts of knowledge and learning. There is not enough space here to engage with the epistemological debates that have raged around the definitions of knowledge applied in previous research (Roos and Von Krogh 1995; Spender 1998). What can be extracted from these debates, however, are the different concerns that researchers have brought to the study of knowledge in a business context. Three major concerns stand out as central to the patterns of researching and thinking that we see in this emerging field.

The first of these we can describe as a concern with *'resourcing'*—in other words, a desire to understand how different forms of knowledge come to act as a resource that organizations can draw on to perform more effi-ciently, effectively, innovatively, and flexibly. Drawing on roots in the fields of business economics and strategy, this view of knowledge as a crucial corporate resource was initially popularized in Nonaka's work on knowledge creation (Nonaka and Takeuchi 1995). Subsequent studies supplied numerous typologies of knowledge forms, establishing that knowledge was a multidimensional resource for the firm (Blackler 1995). Tacit knowledge, for example, was seen as an especially important competitive resource because other firms find it harder to imitate (Reed and Defillippi 1990). Equally, other writers, especially in the area of knowledge management, focused on the firm's ability to exploit its own knowledge-base. Here, the codification of knowledge was seen as crucial to effective exploitation (Stewart 1997).

A second major concern in the literature can be characterized as a focus on the *'organizing'* aspects of knowledge and learning. Here, studies draw more on organization theory and are especially concerned with the interplay between the creation and exchange of knowledge and the development of organizational forms and social relationships. Research shows that organizing, be it in the form of hierarchy, project teams, networks, or markets, does matter for the ways in which knowledge is created and exchanged (Foss 2007; Powell, Koput, and Smith-Doerr 1996). Some researchers have emphasized organizing as a response to the distributed nature of knowledge—that organizational coordination enables groups with different kinds of knowledge to collaborate together towards valued outcomes (Grant 1996; Tsoukas 1996). Others have stressed the role of organizing itself as a route towards creating knowledge. For example, over time repeated organizational activities become enshrined as 'routines', which the organization can deploy more or less flexibly to solve business problems (Nelson and Winter 1982).

A third concern, which runs through much previous work, is informed by studies of cognition and workplace ethnography. It places *'meaning'* in the foreground of the analysis. Knowledge is seen as bound up with the creation and sharing of meanings and identities within and between groups. Some authors here focus on knowledge as a way of making sense of organizational activities (Weick 2001). Other studies, especially those adopting what have been termed 'practice-based' (Nicolini, Gherardi, and Yanow 2003) or 'activity system' approaches (Engeström 1993), emphasize the situated nature of knowledge and learning within particular contexts. These studies sometimes use the term 'knowing' rather than knowledge to emphasize this intertwining with social practices and shared identities.

Figure 1.1 below provides a summary outline of these different concerns. Bringing them together figuratively, however, does not mean that they are easily reconciled. There are obvious tensions, for example, between seeing knowledge as a ready-made resource to be absorbed and transferred and

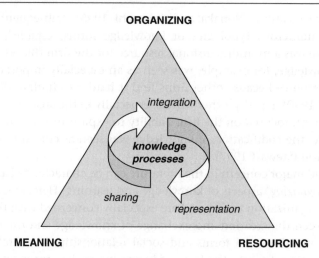

Fig. 1.1. Research on business knowledge—concerns and processes within the existing literature

seeing it as something that is highly context-dependent and emerging from practice. On the other hand, sometimes apparently opposing views are simply different levels of analysis being applied to the same phenomenon. Certainly, many of our existing constructs of knowledge and learning highlight the interplay between the major concerns outlined above. A term such as 'absorptive capacity' (Cohen and Levinthal 1990), for example, underscores the links between organizing and resourcing by showing how an organization's structure affects its ability to absorb and exploit external sources of knowledge. Conversely, the concept of an 'activity system' speaks to the implications of organizing for the understandings that people develop of particular situations (Engeström 1993).

The constructs employed within different studies are defined and reviewed in subsequent chapters. Touching on them briefly here, though, helps to underline the extent to which the EBK programme embodied a 'broad church' approach to the study of knowledge. As this indicates, the definitions of knowledge in use by the EBK research teams reflected a wide variety of theoretical concerns and industrial contexts addressed by the programme. Studies did not follow a unitary construct of 'business knowledge', but rather explored many different permutations of knowledge forms, actors, artefacts, and settings. Thus, some studies were concerned with the creation of knowledge, others with its application. Some were focused on the integration of different kinds of scientific and technical knowledge in a business context. Others explored the development of managerial and organizational forms of knowledge within firms. Collectively, however, they present the integration and application of heterogeneous forms of knowledge not as a special case, but as an intrinsic feature of mainstream business activities.

In part also, the broad church approach means accepting that diversity does not allow for ready comparison or consolidation across empirical studies. When empirical settings range from small businesses to large pharmaceutical firms, from top managers' strategic thinking to new enterprise technologies, there is clearly little scope for the direct empirical comparisons that might be possible for more narrowly focused groups of studies. On the other hand, there is value in the diversity of approaches exhibited here. This includes both a much greater ability to grasp knowledge as a multidimensional construct and an increased awareness of the interplay between such forms of knowledge and different institutional and organizational contexts. Thus, the studies presented here speak to multiple settings in which knowledge is produced, translated, and applied to business challenges.

The problem of 'embeddedness'

One of the important contributions that social science can make when set against existing managerial and policy perspectives is the ability to explore the 'embeddedness' of knowledge in social and institutional contexts (Giddens 1990; Sydow, Lindkvist, and DeFillippi 2004). This aspect tends to be overlooked in these other perspectives because they are mainly concerned with exploiting and spreading knowledge. For example, many managers are attracted by the promise of 'Knowledge Management' (KM) because it claims to enable the capture and sharing of knowledge within their organizations. However, research suggests that these KM systems rarely succeed; simply codifying knowledge into a system does not make it more practically usable for people working in a different time and place (Newell, Scarbrough, and Swan 2001). In short, the managerial pressures to exploit knowledge more intensively are often frustrated by its social embeddedness within particular contexts (Brown and Duguid 2001). New technologies fail to catch on, 'best practice' does not travel, and organizations find it hard to unlearn existing routines (Whipp and Clark 1986). In part, this notion of 'embeddedness' challenges the view that knowledge is an object that can be easily captured, transferred, and used—it reminds us that knowledge is 'sticky' (Zollo and Winter 2002).

But stickiness is only part of the story. The embeddedness of knowledge is also what makes it productive and hard to imitate as a competitive resource. New approaches have to become embedded in the way people work and interact to affect the dynamics of business performance. This is not to say that knowledge is always tied to the status quo or that it remains stuck within a particular context. Ideas, practices, and technologies can be disembedded from their context to create a potential for change and innovation. Some of these may fail because they cannot be absorbed or institutionalized within the existing knowledge and practices of an organization. Those which do catch on, however, seem to be those which can be disembedded from one context and embedded in another. Context, and the interplay between different contexts, continues to matter (Brown and Duguid 2001).

The significance of context and embeddedness, then, is to highlight the paradoxical qualities of knowledge. In one perspective, knowledge may be a tool that is crafted for a specific purpose. In another, it is an insight or idea that can be shared across time and space. Similarly, in one setting it may act as a barrier to change, in another as a powerful driver of innovation. Recognition of these paradoxical qualities has obvious implications for policy and practice. For example, it challenges the view of knowledge as a 'good thing' per se, and questions those approaches that focus solely on creating and spreading knowledge. Simply investing in the production of knowledge, be it in terms of R&D spend, links between academic science and business, or occupational skills development, seems unlikely to be effective on its own in enhancing business performance.

In terms of research, however, this insight suggests that we need to develop approaches that are better able to grasp these paradoxical qualities of knowledge. We can identify some of these approaches in common features of the different EBK projects. For one, these studies take context seriously. Thus, the need to research business knowledge within a particular context, be it an industrial sector or a national business environment, led many of these projects to adopt qualitative and interpretive approaches to research. By relating action (or inability to change) to the ways knowledge is shared and integrated within a defined situation, this approach produced important findings on the way differences in context shape knowledge and business performance.

A second strand has to do with the different processes and mechanisms that allow knowledge to be disembedded from one context and re-embedded in another. Thus, the studies presented here address a variety of such processes and mechanisms, including, for example, knowledge sharing, brokering, integration, and representation. As outlined in Figure 1.1, these processes not only highlight the major concerns found in the existing literature but also underline the interplay between them. For example, studies concerned with knowledge sharing address the way in which the organization of work is linked to the emergence of shared meanings and identities within and between groups.

Third, as noted below, EBK studies were grouped around several different arenas where such embedding/disembedding processes were evident. One such arena can be broadly labelled the study of management and organizational knowledge. This is an important arena for business firms because management and organizational knowledge is seen as key to their ability to continuously reshape themselves to meet the challenges of new markets and new technologies. At the same time, such knowledge is also rooted in the particular circumstances and history of the firm, which may limit the agency of managers and impose constraints on organizational change.

Another arena is that of design and innovation processes. Such processes are central to the firm's ability to reinvent itself. They depend crucially on the ability to integrate specialized forms of knowledge that are dispersed across different groups and settings. Integrating knowledge in this way, however, means overcoming the institutional and organizational boundaries within which groups are located. Actors and artefacts capable of overcoming such boundaries tend to loom large in these studies. Actors provide a brokering function between groups, while artefacts may be an important means of allowing one group to represent its knowledge to another. Important as these boundary-crossing activities are, however, they also need to be related to the social networks and mechanisms, such as trust and reputation, which influence and constrain them.

This last point takes us onto the third arena highlighted in these studies, which is that of inter-organizational relationships. Although such relationships are often presented as channels for the distribution of new knowledge, they rarely offer such unmediated exchange between organizations. A critical issue here then is how to exert influence through inter-organizational relationships. Such influence may serve either to reinforce the status quo or to challenge it, and in that sense is key to the (dis)embedding of knowledge that enables new approaches and technologies to be adopted and institutionalized within particular organizations.

The fourth arena highlighted in the following chapters has to do with those activities and forms of representation that seek to make knowledge an asset for firms. Now, the idea that knowledge constitutes such an asset has become almost an article of faith for some researchers. Practitioners, however, face enormous problems in seeking to translate that idea into practice. Knowledge is difficult to value in economic terms because it is usually non-tradable and, as discussed above, more or less context-dependent. It follows that the usual economic calculus cannot be applied to many forms of knowledge within firms, imposing strict constraints on firms' ability to 'invest' in such knowledge.

As outlined below, this book is organized into sections reflecting these major arenas. Within each section, each chapter gives a flavour of the research and findings for one of the EBK studies. It can, however, provide only a brief overview of that project—more detailed analysis of findings can be found in the journal papers produced by each study.

Part I: Management and Organizational Knowledge

The theme of this part is the emergence and effects of knowledge as a commanding force within firms. As noted above, the role of knowledge in resourcing and organizing business activities is a well-developed strand in the existing literature. The studies outlined here, however, link these concerns to detailed qualitative studies of the shared meanings and identities that shape the evolution of management and organizational knowledge. This approach not only locates such knowledge much more firmly in its organizational context, but also relates it to the activities of managers, employees, and other change agents, thereby suggesting new insights on change and stability in the knowledge-base of the firm.

In Chapter 2, Thorpe and colleagues examine the ways in which managers in SMEs (small and medium-sized enterprises) in North-West England respond to problems such as a financial crisis, losing staff, or acquiring new customers. This study develops an activity-based and situated view of knowledge, which highlights the subjectivity of individual SME managers and the way in which they make sense of the problems facing their firms. For managers in this kind of context, knowledge rarely figures as an available resource: the knowledge that they bring to bear on solving problems is too closely interwoven with their own activities and life experience. As a case example of an individual manager illustrates, knowledge emerges from the personal commitments, informal networks, and the conversations they share with others. Because managers in SMEs are so close to the flow of business activities, what really counts is the ability to leverage their own networks and sense-making capacities. This is made easier where they can find some space, in the midst of all this activity, to be able to reflect on their actions.

In Chapter 3, Storey and colleagues likewise focus on the situated knowing of managers. The contrast here comes from the focus on top management in larger organizations across a range of sectors. The subjective experience of managers is certainly important here. As the authors note, positions towards the top of the corporate hierarchies create expectations that exert a distinct influence on the way these managers draw on available sources of knowledge. Top managers' identities are precariously positioned between the need to appear knowledgeable and in control, on one hand, and yet having to deal with the capricious uncertainties of market forces, on the other. This positioning makes top management highly sensitive to the supply of new concepts and tools by consultants and other intermediary groups that seem to offer a way out of their dilemma. However, it would be wrong to see top managers as passive consumers of these offerings. Not only is the choice of appropriate strategic models highly contested, with multiple ideas in play, but the final realization of any such strategy is dependent on established organizational routines such as corporate planning cycles. These effectively tie management knowledge to the historical evolution of the organization. The chapter explores the way top managers seek to resolve the resulting dilemmas through brief case studies of decision making and change at both industry and firm level.

In Chapter 4, Easterby-Smith and colleagues outline a study of organizational learning and dynamic capabilities. In this chapter, the emphasis shifts away from the role of knowledge in making sense of strategic decisions towards knowledge as a resource underpinning the delivery of such decisions by the organization. This study thus engages with the strategic management literature and particularly the concept of 'dynamic capabilities'. This concept, which highlights the way some firms are able to adapt to change more quickly than others, has become a centrepiece in theoretical explanations of competitive performance. In their study, the Easterby-Smith team developed a new perspective on such capabilities. Much of the work in this field to date has struggled to ground this concept in the way organizations actually work. Where there have been attempts to elucidate the competencies or capabilities of a particular organization, they have sometimes seemed obvious or tautological.

The alternative developed in this chapter is to adopt a socio-political view of organizational learning. This is important because it helps to move the argument beyond the links between abstract constructs such as resources and capabilities towards a better understanding of the relationship between the operational and strategic aspects of the organization. More specifically, the socio-political view of learning outlined in this chapter highlights the means by which management shapes the activities and routines of the firm into the dynamic capabilities that drive organizational performance. From their case material, the authors identify a number of such capabilities which were important for the organizations in their sample. These include, among others, capabilities to do with leadership, networking with other groups, and the ability to cultivate political backing. As the authors indicate, the value of such capabilities lies precisely in the extent to which they are embedded within the situated activities of organizational members.

In Chapter 5, Knights concludes this part on management knowledge by reporting on a study of the dynamics of knowledge production in the business school. Given the findings already outlined, it is hard to sustain the idea that the business school is simply an institution for producing and disseminating management knowledge. However, the absence of such a clear link between academic research and business practice has helped to fuel an intense debate on the role and relevance of the business school, both in the United Kingdom and internationally. Knights outlines the contribution of different strands of the research study to this debate. He does so, however, in a reflective way, which seeks to relate the contributions made by his colleagues to long-running debates. Here, Knights contrasts a 'liberal reformist' approach to the business school's role with the more radical actor-network view adopted in the research strand focusing on academic–business engagement. He suggests that the reformist position is based on a conventional diffusion model of the business school's role. In contrast, an actor-network view would place the demands for relevance as one among a number of actors influencing the development of this institution as an 'obligatory passage-point' for would-be managers.

Part II: Innovation and Design Processes

One consequence of applying a knowledge lens to innovation is to highlight the importance of knowledge integration as a feature of innovation processes. The assumption that firms could manage the innovation process as a linear progression transferring knowledge from R&D lab to the marketplace is now largely discredited. More recent studies have shown that a basic challenge for innovation is how to integrate the knowledge provided by different groups both inside and outside the innovating organization. Now, there are many ways of theorizing that process depending on how we perceive the forms of knowledge involved and the relationships between different groups. The specialist expertise of professional groups, for example, may help to reinforce boundaries to the wider sharing of knowledge within the innovation process. What is undeniable, however, is that it is the processes and actors enabling the sharing of knowledge across such boundaries that take centre-stage in these studies.

In the following chapters, we focus on studies that shed light on some of these processes and actors. One recurrent feature is the role that project forms of organizing—for example, cross-functional project teams—play in bringing groups and different bodies of expertise together. Projects are seen as an important way of organizing innovative activities because they allow project members to escape the steady-state mode of performance. They are equally important, however, as a means of enabling temporary collaborations between different groups and organizations. In certain sectors, most of the major innovation activity is organized in this way precisely because the relevant knowledge is dispersed across an array of different actors and groups, and projects are the only way of applying them to a specific task efficiently. Another recurring issue is the important role of key individuals who are able to develop and manipulate networks to support knowledge integration.

In Chapter 6, Zhang and Baden-Fuller begin with the role of one such set of individuals, termed 'brokers', in the development of high-tech start-up businesses. High-tech sectors pose a range of challenges for knowledge integration. As the authors note, brokers enable knowledge integration in two distinct ways. First, they enable it through specialized support based on their own expertise. Second, they enable integration through a much broader role, which the authors term 'venture development'. The latter encompasses the greater legitimacy that they give to a new business and also their ability to help it overcome the 'liability of newness' by embedding the sectoral knowledge and contacts of a wider range of individuals as board members.

Chapter 7 takes a different sector and a different angle on knowledge integration. Here Lampel and Jha focus on projects in the film industry and highlight the selection of project members as one of the most significant challenges for knowledge integration and innovation in this context. In the film business, the knowledge that makes the difference between success and failure is embodied in individual talents—human capital in other words—which have to be combined effectively to produce a successful outcome. Precisely because it is difficult to evaluate what expertise individuals will bring to a film project, and even more difficult to predict how well they will apply that expertise in practice, the problem of 'member selection' looms very large. This problem is handled by the film director who acts as a knowledge integrator for the project. Here the authors identify two different models that the film director may apply. One, the 'garden model', exploits the greater knowledge of talent produced by repeated interactions. The other, 'market model', is less subjective but also more reliant on the validity of market reputation. The authors extend this analysis beyond the UK film sector through a comparative analysis of a data set that also includes the United States. This produces interesting contrasts in the way market reputations are established in these two countries, with commercial performance being most important in the United States, whereas 'critical performance'—whether reviewers like it or not—dominates in the United Kingdom.

In Chapter 8, Swan and colleagues contribute further to this emerging view of innovation through a multi-level study of the knowledge integration involved in biomedical innovation. This focuses, in particular, on more radical innovations in areas such as tissue engineering and genetics. The challenge of knowledge integration is especially acute here because such innovation involves collaboration between groups who are separated by institutional as well as organizational boundaries. These groups might range from scientists in R&D labs to doctors in hospitals. As highlighted by previous chapters, knowledge integration is closely intertwined with the scope and spread of inter-organizational networks. In the biomedical arena, however, key actors in extending and underwriting such networks are the small number of 'star scientists' whose reputation helps to broker partnerships across the often unpromising terrain of university–industry–government relationships. The importance of this kind of scientific legitimation is distinctive here—certainly compared to the more entrepreneurial contexts highlighted by Zhang and Baden-Fuller. This may be because the knowledge integration process exhibits such high levels of uncertainty, with much of that deriving from the scientific domain.

Swan and colleagues develop this analysis through an account based on their case-study work. This reveals knowledge integration to be a messy, unpredictable activity beset by conflicting performance criteria. It depends not only on integrative capabilities but also on relational capabilities, that is, the ability to collaborate with a diverse set of organizations. In short, knowledge integration in biomedical projects is a long way from being a simple Lego-like assembly. As the authors show in their case analysis, much depends both on the way particular innovation projects are organized, and also on the institutional context for such projects. Here, a comparative analysis of similar projects in the United States and

United Kingdom adds further to our awareness of the distinctive institutional environment of the United Kingdom. While Chapter 7 focused on different cultural and aesthetic norms operating in the film sector of these two countries, this chapter moves the focus on to the institutional divisions between academic science, clinical practice, and business. The deeper gulf between these different communities in the United Kingdom compared to the United States means that it is more difficult to secure the informal and unforced kind of collaboration required by highly interactive innovation processes. This has important policy implications. It suggests that UK policy makers need to pay more attention to mechanisms that 'bond' the various groups together, not simply 'bridge' the differences between them.

In Chapter 9, Whyte and colleagues examine how companies manage new product design processes involving collaboration between a range of supplier and user groups. Their focus is on the use of systems of representation, particularly visual representations, including objects such as blueprints and PowerPoint presentations, to help the sharing of knowledge between these different groups. As in previous chapters, the practice-based lens applied in this study questions the idea that knowledge can be readily transferred through the objects themselves because such objects cannot contain the meanings that they help to evoke. As a result, the study emphasizes the role of objects in *representing*, rather than in codifying, knowledge.

As the authors highlight, visual representations, in particular, play a crucial role as so-called 'boundary objects' in the design process. Here the study builds on previous work to suggest that visual representations perform a range of functions in enabling collaboration between different groups. These functions range from simply enabling technical learning, through a coordination role in the management of project teams, to the legitimation of new ideas. In highlighting these functions, the study also benefits from a comparative analysis of design processes in two different settings: one an architectural practice, the other a high-tech equipment manufacturer. This comparison demonstrates the different ways in which artefacts help to address the problem of creating shared meanings in projects involving multiple groups. In particular, it exposes the 'freezing' and 'unfreezing' of representations as crucial episodes in the way in which such shared meanings are established.

The final chapter in this section by Scarbrough and Amaeshi moves us on from the representation of knowledge to its evaluation. Representations of knowledge feed into the ongoing collaboration between groups.

As with previous chapters in this section, this study does not start from the assumption that such collaboration is, by definition, beneficial. The study focuses on evaluation precisely because innovation involves making decisions on whether or not to engage in collaboration, and if so with what resources. Evaluation practices involve taking a cold, hard look at the potential to be realized from further collaboration. This chapter highlights the distinct character of such practices across a range of settings, including in-house R&D, corporate venturing, and technology transfer offices in universities. In particular, it echoes the distinction made in Chapter 7 between garden and market models by highlighting the different forms of evaluation applied in corporate versus market settings.

Within firms, evaluation is driven by corporate goals and concerns. It is codified through processes such as stage-gate reviews, which rate innovation projects in terms of market potential and feasibility. In contrast, in market settings the evaluation criteria are much harder to specify in detail, and the sheer numbers of innovation opportunities involved are much greater. A typical venture capitalist, for example, might invest in only one in three hundred of the proposals they receive each year. Clearly, in the latter setting, the evaluation practices applied at the front end need to be highly lean and efficient to deal with information overload. Equally, they need to be highly tailored at the back end to deal with the unique features of a specific proposal. The study suggests, however, that the efficiency of these evaluation practices is ultimately dependent not on economic mechanisms, but on the social mechanism of trust. This provides a means both of filtering early stage proposals and of developing the confidence to invest in a particular proposal. This analysis, which can be related to the similarly lubricating role of market reputation outlined in Chapter 7, highlights the different sources of trust available to the investor. Thus, an important source of trust in the initial phase of decision making may be the institutional context of intellectual property rights or the university affiliation of the innovator. This source of trust is cheap and readily available. Later phases might see greater emphasis on the trust arising from the innovator's reputation within social networks, and, later still, on the emergence of trust from interpersonal contacts.

Part III: Inter-Organizational Relationships

The theme of this part is the ways in which inter-organizational relationships—notably between client and consultant, managers and lobby groups, and the users and vendors of new technologies—help to mediate the embedding and disembedding of knowledge within and between groups. We have previously highlighted the role that such relationships play in knowledge integration in discussing the role of network brokering and capabilities. The danger of the network metaphor, however, is that it implies that such relationships are essentially a channel for knowledge flows. As discussed previously, more micro-level accounts put the emphasis instead on their role in enabling collaboration among groups applying different forms of knowledge.

The part begins with Chapter 11 by Sturdy and colleagues, who focus on the dynamics of the relationship between client and consultant. Previous work in this area has suggested that this relationship is an important medium for the transfer of knowledge from consultants to business firms. Although this is a view that consultants would certainly like to promote, by focusing at a level of detail on a small number of consultancy projects, the Sturdy team suggests a more prosaic interpretation of the relationship: consultants are hired to perform specific tasks, and there is little interest—on either side—in transferring knowledge from one organization to another. If such a transfer were to take place, it is just as likely to be from the client to the consultant as vice versa.

But while the Sturdy team reject the simplistic notion of knowledge transfer as central to consultancy work, their study is equally attentive to the dynamics of situated knowledge and learning within such projects. They highlight, for example, the importance of joint project teams, encompassing both clients and consultants, as a genuine site of knowledge creation. Here knowledge of the client's local context is combined with the industry-level knowledge and understandings deployed by consultants. Something new may indeed be learned from this combination. However, this new knowledge is project-centred, meaning that it may not be available to the wider organization, either because the project itself is marginalized or because there is no process through which existing assumptions and recipes can be challenged. This study thus redefines the key aspects of the client–consultant relationship in terms not of bandwidth and knowledge transfer but of the degree of contestation and challenge that it is able to accommodate.

In Chapter 12, Hanlon moves us into the wider set of relationships through which business firms negotiate their legitimacy with representatives of societal concerns and interests. One arena in which such relationships are made particularly visible is that of inter-organizational forums discussing Corporate Social Responsibility (CSR). In this chapter, Hanlon analyses the way in which such forums enable dialogue between large firms and a variety of lobby groups and charitable foundations. He argues that such dialogue does not represent an exchange of knowledge between these groups; their worldviews are too different for such an exchange to be meaningful. However, he also rejects the view that such forums are meaningless or tokenistic exercises that are simply a fig-leaf for corporate power. He argues instead that the conflict and antagonism between business and other groups may actually serve as a stimulus to innovation, and, ironically, a means of deepening capitalist social relations.

In Chapter 13, Knox and colleagues examine information and communicative technologies (ICTs) such as Enterprise Resource Planning (ERP) systems. Adopting insights from social studies of technology, they highlight the extent to which the evolution of business knowledge is bound up with an unfolding sequence of technological applications, exemplified by ERP. As the study outlines, these new technologies reflect a particular form of inter-organizational relationship, which enables the business models and assumptions encoded by the supplier firm to influence practices within the adopting firm. Importantly, their study suggests that these ERP applications not only support new ways of working, but also enable new ways of 'knowing' the organization through greater transparency of organizational activities and roles. The authors argue that this has important implications for management knowledge. ERP makes information and its interpretation more central to management, but simultaneously highlights gaps in the existing information, requiring further standardization and new ways of capturing information. In this way, the chapter speaks to our earlier discussion of the key concerns around business knowledge, by highlighting the interplay among resourcing, organizing, and meaning.

Part IV: Making Knowledge an Asset

This final part focuses on the representation and evaluation of knowledge for purposes of decision making, reflection, and resource allocation. Many academics, consultants, and policy makers have proclaimed knowledge to be the most important competitive asset for business. However, due to its paradoxical relationship with organizational performance, noted earlier, there remain great difficulties in representing knowledge in a way that would be acceptable within conventional accounting systems. One possible way of making progress, though, is to identify the knowledge-based intangible assets of the firm to determine how much they contribute to financial performance and outcomes.

In Chapter 14, Greenhalgh and Rogers deal with this problem by focusing on the role of such assets and intellectual property more broadly in the service sector context. The service sector has been neglected by previous studies of intangible assets mainly because conventional forms of intellectual property, such as patents licensing and R&D spend, are less applicable here. In beginning to make good this deficiency, this chapter focuses on an empirical study of intellectual property assets, notably trade marks, for a large sample of firms in the UK service sector. Among the many important findings from this study, one of the highlights is the positive correlation that the authors have found between the intellectual property activities of firms, such as trade marks, patents, and brand names, and their business performance in terms of stock market value and productivity. As the authors note, this finding has important policy implications. It raises a question as to whether government should support innovation in firms that do not do R&D in the conventional sense, but which may be highly innovative in other ways.

In Chapter 15, Hendry and colleagues develop the focus on intangibles further by exploring the challenges of reporting such assets to external audiences. This study sought to identify the challenges involved in such reporting, both in relation to the innovation arena specifically and when set against a backdrop of shifting government policy. As the authors note, many of the problems of reporting intangible assets have their parallels in academics' desire to develop 'knowledge about knowledge'. Although the term 'intangible assets' seeks to avoid this problem by emphasizing the equivalence of business knowledge and material assets, this only glosses over the underlying difficulties of changing established systems of meaning that are widely grounded in the practices of finance and accounting professionals. Since any information on company assets and performance is subject to these language games, it would be naïve, as the authors note, to believe that any reporting on intangibles would be interpreted literally. They note the paradox that investors are keen to acquire insights on intangible factors such as leadership and are happy to base their investment decisions on such insights. They suggest that investors would be much more distrustful of information on intangibles that was made available publicly rather than acquired privately.

In Chapter 16, Rowlinson and colleagues fittingly complete the empirical studies presented in the book by reframing the way in which companies experience their own histories. Developing knowledge of the firm's history may be seen as an important asset, by, for example, strengthening the firm's brand. Equally, it may be seen as a form of organizational memory. The authors of this chapter outline multiple perspectives on the value of business history, including the contribution of what is termed 'counterfactual history', which posits alternative starting points for historical processes. Their empirical work, however, highlights the way business history is increasingly being captured by business firms themselves as more 'commodified' ways of knowing become important. This work echoes Chapter 12 by underlining the penetration of wider social relations into the way we understand business activities.

Conclusions

One of the contributions of research is to question the assumptions and ideas which we currently bring to a particular topic. As we have outlined in this Introduction, the EBK programme and its constituent studies sought to question many of our assumptions about the way knowledge is created and exploited by business firms. The following chapters will reveal in much more detail what this questioning led to in specific projects. As the Introduction has highlighted, however, the studies presented here reflect the key concerns that have shaped existing debates on the role of knowledge in business; some emphasize the role of knowledge as a resource, while others are concerned with the development of shared understandings or the influence of organizational forms.

Whatever specific view they adopt of knowledge and learning, however, collectively these chapters represent an important challenge to the assumption that economic and competitive success comes simply from ramping up the production and distribution of knowledge. Firms and nations are certainly under pressure to exploit knowledge more intensively. But, without a better understanding of the contribution which knowledge makes to business performance, their efforts are likely to be frustrated by the paradoxical and embedded aspects of knowledge highlighted earlier. The following chapters outline the different kinds of contribution that the EBK studies make to such an improved understanding. Although they range widely in scope, these chapters share a common attention to the importance of context, be it institutional, sectoral, or organizational, in grasping the performance implications of knowledge. By locating their research explorations within and across such contexts, they are correspondingly better placed to expose the social processes and mechanisms that enable knowledge to become an important driver of performance.

The rich picture that they give us of the evolution of business knowledge is certainly hard to square with the stylized imagery of the 'knowledge economy' favoured by politicians and business leaders. The forms of knowledge that make a difference to business performance are rarely 'rocket science'. More often, they are practical understandings that work well in one context but not in another. Even the innovation processes in science-based and high-tech industries are ultimately dependent on the operational routines and capabilities that come from hard-won experience.

In contrast, what is striking about these studies compared to much previous work is their ability to show us how firms extract business value from the sheer variety of different forms of knowledge involved. As the following chapters show, this requires combining multiple social processes including the sharing, integration, representation, and evaluation of knowledge. These processes are central to the ways in which knowledge becomes a resource (or constraint) for business performance. Many authors (e.g. Etkowitz and Leyesdorff 2000; Nowotny, Scott, and Gibbens 2003) argue that the economic and political forces dedicated to making knowledge such a resource are blurring the institutional boundaries between business, science, civil society, and government. If so, it follows that a greater understanding of the social processes involved is likely to be one of the enduring contributions of the EBK studies presented here.

References

Abrahamson, E. (1996). 'Management Fashion'. *Academy of Management Review*, 21/1: 254–85.

Blackler, F. (1995). 'Knowledge, Knowledge Work and Organizations: An Overview and Interpretation'. *Organization Studies*, 16/6: 16–36.

Brown, J. S., and Duguid, P. (2001). 'Knowledge and Organization: A Social-Practice Perspective'. *Organization Science*, 12/2: 198–213.

Burns, T., and Stalker, G. M. (1961). *The Management of Innovation*. London: Tavistock Publications.

Cohen, W. M., and Levinthal, D. A. (1990). 'Absorptive-Capacity: A New Perspective on Learning and Innovation'. *Administrative Science Quarterly*, 35/1: 128–52.

Coombs, R. (1996). 'Core Competencies and the Strategic Management of R&D'. *R&D Management*, 26/4: 345–55.

Engeström, Y. (1993). 'Developmental Studies of Work as a Testbench of Activity Theory: The Case of Primary Care Medical Practice'. *Understanding Practice: Perspectives on Activity and Context*, 64–103.

Etkowitz, H., and Leyesdorff, L. H. (2000). 'The Dynamics of Innovation: From National Systems and "Mode 2" to a Triple-Helix of University–Industry–Government Relations'. *Research Policy*, 29/2: 109–23.

Foss, N. J. (2007). 'The Emerging Knowledge Governance Approach: Challenges and Characteristics'. *Organization*, 14/1: 29–52.

Giddens, A. (1984). *The Constitution of Society: Outline of the Theory of Structuration*. Cambridge: Polity Press.

—— (1990). *The Consequences of Modernity*, Cambridge: Polity Press.

Grant, R. (1996). 'Towards a Knowledge Based Theory of the Firm'. *Strategic Management Journal*, 17 (Winter Special Issue): 109–22.

Lambert, R. (2003). *Lambert Review of Business–University Collaboration*. London: HMSO.

Nelson, R., and Winter, S. (1982). *An Evolutionary Theory of Organizational Change*. Cambridge, Mass.: Harvard University Press.

Newell, S., Scarbrough, H., and Swan, J. (2001). 'From Global Knowledge Management to Internal Electronic Fences: Contradictory Outcomes of Intranet Development'. *British Journal of Management*, 12/2: 97–111.

Nicolini, D., Gherardi, S., and Yanow, D. (eds.) (2003). *Knowing in Organizations: A Practice-Based Approach*. New York: M. E. Sharpe.

Nonaka, I., and Takeuchi, H. (1995). *The Knowledge Creating Company*. New York: Oxford University Press.

Nowotny, H., Scott, P., and Gibbons, M. (2003). 'Introduction: "Mode 2" Revisited: The New Production of Knowledge'. *Minerva*, 41/3: 179–94.

Penrose, E. T. (1959). *The Theory of the Growth of the Firm*. Oxford: Basil Blackwell.

Powell, W. W., Koput, K. W., and Smith-Doerr, L. (1996). 'Interorganizational Collaboration and the Locus of Innovation: Networks of Learning in Biotechnology'. *Administrative Science Quarterly*, 41/1: 116–45.

Reed, R., and Defillippi, R. J. (1990). 'Causal Ambiguity, Barriers to Imitation, and Sustainable Competitive Advantage'. *Academy of Management Review*, 15/1: 88–102.

Roos, J., and Von Krogh, G. (1995). *Organizational Epistemology*. London: Macmillan.

Spender, J.-C. (1998). 'Pluralist Epistemology and the Knowledge-Based Theory of the Firm'. *Organization*, 5/2: 233–56.

Stewart, T. (1997). *Intellectual Capital: The New Wealth of Organizations*. New York: Doubleday.

Sydow, J., Lindkvist, L., and DeFillippi, R. (2004). 'Project-Based Organizations, Embeddedness and Repositories of Knowledge: Editorial'. *Organization Studies*, 25/9: 1475–88.

Taylor, F. W. (1998). *The Principles of Scientific Management*. Mineola, NY: Dover Publications.

Tsoukas, H. (1996). 'The Firm as a Distributed Knowledge System: A Constructionist Approach'. *Strategic Management Journal*, 17 (Winter Special Issue): 11–25.

Weick, K. E. (2001). *Making Sense of the Organization*. Oxford: Blackwell Business.

Whipp, R., and Clark, P. A. (1986). *Innovation and the Auto Industry: Product, Process and Work Organization*. London: Frances Pinter.

Zollo, M., and Winter, S. G. (2002). 'Deliberate Learning and the Evolution of Dynamic Capabilities'. *Organization Science*, 13/3: 339–51.

Part I

Management and Organizational Knowledge

2

The Evolution of Business Knowledge in Smaller Firms

Richard Thorpe, Oswald Jones, Allan Macpherson, and Robin Holt

Introduction

Smaller firms form an important part of any economy. In the United Kingdom, there are 4.3 million firms and 99.8% have less than 250 employees. Small and medium-sized enterprises (SMEs) account for 50% of all UK economic activity and 58.7% of private sector jobs (Tilley and Tonge 2003; SBS 2007). In addition to their contribution in GDP terms, small firms are also important sources of innovation (Tether 2000). Notwithstanding this economic contribution, we still know relatively little about the management processes in smaller firms. It is only relatively recently that they have been taken seriously by academic researchers and afforded the importance they deserve.

Context for the research

Smaller firms have many features that distinguish them from larger firms: absence of complex formal structure, dominance of owner-managers, lack of internal labour markets, environmental uncertainty, and a limited customer base. In addition, managers often find it difficult to remove themselves from operational concerns in order to stand back and focus on longer term strategy, and many are interested, and remain motivated, by independence rather than increases in turnover or profit. Yet these differences should not distinguish smaller firms research as a separate branch of management and organization studies. As firms, they occupy similar institutional structures and experience the same environmental forces as larger firms; larger firms themselves cannot be characterized as homogeneous and unitary forms (indeed many actively seek to constitute themselves as 'flexible' constellations of smaller, flatter units); and smaller firms themselves are informed and organized by many different concerns. Thus, it is very difficult to assign smaller firms a defining, common identity.

Where they are most distinct from larger firms, and have most in common with each other, is in their informality coupled with a view that they are defined very much by the personal commitment of their owners (Gibb 1997; Gartner, Bird, and Starr 1992). This means that as organizations they are likely to be sustained, primarily, by economically significant skills along with successive knowledge claims concerning the viability of those skills. We thus recognize that the evolution of knowledge in smaller firms is likely to be influenced by the development of firm-based resources and capabilities *through activity* rather than the accrual of resources. Thus, our research is positioned with less concern for understanding information acquisition and more attention to an understanding of knowledge, or knowing, through an analysis of the conduct of smaller firm managers.

Empirical study

In this project, we set out to investigate patterns of sense-making across a broad sample of smaller firms. We hypothesized that managers make sense of, as well as shape, their world through a variety of mediating mechanisms that are held in dynamic rather than static relations (Engeström 1999). The constructionist approach we adopted also holds that managers of smaller firms act as 'practical authors' (Shotter 1997; Holman and Thorpe 2002) for whom knowledge represents an understanding of the balance between potential positions and opportunities in the context of their own particular understanding of the environment and the organizations for which they are responsible (Thorpe et al. 2006). We also set out to identify patterns of organizational 'knowing' that we believed would be linked to the recipes, based on size or sector, adopted by managers to ensure their businesses were competitive (Schutz 1976; Spender 1989). As well as sense-making, our research methods were also informed by activity theory (Blackler 1995; Engeström 2000). Our aim through the research was to enhance understanding of the ways in which managers[1] in smaller firms acquired and utilized knowledge as a basis for personal fulfilment, wealth creation, and improved competitiveness. The Parkerprint case is included in this chapter to illustrate a number of the issues central to our research findings.

Parkerprint Ltd

Parkerprint Ltd is a company established twelve years ago by Alan Jones. Originally, a one-man photocopying business, relying on local and passing trade, it now offers design, digital, and litho printing services to predominantly commercial customers, with a turnover approaching a quarter of a million. The company currently employs seven people.

The owner-manager

The growth of Parkerprint as a business has been inextricably linked to the owner's development as a businessman, entrepreneur, manager, leader, husband, and father. The leadership principles that govern Alan Jone's business, his relationships with customers, staff, and the business community have all evolved from his personal convictions and aspirations and from the necessities of running a growing business with its attendant cash flow and customer relationship issues.

Alan was not a high flyer at school, but he enjoyed it. Part of the reason was that it gave him the chance to develop a number of lasting friendships as well as the opportunity to play in the school football team. Before leaving school with three 'O' levels, he had managed to perfect the art of bunking off to play snooker, a game at which he excelled. He became (and remains) something of a local celebrity in the snooker community for his prowess at the game and at one time he seriously considered turning professional. His reluctance to take the leap had much to do with his preference for team sports—notwithstanding the fact that snooker was his talent, he preferred the camaraderie that playing football afforded. This preference for teamwork is an obvious thread in Alan's approach to how he manages his business and a personal quality that has had a profound effect on how the business has grown and on how Alan has brought his people along with him.

Objectives

Under the general research aim of enhancing understanding of ways in which managers in smaller firms create and use knowledge as a basis for personal fulfilment, wealth creation, and improved competitiveness, we had a number of specific objectives:

- to critically investigate if and how knowledge is acquired, generated, shared, absorbed, challenged, and transferred within and between smaller firms in practice
- to investigate enablers and constraints that influence the creation and use of knowledge in smaller firms within a regional context (social, historical, economic, and sectoral factors)

- to investigate whether the formal and informal practices associated with knowledgeable activity create particular patterns of response to critical incidents
- to adopt a methodology that was influenced by both sense-making and activity theory
- to operationalize a mode 2 research design incorporating users of academic knowledge such as practising managers and policy makers.

Fulfilling these objectives required involvement of collaborators at all stages of the research project and feedback of the results in real time in order to capture their views and perspectives.

Methodology and methods

SYSTEMATIC REVIEW

We began by looking at previous research, and this resulted in the publication of two systematic literature reviews. The full versions are now lodged with the UK's Advanced Institute of Management (AIM) and specific studies associated with their findings have formed the basis of two academic papers. One of these investigated how knowledge had been understood in previous studies of small-firm learning (Thorpe et al. 2005). The other examined the specific question of there being avowed links between the possession and use of knowledge assets and small-firm growth (Macpherson and Holt 2007). Major themes identified in earlier research included how smaller firms create and use social capital, their absorptive capacity, and how policy makers can offer appropriate support. Gaps in existing studies included a sectoral bias towards manufacturing and high-tech firms coupled with a lack of research on: (1) the situated nature of knowledge; (2) factors that mediate the adoption of particular systems of organizing; and (3) on how experience, relational competence, and social skills influence both the conception and trajectory of firm performance.

EMPIRICAL RESEARCH, RESEARCH DESIGN, AND DESCRIPTION OF FINDINGS

The study initially engaged 90 smaller firms in Northwest England, which were operating in three sectors: services (media and culture and retail), client-based (bespoke advice and formulaic advice), and manufacturing (high-tech and low-tech). Firms also varied according to what we conceptualized as their levels of maturity: start-up, stable, and innovatory (Appendix 1). In the first instance, the owner-manager or a member of the senior management team was interviewed in each of the firms. These were open-ended, in-depth interviews in which the main questions (focus), follow-ups (more depth), and probes (clarifications) were used flexibly so as to allow us to follow emerging themes (Rubin and Rubin 1995: 146–51). The interviews lasted between one and one-and-a-half hours.

The study was designed to develop an understanding of how managers dealt with 'critical incidents' such as financial crises, losing staff, or acquiring new customers. One item of particular interest was the way in which such critical incidents led to the search for and creation of new knowledge and the associated development of learning processes within each smaller firm. The main questions were framed by what Sole and Edmonson (2002) term 'significant learning episodes'. The term 'episode' conveys a 'response to a series of related activities and decisions unfolding over time' (Sole and Edmondson 2002: S22), and it is an extension of Flanagan's (1954) critical incident technique. Although initially a way of collecting data for quantitative analysis, critical incident technique is now commonly used to orient interviews around particular events that have meaning for participants (Kokkalis 2007; Chell and Allman 2003). Indeed, van-der-Heijden and Eden (1998) recommend the use of interviews to review 'breakdown situations' in order to stimulate managers to reflect on the meaning or import of particular events. By investigating responses to critical incidents, each manager was asked to reflect upon a series of related activities experienced as a 'watershed' in business development; a moment at which their knowledge of existing states of affairs and of future possibilities changed and culminated in a particular insight, a change of direction, or the review and revision of existing understanding.

The interviews were recorded, transcribed, and then analysed using NVivo software, which enabled us to index and structure the accounts into a series of learning episodes linked to specific critical incidents. Each of these claims were then further coded using a theoretical framing *informed* by 'activity theory', an emerging social science research epistemology emphasizing the constructed, dynamic, and open-ended nature of knowledge. An activity-theoretical approach would require a detailed study of actors as they negotiate the development of the object of activity in which they are engaged (Blackler 1995; Engeström 2000). However, in trying to understand the variety of processes, routines, networks, tools, and divisions of labour that act to structure activities and shape the learning process in a variety of smaller firm contexts, we felt it was necessary to adopt a higher level of abstraction in order to compare and so generalize findings into patterns linked to outcomes.

Activity theorists argue that there are six basic elements (see Figure 2.1) of which knowledgeable activity consists: (1) knowing subjects (such as entrepreneurs); (2) meaningful objects of activity (such as creating a product); (3) a wider community of stakeholders upon whom the knowledge is somehow dependent (such as advisors or friends); (4) prevailing norms and values by which the worth of activities is evaluated (such as views of profitability or a firm's ethical responsibility); (5) prevailing systems or divisions of labour by which activities are organized (such as firm structures or legal duties); and finally (6) material and symbolic objects used as tools (such as equipment, logos, communication devices, or buildings). The grounding assumption behind the theory is that it is only by understanding how each of these six elements relates to the other in an activity system that we properly understand what it is that subjects such as smaller firm managers really know, what the limits to their knowledge are, what frustrates their knowing, and the possible benefits from using knowledge more appropriately. These 'elements' of

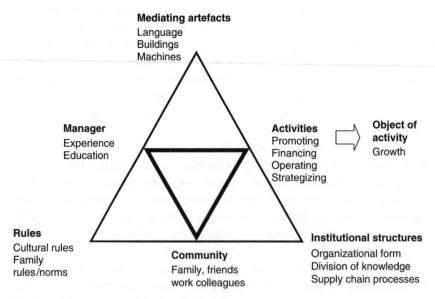

Fig. 2.1. A heuristic model of a smaller firm activity system

the theory were used to guide the coding when trying to analyse each critical incident.

As little work has been done on using the theoretical approach of activity theory in research on smaller firms, we instigated a number of parallel studies critically appraising its potential. First, the systematic review (Thorpe et al. 2005) examined existing uses of activity theory in management and organization studies. Based on this analysis, three further streams of research activity were developed: (1) understanding the small firm as an activity system; (2) understanding the role and influence of mediating objects or tools on entrepreneurial activity; and (3) conceptualizing the entrepreneurial act of founding a business venture as based on an activity system.

Little (1991: 68) argues that the type of ongoing evaluative research process we conducted during these interviews is inherently hermeneutic; claims are 'decoded through imaginative reconstruction of the significance of various elements of the social action or event'. During analysis of the first round of interviews, we were able to populate our conceptual schema with instances of the kind of knowledge being demonstrated, claimed, or sought. Using the six elements of activity theory as a heuristic, we were then able to constitute the conditions in which managers made sense of their activities (see Figure 2.1 above for illustrative codes). We then re-visited sixty of the ninety firms to conduct second interviews and, later, a further thirty firms to conduct third interviews. These two subsequent interviewing phases themselves provided opportunities to further probe the learning events as they had played out over the intervening months in terms of the audiences, their responses, and the implications as the managers experienced and accounted for them. In addition to the above, ten firm cases were also studied in depth in order to provide a more detailed understanding of our concepts.

Analysis of the interview transcripts together with the case-study data identified five factors that appeared particularly important for the creation and evolution of knowledge for smaller firms. First, it was crucial for smaller firms to develop formal systems, procedures, and routines by which new knowledge could be embedded within the firm. Reliance on informality meant the mechanisms for sharing and retaining knowledge were ad hoc and so incurred costs for the firm in terms of repetition. Second, the systems themselves were also found to provide an important trigger to stimulate discussion and debate and, subsequently, the generation of new knowledge. It was through a conscious investment in articulating experience that managers realized the possibility for future innovation. So, for example, for many of the smaller firms it was not the fact that they introduced the *balanced scorecard* or the *business excellence* model that was of importance. Rather it was the implementation of these processes that raised new challenges and, consequently, allowed them to 'think through' issues engendering learning about the business. A related issue was the way in which the system or routine created a 'strategic space' that enabled managers to stand back from 'day-to-day' activities and gave them time to consider and debate longer term issues that supported knowledge renewal.

The third, fourth, and fifth factors relate to the sources of innovation (new products, services, and processes) consequent on—in the main— the managers' human capital. Human capital is found partly in their education but perhaps more importantly in their experience, attitudes, and ability to convert the challenges and uncertainties of business life into tractable problems. The ability to formulate a coherent view in situations that were complex and ambiguous (what in Shotter's theory of practical authorship would be called a 'landscape') was embodied in their 'discursive resources'. In practice, this related to their ability to communicate effectively with a wide range of stakeholders including employees, customers, suppliers, and financiers. Intimately tied to the human capital associated with communication skills came the social capital associated with the extent and quality of links to others. For example, effective managers had the ability and vision to bridge into new networks when they required additional resources such as knowledge and information or the maturity to delegate and encourage others to participate in their venture. These issues we discuss in more detail below.

The absorptive capacity of smaller firms

In many ways the findings of our research support the received wisdom in relation to larger firms in that we found the absorptive capacity of the firm (particularly those elements relating to the quality of the managers' previous experience as well as the involvement of customers) to be important in knowledge acquisition (Cohen and Levinthal 1990). In addition, we found that where there was a diversity of skills and the use of relatively sophisticated management techniques (which included training), managers were making stronger performance claims. This chimes with observations relating to larger firms, which emphasize the importance of constituting an organization using diverse overlapping capabilities (Cohen and Levinthal 1990). This finding is confirmed by the quantitative analysis we have conducted on our data. However, other findings undermined conventional assumptions relating to absorptive capacity. Notably, when applied to smaller firms, the absorptive capacity model developed by Zahra and George (2002) was of limited value, since only rarely was knowledge understood as a 'resource' to be acquired. Rather, absorptive capacity was essentially processual, as it was strongly embedded in the firms' internal and external relationships (see Jones 2006). Managers felt that, when it came to acquiring and using knowledge, it was far more important to create a forum for debate by fostering empathetic listening (Von Krogh 2004) than it was to achieve a somewhat artificial shared understanding. For example, some managers were keen, when they 'had time', to attend networking meetings run by local Chambers of Commerce but had little notion of where these meetings might take them and what opportunities might arise. Serendipity rather than definitive framing governed the acquisition of knowledge; and a flexible approach to its subsequent use meant that knowledge in the form of contacts often lay dormant before suddenly unfurling; or were taken up rapidly and just as rapidly dropped. The sense of the fragile and fragmentary nature of this acquisition was also reflected in the processes they used to further exploit or secure existing knowledge. Often the systems used were idiosyncratic and personalized—for example, a chalk line drawn on a wall to denote levels of stock. Despite the individuality of some systems, our findings reinforce the view that it is important for managers to put in place procedures that help embed knowledge and learning within the firm's activities (Jones and Macpherson 2006).

In terms of both the exploration and exploitation of knowledge, our findings suggest that less positivistic approaches are equally important in conceptualizing the absorptive capacity of smaller firms. Indeed the use of the term 'acquisition' was somewhat inappropriate in relation to the way the knowledge might be said to evolve. On the few occasions where knowledge was spoken of explicitly as a 'resource' or 'asset', it was accounted for in terms of its potential (it did not yet exist) as something that could become useful in some way, such as talking to friends or business consultants to seek advice. Typically, the talk of assets was limited to references to tangible objects such as buildings, machines, or stock that could be sold.

Absorptive capacity

This case illustrates how some managers do learn in a natural way, as a consequence of work-related events rather than through formal courses. For example, business planning was initially something that only took place in Alan's head. However, relatively recently his planning has become far more formalized in terms of targets for turnover, profit, and projected growth. Alan now uses quarterly management accounts to review business activity enabling him to plan ahead, set budgets, and control the business better. External consultants have also been introduced to assist in this area of tendering and financial planning.

Alan also has a much better idea of the type of customer Parkerprint is attempting to attract, those the business should be winning and those they should be keeping in order to develop the business. Alan has worked out, for example, that, based on the firm's records, those customers who have their own brand and history are the one's that he needs to keep. These are the ones that change the information on their letterheads infrequently, which means that each time they reorder their plates are already set up and printing can take place without new set-ups that are time-consuming and costly. Other potential clients that Alan had identified include companies who regularly market themselves using brochures or display materials.

This push to attract more commercial customers has evolved as the Parkerprint brand has developed. The individuality of the brand is now clearly defined both in words and as an image; it is bright and friendly, professional, and reliable with a strong focus on building lasting relationships. In many ways, the brand reflects many of the elements of the owner-manager's own personality. Alan recognizes that there are some elements which militate against business growth in the brand personality that have stemmed from his initially rather too narrow focus on the product as opposed to the relationships that surround the product. This residual anchor he puts down to an element of self-doubt or self-deprecation.

Alan's aspirations for the business have changed significantly over the course of the last twelve years since the business was established on a shoestring budget. In the early days he relied on second-hand machines and organic, slow, and steady growth. At that time Alan spent much of his time in conversation with customers, many of whom eventually became friends. The shop became a magnet for local 'characters' (some would say eccentrics): the local poet, of no fixed abode, had his post delivered to the shop which he collected at the same time as his poetry competition booklets. Alan always had time for a chat with anyone who came in the shop; people liked him and often came back as a result.

Another indication illustrates Alan's ability to adapt to the circumstances (and thus the firm's absorptive capacity) has been the appointment of a female director, Susan, who currently runs her own graphic design business. This has been a big step because, as we have seen, Alan is more comfortable with men than women. This new appointment also heralds a new shift in the business focus as Alan is now beginning to step back from always having to have hands-on control of every aspect of the business. At one time he did his own design. Since taking on a graphic design graduate, not only can he offer customers far more in terms of service, but he now realizes how poor the design was when he did it himself—self-taught. Alan has already mentally made the separation between himself and the business; he now refers to Parkerprint in the way in which employees of large corporations talk about their business (i.e. 'Parkerprint needs to move on . . . ', 'The business needs to . . . ').

Alan and the rest of his employees have also been quick to learn from the new director and he is encouraging others in the business to follow up her ideas as well as delegating far more than ever he used to. Her ideas about branding and profession-alism have brought a new perspective to team meetings and are giving the business a renewed confidence to exploit different markets. The growth of Parkerprint in this way means that the owner-manager now conceptualizes the business as being a design company providing ideas about brand and image rather than a printing company responding to the demands of customers; a collective of experienced experts as opposed to a group of journeymen.

Rediscovering organizational slack: conversational space and boundary objects

The fact that managers of smaller firms were reactive to wider environmental forces did not come as a surprise; that a significant number of managers were able to create *strategic space* was more surprising. We found that con-versational informality was not necessarily a bad thing. What was important was the quality of the relationships managers developed and maintained. Working with professional advisors was seen to be beneficial, since it gave managers the opportunity to work around an intervention whether or not it was the 'right' course of action to take. For example, ISO quality certification was seen as a tool that could be used as an 'artefact' or 'object' around which individuals could debate alternative views of quality, its strategic importance vis-á-vis price and regularity of supply, and how to realize the appropriate levels of quality. So the 'tool' was useful in the way it surfaced contradictions and ambiguities that existed in the firm and its environment rather than because it provided definitive solutions. The ISO 'object' acted as way of abstracting and representing knowledge, but its value lay in its being used to prompt debate across organizational boundaries (both within the firm and with external influences) and so stimulate learning.

In that sense 'boundary objects' provide a potential bridge between organizational and institutional communities. 'Boundary objects' enable conversations between individuals and communities, and the objects promote a range of associated engagements that have the potential to put existing activities under review (Carlile 2002). Thus, objects facilitate social practices through which activities evolve, although they could also be the focus of political games. It is these engagements and activities that lie at the heart of communicative actions (Orlikowski 2002) and which serve to create and transform knowledge rather than the mediating artefacts or boundary objects themselves. We found it was important to understand both 'spaces' and 'objects' and their associated social practices in order to understand the social construction and transformation of knowing within our sample of firms. In this sense, knowledge transformation is fundamentally influenced by the creation of social learning spaces. One machining company, for example, hired a consultant to train staff in set-up reduction. The three days that staff spent on the exercises incurred costs in terms of lost production as well as consultant's fees, but the outlay was more than repaid when they presented their own ideas to improve efficiency to the owner-manager. In many cases, creation of such social learning spaces were linked to the use of boundary objects (such as computer-based training courses, ISO9002, or SWOT analyses), which promoted discussion and debate throughout the firm (see Macpherson, Jones, and Oakes 2006). There needs to be a pragmatic commitment to new activities which occur, not through mediating artefacts (or boundary objects) themselves, but through the engagement and activities of those within and between communities *using* those objects (Macpherson and Jones 2008). It has also been noted that outside agencies, such as academic institutions, customers, suppliers, or professional advisors are in a position to influence these conversations by both creating space (the purpose of the majority of development interventions based on action learning) and through the use of objects (the approach at the heart of the use of tools such as the balanced scorecard or Investors in People) (cf. Bell et al. 2002; Macpherson, Jones, and Oakes 2006) around which knowledge evolution can be stimulated and accelerated to encourage the institutionalization of new activities (Jones and Macpherson 2006). This finding suggests that objects and their associated social activities and discursive practices are an important pragmatic way of stimulating strategic renewal and the evolution of knowledge in small firms.

Understanding knowledge claims rhetorically

Through a number of our case studies we were able to understand that the effective use of knowledge is in many ways dependent on the ability of managers to create what we refer to as a rhetorical rapport between themselves and their constituents. We suggest that knowledge claims made by managers (for example, to customers and employees) can be understood very much as exemplars of rhetorical practice. The successful organization of firm activity, whether it be a move of premises, an attempt to involve suppliers in new working practices, or a change to shift patterns, relies significantly on the ability of managers to convince 'others' of the legitimacy of their knowledge claims. Why does the change have to be made? Why should it be done this way? Rhetorical analysis of a number of narrative accounts showed how, despite the privileged role each manager held within their firm, a response to the inherent ambiguity of change required that the business case be understood as more than simply a consequence of economic logic. If managers simply made a claim on the grounds of cost-effectiveness or market pressure, their claims were treated with more suspicion and, generally, were less well heeded than if they were coupled to the claimants' self-awareness (were they credible people whose claims others could trust?) and to the worldview of their audience (what interests were they appealing to when making the claims and were these interests sufficiently distinct to require differing modes of address to, say, employees and customers?). We found that where knowledge claims attended to the influence of all three aspects of the case being made (namely, the inherent logic of the argument, the importance of being a credible claimant and hence a believable source of knowledge, and a sensitivity to different interests and perspectives amongst audience to the claim), then the outcomes were better realized (Holt and Macpherson 2007).

An understanding of the concept of maturity

Focusing on managers' frustrations with both sourcing and using knowledge, we initiated a parallel stream of research using a novel e-postcard method of data collection (Gold 2007) from 104 entrepreneurs within our own sample and beyond. The object was to ascertain in a quick and informal manner the primary sources of this frustration to knowledge acquisition and use. We theorized this struggle as one which the philosopher Immanuel Kant termed the struggle for enlightened 'maturity'. For Kant, an unenlightened condition was one governed by guardians (he singled out the physicians, politicians, clergymen as likely guardians) who possessed the authority of ready-made solutions that they sought to impress upon those with whom they came into contact. The mature are those able to resist such uncritical absorption of orthodoxy and who, instead, constantly test things. In Kant's terms, they dare to know. In the context of this research on smaller firms, potential guardians might include the banks, business advisors, government regulators, and so on (Thorpe et al. 2006). What we wished to explore was the extent to which managers felt such voices were actually constraining rather than enhancing their knowledge and hence performance.

Our findings were threefold. First, we found the e-postcard method a great success and extremely useful in gaining an understanding of entrepreneurs for researchers working within a social constructionist paradigm. From a Mode 2 perspective (Gibbons et al. 1994), a number of entrepreneurs commented on how useful the insights had been for them personally. Second, we found that while many managers did indeed wish to strike out—showing in Kant's terms 'no fear of phantoms'—this quality was easily threatened. As Kant also argued, 'It is so convenient to be immature.' We found the onus to be on the managers to ensure they have a balance in their life roles to encourage a wider value base and to make sure conflicting roles do not lead them back to immaturity. Maturity is, therefore, at times a precarious quality, which was easily lost when 'buying into' established procedures and remedies for matters of availability, convenience, and even commercial pressure. We found that this tendency was best countered by managers simply meeting one another to share experiences; supporting Rae's (2000) emphasis on recognizing the influence 'others' may have in managers remaining 'mature'. By allowing managers to contextually test out their thoughts in relation to an entrepreneurial idea with 'mature' others, this leads to a form of experiential learning, consistent with much of the entrepreneurial learning literature, where the general consensus is that entrepreneurial learning is action-based (e.g. Deakins and Freel 1998; Gibb 1997). Third, from a policy perspective, the analysis showed the dangers of offering advice and preprogrammed external assistance. Indeed, managers identified hindrance to knowledge-use as emanating from 'higher' authorities, who wished to elicit obedience in exchange for grants or funding. There is a common complaint about 'red tape', but also the failure of government to provide 'real' help; and this complaint might be extended to institutional finance. There remain real doubts about attempts to create the environment of support that can be called an 'enterprise culture' using stipulative, guardian-like advice that focuses on content. Much better, we suggest that efforts should be made by higher authorities to afford smaller firm managers the opportunity to share their experiences, test ideas, and network with other like-minded individuals encouraging the retention and development of maturity among entrepreneurs, for it is they, and not 'outside' guardians, who have intimate knowledge of what has worked and why. Furthermore, policy makers perhaps need to develop an empathy with the needs of smaller firm managers so as not to impose structures or shape entrepreneurial environments in accord with their own convenience and experiences rather than those of the small firms.

Future directions

Alan measures the success in his business by healthy profit margins and happy customers. His job satisfaction comes from the contribution he makes to the business by, for example, bringing in new customers and spreading the Parkerprint message. He expects the same from his staff; he has high expectations from all of them and has often been disappointed when others have failed to share his passion for growing the business. Despite these disappointments and setbacks, Alan continues with his team-based leadership style. When he talks about his business, his accounts of how the business is progressing are peppered with the words, 'we' and 'the team'. He rarely takes sole credit for anything, preferring to tell others about the achievements of the Parkerprint team; implicit in this is his role in building and leading this team. He knows that he relies on his staff to provide a service that customers will buy; he finds it easy to trust them but difficult to take the disappointment that having one's trust misplaced sometimes brings. Notwithstanding this, he continues to believe in them and to give them a chance to prove themselves.

Ironically, one of the reasons why he originally established the business was because he didn't enjoy working for others—the clerical jobs he'd had since leaving school both frustrated and bored him. He believed that he would open a chain of printing shops moving on from copiers to presses and then into the more commercial markets. Now, his overarching goal still is to be able to retire in the belief that he has achieved something. His current more immediate goal is to reach a million pound turnover with a 10% profit and retire by the time he is 55, selling the business to someone who has the ambition to develop it further.

The importance of social capital

Another important research finding was to confirm the importance of social capital to smaller firms. Business networks and professional advisors were influential for dynamic firms and were often cited as sources of new knowledge. In this context the recruitment of senior managers was important because of the new human and social capital they brought into the businesses. We found that firms with stronger performance claims that had created a complementary range of capabilities through the development and recruitment of staff had also had increased access to social capital. Again, the capacity for 'self-awareness' discussed earlier came to the fore. It was clear that successful outcomes were linked to managers' capacity to devolve responsibility by employing others with necessary skills and hence contacts with significant sources of external knowledge (Zhang, Macpherson, and Jones 2006). In addition to the appropriate social and rhetorical skills, managers needed the motivation to identify wider resources and opportunities by establishing new network linkages. Furthermore, the more effective managers were able to turn those linkages into resources for their businesses by developing higher levels of trust with external actors. Within the social capital literature, this process of turning weak ties into stronger ties (Granovetter 1973) is known as 'bridging' and 'bonding' (Davidsson and Honig 2003).

We could also see evidence of the opposite case, and we noted that a lack of social capital and a lack of ability and/or motivation to extend networks was a source of frustration. With respect to these social networks, we were more concerned with the agency rather than the structure through which know-ledge was found. Thus, the aspect of social capital we believed important was cognitive social capital (Nahapiet and Ghosal 1998), which refers to managers' interpretive frameworks based on shared language, codes, and narratives (Lee and Jones 2006). The suggestion is that rather than regard social capital and absorptive capacity as distinct 'possessions', it is better, in smaller firms, to emphasize their being the mutual creations of managers' relational skill.

Social capital

Four years ago, Alan was persuaded, by his accountant, to join a networking organization called Business Networking International. The group met every Friday morning for breakfast and worked on the premiss that members of the group would give each other business referrals from their wider network of contacts. At each meeting, each member also had to give a one-minute presentation about their business and every so often, each member is called upon to run a ten-minute session on a current topic of importance. When Alan first joined the club, the thought of standing up for one whole minute in front of twenty-five other experienced managers terrified him. Thursday evenings were consumed by preparation and the search for new and novel ways to talk about the firm. Rarely having to speak in public before, he was self-conscious both about the way he projected himself and about how he might sum up the business in just a minute. The discipline of trying to tell others what his business was about was a significant developmental experience for Alan, as his previous experience was that the majority of his day was spent chasing and completing jobs. What the Business Networking International provided was an opportunity to reflect on what the firm was actually about and where it was going. The very process of talking aloud to others about the business was profoundly thought-provoking and he began to find that after each presentation he would spend his time on the way back to the shop thinking about what he had said or talking to his wife or a friend about it. These critical reflections of the sense he was trying to make of his own business in one-minute bites and the comparison he made between his presentation and the others, gave Alan valuable insights into where the company should be going and this fed his ambition.

For the next three years, Alan was devoted to the BNI. The friendships he was developing and the contacts he was making were extremely useful. He had in his own words built trust and respect. Members (friends) often used each other as sounding boards outside meetings, encouraging each other to take risks and this gave them confidence as well as a certain amount of 'if he can do it, then so can I' attitude. He soon found that other people's businesses became an integral part of his

---

life. Not only were they his customers, but the people who ran them were also his friends. Alan's social life now had a distinctly 'BNI' focus. The camaraderie and support that he found completely suited his team-focused approach, and according to his wife, with very few women members, there was also a real blokey feel to the whole set-up. This again suited Alan, who felt much more at ease in male company.

In April 2005, Alan Jones took on the Directorship of the BNI Chapter. He did so with a certain amount of pride and a determination that he would like to take the chapter to new heights. However, his main motivation for taking on the role of director was that he felt he owed the group a debt and he wanted to give something back. During his year as director, Alan's enthusiasm for BNI waned dramatically. The nervous Thursday evenings spent in preparation were long gone—speaking for a minute he could now do without preparation and often even ten minutes wasn't long enough to tell the assembled group what Parkerprint had to offer. He also about this time became aware that the chapter members were less like kindred spirits than they had been—he thought there are just too many one-man bands. What had happened was that, in effect, Alan had moved on to another level of personal and business development and his problems and concerns now were very far from those he had faced when he had first joined, and in the majority of cases different from those of the other members. It was also the case that the potential for new customers that might emanate from BNI was diminishing and opportunities that did present themselves were unlikely to meet the new and developing objectives of the business. He served his year as director and, although is still a member of the chapter, he now takes much more of a backseat. He still counts as friends many of the co-founders of the chapter, many of whom have now formed their own networking and support group outside the formal meetings structure. Many of the business issues that gave them a common identity and focus four years ago are still there (cash-flow, staff issues, and work–life balance), but the dynamic is now different.

Discussion

Conceptualizing the evolution of business knowledge

Drawing these strands together, we are better able to conceptualize the links in our work. Figure 2.2 focuses on the implications of our research for researchers, practitioners, and the user communities more generally, including policy makers. The research highlights the idiosyncratic nature of success and how this view impacts on the way in which performance might be viewed and measured—a finding that mirrors earlier research on the printing industry in Northwest England (Thorpe 1988).

To effectively exploit their unique knowledge environments, all small firms depend on the human capital of key actors (usually the owner-manager), the firm's absorptive capacity (systems, structures, and

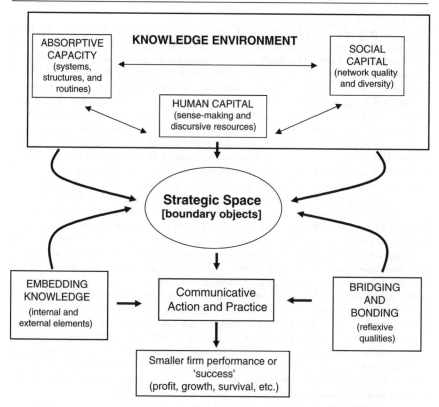

Fig. 2.2. Conceptualizing knowledge in smaller firms

routines), and social capital (network size, quality, and diversity). The model represents an acknowledgement that human capital (incorporating sense-making and discursive resources) is the key influence on smaller firms' social capital and absorptive capacity. Viewed in this way, knowledge and knowing are seen as being embedded within the structures and relationships that exist within the firm's ambit. In addition, this knowledge capacity is continually renewed though interaction, engagement, and activities that are in part structured by existing social relationships. In order for knowledge renewal to take place, 'strategic space' has to be created through a variety of mechanisms in order to allow existing activities or 'objects' to be put under review. Thus, at the heart of knowledge creation and use in smaller firms are the communicative actions and practices that encourage 'bridging' and 'bonding' with new networks while also exploiting what is already known within collective activities.

Moreover, it needs to be acknowledged that activity takes place in an institutional context, one which influences what is possible. As a consequence, current arrangements, market conditions, and changing institutional pressures influence the evolution of knowledge and knowing within smaller firms. Although this model is not intended to suggest causality, it does serve to map the types of processes involved in the evolution of business knowledge in small firms. The Parkerprint case provides a useful illustration of how the elements of the model are deeply entwined and potentially how idiosyncratic the evolution of business knowledge is in smaller firms.

At Parkerprint, Alan Jones is the driving force behind the business, and it is his experience and energy that sustained the business in the early years. In the early stages, the knowledge environment in his firm also consisted of the informal routines of operation and management, and the informal business network that he developed. A critical turning point was his accountant's encouragement to participate in BNI. Once he extended his network to 'bridge' into and 'bond' with others in BNI, he extended his social capital and he was able to share his ideas and problems with others. The presentations to his peers act as boundary objects that allow him to communicate with others about the nature of his problems and his business goals. This process required his motivation and capabilities to discuss, share and articulate his ideas about the nature of success and how he might achieve a sustainable and respectable business. At the same time, these networking events create time for him to reflect. The presentations he makes become events through which he engages with others and to which he gives time energy to critically evaluating his strategic direction.

In developing his business, he further extends the knowledge environment by appointing a director (Susan) to develop the graphic design part of the business and by hiring a graphic design graduate. These two acts create further 'strategic space', as he is now able to delegate responsibilities that allow him to assess the strategic direction of the firm by focusing on larger, more stable clients. While initially his systems of management were very informal, over time he has changed those systems to allow others to take over his operational roles. He has institutionalized new procedures. These new systems also help to creat 'strategic space' for business development. In other words, it is his actions in engaging with others, that created opportunities to reflect critically on current practices, which supported a change in work practices and a change in strategic direction.

The knowledge environment at Parkerprint is now in constant need of renewal. Alan has recognized this in his disengagement from his old business club, his seeking out of new corporate clients, and his development of a new 'business network'. It is also interesting to note that his notion of success and performance has changed over the years. While he is still keen to develop a team and he is focused on 'happy customers', other success factors have changed. From being content to give up a boring day job and 'be his own boss' he has now set his sights on growing the business to a turnover of £1M. It is this goal (or identity) that influences his actions, practices, and with whom he engages.

Implications for policy and practice

The findings from the project suggest three profound implications for policy and practice. First, managers must be able to create 'strategic space' if their firms are to survive and prosper in the longer term. Many managers in our sample were able to do so by delegating internal responsibility and 'opening up' to external sources of information. Entrepreneurial actions are directly related to the embeddedness of activities, experiences within specific communities, and the space to reflect on the long-term viability of their business. Managers in smaller firms have to be willing to delegate authority, recruit new talent, to implement new systems or develop technologies that provide space to focus on strategic renewal and change. Thus, significant rigidities in terms of resources, time, and existing practices may need to be unblocked before the firm can change. Creating opportunities and the 'strategic space' for managers to be able to reflect on their business is important if critical thinking is to be effective in generating strategic renewal. Creating strategic space incorporates those activities that provide the time, resources, motivation, and capabilities needed for owner-managers to reflect on and review existing practices. Unblocking rigidities and creating strategic space may also require both the power and political influence of critical actors, such as the owner, customers, or regulatory bodies to create both the desire and direction for change. The more active managers are in seeking out different communities, the more likely such interactions are to provide resources for reflecting on current activities.

This brings us to the second key point. Learning within the firm is more effective if it is problem-centred and learner-centred incorporating 'boundary objects' (such as business analysis tools, problem-solving forums, or soft process technologies) to assist engagement and dialogue across internal and external boundaries. It is the use of flexible, unstructured, and socially-embedded experiences and relations that exemplify the knowledgeable and knowledge-creating entrepreneur. Thus, in order to support the evolution of knowledge in small firms, interventions should be activity-based and focused on 'real' problems. The implication is that more attention needs to be placed on problem solution and practice. This includes attention to the discursive skills (mentioned above) of the manager, acknowledgement that prevailing discourses will limit understanding of what is appropriate, and a deeper understanding of how 'boundary objects' might provide a focus for collective action such that they create 'learning spaces' where dominant discourses are challenged. The importance of developing critical thinking skills is key to 'opening up' to alternative possibilities of organizing (including delegation of responsibilities) and for the ability to manage change (Anderson and Thorpe 2005, 2006). Development of KTPs (knowledge transfer partnerships) and the critical role that university staff play alongside KTP associates in monthly strategic management meetings to challenge current thinking are also important. Other schemes to get graduates into businesses as new sources of knowledge as well as challenges to current orthodoxy might also be considered.

Third, the interconnected nature of the evolution of knowledge and the learning processes identified in this study underlines concerns that a 'small firm' is less typical than current categorizations based on age, size sector, and turnover assume. It is important, therefore, that government agencies and other funding bodies reconsider the classification of smaller firms simply in terms of size (number of employees or turnover and so on) and instead focus more on the owner-manager's human and social capital and the firm's absorptive capacity, as firms with higher levels of potential absorptive capacity are far more likely to respond positively to external advice and support. Structures, process, human capital, networks, and institutional arrangements differ between firms. These could be used to identify and contrast the 'learning orientation' of small firms or to identify their specific ability to absorb new knowledge through the structures and activities in which they participate.

These implications indicate that there can be three main 'points of entry' for policy support that are intertwined: the social architecture and relationships that mediate interactions, the structures and availability of human and social capital, and the context of institutional and market conditions within which the firms reside and which may shape the way policy support is delivered. Using these characteristics, an alternative classification process could be linked to a more sophisticated heuristic in order to target policy initiatives. Alternatives might include the capacity, willingness, and openness of the owner-manager to develop the firm; the available structure of social capital and the network possibilities the firm might have; the degree of sophistication the entrepreneur-manager and employees have for accepting new knowledge (absorptive capacity); and their views on delegation and subsidiarity (maturity). These classifications could be used to target firms in need of specific help, or that were more open to change, in order that policy funds might be more effectively applied.

Conclusion

In summary, this project examined the evolution of business knowledge in SMEs based in Northwest England. As stated in our original proposal, the research was designed to enhance the understanding of ways in which managers in SMEs acquire and utilize knowledge as a basis for wealth creation and improved competitiveness. Our focus on smaller firms in Northwest England was important because entrepreneurial and organizational 'knowing' (the creation and use of knowledge) is influenced by social, historical, economic, and sectoral context. A further reason for undertaking this project was related to the relative marginalization of SMEs in research terms despite their significance within the UK economy. Our research confirms the importance of social capital and absorptive capacity to those smaller firms in which managers have a vision for the longer term viability of their businesses. While such a claim is not particularly revolutionary in the understanding of smaller firms, we are able to provide evidence based on a longitudinal analysis of ninety firms representing a wide range of sectors and sizes. Of more significance is our data, which indicates the way in which managers in our sample actually created social capital and absorptive capacity. As indicated above, managers who were the most effective in managing their businesses had well-developed rhetorical and social skills. These skills were important in managing their employees but much more importantly they provided access to additional resources through the development of new networks (bridging and bonding). A related finding confirmed the importance of the linked concepts of 'strategic space' and 'boundary objects'. Once again, effective managers were able to stand back from day-to-day activities and consider longer term issues that impact on their businesses. As discussed above, boundary objects promote conversations between managers, employees, and other stakeholders, which have the potential to create and disseminate knowledge throughout the organization. Links between delegation and the performance of SMEs is well established in the literature (Jones 2003). Similarly, the role of boundary objects and mediating artefacts in organizational learning have been identified by a number of writers (Engeström 2004; Carlile 2002). Our clear contribution is to bring together a range of elements (human capital, social capital, absorptive capacity, strategic space, and boundary objects) into a coherent conceptual framework (Figure 2.2) for understanding the management of knowledge in SMEs.

Acknowledgements

We would like to acknowledge assistance of Lisa Anderson who conducted the case study and Adnam Ghecham who assisted with the quantitative data analysis.

Note

1. The terms 'management team' and 'managers' are used throughout this chapter as shorthand for the full range of smaller firms from micro firms with owner-managers to medium-sized firms with functional structures.

References

Anderson, L., and Thorpe, R. (2005). 'New Perspectives on Action Learning: Developing Criticality'. *Journal of European Industrial Training*, 28/8–9: 657–69.

———— (2006). 'Putting the C in HRD', in C. Riggs, J. Stewart, and K. Trehan (eds.), *Behind and Beyond Critical HRD*. London: Pearson.

Bell, E., Taylor, S., and Thorpe, R. (2002). 'Organizational Differentiation through Badging: Investors in People and the Value of the Sign'. *Journal of Management Studies*, 39/8: 1071–85.

Blackler, F. (1995). 'Knowledge, Knowledge Work and Organizations'. *Organization Studies*, 16/6: 1021–46.

Carlile, P. R. (2002). 'A Pragmatic View of Knowledge and Boundaries: Boundary Objects in New Product Development'. *Organization Science*, 13/4: 442–55.

Chell, E., and Allman, K. (2003). 'Mapping the Motivations and Intentions of Technology Orientated Entrepreneurs'. *R & D Management*, 33/2: 117–34.

Cohen, W. M., and Levinthal, D. A. (1990). 'Absorptive Capacity: A New Perspective on Learning and Innovation'. *Administrative Science Quarterly*, 35/1: 128–52.

Davidsson, P., and Honig, B. (2003). 'The Role of Social and Human Capital among Nascent Entrepreneurs'. *Journal of Business Venturing*, 18/2: 301–31.

Deakins, D., and Freel, M. (1998). 'Entrepreneurial Learning and the Growth Process in SMEs'. *The Learning Organization*, 5/3: 144–55.

Engeström, Y. (1999). 'Innovative Learning in Work Teams', in Y. Engeström, R. Miettinen, and R. Punamäki (eds.), *Perspectives on Activity Theory*. Cambridge: Cambridge University Press.

—— (2000). 'Activity Theory and the Social Construction of Knowledge: A Story of Four Umpires'. *Organization*, 7/2: 301–10.

—— (2004). 'New Forms of Learning in Co-Configuration Work'. *Journal of Workplace Learning*, 16/1–2: 11–21.

Flanagan, J. C. (1954). 'Critical Incident Technique'. *Psychological Bulletin,* 51/4: 327–58.

Gartner, W. B., Bird, B. J., and Starr, J. A. (1992). 'Acting As If: Differentiating Entrepreneurial from Organizational Behavior'. *Entrepreneurship: Theory and Practice,* 16/3: 13–31.

Gibb, A. (1997). 'Small Firms' Training and Competitiveness: Building upon the Small Firm as a Learning Organization'. *International Small Business Journal,* 15/3: 13–29.

Gibbons, M., Limoges, C., Nowotny, H., Schwartzman, S., Scott, P., and Trow, M. (1994). *The New Production of Knowledge.* London: Sage.

Gold, J. (2007). 'e-Postcards', in R. Thorpe and R. Holt (eds.), *The Sage Dictionary of Qualitative Research in Management.* London: Sage.

Granovetter, M. (1973). 'The Strength of Weak Ties'. *American Journal of Sociology,* 78/6: 1360–80.

Holman, D., and Thorpe, R. (2002). *Management and Language: Managers as Practical Authors.* London: Sage.

Holt, R. and Macpherson, A. (2007) 'Rhetoric, Knowledge Claims and Creating Organizations', European Academy of Management Conference, Paris, 16–19 May.

Jones, O. (2003). 'The Persistence of Autocratic Management in Small Firms: TCS and Organizational Change'. *International Journal of Entrepreneurial Behaviour and Research,* 9/6: 245–67.

——(2006). 'Developing Absorptive Capacity in Mature Organizations: The Change Agent's Role'. *Management Learning,* 37/3: 355–76.

——and Macpherson, A. (2006). 'Inter-Organizational Learning and Strategic Renewal in SMEs: Extending the 4I Framework'. *Long Range Planning,* 39/2: 155–75.

Knights, D., and Morgan, G. (1991). 'Strategic Discourse and Subjectivity: Towards a Critical Analysis of Corporate Strategy in Organizations'. *Organization Studies,* 12: 251–73.

Kokkalis, P. (2007). 'Critical Incident Technique', in R. Thorpe and R. Holt (eds.), *The Sage Dictionary of Qualitative Research in Management.* London: Sage.

Lee, R., and Jones, O. (2006). 'The Role of Cognitive Social Capital in Entrepreneurial Learning'. Organizational Learning, Knowledge and Capabilities Conference, Warwick University, 20–22 March.

Little, D. (1991). *Varieties of Social Explanation: An Introduction to the Philosophy of Social Science.* Oxford: Westview.

Macpherson, A., and Holt, R. (2007). 'Knowledge, Learning and SME Growth: A Systematic Review of the Evidence'. *Research Policy,* 36/1: 172–92.

——and Jones, O. (2008). 'Mediating the Object of Activity: Strategic Renewal and Learning in Mature Organizations'. *Management Learning* (forthcoming).

——Jones, O., and Oakes, H. (2006). 'Mediating Artefacts, Boundary Objects and the Social Construction of Knowledge'. Organizational Learning, Knowledge and Capabilities Conference, Warwick University, 20–22 March.

Nahapiet, J., and Ghoshal, S. (1998). 'Social Capital, Intellectual Capital, and the Organizational Advantage'. *Academy of Management Review*, 23/2: 242–66.

Orlikowski, W. (2002). 'Knowing in Practice: Enacting a Collective Capability in Distributed Organizing'. *Organization Science*, 13/3: 249–73.

Rae, D. (2000). 'Understanding Entrepreneurial Learning: A Question of How?' *International Journal of Entrepreneurial Behavior and Research*, 6/3: 145–59.

Rubin, H., and Rubin, I. (1995). *Qualitative Interviewing: The Art of Hearing Data*. London: Sage.

SBS (2007). <http://www.sbs.gov.uk/smes>.

Schutz, A. (1976). *Collected Papers*, vol. ii. *Studies in Social Theory*. The Hague: Nijhoff.

Shotter, J. (1997). 'Dialogical Realities: The Ordinary, the Everyday, and Other Strange New Worlds'. *Journal of the Theory of Social Behaviour*, 27/2: 345–57.

Sole, D., and Edmonson, A. (2002). 'Situated Knowledge and Learning in Dispersed Teams'. *British Journal of Management*, 13, special issue: 17–34.

Spender, J. (1989). *Industry Recipes: The Nature and Sources of Managerial Judgement*. Oxford: Basil Blackwell.

Tether, B. (2000). 'Small Firms, Innovation and Employment Creation in Britain and Europe: A Question of Expectations'. *Technovation*, 20/2: 109–30.

Thorpe, R. (1988). 'An Exploration of Small Business Success: The Role of the Manager'. Ph.D. thesis, University of Lancaster.

——Gold, J., Holt, R., and Clarke, J. (2006). 'Immaturity: The Constraining of Entrepreneurship'. *International Small Business Journal*, 24/3: 232–50.

——Holt, R., Macpherson, A., and Pittaway, L. (2005). 'Knowledge Use in Small Firms: A Systematic Review'. *International Journal of Management Reviews*, 7/4: 257–81.

Tilley, F., and Tonge, J. (2003). 'Introduction', in O. Jones and F. Tilley, *Competitive Advantage in SMEs: Organising for Innovation and Entrepreneurship*. Chichester: Wiley.

Van-der-Heijden, K., and Eden, C. (1998). 'The Theory and Praxis of Reflective Learning in Strategy Making', in C. Eden and J. Spender (eds.), *Managerial and Organizational Cognition: Theory, Methods and Research*. London: Sage.

Von Krogh, G. (2004). 'Knowledge Sharing and the Communal Resource', in M. Easterby-Smith and M. Lyles (eds.), *Handbook of Organizational Learning and Knowledge Management*. Oxford: Blackwell.

Wilkinson, A., and Willmott, H. (1995). 'Total Quality: Asking Critical Questions'. *Academy of Management Review*, 20/4: 789–91.

Zahra, S. A., and George, G. (2002). 'Absorptive Capacity: A Review, Reconceptualization, and Extension'. *Academy of Management Review*, 2: 185–203.

Zhang, M., Macpherson, A., and Jones, O. (2006). 'Conceptualising the Learning Process in SMEs: Improving Innovation through External Orientation'. *International Small Business Journal*, 24/3: 299–321.

APPENDIX 1

THE SAMPLE STRUCTURE

The six industrial sectors

	Services			Manufacturing	
		Client-based			
Culture and leisure	Retail	Bespoke advice	Formulaic advice	Low-tech	High-tech
This type of firm will provide products (other than internally manufactured items), services, or support to the media, entertainment, and leisure industries. This includes sports, travel, and hobbies, and includes any activity through which customers either support or participate in these types of activities.	This industry includes any firm that provides goods or services directly to the public involving face-to-face interactions with the customer. This excludes companies that only provide electronic outlets over the Internet or through catalogue and call-centre–based operations.	This involves the provision of consultancy or support in the delivery of idiosyncratic solutions. Typically this type of firm would provide a bespoke approach to each of its customers taking into account a variety of possibilities and providing creative, contextually sensitive advice. Outcomes are likely to be intangible as well as tangible.	This involves the provision of formulaic 'best practice' or derivative solutions provided by 'experts' in a field of business or related professional activity. While the product or service may vary between customers, this will usually be within a typical professional or business framework and rely on tried and trusted methods for product or service solutions.	This is conceived as a firm that provides manufactured goods, either as components or finished products, as its primary activity. The goods will be in any sector, but they will rely on readily available technology, processes, and systems during manufacture.	A firm operating in this sector will either be using highly technically complex manufacturing systems that are not readily transferred, or they will be manufacturing products that are technically complex and idiosyncratic (these may be protected by IPR). That is, the materials, processes, or products will be developed to a high level of specification and provide a leading-edge technological solution.

The three outlooks

Start-up	Stable	Innovative
Typically, a company in this category will be within the early stages of its initial business venture and will be searching out or developing its market potential. The systems and processes will still be in the process of development, and the company will be establishing its identity within its market place.	This type of company will have been established for any length of time. However, for a significant period it will have continued to trade in existing markets, providing the same or very similar products and services, using a stable array of production techniques or organizational systems. A firm in this category may be defending or exploiting a particular market niche.	This company may have been established for any length of time and demonstrates periods of organizational renewal, either through the development of new products and services or new processes. The rate of change may be either adaptive or revolutionary. Evidence of experimenting, risk taking, or development would be expected, which may include diversification or simple adaptation. The renewal may have facilitated survival or growth, but this would depend on the context or market within which this firm operates. A firm is likely to be strategically predisposed to technical or market leadership, and provide evidence of a responsive and flexible approach to new opportunities identified in the market.

3

Executive Directors' Knowledge

John Storey, Graeme Salaman, and Richard Holti

Introduction

The research reported in this chapter explores the knowledge work practices of directors and other senior managers. It examines the ways in which senior managers use knowledge and the ways they help to adapt and create knowledge. Through close and detailed examination of senior managers' doing and knowing, it becomes possible to shed some light on what, and how, knowledge is used at the strategic apex of organizations. There are a number of crucial questions for which research to date has not yet provided adequate answers: What knowledge do executive managers use? What knowing is involved in management? In so far as contributing to strategy is an expectation, how is this accomplished and what knowing is required for this?

The processes involved in senior managers' knowing and the ways in which they draw upon that knowing are shaped by multiple forces. Not least, there is the range of ways in which different types of knowledge (including knowledge of suppliers and of customers, of processes and of support services, of science and technology) and the different requirements for knowledge are distributed in complex organizations. There is also a network of social relations and expectations in which these types of knowledge are embedded and a range of routinized and institutionalized practices, such as board meetings and annual business planning cycles, in which they are embroiled. Each of these can limit and inhibit the dispassionate use and scrutiny of knowledge.

These are some of the features that make higher echelon knowledge distinctive and problematic compared with more operation-level knowledge and practice, which to a much greater extent can be subjected to routines—albeit ones that nearly always require some element of additional tacit knowledge. Previous work (e.g. Whitley 2004) has noted that management knowledge is especially contextualized. This makes it less amenable to abstraction and professionalization. Our purpose was to probe further the nature of this embedded and contextualized knowledge and the social practices that sustain it. We found that executive managers were caught within a set of competing values and expectations. They were expected to be 'leaders' in the sense of knowing where to take the organization. They were expected to use rational decision-making tools. They were expected to adopt a corporate perspective and yet also lead their specialist divisions. They were expected to be alert to changes of myriad kinds and yet also to maintain a steady hand on the tiller. The 'technologies' available to them, such as the various business planning tools, seemed to be of limited practical value: they offered frameworks that required a great deal of additional practical knowledge to make them useful. One of the dominant meta-level business themes of our time is the notion that 'agility' is the ultimate capability. Yet, except in times of unambiguous crisis, the executive managers we studied were deeply influenced by prevailing organizational routines and knowledge. While such *embeddedness* blunts organizational *agility*, and even undercuts attempts to develop strategy as a rational process of decision making, in many circumstances it ironically gives greater resilience to top management action in the long run.

Context for the research

We were especially interested in the kind of *knowing* required in order to 'do' strategizing, because this, using the term in its widest sense, is what makes top-level management distinctive from other organizational participants. But, despite the pervasive use of the term 'strategy', it is notoriously difficult to circumscribe the use of this term even within the strategic management literature itself.

The strategy-as-practice perspective enables an approach to strategy as a contingent form of knowledge involving historical and culturally specific ways of thinking. It is helpful when studying higher echelon players, such as directors and senior managers, because it directs our attention to the different 'levels' of knowing and the different 'levels' of practice. For example, it has been suggested that the idea of 'strategic management' is an essentially Anglo-Saxon phenomenon and that it is perceived and used differently in other cultural settings. Our work with Ethiopian managers supports this point (Woldesenbet, Storey, and Salaman 2006).

It is not just that 'strategy' may be constructed retrospectively (though we found this does appear to happen), but further, there can be different versions of what the strategy is and what it ought to be—and indeed whether there really is a strategy. Rather than seek to arbitrate between the various 'schools' (e.g. see Mintzberg 1990), our approach was to examine empirically how senior managers themselves behave in relation to their work. To what extent would they define it as 'strategic', and, in so far as they did, what would they mean by this? What were they doing when they claimed to be strategizing? Who would they regard as primarily responsible for strategy? With regard to business knowledge, three main interrelated questions are addressed:

(1) What kinds of knowledge do senior managers draw upon and deploy?
(2) How do they access, adapt, and develop this knowledge?
(3) How do they use it?

To varying degrees, these questions are amenable to empirical enquiry.

The strategy-as-practice literature, according to Whittington (2006), has concentrated so far on just two main 'levels' while neglecting a third. He contends that studies have focused either on interpersonal interactions, on the one hand, or societal level interpretations, on the other, while the organizational level has been neglected. The notion of levels is useful but problematical. There are potentially numerous levels that could be conceptualized, the boundaries are fuzzy and practice often operates at multiple levels simultaneously. Thus, an activity episode at any one time may appear to be directed at the interpersonal level, but it may also carry implications and derive meaning from organizational, industry sector, national, and international levels. In the analysis that follows, we show the interconnections between macro-level business knowledge (including, for example, narratives built around 'enterprise', 'globalization', 'agility', and so on); sector level (such as industry recipes); organizational level (business models); individual executive; and action-episode level. But, for ease of presentation given the space constraints in this chapter, we focus on just two levels—micro and macro. The micro refers to practical activity within organizations; the macro refers to interpretations and practices at the supra-organizational level—including sector and societal levels. Our aim is to reveal the interpenetrations of knowing across these levels.

It is possible to conceptualize *societal-wide* 'knowledge' as 'paradigms' or 'cosmologies' (Kuhn 1966). At the *industry sector level*, Spender (1989) has analysed 'industry recipes', at the *organizational level*, others have explored 'dominant managerial logics' (Prahalad and Bettis 1986). In a later article (Bettis and Prahalad 1995), dominant logic is seen as a 'frame of reference' that filters data and information.

We encountered many instances of pervasive, well-rehearsed accounts and schemas that 'made sense' of perceived trends and emergent realities. While some managers perceived continuity, time and again we heard tell of long-established business models coming under strain while ways of doing business that had for many years been taken for granted were said to be viable for not much longer, or even more dramatically, that the industry model was 'broken'. This was encountered, for example, in sectors as varied as pharmaceuticals, construction, graphics and print, education, and so on. Indeed, the 'broken' industry model was found sufficiently widely that it too appears to be a meta-narrative at the societal level.

A little more probing, however, revealed other levels of knowing. One level was the meta-narrative rehearsed at major sector conferences and embellished by leading management consultants in the respective sectors. These accounts were often framed in terms of the 'paradigm shift' language. But another level was the knowledge about the organization and the sector as held by different directors and senior managers. These interpretations of the 'required business model' often varied in significant ways and thus by implication challenged the paradigm shift notion. In this chapter we seek to illustrate how strategizing, and the associated business knowledge on which it was based, were found to operate at these different levels, and most essentially, how knowledge was translated between and within these levels.

The strategy-as-practice perspective seems potentially helpful in this regard. This approach to strategy research treats strategy as something that is done and therefore something that can be observed. The need and relevance of attending to the micro aspects of practice stem ironically from changes in the economic context. The faster pace of change means that strategy-making is no longer something occasionally undertaken in elaborately planned episodes: change is constant and so more people are involved in strategy and do so more often (Johnson, Melin, and Whittington 2003: 5). Process research has arguably not delved deeply enough into actual practices. Brown and Duguid (2000) argue that practice is what occurs inside processes. They suggest that while the process perspective has been insightful, it has failed to address a number of aspects that a practice perspective could help illuminate. These include: what managers actually do and with what techniques (and we would add with what knowledge), the extent of agency, and the extent of institutional and societal forces. Each of these, singularly and together, affect strategic decision making. The agenda and challenge for activity/practice research is set by the shortcomings in the process approach.

Managers draw on (some of) these wider knowledge resources and at the same time they contribute creatively to them. They adapt existing knowledge and in the practice of its attempted utilization they create new knowledge. Information and knowledge does not always travel smoothly, it has 'sticky' properties (Von Hippel 1994; Szulanski 2003). Nonetheless, managers are the ultimate arbiters of guru concepts and frameworks: if they purchase them and use these forms of knowledge, then that patronage ensures the growth of that business knowledge. If they ignore even the most well-argued frameworks, then these theories will struggle for survival. In the marketplace of ideas, even the most heavily subsidized modes of 'best practice' are frequently largely ignored by practising managers.

When strategy does become explicit, this may be because of a breakdown or threat to the normal order. But the nature of that 'threat' may be as much perceived as real. It may be prompted by critical questioning from powerful stakeholders, for example, new shareholders, new non-executive directors, a regulator, and so on. It may well be that it is when organizational identity is threatened that strategists 'begin to invoke purposeful ideas so as to restore consistency and recover identity' (Chia and Holt 2006: 649). But the way in which this is then accomplished is of great interest because these periods tend to force the surfacing of previously unarticulated knowledge. This is the opportunity to study managers' attempts to articulate their understandings of strategy. Divergent statements stimulate enquiry as to the sources of difference. This is the ideal time to explore the nature of top managers' business knowledge. Divergence often results in fracture. New distinct positions (and meaning systems) are identified. 'Fractal distinctions' create a sense of evolution of knowledge (Abbott 2000).

The empirical study

The chapter draws on case studies across a range of sectors including retail, construction, business services, health care, engineering consultancy, graphics, print, and banking. We observed executive boards in action and conducted one-to-one interviews with executive directors. The research project concentrated on executive teams. There were three phases to the casework. The first phase involved initial scoping visits to some fifteen organizations in order to gain intelligence about critical issues and the extent of challenge to existing business models. The second phase was more detailed work with six selected cases. The third phase was the most intensive and this involved action research with three of the organizations.

The knowledge work undertaken by the chief executive and the other executive directors was the focus of attention. The strategy-as-practice perspective was useful because it encouraged dual engagement with what these managers did and said. As knowledge cannot be seen, we had to infer it from action and explanation of action. Hence, with respect to the case studies and the action research sites, three mutually reinforcing methods formed the heart of the study: in-depth one to one interviews with each member of the respective executive teams; direct observation of management board meetings; and scrutiny of secondary sources, including, most notably, executive board agendas and minutes plus internal company reports. The observations of executive board meetings allowed insight into the naturally occurring conversations of directors and senior managers and facilitated the observation of non-verbal signals.

Our empirical work included two sector-level organizations. One was an association of premier companies in the construction industry; the other was an association of leading companies in the cleaning and support services industry. Each of these organizations was seeking actively to change the business models of their respective industries. Each allowed us high-level access to senior executives who were grappling actively with ideas about fundamental sector-level change in these respective industries. We were able to observe these senior players in debate and negotiation with each other and were able to interrogate them further about their views and actions following these meetings. We begin with the construction companies and then compare the situation with the large cleaning and support services companies.

Changing the business model in construction

The influential figures on the body we studied were clear that the organization is on a mission to change the nature of the industry—or at least that top segment of the industry that is represented by its members. The degree to which these industry figures believed or knew such a change to be feasible was a point of contention. The organization stands for 'new ways of working'—by which is meant collaborative working between all component parts of the supply chain from architects to clients. Proponents of such change believe that the new ways can deliver mutual gains and allow learning from previous experience instead of the business as usual model, which was described as 'screwing each other in the same old way'. They seek to influence the industry—big clients, their agents, architects, and other suppliers and other contractors in the supply chain. Clients in both the public and private sectors are targeted, most especially the big repeat procurers.

The organization has a mission to move the industry from an adversarial and litigious model to one that focuses on a value stream of 'collaborative working' to integrate the supply chain. Members of the association were expected to be committed to that agenda. The methods for change included programmes of training events, demonstration projects, communication of best practice, measurement and self-assessment tools, and action research initiatives.

There were, however, a range of views as to the precise nature of the new model. Often, it was described as 'the Egan model' following Sir John Egan's report, which recommended a Toyota-style reform in construction, drawing on lean practices in the motor industry, including elements such as just in time, process management, and so on. But some senior figures in the construction association claimed that the motor industry analogy was inappropriate and that, in any case, the main features of the Egan model had already been proven in a major construction project in the City of London at Broadgate. This was cited as already demonstrating the value of collaborative working with benefits realized in health and safety, reduced conflict with the workforce, and less confrontation with other contractors and suppliers.

We learned a number of lessons pertinent to our knowledge study through our engagement with these players. One lesson was that even those senior managers who apparently 'knew' that the current ways of working were costly and inefficient were still prepared to conspire in their prolongation in their everyday work. One justification offered was that it is only possible to shift if all the players in the supply chain agree and develop the necessary capabilities. However, here was a group of major players at the pinnacle of the industry who 'knew' that the model they operated within was inefficient and costly and who also had knowledge of a viable, preferred, alternative—yet they find it enormously difficult to shift from one to the other.

This case illustrates the indeterminate and contested nature of business prescriptions as well as the gap between their espousal and their implementation. It suggests that the work and 'knowing' of senior managers concerns coping with such conditions, rather than the straightforward application of clearly validated strategic 'knowledge'. Senior managers in the construction contracting firms were were torn between their 'knowing' as senior figures at sector level and their localized 'knowing' as participants in ongoing organizational routines and power structures.

Changing the business model in cleaning and facilities management

The organization we studied in this sector was the leading trade body for cleaning and support services companies. There were many similarities with the construction case. This again was a fee-based membership body that employed a salaried chief executive and a secretariat. The executive board was likewise intent on changing the industry business model. It wished to move the industry from a low-cost, low quality, low margins, and low pay model to an enhanced value-added service model. To mark this shift, they aspired to a new 'Kitemark' of quality that would distinguish the leading players from the rest. To qualify for the Kitemark, members would need to pass a range of 'tests', including high quality processes and services, accredited technical ability, a code of conduct, evidence of a training policy and good training practice, health and safety practices with evidence of operator qualifications, quality assurance procedures, appropriate staff terms and conditions, and evidence of managerial capabilities. Other elements of change they envisaged were an expansion in the range of service offerings. For example, in addition to the core cleaning services, there could be such additional services as meeting room management, including the booking of rooms and the provisioning of water, stationery, the setting up of audio-visual equipment and other requirements. In addition, other services could also be 'bundled' into the contract essentially amounting to a new, enhanced, form of property management services.

Some members of the executive, including the director general of the association, believed that such a fundamental shift was feasible. The aspiration was to raise the quality and the image of the service and the industry. But some members of the association were sceptical. Their knowing of the industry—most especially of the clients and other contractors—suggested to them that it would be very difficult if not impossible to shift the business model in this way, except perhaps for a few niche players in very particular circumstances. Thus, the debate hinged on different conceptions of what 'the market' was 'really like'. It also hinged on contention concerning the extent to which it is feasible to reconfigure 'the market'.

These two different modes of knowing about the business environment and the business models were explored in our research both with clients as well as a range of contractors. There was evidence that at least some clients wanted to see a move to the high-value model. Clients were under pressure from campaigning groups and trade unions complaining about low pay, especially in Canary Wharf and the City of London 'zones'. Equally, in specialist sectors, such as among the pharmaceutical client firms, or those in hospitals and high-capital intensive specialist settings, the facilities managers needed high-value-added reliable services rather than the lowest cost services.

In summary, executive directors in the cleaning and facilities management contracting firms were torn between competing models of how the sector 'really worked'. They had different interpretations of how the market operated; they drew upon different knowledge about what mattered most to clients; and they drew upon different knowledge systems concerning how the cleaning business model had to be—or could be.

The engineering consultancy company

We now turn from the sector level of analysis to the organizational level. For illustrative purposes here, we will discuss findings from a very successful consultancy firm and in the next section from a large retailer.

Eng-Con with 300 staff provides the engineering services required for the design of buildings of all types: hospitals, arts centres, airports, and so on. Structural, civil, and building services engineering teams are employed. Eng-Con directors expect 30% UK and 200% overseas growth in 2006. The firm's business plan involves recruiting 200 new staff. Its staff turnover is half the industry average. By any measure, this company is highly successful and is a respected leader in its sector.

The knowledge for success underpinning the business model was based on a notion of 'enterprise'. This was regarded by senior management as central to the organization's culture, strategy, and business approach. The directors/partners talked in a consensual way about their desire to 'look at every engineering problem with a fresh outlook', they maintained there was 'a freshness about us . . . and an enthusiasm for what we do'.

Enterprise and talent were achieved and supported at the individual and the organizational level. The source of enterprise at the individual level is the people who are recruited and the way they are then 'managed'. Recruitment is a key factor but so is retention, and both are the result of deliberate policies and practices. Organizational structuring and business strategies are designed in ways that take into account this aspect of the business model. Senior managers, including the founder CEO, see themselves as enterprising, and they try deliberately to recruit others who share this quality. The directors shared an antipathy to 'bureaucracy'.

The directors were aware of the discrepancies between their own business model and what they perceived as conventional business. They were willing to learn about and explore more systematic approaches and to this end had invited in consultants and advisers from Business Link and other service providers. But they remained doubtful about the transferability of these models to their own firm. They were comfortable in taking their organization forward in a state of some ignorance about the professional norms of management, in contrast to their deep commitment to ideals of engineering professionalism. This case illustrates that skilled practice of senior managers can involve operating without the guidance of generic management knowledge.

Retailing Co

Retailing Co is a major retailing company that owns a number of significant retailing businesses on the high street. We studied senior managers within the constituent businesses and at corporate level. A high level of tacit consensus existed within the top team based on shared but largely un-surfaced, well-established historic assumptions. There was considerable agreement about what the business needed to be like in order to pursue its proper historic role and objectives. These assumptions centred on a highly distinctive normative model of organizations and employment relations, with a consequent emphasis on service and quality with respect to customers.

Because executives shared so many assumptions and beliefs, they found it hard to envision new possibilities or ways in which such innovations could be generated. But some signs of declining performance relative to major competitors were addressed by two types of activity. First, there was piecemeal introduction of modern management processes. These included development and training, executive team-building initiatives, and performance-management and supply-chain redesign. These did not generally constitute a significant change in the assumptions underlying the business model and therefore were broadly acceptable to all members of the top team. A second initiative was to revive, refresh, and re-emphasize the historic values and unique features of the organization through a relaunch of these and their communication throughout the business. In short, a major strategy was to surface, revive, and reassert the historic assumptions and models. This initiative could be seen, in terms of the model used here, as an attempt to make the tacit model more explicit. So strategy issues were resolved simply by invoking the accepted and taken-for-granted models. There were thus changes and yet, in another sense, no change.

Discussion

It is often claimed that the nature of business and business environments has become subject to rapid and far-reaching change. The pervasiveness and extent of such changes is indicated by the frequent use of the term 'paradigm shift' in various sectors. Product life cycles are shorter, markets are more global, industry boundaries are increasingly blurred, and business organizations are tending to compete beyond conventional boundaries through strategic alliances and various forms of collaboration. The way managers handle these changes is often regarded as indicative of the evolution of business knowledge.

But these kinds of accounts are usually presented as an admixture of descriptions of business practice and prescriptions for action. Less well observed has been the way in which the senior practitioners, who are crucial players in this unfolding drama, themselves interpret their situation. What knowledge do senior executives (whose job it is to steer and lead these businesses) have of these 'trends', 'shifts', and 'evolutions'? How do managers use their knowledge to weigh and calculate the implications for their organizations?

The construction and cleaning contractors were versed in a brave new narrative, and they were aware of the deficiencies of their current sector business model. But they seemed incapable of acting in a different way. In the engineering consultancy, the managers had knowledge of institutionalized modern management methods, but they wanted to avoid them or at least treat them with great caution.

Paradigm shifts are often presented as supra-sector trends. They also find reflection in many sector-level analyses. Thus, for example, in graphics and print there are insistent depictions of far-reaching transformations of the industry. The new conventional wisdom is based on notions of a shift

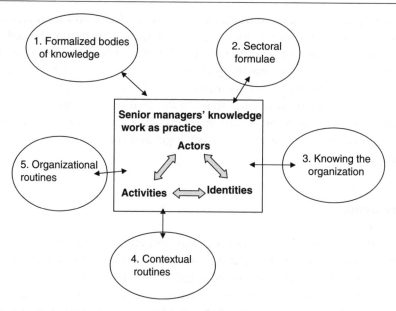

Fig. 3.1. Executive managers' fields of knowing

to a new paradigm. The drivers are depicted as increased price competition, globalization, new technology, demand for additional services from customers; the outcomes and consequences are described as just-in-time delivery, shorter print run capability, reduced stocks, and greater customer orientation. This at least is the 'official' view.

A synthesis of the diverse strands of literature described in the introductory section of this chapter allied with the findings from our empirical enquiries is shown in Figure 3.1.

The central circle of the diagram emphasizes senior managers as participating actors using, and being defined by, *practices*. These are socially constituted streams of activities, such as board meetings, strategic planning workshops, or annual budget-setting rounds. Managers' knowing derives from learning over a period of time—it is a consequence of an intellectual journey. This accumulated knowledge becomes part of identity and is in turn constructed through practical action, while practical action in turn shapes identity.

The outer five circles of the diagram summarize social phenomena that we found influence and are influenced by senior management knowledge work. Circle 1 denotes codified bodies of abstract knowledge, often available in published form, which senior managers draw on. Circle 2 refers to those practices in play outside the formal boundaries of the focal organization that are concerned with overtly influencing how senior managers think about and perform their work. As we found in the construction and cleaning services sectors, there are in circulation particular formulae and archetypes that promulgate reformed business knowledge. As institutional theorists argue (see e.g. Greenwood and Hinings 1996), these may acquire legitimacy and so become powerful influences on local practice. Some formulae for organizing—of the 'new paradigm' variety—may be under-specified at a detailed level. But even in these cases, an important aspect of senior management knowledge work is to find a way of engaging with these legitimated isomorphic forces. Other formulae for organizing may be promulgated by well-developed networks of actors, for example, business process re-engineering. In these cases, senior management practice involves engaging with purveyors of alleged improvement techniques and deciding if and how to let them into their organization. Application of such institutionalized practice generally requires tacit knowing. Through managerial actors, there is considerable scope for variation in interpretations of tools and techniques, as well as variation in the knowing about and indeed knowing what needs to be done as well as how things ought to be done. Thus, in the cleaning contractors and the construction contractors we studied, the applications of the sector-level knowledge shifts were variegated.

Circle 3 refers to the sets of recipes for action and common understandings that become established through processes of learning within an organization. Such practices can be understood as accumulated knowledge or even as 'intellectual capital'.

Circle 4 denotes the routines of interaction that become established with actors in external agencies, such as customers, suppliers, and regulators. It reveals how networks of practice cross the boundaries of the focal organization. It is through these that senior managers can claim to 'know the context' in which they are managing. Boundary-spanning routines, such as annual report press conferences for city journalists, set the context and framework for senior management debates and decision making.

Circle 5 refers to organizational routines and the ostensible 'knowledge resources' available within the focal organization. The case organizations all had written instances of 'organizational knowledge', such as organization charts and analyses of market intelligence and market share. Senior management knowledge work involves drawing on these, as well as contributing to their further development.

Drawing on our data in relation to this framework, we can now proceed to summarize some of the main characteristic features of senior managers' knowledge in its embedded practical sense. This is presented in three segments: knowing the strategy, knowing the organization, and knowing the context.

Formalized bodies of knowledge and their implications for strategy: Circles 1 and 2

One of the findings from the casework was the realization that senior managers were often very unsure about many aspects of strategy. This uncertainty included the meaning of strategy, what the strategy of the organization could be said to be, or even whether their organization really did have an agreed strategy. Moreover, there was expressed lack of knowledge about how they and their management boards should go about formulating strategy. To compensate for this we found they fell back on two forms of knowledge: explicit process knowledge about strategy formulation and formulae derived from sector-level bodies and networks.

Often, leading management consultants would be hired to help with a strategic review, and they would leave behind a conceptual framework, a new language, and a suggested market position. Work streams and action plans would follow and responsibilities would be allocated. To this extent, these senior teams could then say that (for the time being) they now truly did have a strategy. How much difference in practice this made to actual behaviour (and its deeper level of business knowledge) was often questionable.

Different directors often gave incomplete or differing accounts of what they saw as 'the strategy'. Both the nature of the supposed current strategy and the preferred nature of a future strategy triggered competing versions. There was also the recurring problem of achieving even a corporate view. Using knowledge to reassess strategy in any fundamental way may be simply too threatening and too difficult. Instead, displacement activity occurs to fill the time at executive board meetings: information sharing, reporting, scrutinizing budgets, commenting on functional papers, and reviewing bids for capital expenditure.

'Away days' and team process analysis events we found to be very common—almost universal in the large organizations. But senior managers often criticized them as being too much about individual styles and complementarities. Attempts to 'know the mission' through brand identity exercises, values-clarifying workshops followed by statements of values, and the like seemed to have limited effect. It was common for organizations to seek to encapsulate their purpose or 'essence' in six or so adjectives or adverbs but there was also scepticism among executives about the meaningfulness of these. This is one illustration of the elusiveness and ambiguity of senior management 'knowledge' of business.

Because the search for clarity and consensus was not quite so easily accomplished, a crucial aspect of the knowing about strategy was that such knowing was often contested. Statements—in effect knowledge and truth claims—about what the organization should 'really' be doing, 'really' be prioritizing, or 'really' be like, frequently pointed in different directions. While some top team members thought the organization should 'stretch the brand', others were convinced that it should 'stay focused'. Because senior managers knew these kinds of debates would lead to fundamental differences, because they knew these were difficult issues, and because they knew that they had little in-depth knowledge about them, they usually preferred to avoid having the debates at all.

Knowing the organization: Circle 3

There was contestation in knowing about organizational design. This could take place over many aspects: how much centralization or decentralization was appropriate; how much formalization versus informality; how much insistence on standard operating procedures versus a leaning towards flexibility and adaptability? Intense debates also occurred over the nature, purpose, and extent of central control. Most senior managers in divisions of multidivisional companies questioned the contribution of the corporate centre. What was 'the value-add' they would ask. Knowledge about the work of the corporate centre was limited from a divisional perspective. Conversely, knowledge about how the divisions were behaving in practice was obscure from a corporate perspective.

Given these tendencies, knowing about the organization in a different way—i.e. in terms of its key members—is a vital form of knowledge. This kind of knowledge covered assessments and judgements about which key individuals were supported by whom and which were opposed by whom; understanding about which figures were in the ascendancy and which on the wane; which cabals granted shelter and which threatened ridicule and exposure.

Knowledge of important new developments in the external context could be more problematic. Despite the routine 'market intelligence/ news' made available by ICT departments, some executives gained critical advantage from their superior knowledge of the really crucial developments made known to them through their networking with analysts, professional association colleagues, peers in other companies, and so on. This kind of knowledge, heralding perhaps significant new directions in the market for the organization's services could be crucial.

Knowing about the organization had various elements. Knowing about organizational routines was important as was knowledge about performance through the interpretation of various sorts of information. With advances in ICT, the availability of, and access to, information of many kinds has multiplied. Organizational intranets allow access to policy documents, committee papers, organizational profile data, performance indicators, customer information, and so on. Thus, the skill is to know how to be selective about this overwhelming amount of information and data.

Part of the skill was also to know how to make sense of it: that is, to construct a meaningful picture from it. The ready availability of data and information via electronic technologies has meant that it seems less important to know the detail in quite the same way as was perhaps once expected. Because now 'everyone has it' the special advantage derived from having and displaying knowledge of this sort of information is often diminished. Indeed, the game had changed to such an extent that the sheer availability of information became a source of complaint. Few were satisfied that they knew which measures to pay regard to in their monthly meetings. There was usually some concern that there were too few measures or too many. And there was a concern that the measures that were presented were perhaps not the 'right' ones. The search for the holy grail of the few, relevant metrics was ongoing in the majority of senior executive teams.

Even when ample financial performance data was made readily available in monthly board meetings, there were important moments when a manager would claim that some figures and some ratios but not others were giving a 'truer picture' of the organization's real performance. This controversy about simply knowing how the organization was performing was in fact a major source of contention. Markedly different accounts about organizational health (including interpretations of progress versus decline) were allowed to circulate in a number of these organizations. Thus, for senior managers even to know 'how we are doing' could be very problematical.

Routinized knowledge: Circles 4 and 5

Senior managers' knowledge systems were deeply embedded. They had arrived at the top because they had worked within, understood, and supported a business model that had resulted in some measure of success. The implicit business models in the case organizations had accrued their own attendant and supportive routines. Hence, asking managers to subvert such knowledge would be to ask a great deal. Senior managers were usually wedded to an interlocking set of 'knowledges' about market opportunities and organizational characteristics.

Within this overall net of organizational routines, senior management knowledge work is shaped and reinforced by the established routines of strategy development and organizational review. This does not necessarily entail stasis: at any point in time, we can see the actors within these routines as capable of undertaking review and innovation (Feldman and Pentland 2003). As we found, there is a strong 'performative aspect embodied in the specific actions of specific people at specific times and in specific places' (2003: 94). Patterns of action reflect 'practical mastery'.

To break out of these routines in any significant way, it is frequently thought that the recruitment of new top management from outside the prevailing framework of experience is necessary. This may be one way to introduce a new knowledge system—a new set of realizations and new priorities. A new chief executive may be expected to bring a ready-made constellation of diagnosis, values, guiding principles, and solutions that are unfettered by the previous knowledge constraints of the previous regime. In one of the cases, in the search for knowledge that the 'right candidate' was chosen, there was a scramble for confirmatory evidence. A string of poor performance data may be forgiven as part of the 'medicine' and part of the pain of the turnaround process.

In spite of all this, or perhaps because of a realization of these considerations, a large proportion of top teams seemed intent to project an impression that they are nearly always 'driving change' of some kind or another. Indeed, being seen to actively drive change (rather than being driven by it as an object) is one of the more notable refrains in the discourse of senior managers. It is evident from senior managers' talk (as revealed both in the interviews and in the observed meetings) that change and action are highly valued notions. It was apparent that almost anything was better than the impression that the board was presiding over a static situation or that it was a hapless victim of drift. It was vital to be seen to 'manage' events.

In the main, senior managers wanted to maintain a conceit that change was under control, that there was a purposefulness and indeed an urgency about the top team and they were able and willing to 'drive forward' with change. And yet there was sufficient continuity—extending over such long time periods—that reassurance could also be found. The executives needed to know what to change and what to preserve.

Conclusions

The research discussed in this chapter reveals the nature and use of knowledge by senior managers as they undertake their executive work—and most notably their strategizing work. The chapter contributes to the growing literature using an activity-based view of strategy. A crucial part of this activity is discourse: senior management work is to a very large extent constituted by discourse (Heracleous 2006). Executives are exposed to multiple and competing sense-making narratives ranging from the service-profit chain, lean, agility, process re-engineering, and many others. Various business models that reveal a recursive relationship between market-related strategies and organizing strategies were constructed by the senior managers in the case organizations. The analysis reveals that the dominant sense-making paradigms provide, at best, loose and incomplete guides to action. Likewise, each knowledge-informed solution can usually be countermanded with another. Accordingly, senior management work is constituted by discourse that seeks to surface and then clarify, resolve, and reconcile differences, and then to navigate an 'agreed' way forward. This work rarely involves full or systematically structured debate of the range of perceived possibilities. Different power positions, division of responsibility, and legacy issues conspire to produce adopted stances, which represent political settlements. Strategy-as-practice in the cases studied reveals the recursive interplay between knowledge of the moment (e.g. the service-profit chain, global sourcing, employee engagement) and long-established, embedded practices, organizational values, and power considerations, such as succession opportunities into top posts. With this type of understanding, we may conclude that key aspects of the skilled practice of senior managers include operating without precise knowledge. We found that senior managers on occasions considered that explicit strategic debates are best avoided, that rhetoric needs to be asserted and inconvenient reality ignored, and ambiguity about the nature of a strategic direction or the state of organizational performance needs to be preserved. Rather than making judgements that these are features of 'bad strategic management', we can instead see these as important elements of senior management practice. The ability to work in this way can even be seen as a kind of enacted knowledge that senior managers acquire.

In varying degrees, virtually all senior managers working within large corporations in the UK environment, whether of British or other national origin, can loosely articulate their company's strategy and most can also reflect critically upon it. They are also usually broadly familiar with the central ideas embedded in the generic paradigm shift models. They know about globalization and agility, about enterprise and empowerment, customer focus, about shorter product life cycles and the need for responsiveness. Whether the term was deployed or not, it was not difficult to make these understandings of a changing world fit with the notion of a new paradigm. But, in order to preserve their connection with these ideas, our senior managers seemed at times to conduct themselves in ways that suggested they had unresolved differences about the nature of the 'new paradigm', which they were further uninterested in resolving. These findings accord with Chia and Holt's (2006) notion of strategy as practical coping. Strategy reflected a disposition to act 'in a manner congruent with past actions and experience' (p. 636). One, optimistic, reading consistent with Chia and Holt's would be that 'not having a fully articulated strategy is strategic' (p. 649), which reflects a 'kind of flexible responsiveness to a situation as it unfolds'. A less optimistic reading suggests that senior managers are sometimes incapable of agreeing a coherent and consistent position and so they proceed with a series of routines and heuristics that have served them well in the past but may mislead them in the changing present and future. A third position is that the ability to maintain an apparently coherent position while maintaining awareness of unresolved strategic differences is actually a key feature and strength of senior management practice. While embeddedness undercuts attempts to develop strategy as a rational process of decision making, it ironically gives greater resilience to top management action in the long run.

References

Abbott, A. (2000). *Chaos of Disciplines*. Chicago: University of Chicago Press.

Bettis, R. A., and Prahalad, C. K. (1995). 'The Dominant Logic: Retrospective and Extension'. *Strategic Management Journal*, 16: 5–14.

Brown, J. S., and Duguid, P. (2000). 'Organizational Knowledge'. *California Management Review*, 40/3: 90–111.

Chia, R., and Holt, R. (2006). 'Strategy as Practical Coping: A Heideggerian Perspective'. *Organization Studies*, 27/5: 636–55.

Feldman, M. S., and Pentland, B. T. (2003). 'Reconceptualizing Organizational Routines as a Source of Flexibility and Change'. *Administrative Science Quarterly*, 48: 94–118.

Greenwood, R., and Hinings, C. R. (1996). 'Understanding Radical Organizational Change: Bringing Together the Old and New Institutionalism'. *Academy of Management Review*, 21/4: 1022–54.

Heracleous, L. (2006). 'A Tale of Three Discourses: The Dominant, the Strategic and the Marginalized'. *Journal of Management Studies*, 43/5: 1059–87.

Kuhn, T. S. (1996). *The Structure of Scientific Revolutions*, 3rd edn. Chicago: University of Chicago Press.

Johnson, G., Melin, L., and Whittington, R. (2003). 'Micro-Strategy and Strategizing: Towards an Activity Based View'. *Journal of Management Studies*, 40: 3–22.

Mintzberg, H. (1990). 'Strategy Formation: Schools of Thought', in J. Frederickson (ed.), *Perspectives in Strategic Management*. New York: Harper Business.

Prahalad, C. K., and Bettis, R. A. (1986). 'The Dominant Logic: A New Linkage between Diversity and Performance'. *Strategic Management Journal*, 7: 485–501.

Spender, J. C. (1989). *Industry Recipes*. Cambridge, Mass.: Blackwell.

Szulanski, G. (2003). *Sticky Knowledge: Barriers to Knowing in the Firm*. London: Sage.

Von Hippel, E. (1994). 'Sticky Information and the Locus of Problem-Solving'. MIT Sloan School of Management, Working Paper no. 40.

Whitley, R. (2004). 'Managing Competences in Entrepreneurial Technology Firms: A Comparative Institutional Analysis of Germany, Sweden and the UK'. *Research Policy*, 33: 89–106.

Whittington, R. (2006). 'Completing the Practice Turn in Strategy Research'. *Organization Studies*, 27/5: 613–34.

Woldesenbet, K., Storey, J., and Salaman, G. (2006). 'Senior Managers' Business Knowledge in a Transition Economy'. British Academy of Management, Belfast, 12–14 September 2006.

4

Organizational Learning and Dynamic Capabilities

Mark Easterby-Smith, Elena Antonacopoulou, Manuel Graça, and Jason Ferdinand

Introduction

Two external dynamics have impacted on us within the last 12 or 18 months quite dramatically. We had two major customers, big customers that were both our competitors and in the space of 18 months they've practically stopped buying from us. One of them because they've got their own internal capacity for production so they're doing that internally. The other main competitor has got associated with the other dynamic, which is cheap imports from Asia. So these customers have changed their strategy and they're pretty well sourcing from Asia as quickly as they possibly could.

Now I believe that both of these big customers have accelerated the implementation of these strategies because of the fact that we've changed our strategy and we've now gone down the value chain. (This new) environment is affecting our innovation effort. Before, it was heavily directed towards looking at the market place and seeing incremental improvements in performance that the market place wanted. So customers needed chemicals that could speed up their own processes. So if we could do that it's a new product and we're keeping ahead of the cheaper competition.

Now the market is not asking for these sort of things very much at all just now, its all about cost, cost, cost, cost and we just want the lowest cost product ok. So our innovative capability now concentrates on radical breakthroughs, and this is demonstrated that by 2002, 51% of our sales were new products.

(CEO ChemCo)

In the quotation above, the chief executive is reflecting on the strategic impact of major competitive changes in his industry over the last few years. These changes contain many dynamic elements, including the interplay of existing global competitors trying to outmanoeuvre each other and the evolution of new markets and competitors. The central response of his company was to build up their capacity for radical innovation, and as we will see below, they have achieved this through internal training and development interventions and external political pro-activity. For the time being, this is giving them the flexibility, or *dynamic capability*, to stay ahead of the competition.

The aim of this chapter is to understand more about these dynamic capabilities, what they are and how they might vary in different contexts. We base this on fieldwork conducted in four European organizations: a hospital trust in the United Kingdom, a small business in the high-tech industry, a multinational in the chemical industry, and a water treatment company. We use data from this fieldwork in order to test and extend ideas about dynamic capabilities, which adds to the theoretical literature by providing detailed views of the inside workings of organizations, and in a context away from the United States, which has previously been the main site for studies on dynamic capabilities. Moreover, by drawing on a range of diverse contexts, we demonstrate the pluralistic ways in which dynamic capabilities manifest themselves, the various features that they share, and the processes that constitute them.

Our project makes several distinct contributions to the wider EBK project. First, it highlights the issues of learning within and between organizations, which are regarded as critical elements in the development and dissemination of organizational knowledge, and this provides a new theoretical perspective on business knowledge. Second, the link to dynamic capabilities provides an emphasis on the relationship between strategic change and operational realities. This sets a broader context for understanding the role of business knowledge and also grounds it in specific practices.

We start with brief reviews of the literatures on dynamic capabilities and organizational learning, demonstrating some weaknesses of the former and the potential benefits of combining it with the latter. We then explain the methodology and research design, and provide illustrative results from our cases, which lead to the identification of six major sources of dynamic capability. We conclude with a summary of theoretical and practical implications.

Context for the research

What are dynamic capabilities?

The idea of dynamic capability is often claimed to provide the secret to sustained competitive advantage. With increasing global competition, and the potential destabilizing of an economic order dominated for so long by the United States, the sources of sustained competitive advantage have attracted the attention of both academics and senior managers. Most of the writings about dynamic capabilities concentrate on the ways in which companies can establish and reconfigure their assets (resources) (Feldman 2000; Teece, Pisano, and Shuen 1997), and how they can establish business processes (routines) that will guarantee flexible deployment of resources (Cohen and Bacdayan 1994; Winter 2003). In the last few years, leading academics have pointed out that sustained competitive advantage must result from a learning process, and the idea of organizational learning has been added to the equation (Zollo and Winter 2002). Eisenhardt and Martin (2000) provide an additional angle by distinguishing between moderate and high velocity markets. They suggest that in moderately dynamic markets, dynamic capabilities derive from routines that are complicated and analytic relying on linear implementation of existing knowledge; whereas in high velocity markets they derive from 'simple, experiential, unstable processes that rely on quickly created new knowledge and execution to produce adaptive but unpredictable outcomes' (Eisenhardt and Martin 2000: 1113).

Despite the amount of academic literature on the subject, there remains a lack of clarity and several unresolved disagreements. For example, there is a 'chicken and egg' problem: does dynamic capability reside in the ability to move assets and resources around flexibly and rapidly, with routines in support, or does the key lie in the ability to modify and change routines, which then impact on resources? There is also uncertainty over the difference between capability and dynamic capability. For example, if a company has a distinctive capability in conducting Internet sales, then the dynamic capability would require them to be able to change the way they conducted Internet sales. But what kind of change would need to be undertaken in order to demonstrate that it is *dynamic*? And how long do these changes need to continue in order to demonstrate that they are sustained?

In our view there are several problems with the literature and with prior research into dynamic capabilities. First, the bulk of it has been conducted through gathering superficial data from large numbers of organizations and by looking at strategic changes across industries. It is still relatively rare for the studies to look inside organizations in order to understand what behaviours actually constitute dynamic capabilities. Second, most of the studies have been conducted in industries, and during times, which have been obviously dynamic. The development of Silicon Valley in the 1980s is one classic setting for research into dynamic capabilities (Saxenian 1994); likewise the development of biotechnology during the 1990s has been another fertile setting (Powell 1998). However, there have been few studies looking at dynamic capabilities within 'normal' organizations operating in normal degrees of competitive change.[1] Third, the bulk of studies have been conducted in the United States, and it is possible that the procedures and conceptual frameworks (for example, the emphasis given to routines and business processes) may be more appropriate within US cultural settings than they are elsewhere.

For these reasons, our study looks at European organizations, and we have also selected a sample covering both large and small companies, and both public and private sectors. Our approach to the research in those organizations is discussed later on in the methodology section.

The role of organizational learning

The field of organizational learning has become very extensive in the last two decades, and this reflects a growing interest in learning processes as key drivers of organizational and economic development. In this section, however, we do not seek to review this literature as a whole. Instead, we focus on identifying a few concepts that are relevant to our inquiry into dynamic capabilities, and to explain in what ways these concepts are likely to contribute to the relevant literature.

As with dynamic capabilities, there has been much debate about how to define and delineate the field of organizational learning. In recent years this has settled down into acceptance of three major perspectives: cognitive, behavioural, and socio-political views. The *cognitive* perspective is influenced by psychological views of learning, which concentrate on the acquisition, dissemination, and interpretation of knowledge, which assumes that organizational learning is based on some compilations of individual learning. Representative examples are to be found in the work of Huber (1998), March (1990), and Argote and Darr (2001). The *behavioural* perspective is less concerned with the knowledge that people in the organization possess, concentrating more on the actions of individuals and the routines that are embedded in the organization (Cohen and Bacdayan 1994; Cyert and March 1963). Key ideas in this stream of work include concepts such as the 'experience curve', which demonstrates statistically the more that a company produces a particular product, the less the cost of that product becomes (Argote, Beckman, and Epple 1990). The *socio-political* perspective was developed to rectify shortcomings of the cognitive view, especially the emphasis it gives to the cognitions of individuals. The essence of this perspective is that learning takes place through social interactions between individuals, and that knowledge is therefore co-created, and to some extent exists in the spaces between people (Brown and Duguid 2000; Cook and Yanow 1993; Nicolini and Meznar 1995). One important feature of this perspective is the idea that knowledge is linked to power, and that learning often incorporates political processes (Coopey 1995; Lawrence et al. 2005). This means that learning, whether pursued by actors individually or in community, is always reflecting a set of tensions about the competing priorities that need to be accommodated. Recent empirical evidence shows that these tensions reflect political behaviour in efforts to institutionalize the desirable approach to learning within specific organizational contexts. In such instances the political nature of learning is reflected in efforts to 'fit in'. And the choices of individuals are equally political when they seek to preserve their power to be 'in control' of their learning and thus challenge rather than comply with the status quo (see Antonacopoulou 2006).

In our view, organizational learning theory can add a number of insights into the nature of dynamic capabilities because it provides a focused examination of the learning processes that are being identified by authors on dynamic capabilities, but generally without wider knowledge of the area. First, research into organizational learning has generally looked at groups and teams, and the resulting 'micro' perspective both complements, and potentially rectifies, the over-reliance on macro forms of analysis within dynamic capabilities research. Second, aspects of organizational learning theory correspond to some of the dominant concepts of dynamic capabilities. For example, the cognitive perspective, which emphasizes the collection and retention of knowledge, has links to the resource-based view of dynamic capabilities. Third, there are parallels, such as the idea that learning can be conceptualized at different levels where successive levels imply an ability to learn about the previous level (Bateson 1973; Easterby-Smith 1997); and this kind of thinking attempts to clarify concepts of dynamic capabilities (Winter 2003). Fourth, there are insights into the socio-political aspects of organizational learning that can shed light on existing theories of dynamic capabilities, which tend to be depersonalized and mechanistic in as much as they are positioned as 'solutions' rather than possibilities.

For these reasons, we think it is valuable to use concepts from learning theory to make sense of dynamic capabilities. However, since the primary focus of this chapter is on dynamic capabilities, we make reference to organizational learning theory only where it helps to clarify, or add further insight, into the primary discussion.

Empirical study

Research design and methodology

One of the main aims of this research was to explore empirically the nature of dynamic capabilities in a range of contexts. In doing so, we sought to identify the features and sources of dynamic capabilities, a point that hitherto has received limited treatment within the dominant research tradition on dynamic capabilities. We therefore thought that it was appropriate to conduct detailed case studies in a small number of organizations that were considered by informed observers to be reasonably 'dynamic'. The data collection strategy was to start with a list of general concepts and questions (see below) but also to be open for the identification of new concepts and questions as the research progressed. We therefore tried to combine the more traditional perspectives on case study research (Eisenhardt 1989) with the emergent tradition of grounded theory (Locke 1997).

Our sample included two larger organizations, a hospital trust (HealthCo) and a European chemical company (EuroChem); and two smaller organizations, an Internet business (WebCo) and a relatively new venture in the water treatment business (WaterCo). Each had done very well over recent years. HealthCo had achieved a turnaround in external judgements of its performance within the space of two years; ChemCo had survived despite major increases in external competition and some hostility within the parent company; WebCo had grown rapidly during a period when most of its competitors were failing; and WaterCo was regarded by its parent company as the most successful of nearly thirty recent new business ventures.

Agreements for access had been secured from senior management in each case before the research project began. We therefore started fieldwork in each case by talking to senior managers about the recent history of the organization, the current corporate strategy, major threats and opportunities, core competencies, whether they thought they had any dynamic capabilities, and major innovations or changes that had taken place recently. These conversations led to the identification of at least two operational units, one of which was regarded as particularly 'dynamic' and the other was regarded as significantly less so. Within each company, therefore, we had two potential dimensions of analysis: first between the strategic and operational levels, and second between the operational units that were regarded as more or less dynamic.

In addition to the comparisons within each organization, we also had potential comparisons between the full organizations, including large/small firms, UK/European firms, and public/private sector organizations. Our initial analysis, which is reported in this chapter, concentrates on each organization as the primary unit of analysis, and we illustrate our main points by selecting brief but detailed incidents from within each organization.

Data collection was mainly through semi-structured interviews. With senior managers, we discussed the strategic issues listed above, while the interviews with members of the operational units concentrated more on specific innovations, procedures, successes and failures, and more generally on their perceptions of the strategic issues that we had previously discussed with senior management. As the interviews progressed, we identified additional themes for investigation. These included issues such as: the leadership style, the impact of different structures, and the role of external networks. Once each of the new themes was identified, we continued investigations within the same organization, and then explored their relevance to the other three organizations.

As the fieldwork progressed, the methods became iterative and involved sense-making from multiple perspectives. Due to the complexities of organizing specific interviews and meetings, we found that primary data collection took several months in each case, and follow-up meetings aimed at clarifying specific issues and technical points sometimes took a further four or five months to organize. Once we had completed the primary fieldwork in each organization, we provided a brief summary to our key contacts and asked for their reactions and whether they felt there were further issues that we should investigate. These two features led to intermittent, but extended, contact with each organization, which enabled us both to observe strategies and procedures as they evolved, and to track the rise and fall of particular projects and initiatives over a period of at least two years. This longitudinal approach led us to be much more aware, for example, of the variability of performance data over time, and the political processes which lead to judgements of success and failure of specific initiatives and projects.

Analysis and interpretation

Our data analysis concentrated on the most significant features of dynamic capability in each organization. In identifying dynamic capabilities, we used a range of methods including structured codification of individual interviews, thematic analysis of all four companies, and open debate among ourselves. We sought to account for the differences between each organization, the differences between different parts within each organization, and the variability in terms of capabilities and performance of units and projects over time. This has led us to six dynamic features, which appeared to be critical to the success of these organizations, or part of them. We arrived at these six features by systematically accounting for what companies did that was distinctive and was seen to contribute to their changing operational and strategic activities over time. However, as we can see below, these features appeared to be different for each organization, and no organization appeared to be particularly strong on all six. We discuss the theoretical and practical implications of this observation later on in the chapter, but for the time being, we summarize these six features as sources of dynamic capability and illustrate them with anecdotes from our case studies.

In Table 4.1, we have provided a summary of how each company rated against the six sources of dynamic capability. A 'high' rating implies that

Table 4.1. *Mapping of dynamic capabilities across four organizations*

	HealthCo	EuroChem	WebCo	WaterCo
Strategic and operational leadership	High	Neutral	Medium	Medium
External networks	High	Negative, later medium	Low	Low
Political backing	Very negative, later medium	Negative	Medium	High
Flexible structure	Negative	Negative	High	Medium (threatened)
Leverage expertise	Low	Low	Negative, later low positive	High
Innovation culture	Negative	High	Low	Low

in our view this feature is critical in the ability of the organization to respond to external competitive pressures. Medium and low ratings suggest that the feature is present, but that it is not so significant; whereas a negative rating suggests that this feature is a hindrance to adaptability, thus acting as a kind of core rigidity (Leonard-Barton 1992).

The rating is not intended to reflect a precise measure but an indication of how the same features manifest themselves to different degrees of significance in different contexts. They are based on our own judgement derived from a number of sources and experiences, including independent notes made by interviewers, discussions between pairs of interviewers on the journey back from company visits, and reflections about the similarities and differences between the different companies. Where we rated something as high, that means that it was a dominant feature that was mentioned by over one-third of the informants at different levels of the organization; similarly, where a feature was very negative this was also mentioned repeatedly in different interviews. The range of ratings is also relative to the four companies we have observed, and it is therefore highly likely that there will be a few companies that exceed this range in both dimensions.

In the next section of the chapter, we will concentrate on the 'high' features, since we are attempting to build up a model of what might constitute dynamic capabilities, and we will therefore pay less attention to the lower rated features. Subsequent analysis of the middle of the scale will help elaborate on some of the more subtle features of these dimensions, but that is outside the scope of the current chapter.

Six types of dynamic capability

As explained above, these are the most prominent features that we noticed when conducting fieldwork in organizations. At this stage, we are calling them 'dynamic capabilities', although this should perhaps be a tentative classification, since we will be returning at the end of the chapter to reflect on how particular definitions relate to the established literature on dynamic capabilities. For each of these six features, we explain briefly the principle and then provide one or two illustrations from our case study companies.

STRATEGIC AND OPERATIONAL LEADERSHIP

This feature reflects an ability to combine contradictory leadership tendencies of being highly directive and very consultative at the same time. It was most noticeable in HealthCo and WebCo, and to a lesser extent in WaterCo. In HealthCo, in particular, the chief executive who was appointed to rescue the Hospital Trust from a major crisis managed to combine an autocratic style of decision making with energetic consultation at all levels of the hospitals and the local community. An aggressive style was experienced most severely by senior managers, on the hospital board, who found the CEO to be quite adamant in pushing forward her own ideas. At the same time, she established a number of mechanisms for fully consulting the opinions of clinical and nursing staff. Many of these mechanisms she fronted herself; but she also expected senior colleagues to play a major role in consultation exercises. One of the first things she did after arriving was to schedule personal meetings with all 120 clinicians in order to listen to their grievances about the previous regime and to enlist their ideas and support for developing the future of the Hospital Trust. This meant that she was similarly well informed about operational matters and was able to incorporate these ideas into strategic decisions.

In WebCo, there was a single similar pattern of leadership that moved easily from strategic to operational levels, although it was much less personalized than in the case of the chief executive of health care. This was a relatively small company, which sold Internet technologies to commercial clients and which grew very rapidly in the early 2000s, just as the dot-com boom was collapsing elsewhere. Indeed, because they started off with a strong cash position, they did very well out of acquisitions of other failing Internet companies. In this case, the senior management group operated as an informal team providing strategic direction to the company, but they all maintained very close personal contacts with the staff in the operating sections, occasionally working alongside account managers in dealing directly with customers. This meant that on a number of occasions they were able to spot new products and business opportunities from direct contact with customers and operational staff.

EXTERNAL NETWORKS

Three of the companies had only modest contact with the outside world, but the professional networks and personal contacts, that the Hospital Trust maintained, made it stand out in this respect. The chief executive of HealthCo had dismissed most of the incumbent directors within her first week in office and appointed a new team from outside the Trust. Each one of the new appointees had exceptionally good external contacts, some to senior members of the regional health authority. In one case, a key contact was responsible for funding decisions and performance evaluations across the region. Another person was recruited from the UK Department of Health, and the Finance Director was recruited from one of the most successful performing Trusts in the country. This meant that the Trust, which was physically located in an isolated part of the country, had abruptly acquired very good communication links with regional and national domains. At a strategic level, they were therefore in close contact with national policy and also able to anticipate new initiatives to which they could respond very rapidly.

But we also observed a similar transitional story about external networks within EuroChem. At the outset of the research the plant, which is located in a northern city of the United Kingdom, was trying to persuade the parent company in Switzerland to invest in the development of some radical process innovations for which a small research team had already demonstrated good potential. However, the development plan requested a substantial amount of funding during a period when cash squeezes for the company were significant. The response of the managing director was to put in a lot of effort into building networks amongst scientists in the head office and politicians in the north region of the country. The former involved numerous visits and short secondments in both directions of key researchers so that head office technical staff would be more likely to appreciate the viability of the new process, and the latter involved making the obvious link between core investments and local jobs. Eventually he was successful in obtaining matched funding from local government, which put sufficient pressure on the headquarters to provide full backing for the new innovation. The creation and establishment of substantial external networks contributed to radical turnaround in the fortunes of both organizations.

POLITICAL SUPPORT

In two of the cases, the establishment of positive political support was largely an outcome of the establishment of good external networks. However, in the other two companies there was an additional feature to the way political support operated. In WaterCo, in particular, the business was set up by the parent company following a week-long seminar aimed at developing major new projects and products. The president of the parent company took a close interest in these fledgling businesses, and in the case of WaterCo he recognized that it would only flourish if it was not constrained by the normal procedural and contractual rules that operated across the wider company. He therefore established a dotted-line relationship between himself and the director of the new business and authorized negotiation of financial and contractual procedures that were unique to the new business. Although this decision caused irritation in some other parts of the company, it created an unprecedented degree of freedom and flexibility about how they operated.

A similar degree of freedom operated within WebCo, but in this instance it was because the main shareholder of the business worked as a member of the executive team on the same site. In his role as the managing director, he had the authority to approve and implement radical products and strategic changes without further reference (beyond a brief phone call to the chairman in London). In both of these cases, we can see that clear political support can act as a kind of umbrella that encourages and legitimizes local creativity and initiatives.

FLEXIBLE STRUCTURE

One of the consequences of political support for WebCo was that structural changes were extremely easy to implement. There was acceptance that regular reconfiguration of group and functional boundaries was one of the best ways of keeping up with the demands and opportunities of the marketplace. Consequently, as researchers we noticed on each subsequent visit that the layout of groups and departments within open plan offices changed very frequently, and we usually started each visit by poring over organizational charts with the training and development manager in order to work out where our various interviewees had moved to.

In WaterCo a different kind of flexibility was built into its strategic development plans. Because the key idea of the business was to expand a French company into a global business very quickly, a decision was taken not to establish new businesses in other countries, but to enter into exclusive partnership agreements with existing businesses in each country.[2] This meant that new national businesses would be established very quickly with minimal outlay of capital from WaterCo, and if they did not work, then alternative arrangements could be made. The key point about this arrangement was that it provided a structure that in itself created greater strategic and operational flexibility.

LEVERAGING EXPERTISE

WaterCo was also distinct from the other three organizations in the way it attempted to leverage knowledge and expertise across the organization. Thus, the technical expertise of the original French company was disseminated to national partners in a series of workshops, secondment, visits, and one-to-one enquiries. But the flow of information was not only outwards; local partners started to offer new technical and operational ideas (for example, about how to deal with the effects of high temperatures in the Middle East on water processes) back to the technical centre in France, which could then be disseminated elsewhere.

Direct contact with the national partners was maintained by a team of five regional sales managers, each of whom looked after several countries. These regional sales managers both worked closely with their national partners and also met every other month with each other to share new ideas about business practices and potential clients. In a number of cases, this also involved sharing knowledge about multinational clients where a contract had been established in one country, but where there was potential to expand the business into another country (for example, from France to Romania). Thus, the regional sales managers acted as a social process of organizational learning and as a conduit for the transfer of knowledge across national and organizational boundaries. (For further information on this company, see Prieto and Easterby-Smith 2006.)

INNOVATION CULTURE

As we have seen above, there was an expectation in both WebCo and WaterCo that employees would look both for new business opportunities and for new technical processes, and that they would share this information with others—although in both cases this was one of a number of other initiatives taking place simultaneously. In this respect, EuroChem was distinctive because it placed a central strategic emphasis upon innovation. Not only did it maintain a large facility (8% of the employees on the production site worked full-time in R&D), but the spirit of innovation was permeated through all levels across the whole site. The message behind this principle was simple: that without successful efforts at both incremental and radical innovation the plant would be unable to compete with similar products now being manufactured more cheaply in Asia and would almost certainly be closed. This imperative was supported by regular 'creativity' workshops involving both diagonal slices across the plant, and natural work groups, which were co-ordinated by a senior technical manager. They already had a tradition of successful incremental innovation, with process improvements over the preceding twenty years leading to a tenfold increase in productivity. But radical innovation became increasingly important and by 2002, over half of their sales were new products, and in 2003 it was still over one-third.[3] The major R&D project described above was part of the attempt to sustain this performance.

Discussion

Theoretical implications

In this section we focus mainly on the nature of dynamic capabilities and use our fieldwork examples to reflect back on the conceptual discussion, which was based on a summary of relevant literature. First, if we look at the six dynamic capabilities identified here, they do not fit easily into the debate between resources and routines, which was discussed at the beginning of the chapter. Perhaps the last two, leveraging expertise and innovation culture, could be regarded as routines because there is considerable effort within WaterCo regarding the dissemination of business and technical knowledge around the company, and within EuroChem a number of routine activities and procedures were established to generate and nurture the innovative culture. Routines were also evident in the way a range of consultative processes and structures were established in order to incorporate the views of employees in strategic directions, but this is only one part of their particular story.

The principle of flexible structures was most obviously linked to generating flexibility in resource allocation and dispositions, at least in the way it operates in WebCo, and to a lesser extent in WaterCo. The remaining dynamic capabilities, external networks and political backing, do not relate either to resources or routines; rather, they are primarily about influencing the environment within which the business operates, and they have a common theme about pro-activity or enactment (Weick 2001). Similarly, the story from HealthCo demonstrates a concerted attempt to build the capacity to influence the environment and to change assessments of the Hospital Trust both within funding bodies and the local community.

In some respects, it is not surprising that these six features do not fit directly with established models of dynamic capabilities: they have been derived from direct observations within specific organizations, rather than being inferred indirectly from large-scale studies across organizations. But they do fit quite well Eisenhardt and Martin's (2000) pragmatic definition of dynamic capabilities in normal dynamic markets as being: 'specific and identifiable processes such as product development, strategic decision-making, and alliancing' (p. 1113). A further question here is whether we have identified capabilities or *dynamic* capabilities. To some extent these six may be seen as having the potential to create other capabilities within the organization, and this is probably most clearly seen in the case of political backing, which creates the freedom for new processes and capabilities to develop the innovation culture, which by definition leads to new processes. The six capabilities can be linked to the creation of organizational flexibility and the potential to respond quickly to new environmental or competitive information.

The six dynamic capabilities could also be seen to be closely linked to learning processes. The strategic and operational integration, leveraging expertise, and the innovation culture are all closely linked, and dependent upon, learning taking place within the organization; and the relevance of external networks is primarily in ensuring that the organization has the absorptive capacity to learn from its environment. In each case, organizational learning is located mainly in social and political processes, although there is an element of behavioural learning in the routines associated with leveraging expertise and innovation culture.

Practical implications

The key practical implication from our work is that organizations become dynamic in different ways and for different reasons. When assessed against the six dynamic capabilities, each of the organizations had a very different profile, and it is therefore likely that the 'ideal' for any organization will be unique to itself and dependent upon factors such as its history, competitive environment, technology, national culture, and dominant personalities. There is an element of path dependency here, in the sense that current policies and strategies must be constrained by previous histories and structures of the organization, but it is also noticeable that each of the four organizations developed these capabilities substantially during the period of our study. So even if there is a degree of inevitability, there also needs to be active agency from managers determined to implement a particular process or strategy. As such, we think that dynamic capabilities may be more under the control of individual managers than has previously been suggested.

Although we have not discussed this point particularly in the chapter, it is evident that each of the four organizations changed significantly during our period of observation, which included the evolution of new dynamic capabilities. For example, both HealthCo and EuroChem developed significant external networks. At the same time, the absence, or weakness, of a particular capability may lead to significant lack of flexibility and dynamism in the organization. So it is not just a matter of adding dynamic capabilities into the existing repertoire of the organization, it is also essential that companies identify the core rigidities, which may be indicated by weakness or absence in particular dynamic capabilities.

Finally, the immediate implication of all this is that there is no single ideal pattern for achieving dynamic capabilities. Clearly the features we have identified are important in the four companies we investigated. But there may be other features that we have not identified, which will be more important in other circumstances. We therefore suggest that, rather than using these six dynamic capabilities as a rigid template, they should be used as an open-ended checklist against which companies can review and examine their own strengths and weaknesses, and then decide how best to rectify them.

Conclusions

A number of academics have been sceptical about the idea of dynamic capabilities on the grounds that it is vague, tautological, and of limited practical value. In our view these problems can be addressed through research based on live data, and in particular, we believe that case-based, longitudinal research is necessary in order to make sense of supposedly dynamic processes. Moreover, we also suspect that this is a matter of 'horses for courses', in the sense that different kinds of research methodology will yield different theoretical results.

In the case of our project, by using qualitative case studies in different settings we have identified some processes that appear to be important, such as the tension between direction and consultation, the importance of pro-activity, and the apparent uniqueness of dynamic capabilities in any single organization. We suspect that further qualitative research in this area will yield some additional capabilities, but will also start to confirm the patterns we have identified. In particular, we think that there is an opportunity to explore further the relationship between learning processes and dynamic capabilities, since the only way to sustain a flexible organization is to learn from the processes that generate flexibility. These are our recommendations regarding future research directions in this field, and we believe that if they are followed the resulting theoretical and practical insights will have considerable value.

Notes

1. Saxenian's identification of open inter-organizational networks in California as the key to innovation is, however, made more potent by contrast with the poor links between the established firms in Boston's electronics industry clustered along Route 128.
2. The principle of having one exclusive agent in each country worked well everywhere, except for Italy where, due to regional differences, it was necessary to establish seven separate partnerships.
3. In this part of the chemical industry, a new product is defined as something that has been developed and launched in the last five years.

References

Antonacopoulou, E. P. (2006). 'The Relationship between Individual and Organisational Learning: New Evidence from Managerial Learning Practices'. *Management Learning*, 37/4: 455–73.

Argote, L., and Darr, E. (2001). 'Repositories of Knowledge in Franchise Organisations: Individual, Structural, and Technological', in G. Dosi, R. Nelson, and S. G. Winter (eds.), *Nature and Dynamics of Organizational Capabilities*. Oxford: Oxford University Press.

—— Beckman, S. L., and Epple, D. (1990). 'The Persistence and Transfer of Learning in Industrial Settings'. *Management Science*, 36/2: 140–54.

Bateson, G. (1973). *Steps to an Ecology of Mind*. London: Paladin.

Brown, J. S., and Duguid, P. (2000). *The Social Life of Information*. Boston: Harvard Business School Press.

Cohen, M. D., and Bacdayan, P. (1994). 'Organizational Routines Are Stored as Procedural Memory: Evidence from a Laboratory Study'. *Organization Science*, 5/4: 544–68.

Cook, S. D. N., and Yanow, D. (1993). 'Culture and Organizational Learning'. *Journal of Management Inquiry*, 2/4: 373–90.

Coopey, J. (1995). 'The Learning Organization: Power, Politics and Ideology'. *Management Learning*, 26/2: 193–213.

Cyert, R. M., and March, J. G. (1963). *A Behavioral Theory of the Firm*. Englewood Cliffs, NJ: Prentice-Hall.

Easterby-Smith, M. (1997). 'Disciplines of Organizational Learning: Contributions and Critiques'. *Human Relations*, 50/9: 1085–113.

Eisenhardt, K. M. (1989). 'Building Theories from Case Study Research'. *Academy of Management Review*, 14/4: 532–50.

—— and Martin, J. A. (2000). 'Dynamic Capabilities: What Are They?' *Strategic Management Journal*, 21/10–11: 1105–21.

Feldman, M. S. (2000). 'Organizational Routines as a Source of Continuous Change'. *Organization Science*, 11/6: 611–29.

Huber, G. P. (1998). 'Synergies between Organizational Learning and Creativity and Innovation'. *Creativity and Innovation Management*, 7/1: 3–8.

Lawrence, T. B., Mauws, M. K., Dyck, B., and Kleysen, R. F. (2005). 'The Politics of Organizational Learning: Integrating Power into the 4I Framework'. *Academy of Management Review*, 30/1: 180–91.

Leonard-Barton, D. (1992). 'Core Capabilities and Core Rigidities: A Paradox in Managing New Product Development'. *Strategic Management Journal*, 13: 111–25.

Locke, K. D. (1997). 'Re-writing the Discovery of Grounded Theory after 25 Years?' *Journal of Management Inquiry*, 5: 239–45.

March, J. G. (1990). 'Exploration and Exploitation in Organizational Learning'. *Organization Science*, 2/1: 71–87.

Nicolini, D., and Meznar, M. B. (1995). 'The Social Construction of Organizational Learning—Conceptual and Practical Issues in the Field'. *Human Relations*, 48/7: 727–46.

Powell, W. W. (1998). 'Learning from Collaboration: Knowledge Networks in the Biotechnology and Pharmaceutical Industries'. *California Management Review*, 40/3: 228–40.

Prieto, I. M., and Easterby-Smith, M. (2006). 'Dynamic Capabilities and the Role of Organizational Knowledge: An Exploration'. *European Journal of Information Systems*, 15/6: 500–10.

Saxenian, A. L. (1994). *Regional Advantage: Culture and Competition in Silicon Valley and Route 128*. Cambridge, Mass.: Harvard University Press.

Teece, D. J., Pisano, G., and Shuen, A. (1997). 'Dynamic Capabilities and Strategic Management'. *Strategic Management Journal*, 18/7: 509–33.

Weick, K. E. (2001). *Making Sense of the Organization*. Oxford: Blackwell.

Winter, S. G. (2003). 'Understanding Dynamic Capabilities'. *Strategic Management Journal*, 24: 991–5.

Zollo, M., and Winter, S. G. (2002). 'Deliberate Learning and the Evolution of Dynamic Capabilities'. *Organization Science*, 13/3: 339–51.

5

What Knowledge or Knowledge for What? Reforming/Reinventing the Business School

David Knights

Introduction

Although knowledge is clearly a key management resource, until the recent fashion for 'knowledge management' (*Harvard Business Review* 1998; Little, Quintas, and Ray 2002) little research has been conducted on how management knowledge is produced, developed, and disseminated (Suddaby and Greenwood 2001). In reporting on some of the deliberations and findings of our research, this chapter provides a limited correction to this dearth of research on the conditions and consequences, and the contexts and content of management knowledge and the relationships surrounding it within business schools.

The university has historically been an important site of knowledge production. However, the changing dynamics of the knowledge economy and society have meant that the university's privileged knowledge role has been increasingly challenged (Delanty 2002). Yet some conventional wisdoms would see the business school as having the potential to become a leading site of knowledge production and dissemination, education and/ or professional training just so long as it is responsive to the changing contours and processes of an increasingly demanding public within a 'knowledge-based' economy. For this to occur, however, they will have to subject themselves to substantial reform or to use a more topical language—to reinvent themselves. Nonetheless, there is no shortage of prescriptive advice from critics who question the practical relevance of management research or teaching but remain tied to a neo-positivist view of knowledge (e.g. Mintzberg 2004; Pfeffer and Fong 2002, 2004; Goshal 2005). Others, including some of our research team (Currie 2005; Starkey and Tiratsoo 2007; Wright et al. 2005), feel that a more radical reform is called for if the business school is to occupy the area of the academy at the centre of debates about the nature and the needs of knowledge production and transfer in today's society and economy.

Business schools are analysed theoretically and empirically by focusing on their pedagogic and research networks and establishing how debates and discourses about policy and practice are mobilized in their construction. Theoretically, the chapter engages with debates on the relevance and value of business school research and education, particularly the comments of some leading critics (e.g. Hambrick 1994; French and Grey 1996; Tranfield and Starkey 1998; Beer 2001; Grey 2001, 2004; Starkey and Madden 2001; Hodgkinson 2001; Currie and Knights 2003; Mintzberg and Gosling 2002; Mintzberg 2004; Pfeffer and Fong 2002, 2004; Bennis and O'Toole 2005; Goshal 2005). This debate is part of a broader debate about the role of the university in what is being called the 'knowledge economy'. While the debate encompasses a wide spectrum from excessive optimism (Bok 1990, 1996) to messianic pessimism (Readings 1996), the question revolves around what kinds of power–knowledge relations legitimize the business school (and the university) at a time when knowledge is becoming commodified and where there is not only competition from corporations that establish their own universities but also from consultants, government departments, NGOs, think tanks, and pressure groups—all seeking a claim on expertise and information services. Such an analysis cannot, however, be conducted in the absence of an examination of knowledge itself—something that is far too often taken for granted as self-evident.

In the context section, I examine current concerns with reform of the business school through, respectively, a conservative, liberal, and radical lens. In the empirical section, I discuss (1) the role of the business school in terms of the entrepreneurial networks that are involved in patented knowledge and technology transfer and their significance for business practice; (2) business school research knowledge networks that are seeking to transcend the walls of the ivory tower; and (3) how MBA pedagogic networks are changing as they respond to a changing student marketplace and the demands from several quarters for knowledge relevant to business practice. In the conclusion, actor network theory is drawn upon more thoroughly to suggest possible developments that may render business schools less vulnerable to contemporary criticism. While precarious, unstable, and often transitory, business schools can become 'obligatory passage points', where an increasingly heterogeneous and diverse range of stakeholders feel a need at least to pass through, if not remain permanently and irreversibly locked into, their networks.

Context for the research

Theorizing the 'knowledge economy'

As researchers in an ESRC programme on the Evolution of Business Knowledge, we are all participants in a network mobilized to secure (or challenge) the legitimacy and power of knowledge. We cannot, therefore, be seen as independent or detached producers of accounts or stories 'about' business or management knowledge, claiming little more than telling it how it is. For clearly our accounts are not, 'in any sense "neutral" or "innocent"— that is to say, un-"polluted" by economic, political, cultural or other interests' (Knights et al. 2002: 99). On the contrary, they enact specific business knowledge agendas. We are simply 'professional' producers and consumers of stories 'about' business knowledge, its role and consequences.[1]

If only because our funding agent—the ESRC—is embedded in establishment institutions such as the Cabinet Office, the DTI, and the Treasury, many if not most of the narratives that populate this programme are positive descriptions or where negative, produced as part of an attempt to prescribe *reforms* that would mitigate or ameliorate that which fails to live up to cultural expectations of knowledge in the 'knowledge economy'. As we shall see later, our research contribution to the EBK programme falls mostly into this category of reform, but let me elaborate first on why I feel it is necessary to place scare quotes around the 'knowledge economy'. It is because once again the description is not independent of what it anticipates—the vision of the knowledge economy and the discourses and practices that are perceived to make it possible and perhaps inevitable is invoked precisely to bring it about. It serves to enrol and mobilize significant actors and material resources in networks (Callon 1986; Latour 1987) that reproduce themselves through a commitment to realizing the very vision that they claim already to exist—namely, the knowledge economy.

Some accounts of business knowledge, however, refrain from adopting a positive and celebratory stance not merely to invoke the reforms that can remove the weaknesses, repair the leaks, and transform damaging gaps in cultural expectations into positive and productive outcomes. Critical management studies (CMS), for example, raise fundamental criticisms of management and business knowledge because of its neglect of political and ethical matters (Anthony 1986; Alvesson and Willmott 1996; Grey, Knights, and Willmott 1996; Grey 2002, 2004). The claim is that such knowledge invariably serves to reinforce and reproduce existing systems of global domination and inequality, and often supports economic and political exploitation at the expense of environmental sustainability and world peace (Knights and Willmott 2007). For example, issues of human life and sustenance in developing countries, animal life within factory farming, and environmental sustainability are often marginalized or treated as 'political' or 'ethical' matters that are beyond the scope of business or management knowledge. Despite this apparent concern for 'real-politics', few of these critics (c.f. Bojé at <http://business.nmsu.edu/~dboje/nike/nikemain.html>) engage in any practical sense with the issues. Instead they remain steeped in the business of academic credibility through publishing in prestigious journals and books within their own narrow discipline. As it was expressed more than a decade ago: 'With so little countervailing pressure from the profession, faculties have felt free to pursue the rewards of academic prestige by emphasizing the teaching and scholarship favored by their parent disciplines with scant regard for their relevance to the real world of business' (Bok 1990: 113).

This focus may give the impression that students of business or management knowledge are either critics or reformers, whereas there are other responses. There are traditionalists who have a romantic sense of a glorious past when the distinction between business education and practice was much more blurred because most of the educators were part-time or ex-business people. These were the days when successful business entrepreneurs simply taught what they knew in a more or less anecdotal fashion (Fayol 1916/1949; Barnard 1938; Urwick 1956), reflecting an identical set of values and identification with management practitioners; they might be inclined to view contemporary thinking about business knowledge or the knowledge economy as simply old wine in new bottles. A more scientific or academic version of this comparatively unquestioning stance is the modern managerial[2] academic who celebrates and supports (and could even be an apologist for) business knowledge and the so-called knowledge economy. There is a general belief among such academics that the purpose of academic research and education is simply to act, in the words of Baratz (1960), as 'servants of power'—that is, providing contemporary management and business with tools or knowledge that makes their job as managers easier or helps them manage better.

While these different approaches to business knowledge provided us with important background material for our study of the business school, industry–academic collaboration and knowledge transfer activity, I have concentrated here on reform of the business school and its relationship to management knowledge in theory and practice. But reform or criticism designed to bring about improvements in the business school and its external relations assumes different political stances: it can be conservative, liberal, or radical. Clearly there is some degree of overlap between some of these positions and those discussed above as we shall see when presenting the findings of our project, where all three of the perspectives in this spectrum are represented.

Conservative reformers

Several researchers who have been highly critical of business schools fall into the category of conservative reformers despite appearing at times to be closer to the critical management students or at least the radical reformers. This is because they seek to eradicate the weaknesses but retain the form through which the business school operates. Beer (2001) has reported on how business has been disappointed repeatedly with the absence of any help from academics in implementing new ideas. This is the major reason, he argues, why 'approximately 70% of corporations are disappointed with the effectiveness of total quality management (Spector and Beer 1994)...and...a similar percentage of companies are disappointed in the results of reengineering efforts (Hall, Rosenthal, and Wade 1993). It cannot be said that inadequate theory or lack of rigorous research is the cause of implementation failures' (Beer 2001: 59). The reform that he is suggesting is simply to cajole academics to take responsibility for implementing their theories and prescriptions on the basis that it is their duty to provide managers with solutions to their problems. This managerial perspective broadly is taken for granted by conservative reformers but some believe the reform required is more substantial.

Pfeffer (1993) has sought to render management and organizational knowledge more coherent and less fragmented—a condition that they attribute, perhaps exaggeratedly, to economics.[3] His position is grounded in the belief that a theoretical consensus is a necessary condition for a science to have impact, secure resources, and gain status and respect especially of a professional nature. In later work (Pfeffer and Fong 2002, 2004), the critique of business schools has become ever more stringent broadly based on the view that their work is too analytical and insufficiently integrated or concerned with developing practitioners in terms of the 'softer' skills and leadership. Based on a review of existing findings and a statistical survey, these authors condemn business schools for failing to develop knowledge that is relevant for practitioners who are seeking to develop their businesses or students who expect to improve their career and earnings success (Pfeffer and Fong 2002, 2004). Their solution is that business schools develop a more 'professional ethos and an appeal to students that does not sell business education primarily as a way to make more money' (2004: 1157).

There are some parallels here with a much earlier analysis (Simon 1967) in that the primary objective is to reform business school knowledge so it resembles the more scientific disciplines. Simon (1967) had also been concerned about the failure of any integration between scientific analysis and the concerns of professional practice to synthesize a range of actions, processes, or structures 'to serve some specified purpose' (ibid. 14). His solution was to make professional practice more scientific by 'developing an explicit, abstract, intellectual *theory* of the processes of synthesis and design' (ibid. 15, author's emphasis), so that it can be taught as a fully respectable academic subject in university. His major concern was to avoid the separation of those in the faculty who are academically or discipline trained from those professionally trained, since integration is the best way for the business school to carry out its teaching and research effectively (ibid. 12).

Some of those who advocated a more professional role for business schools believed it already existed (Chandler, McCraw, and Tedlow 1996), whereas others sought its promotion (Bennis and O'Toole 2005). The latter also supported Simon's plea for integration between discipline-based knowledge and the requirements of business practice (ibid. 102) to avoid scientific rigour displacing all other forms of knowledge. Another conservative reformer who believes in the potential of a professional route out of the difficulties that business schools find themselves in is Peter Drucker. But whereas those I have discussed so far understand research as an essential component of this development, Drucker (2001) believes business schools should concentrate on teaching and, like other professional schools, such as law or medicine, seek simply to improve the profession.

Business schools could not readily generate a mimesis of professionalism in the strong sense of its meaning, where the profession is capable of policing its members and the practitioners are able to control the definition of the relationship between themselves and clients (Johnson 1976). This is because we are never likely to come even close to reaching a public consensus about business in the way that there is broad agreement about what is, and the value of attaining, a healthy body or legal system fit for purpose. Emulating the professions is then problematic, since without this consensus it would be difficult if not impossible to develop a set of qualifications that were an obligatory condition of practice and a means of controlling entry. It is also unlikely that any professional body in business or management would be able to prevent those not maintaining professional standards from practising. In the rather weaker sense of professionalism, of course, business school academics could attain high standards of pedagogy, ethical practice, and levels of research competence. But this kind of professionalism is no more than one in which business school academics behave as competently as possible and display a strong commitment to providing a good education for their students as well as conducting research at a high standard of rigour and scholarly accomplishment. It cannot ensure that any professional association is able to control its members, prevent them from practising when they do not meet certain standards, preclude them from entering the profession, or perhaps most importantly, control entirely the definition of the relationship between academics and their students.

Liberal reformers

Liberal reformers also begin by criticizing business schools for failing to provide research or teaching materials that are relevant to a business community (Tranfield and Starkey 1998; Starkey and Madan 2001). Some simply demand that business research and teaching begin to adopt a less abstract and esoteric style (Kelemen and Bansal 2002) and develop their research from a more interdisciplinary perspective (Burgoyne et al. 1997; Tranfield and Starkey 1998; Beer 2001; Hodgkinson 2001; Bennis and O'Toole 2005). Another group (Hodgkinson, Herriot, and Anderson 2001; Huff and Huff 2001; Starkey and Madan 2001; Starkey and Tempest 2005) are concerned that business schools take account of a 'wider group of stakeholders than corporate business' (Currie 2005: 10). In the light of numerous recent corporate scandals, however, a more stringent critique has revolved around the business preoccupation with shareholder value legitimized by business schools that have failed to challenge it or give adequate attention to business ethics (Mintzberg 2004; Goshal 2005; Knights and O'Leary 2006).

Mintzberg (2004) focuses more of his attention on the MBA, criticizing it for failing to deliver education that is relevant for practising managers but also for attracting the wrong kind of students and teaching the wrong kinds of material. His solutions are rather more radical than the conservatives because he does believe in disrupting the tradition of establishment MBA education. Indeed, with a UK colleague (Mintzberg and Gosling 2002), he has established an alternative to the MBA called the Master for Practising Administrators (MPA). They offer a framework of five interventions that are deemed necessary for improving management and leadership:

- Managing self: the reflective mindset
- Managing organizations: the analytic mindset
- Managing context: the worldly mindset
- Managing relationships: the collaborative mindset
- Managing change: the action mindset.

These mindsets have been constructed largely out of the authors' own experience of developing and delivering management education programmes. Their framework is about creating 'structures', nurturing conditions, and shaping attitudes for purposes of getting things done and that this requires an action mindset that is alert to, and facilitative of, change. In order to develop an effective structure of activities or to manage change, contexts and relationships need to be examined analytically and this is best achieved when the self is managed reflexively in ways that challenge and develop the other mindsets.

Introducing these different mindsets and their interrelationships is a more appropriate response to the question of relevance than the standard knee-jerk reaction to have a closer relationship with practitioners. It is more all-embracing than simply working with practitioners whose economically instrumental preoccupations are unlikely to be extended in self-reflexive ways in the direction of analysis, global impact, collaboration, and in terms of change unless they are freed from their everyday tasks for a significant period. However, despite the MPA having this opportunity to release managers from their immediate tasks for significant periods, Mintzberg and Gosling subordinate the mindsets to the tasks of 'getting things done', and thus the potentially radical nature of the framework is sacrificed at the altar of conventional understandings of organizational practice that involve an instrumental, pragmatic pursuit of material wealth. The MPA programme does not seem to consider how self-reflection could challenge the dualistic separation of mind (self) and matter (getting things done) and/or this focus on calculable events and outcomes (getting things done).

Radical reformers

It has been argued quite consistently that business schools need to 'do some very hard thinking about the future, if there is to be a future' (Grey 2004: 184). The idea that technologies of management can be seen simply as reflecting morally and politically neutral scientific knowledge has begun to seem naive. Yet some critical management studies (CMS) academics concerned with critical management education (CME) have resisted a blanket condemnation of the exploitative practices of business (Bojé and Dennehy 1993; Alvesson and Willmott 1996) but have sought to stimulate a more radical reform of business school education than we have witnessed so far. Partly through the legitimacy provided by both conservative and liberal critics of business schools and the MBA, these radical critics have promoted a more socially and environmentally conscious pedagogy that is reflective of how business in the West tends to reflect, reinforce, and reproduce social and environmental inequality, injustice, and irresponsibility on a global scale. However, these critics (Roberts 1996; Currie and Knights 2003; Grey 2004; Knights and Willmott 2007) have also been concerned to promote a critical view in teaching not by simply imposing an alternative politics on their students that is likely to be endorsed only for the purpose of passing exams and then immediately forgotten. Instead, they have sought to expose students to the complex and contradictory experiences of business practice through case studies and group consultancy projects. The students experience the moral and political tensions that are evident in almost all business decisions and practices at sufficient distance to allow space for a self-reflexivity that refuses to deny, marginalize, or subordinate them to 'bottom line' or utilitarian pragmatics. Through having to work through them collectively in the context of providing consultancy advice, the students are confronted with moral dilemmas and insights into the politics of organization. This sensitizes them at an experiential level to alternative ways of thinking and self-reflection of the kind advocated by Gosling and Mintzberg, but without these being overridden by utilitarian managerial demands to 'get things done'. However, despite limited support from some prominent academics (e.g. Dehler, Welsh, and Lewis 2001; Zald 2002; Pfeffer and Fong 2004) and its practice in a number of business schools in the United Kingdom (e.g. Cambridge, Essex, Exeter, Keele, Lancaster, and Manchester), it is unlikely that CME will become a central part of MBA pedagogy in the immediate future.

An alternative suggested by Delanty (2002) is that the university be reconfigured to link cultural and societal communications to the 'production, organization and diffusion of knowledge' as a means of 'cultivating technological and cultural forms of citizenship' as it has done social citizenship in the past (ibid. 9–10). Translating some of this to the particular focus of management education, Starkey and his colleagues argue that the business school should act as a knowledge broker and 'as a forum *par excellence* for promoting constituent interplay and debate' (Starkey and Tempest 2005: 79). Despite having advocated closer links with business (e.g. Starkey and Madan 2002), they also take a well overdue sideswipe at the bandwagon belief that a closer relationship with industry is the solution to business school problems, especially those of a financial nature (Starkey and Tempest 2005: 79). For if business begins to fund business school research, faculty, and buildings, it can erode the academic autonomy that is a condition of independent and critical thinking about business and its role in society. Business school academics should adopt the role of sage rather than scribe, so that they can 'help inform a vision of sustainable business practice' in a world fraught with complexity, risk, and uncertainty (ibid.; see also Starkey and Tiratsoo 2007).

These radical reformers could all be seen as revitalizing the argument made by Robert Lynd (1939) when he posed the question 'knowledge for what' in discussing the role of social science in American culture, as well as reflecting the mood of Gouldner (1973) when in discussing deviancy he argued that it is not for us to take sides between the underdog against the powerful or, in our case, between the supporters and critics of corporate business but to take the side of reason. While this broad sweep and grand narrative approach can appeal as rhetoric, it is short on detail in terms of pedagogic suggestions for critical management education policies and practices. I turn now, therefore, to the findings of our ESRC project, 'The Dynamics of Knowledge Production in the Business School'. Different parts of the project have been identified in relation to our political typology, but the potential for each contribution to be more radical has been accomplished by reinterpreting the data through the lens of actor network theory.

Empirical study of knowledge production

Knowledge transfer and entrepreneurial networks

The objective of this part of the dynamics of knowledge production in the business school was to address two specific research questions:

1. What roles do business schools play in the development of academic entrepreneurship?

2. What are the barriers to business schools contributing to the development of academic entrepreneurship?

Data were collected in two ways. First, background data on the technology transfer process and the nature of the business school were collected from published sources and from the universities themselves. Second, detailed data on the role of the business school were collected through in-depth, face-to-face interviews with respondents from case studies in eight universities. Each case study involved semi-structured interviews with the head of the university technology transfer office (TTO) or equivalent, and members of the business school (notably the deans plus members specifically involved in academic entrepreneurship activities). Members of science departments involved in academic entrepreneurship activities were also interviewed. In total, forty-two interviews were conducted.

Knowledge transfer and entrepreneurial networks are largely concerned with the commercialization of university activities through the exploitation of science and technology, and sometimes, patented inventions. Attention in the project was particularly focused on the role of the business school in disseminating knowledge to other areas of the university to facilitate the commercial potential of the diffusion of knowledge. One way of accomplishing this potential is to develop start-up companies that can spin-out practical solutions and entrepreneurial ideas based on intellectual property (IP) rights from knowledge generated in the university.

So far it would seem that little success has been recorded largely because there is a significant skills gap that obstructs the realization of commercial objectives within universities. As the UK Treasury commissioned Lambert Review (2003) has argued, a key issue is how to develop the skills required to promote academic entrepreneurship. Because academic scientists are not usually skilled in translating knowledge into practical or commercial ventures (Franklin, Wright, and Lockett 2001), government has intervened to promote courses on entrepreneurship for both students and faculty (OST 2000). The skill gap is not confined to the academics, since those employed specifically to facilitate the commercialization of university research—the technology transfer officers (TTOs)—also require substantial training, although it would help matters if individuals with an industry background and experience were also recruited (HM Treasury 2004).

From the detailed field studies and interviews, the EBK researchers found that business schools are involved more in the transfer of generic knowledge prior to, rather than after, the commencement of active academic entrepreneurship (Wright et al. 2005, forthcoming; Wright, forthcoming; Wright and Lockett, forthcoming). There would appear to be a need to develop internal university processes and policies that facilitate links between the networks of business schools, TTOs, and science departments. Such processes may be enhanced by the explicit recruitment of boundary spanners where the primary task is to integrate activities across boundaries and to reconcile divisions and conflicts. An alternative and perhaps more effective way of developing the commercial potential of university work is to train the scientists and engineers in marketing, finance, and other management skills rather than complicating the networks by introducing boundary-spanning functions.

However, a major problem for academics is that technology transfer and entrepreneurial activities are not part of the culture, even in business schools in the United Kingdom, largely because of the Research Assessment Exercise, which elevates top-ranked refereed journal publications above most other activities. Consequently, academic entrepreneurship tends to be marginalized and, unless parallel career structures are developed to recognize work of this kind, it is unlikely to attract much support. Financial rewards can, of course, oil the wheels, but academics often elevate intellectual interests above money resulting in incentives having a limited effect in promoting entrepreneurial developments. The decentralized, multi-objective nature of universities also tends to pose problems for knowledge transfer, since diverse goals relating to teaching, research, and academic entrepreneurship are often in conflict both within and between different parts of universities.

The research that has been conducted in this area has tended to follow a conservative reformist tradition, but it could be reinterpreted in a more radical fashion by adopting actor network theory (Callon 1986, 1991; Latour 1987, 1993) as a mode of analysis. The radical nature of this reinterpretation is to admit non-human actors in these entrepreneurial knowledge networks and to recognize that knowledge is *not fully formed* at the point of its so-called transfer or dissemination. While realizing that sometimes an invention has already been patented prior to going to market, there is still a substantial distance between an invention or innovation, even when patented, and its commercial viability. Many fail in the translation process probably because of poorly developed actor networks. This has implications for the way the reform is understood and translated.

For example, the boundary spanners may be seen as non-human entities such as the prestige of the university, the reputation for collaborating or (net)working with industry, knowledge track record, associated networks, and links with government and other bodies such as the regulators, consumer groups, trade associations, and so on. Boundary spanning is less about converting the so-called knowledge into commercial form than building the networks around the problems and interests that then perform the task of developing and translating knowledge with practical intent. This is accomplished through enrolling key supporters and mobilizing resources to produce knowledge networks of some durability, if not irreversible status. This reinterpretation is now clarified by another part of the project where actor network theory served as the framework for examining business school collaborations with industry.

Industry–academic collaboration

The objective of this part of the project was to assess academic/practitioner networks in terms of their success or failure to survive and produce knowledge of relevance and utility to both academics and practitioners. Out of an estimated forty-one UK business school/industry collaborations of various types, there appear to be only around seventeen business schools currently hosting academic practitioner research networks or best practice clubs. Empirical research was conducted in eleven of these, which represented the full range of activities conducted by the whole sample. These different forms cover: research networks, best practice clubs, and networks dedicated to policy, international, or local regional development. Within these eleven networks, three were selected for in-depth research involving interviewing not only the founder and/or coordinator of the network but also practitioner members (twenty-one in all), attending network events, participant observation in one research network in financial services and a virtual network dedicated to performance management.

A major problem for business schools is that in the search for scholarly respectability and reputation from their university peers, they have tended to separate theory from practice and produced increasingly more esoteric output that is beyond the capability let alone interest of all but a few fellow academics (Hambrick 1994). This anxiety about their academic and intellectual credentials was stimulated by a report in the United States in the early 1960s that criticized business school research for its low scholarly standards and the absence of a 'strong scientific foundation' (Zimmerman 2001: 2, quoted in Pfeffer and Fong 2002: 79). A significant group of critics, and these extend beyond the confines of business school research, have strongly challenged this theory–practice dichotomy associated with traditional 'pure' conceptions of science. Accordingly, they have sought to break down the disciplinary boundaries, the separation of knowledge production from its application (Gibbons et al. 1994; Pearce 1999; Nowotny, Scott, and Gibbons 2001; Adler, Shani (Rami), and Styhre 2004) and also to draw in a much wider array of stakeholders (Hodgkinson, Herriot, and Anderson 2001; Huff and Huff 2001; Starkey and Madan 2001).

As a result of these continuous criticisms, business schools have been suffering lately from something of a crisis, and this has been instrumental in encouraging some academics to seek to bridge the theory–practice divide. This has taken different forms but one approach has been to build industry–academic collaborations through networks of various kinds. Our research demonstrated that the precariousness and often demise of these networks partly could be attributed to a shortfall in self-analysis or self-reflection on networking (Alferoff and Knights 2006; Knights et al. 2007). The reform that advocates industry–academic collaboration remains liberal rather than radical, since it continues to believe that knowledge can be diffused through this mechanism. It seeks to modify academic and commercial organizations at the margins so that they are more compatible with one another. It may be argued that this is partly what leaves these industry–academic networks extremely precarious and vulnerable to disruption and demise.

Actor network theory provides a more penetrating analysis of the precariousness of the various academic–industry networks. Partly this is because it departs from the modern view of knowledge as something that is fully formed prior to its dissemination or diffusion—a view that is often still subscribed to even by radical reformers.[4] Since the hard sciences and engineering do not generally view knowledge production and use as distinct activities, it is strange that social scientists should do so. However, the promotion of the co-production of knowledge (Gibbons et al. 1994; Nowotny, Scott, and Gibbons 2001; Starkey and Tempest 2005) could be seen as breaking with this tradition, but unfortunately their departure is not because of ontological and epistemological misgivings about modernist separations of nature (facts), society (power), and their deconstructions (discourse) as separate and irreconcilable entities (Latour 1993: 6).

An actor network analysis indicates that industry–academic knowledge networks cross these borders and are thus recognized as not simply one or other of the three distinct entities—objective (like nature), social (steeped in power), or effects of discourse (endless significations), despite being *simultaneously* 'real, and collective and discursive' (ibid.). While acknowledging that knowledge is socially constructed, it can never simply be reduced to the social dimension because society is already 'populated by objects' (nature) 'mobilised to construct it' (ibid.). Accordingly, knowledge may be seen as a hybrid of objects, social artefacts, and discourses that are organized (or disrupted) through networks of actors and intermediaries mobilized for purposes of securing it. This reflects von Humboldt's view of knowledge as 'something not yet entirely found and never completely findable' (Friese and Wagner 1998: 30). 'Know-ledge' is perhaps always on the ledge or edge of knowing—forever embryonic, in transition, or unfinished. This is anathema to a diffusion model because if knowledge is elusive and transitory, it can hardly be diffused or disseminated in the conventional sense.

Actor network theory not only provides a valuable critical understanding of industry–academic collaborations, but also potentially could assist them in pursuing their objectives, since it describes how networks secure themselves. In this sense, it may be seen as a theory and methodology that has radical reform implications for knowledge discourses and practices, including the business school and their relations with other stakeholders. In particular, it forces academics who enter industry–academic networks to rethink their relations and to work harder at rendering their ideas more accessible to those who have not spent a lifetime poring over academic papers, archives, books, or data files. It may also contribute to their becoming more professional at least in the weak sense discussed earlier, since there are demands that are made of the researchers from those whose future does not depend on how they are judged by the academics. This is not so in the protected cloisters of the university where students, despite attempts to bureaucratize the relationship in order to protect them from arbitrary judgements, always feel vulnerable to the power of academics to grant them awards and certificates. However, our research drew the conclusion that one of the most important vehicles for making business school knowledge relevant to practitioners was through teaching the MBA.

MBA pedagogy

If patented knowledge and collaborative research falls well short of the impact desired of them, what of teaching in business schools? The Master of Business Administration (MBA) has for some time been subjected to criticism from two often mutually incompatible positions (Porter and

McGibbin 1988; Hambrick 1994; Mintzberg 2004). Either it is seen as insufficiently rigorous intellectually or it fails to offer knowledge that is relevant to management practitioners. Mindful of these criticisms, the aim of this part of the project was to examine the role of the MBA as a conduit for the (co)production and transfer of knowledge (Currie 2005; Currie, Tempest, and Seymour 2006; Tempest, Currie, and Wright 2006).

Comparative cases of full-time MBA provision in four leading UK business schools were conducted between 2004 and 2006 encompassing sixty-six interviews with MBA students, twenty interviews with faculty within the four in-depth cases, and outside the in-depth cases a further sixteen interviews with Deans and MBA Directors, and 290 hours observation of MBA teaching. The business schools were selected on the following basis: business school A (close to practice); business school B (critical); business schools C and D (typify those business schools that are research-led but seek to develop links with industry/commerce/public sector). These schools were all ranked in the top 100 of the *Financial Times* league table of MBA providers and had or were in the process of radically reconfiguring their MBAs (process and content) in the face of declining demand from students.

Business school Deans pay considerable attention to the MBA, since its 'performance' (measured largely by salary increase for students on graduation) provides the basis of league tables of business schools and thereby ranking, which is important not only for recruitment (both students and staff) but also as the main determinant of the size of student fees. However, the research found that business schools had to adapt to a number of challenges, not least of which is declining applications for the full-time MBA. The general trend within the four case studies indicated them moving closer to management practice through, for example, consultancy-type projects. Diverse pedagogical approaches were evident within each case, but this appeared to be largely a function of the academic discipline. For example, courses in organizational behaviour were generally more critical than other offerings. Institutional characteristics appeared less influential: for example, the more critical business school (B) paradoxically exhibited pedagogy closer to the 'needs' of management than the schools that espoused such virtues. A range of pedagogical interventions was evident. Only business school D relied upon a more traditional didactic and stand-up lecture approach to teaching and learning. The other three cases used teaching cases (most notably in strategy), syndicate learning (all three modules), and consultancy projects (most notably in entrepreneurship). Criticism that the MBA is neither rigorous nor relevant can be challenged, since there were numerous examples of good practice regarding relevance (syndicate learning combined with consultancy projects) and rigour (critical approaches to use of teaching cases). Until recently there has been an increase in the proportion of international students, particularly from South and East Asia, participating in full-time MBA programmes. MBA programmes generally appear slow to respond pedagogically to this market change, although the case studies revealed some examples of good practice to accommodate cultural asymmetry.

This research has generally followed the liberal view that the MBA should respond to the relevance critique by becoming more involved with business practice but also with a much broader group of stakeholders (Currie 2005: 10). However, it also subscribes to a liberal pluralist view of recognizing that reconfiguring the MBA cannot follow some universal standard or model, since it 'is more influenced by local level factors, such as the institution's history, and distinctive reputation and existing competences and perspectives of its faculty' (ibid. 9). In all four case studies, declining student demand and perhaps sensitivity to the critique of relevance seems to have resulted in a process of reconfiguring and reforming their offerings both in terms of delivery and in relation to the content of their syllabuses. One way in which a closer link with management practice was being sought was through involving students in consultancy type projects (Roberts 1996).[5]

The approach taken in this research has been a conventional liberal analysis where business schools are seen as discrete organizations or institutions through which knowledge is diffused to students. Rather than accepting the relevance critique at face value and thereby encouraging in theory, and seeking in practice, to develop a closer relationship between the MBA and business practice, as well as other stakeholders, this analysis could be reinterpreted through actor network theory in ways that would perhaps have more radical implications. It could reasonably be argued that the MBA has become an obligatory passage point for large numbers of managers and perhaps the development of further industry–academic collaborative networks would consolidate this durability to render the networks around which business school education has been sustained irreversible. If the networks are comparatively durable, the kind of 'crisis talk' that has accompanied blips in MBA student demand and the threats generated by critiques of relevance and ethical failure can be summarily dismissed. This is because such talk invariably has the effect of consolidating existing networks (e.g. Porter and McGibbin 1988; Hambrick 1994) or enrolling people and mobilizing resources both human and non-human around alternative pedagogic networks for managers (e.g. Mintzberg and Gosling 2002; Mintzberg 2004). The existence of critique or alternatives is evidence of the durability of business education networks not a sign of their demise. The demand for relevance is just one more non-human mobile (alongside, for example, government exhortation, the alumni, league tables, and research credibility) that helps to consolidate business education networks (Alferoff and Knights 2006). Academic–industry collaborations also serve to strengthen business schools further perhaps to render business pedagogic networks irreversible (ibid.).

Discussion and conclusion

Whether they are based on innovation patents, collaborative research, or educational practices, our research on networks associated with the business school (Alferoff and Knights 2006) suggests that they are invariably 'hybrid' rather than 'pure' in the Latourian sense of the term. That is to say, these knowledge networks involve natural, social, and discursive 'objects' simultaneously and therefore cannot be analysed purely by drawing on any single one of the perspectives associated with such objects. Hybrid phenomena demand hybrid analytical frameworks that recognize the complex mutual interdependencies of material artefacts, social relations, and the discursive nature of meaning in which they are embedded. It has been suggested that if business schools are in need of reform, actor network theory can assist in reinterpreting research on patented knowledge, industry academic collaborations, and teaching practices.

The chapter began with an analysis of how research under the programme for the Evolution of Business Knowledge has a close affinity with the so-called knowledge economy or society but that accounts of it cannot be seen as independent of specific business knowledge agendas. That is to say, while pretending political and ethical neutrality, they cannot escape describing precisely what is aspired to or anticipated. In short, the research is invariably informed by a vision of business knowledge and the discourses and practices that are perceived to make it possible, and perhaps inevitably invoked precisely to bring it about. For this reason, I concentrated on examining different programmes of reform for the business school on the basis that there is then no attempt to conceal the political nature of research and writing. Separating the reforms into three kinds of politics—conservative, liberal, and radical—and concluding that if the business school is to have a future it probably needs to be radical in its reform or reinvention clearly identifies my own politics.

In teaching, research collaboration, or patented knowledge, successful outcomes are dependent at least on the network becoming an obligatory passage point that it is essential to pass through in order to manage the problems it represents. Ultimately, this can lead to a network enjoying the condition of irreversibility, where the network becomes highly durable and stable. This latter condition depends largely on the degree to which all alternative or competing ways of arousing interests and resolving particular ecological, economic, cultural, technological, and ethical problems have been driven from the collective memory. Irreversible networks of this kind occur only when significant human actors and material artefacts are enrolled and then mobilized to institutionalize network construction and reproduction. This is facilitated by inscribing identities in the specific practices and objects surrounding the resolution of these problems, through enrolling significant numbers of supporters of comparatively high status, and in mobilizing resources that are then difficult to detach from the network and its continued durability and potential permanence.

Clearly in writing this chapter, I anticipate the future of the business school to coincide with the reforms advocated here, but there is no sense that this at present constitutes a network that will enrol significant supporters or mobilize material and human resources that render it effective. Nonetheless, those engaged in securing an entrepreneurial role for the business school, those participating in industry–academic collaborations and business school teachers and faculty more generally may see actor network theory facilitating their practices and giving insights to their reform programmes, where they exist, and encouragement to reform, where not.

Acknowledgements

The project was conducted by Ken Starkey (Principal Investigator); co-investigators Graeme Currie, David Knights, Andy Lockett, Sue Tempest, and Mike Wright; and research assistants Catrina Alferoff, Annette Knight, Alison Seymour, and Nic Tiratsoo. The chapter draws on research from the project as a whole, but the arguments are those of the author and may or may not directly represent the team's views. Thanks also go to the secretary to the project, Laura Pearson.

107

Notes

1. Although applied here to business knowledge rather than technology, the last two sentences are also a paraphrasing of Knights et al. (2002: 99).
2. Managerial is perhaps a more neutral term than *managerialism*, which is deployed pejoratively by critics who see management researchers unreflectively espousing or taking for granted the values and goals of practising managers.
3. In Europe, at least, it has for years been joked that there are as many positions in economics as there are economists, which hardly reflects a model of coherence and consensus that Pfeffer believes we can import into management and organization studies.
4. It may be unfair to criticize Delanty (2001: 9) for using the term 'diffusion of knowledge' in relation to the university and Starkey and Tempest (2005: 70) with respect to the business school, but our language cannot avoid betraying our thinking and the diffusion model remains the conventional wisdom.
5. Roberts (1996) was probably one of the earliest teachers to incorporate consultancy projects into the MBA programme, and indeed from a critical perspective where students were expected to analyse how social inequalities and the exercise of power condition performance. His approach draws on a critical sensibility and seeks to develop it through his students conducting live consulting projects in real time (Roberts 1996, reported in Grey 2004: 183).

References

Adler, N., Shani, A. B., and Styhre, A. (2004). *Collaborative Research in Organizations*. Thousand Oaks, Calif.: Sage.

Alferoff, C., and Knights, D. (2006). 'Making and Mending Your Nets: The Management of Uncertainty in Academic/Practitioner Knowledge Networks'. Unpublished paper, Institute of Public Policy and Management, University of Keele. *British Journal of Management,* forthcoming.

Alvesson, M., and Willmott, H. C. (1996). *Making Sense of Management: A Critical Introduction*. London: Sage.

Anthony, P. D. (1986). *The Foundation of Management*. London: Tavistock.

Baratz, L. (1960). *The Servants of Power*. New York: Wiley.

Barnard, C. I. (1938). *The Functions of the Executive*. Cambridge, Mass.: Harvard University Press.

Beer, M. (2001). 'Why Management Research Findings Are Unimplementable: An Action Science Perspective'. *REFLECTIONS,* Society for Organizational Learning and the Massachusetts Institute of Technology, 2/3: 58–63.

Bennis, W. G., and O'Toole, J. (2005). 'How Business Schools Lost Their Way'. *Harvard Business Review*, 83/5: 96–104.

Bojé, D. M., and Dennehy, R. F. (1993). *Managing in the Postmodern World: America's Revolution against Exploitation*. Dubuque, Ia.: Kendall/Hunt Publishing Company.

Bok, D. (1990). *Universities and the Future of America*. Durham, NC: Duke University Press.

—— (1996). *Beyond the Ivory Tower: Social Responsibilities of the Modern University*. Cambridge, Mass.: Harvard University Press.

Burgoyne, J., Knights, D., and Willmott, H. (1997). 'Introduction', in J. Burgoyne, D. Knights, and H. Willmott (guest eds.), *British Journal of Management*, 8/1 (March): 1–118.

Callon, M. (1986). 'Some Elements of a Sociology of Translation: Domestication of the Scallops and the Fishermen of St Brieuc Bay', in J. Law (ed.), *Power, Action and Belief*. London: Routledge and Kegan Paul.

—— (1991). 'Techno-Economic Networks and Universality', in J. Law (ed.), *Essays on Power, Technology and Domination*. London: Routledge.

Chandler, A. D., Jr, McCraw, T. K., and Tedlow, R. S. (1996). *Management Past and Present: A Casebook on American Business History*. Cincinnati: Southwestern Publishing Company.

Currie, G. (2005). 'Alternative Models for Business Education'. Paper presented at the Joint Advanced Institute of Management/ESRC Evolution of Business Knowledge conference on the Future of the Business School at Warwick Business School, University of Warwick, 13 December.

—— and Knights, D. (2003). 'Reflecting on a Critical Pedagogy in MBA Education'. *Management Learning*, 34/1 (March): 27–50.

—— Tempest, S., and Seymour, A. (2006). 'The Development of "Impoverished Souls": A Critical Appraisal of the Case Method within UK MBA Programmes'. Unpublished paper, Nottingham University Business School.

Dehler, G., Welsh, A., and Lewis, M. (2001). 'Critical Pedagogy in the New Paradigm'. *Management Learning*, 32: 493–511.

Delanty, G. (2001). *Challenging Knowledge: The University in the Knowledge Society*. Buckingham: Society for Research into Higher Education/Open University Press.

Drucker, P. (2001). 'Taking Stock'. *BizEd*, November–December: 13–17.

Fayol, H. (1916/1949). *General and Industrial Management*. London: Pitman.

Franklin, S., Wright, M., and Lockett, A. (2001). 'Academic and Surrogate Entrepreneurs and University Spinout Companies'. *Journal of Technology Transfer*, 26: 127–41.

French, R., and Grey, C. (1996). *Rethinking Management Education*. London: Sage.

Friese, H., and Wagner, P. (1998). 'More Beginnings than Ends: The Other Space of the University'. *Social Epistemology: A Journal of Knowledge, Culture and Policy*, 12/1: 27–32.

Gibbons, M., Limoges, C., Nowotny, H., Schartzman, S., Scott, P., and Trow, M. (1994). *The New Production of Knowledge*. London: Sage.

Goshal, S. (2005). 'Bad Management Theories Are Destroying Good Management Practices'. *Academy of Management Learning and Education*, 4/1: 75–81.

Gouldner, A. W. (1973). *For Sociology.* Harmondsworth: Penguin.

Grey, C. (2001). 'Re-imagining Relevance: A Response to Starkey and Madan'. *British Journal of Management*, 12 (December special issue): S27–S32.

—— (2002). 'What Are Business Schools For? On Silence and Voice in Management Education'. *Journal of Management Education*, 26: 496–511.

—— (2004). 'Reinventing Business Schools: The Contribution of Critical Management Education'. *Academy of Management Learning and Education*, 3/2: 178–86.

—— Knights, D., and Willmott, H. (1996). 'Is a Critical Pedagogy of Management Possible?' in R. French and C. Grey (eds.), *Rethinking Management Education*. London: Sage.

Hall, J., Rosenthal, J., and Wade, J. (1993). 'How to Make Reengineering Really Work'. *Harvard Business Review,* 71: 119–31.

Hambrick, D. C. (1994). 'What If the Academy Actually Mattered?' Presidential Address to the Academy of Management, 1993. *Academy of Management Review,* 19: 11–16.

Harvard Business Review (1998). *On Knowledge Management.* Boston: Harvard Business School Press, originally published 1987.

HM Treasury (2004). 'Science and Innovation Investment Framework 2004–2014'. DTI/Department for Education and Skills, HMSO.

Hodgkinson, G. P. (ed.) (2001). 'Facing the Future: The Nature and Purpose of Management Research Re-Assessed'. *British Journal of Management*, 12 (December special issue): S1–S2.

—— Herriot, P., and Anderson, N. (2001). 'Re-Aligning the Stakeholders in Management Research'. *British Journal of Management*, 12 (December special issue): S41–S48.

Huff, A. S., and Huff, J. O. (2001). 'Re-Focusing the Business School Agenda'. *British Journal of Management*, 12 (December special issue): S49–S54.

Johnson, J. (1976). *Doing Field Research.* New York: Free Press.

Kelemen, M., and Bansal, P. (2002). 'The Conventions of Management Research and Their Relevance to Management Practice'. *British Journal of Management*, 13/2: 97–108.

Knights, D., and O'Leary, M. (2006). 'Leadership, Ethics and Responsibility to the Other'. *Journal of Business Ethics*, August. DOI 10.1007/s10551-006-9008-6, pp. 1–13.

—— and Willmott, H. (eds.) (2007). *Introducing Organization Behaviour and Management.* London: International Thompson Press.

—— Alferoff, C., Starkey, K., and Tiratsoo, N. (2007). 'Bridging the Academic–Practitioner Divide: A Case Study Analysis of Business School Collaboration with Industry', in R. Shani et al. (eds.), *Handbook of Collaborative Management Research*. London: Sage.

—— Noble, F., Vurdubakis, T., and Willmott, H. (2002). 'Allegories of Creative Destruction: Technology and Organisation in Narratives of the e-Economy', in S. Woolgar (ed.), *Virtual Society? Technology, Cyberbole, Reality*. Oxford: Oxford University Press.

Latour, B. (1987). *Science in Action: How to Follow Scientists and Engineers through Society*. Milton Keynes: Open University Press.

——(1993). *We Have Never Been Modern*. London: Longman.

Little, S., Quintas, P., and Ray, T. (eds.) (2002). *Managing Knowledge: An Essential Reader*. London: Sage.

Lynd, R. (1939). *Knowledge for What? The Place of Social Science in American Culture*. Princeton: Princeton University Press.

Mintzberg, H. (2004). *Managers Not MBAs*. London: Pearson Education.

——and Gosling, J. (2002). 'Educating Managers Beyond Borders'. *Academy of Management Learning and Education*, 1/1: 64–76.

Nowotny, H., Scott, P., and Gibbons, M. (2001). *Re-Thinking Science: Knowledge and the Public in an Age of Uncertainty*. Cambridge: Polity Press.

OST (2000). *Excellence and Opportunity: Science Enterprise Challenge*. Science and Innovation Policy White Paper.

Pearce, J. A., II (1999). 'Faculty Survey on Business Education Reform'. Academy of Management Executive, Report Cards, May, pp. 105–9.

Pfeffer, J. (1993). 'Barriers to the Advance of Organizational Science: Paradigm Development as a Dependent Variable'. *Academy of Management Review*, 18: 599–620.

——and Fong, C. T. (2002). 'The End of Business Schools? Less Success than Meets the Eye'. *Academy of Management Learning and Education*, 1/1: 78–95.

————(2004). 'The Business School "Business": Some Lessons from the US Experience'. *Journal of Management Studies*, 41/8: 1501–20.

Porter, L. W., and McGibbin, L. E. (1988). *Management Education and Development: Drift or Thrust into the 21st Century*. New York: McGraw Hill.

Readings, B. (1996). *The University in Ruins*. Cambridge, Mass.: Harvard University Press.

Roberts, J. (1996). 'Management Education and the Limits of Rationality: The Conditions and Consequences of Management Practice', in R. French and C. Grey (eds.), *Rethinking Management Education*. London: Sage.

Simon, H. A. (1967). 'The Business School: A Problem in Organizational Design'. *Journal of Management Studies*, 4: 1–16.

Spector, B., and Beer, M. (1994). 'Beyond TQM Programs'. *Journal of Organization Change Management*, 7: 6–14.

Starkey, K., and Madan, P. (2001). 'Bridging the Relevance Gap: Aligning Stakeholders in the Future of Management Research'. *British Journal of Management*, 12 (December special issue): S3–S26.

——and Tempest, S. (2005). 'The Future of the Business School: Knowledge Challenges and Opportunities'. *Human Relations*, 58/1: 61–82.

——and Tiratsoo, N. (2007). *The Future of the Business School*. Cambridge: Cambridge University Press.

Suddaby, R., and Greenwood, R. (2001). 'Colonizing Knowledge: Commodification as a Dynamic of Jurisdictional Expansion in Professional Service Firms'. *Human Relations*, 54: 933–53.

Tempest, S., Currie, G., and Wright, M. (2006). 'Entrepreneurship Education and the MBA'. Unpublished paper, Nottingham University Business School, to be submitted to *Entrepreneurship Theory and Practice*.

Tranfield, D., and Starkey, K. (1998). 'The Nature, Social Organization and Promotion of Management Research: Towards Policy'. *British Journal of Management*, 9/3: 341–53.

Urwick, L. (1956). *The Pattern of Management*. London: Pitman.

Wright, M. (forthcoming). 'University–Industry Linkages: Regional Policies and Initiatives in the UK', in S. Yusuf (ed.), *University–Industry Linkages and the Regions*. World Bank, September.

——and Lockett, A. (forthcoming). 'Risk Capital, Resources and University Spin-outs', in B. Clarysse et al. (eds.), *Entrepreneurship and Innovation*. London: Edward Elgar.

————Alferoff, K., and Mosey, S. (2005). 'Academic Entrepreneurship, Knowledge Gaps and the Role of Business Schools'. CMBOR Working Paper, University of Nottingham.

————Clarysse, B., and Binks, M. (forthcoming). 'University Spin-offs and Venture Capital'. *Research Policy*.

Zald, M. (2002). 'Spinning Disciplines: Critical Management Studies in the Context of the Transformation of Management Education'. *Organization*, 9: 365–85.

Zimmerman, J. L. (2001). 'Can American Business Schools Survive?' Unpublished manuscript, Simon Graduate School of Business Administration.

Part II

Innovation and Design Processes

Innovation and Design Processes

6

Knowledge Brokering in High-Tech Start-Ups

Joanne Jin Zhang and Charles Baden-Fuller

Introduction

It is well established that brokers (boundary-spanning individuals) add value to organizations because they bring together in the course of their brokering activities much needed knowledge (Burt 1992), including information and know-how (Kogut and Zander 1992). Studies in different research streams have emphasized that this knowledge is typically technical or rare and has a measurable influence on the actor's survival and success, see for instance the work on intra-organization technical communication (Tushman and Scanlan 1981), project-based television and film talent recruiting (Bielby and Bielby 1999), and employee recruiting (Finlay and Coverdill 2000).

Scholars have not only linked brokerage with creativity and innovation in a wider perspective but also noted that the level of brokerage through which a person could create value may vary. Based on an extensive literature review, Burt (2004) suggested that brokers who are resourceful and skilful in bringing together different types of information and knowledge from various domains are more likely to have good ideas, as they benefit from being the first to see new opportunities or visions otherwise unseen. Moreover, he observed various levels of brokerage. At the lower level, a broker may help to communicate issues between groups or to translate the belief or practice of one group into language digestible by the other. At the higher level, a broker may see potential value-creating opportunities by linking unrelated groups or by synthesizing different beliefs or behaviours from both groups.

Despite the emergent interest in the role of brokering in knowledge management, the extant literature seems to be at odds with Burt's observations. First, most brokering literature focuses on either individual-level (Allen 1977; Aldrich and Herker 1977; DiMaggio 1992; Rodan and Galunic 2004; Burt 2004) or firm-level brokering relationships (Hargadon and Sutton 1997; Lorenzoni and Baden-Fuller 1995). As we know, knowledge resides in individuals (Polanyi 1966). To understand how organizations learn through brokering activities, we need to look at the relationship between individuals and organizations. Secondly, emphasis on the micro–macro link points to the importance of managerial choice (Felin and Foss 2006). However, the extant literature on the motivation of individual brokering is scattered in various research streams. Taking a social identity perspective, some scholars have suggested that the boundary-spanning function is subject to conflicting roles as 'representative' vs. 'gatekeeper' (Khan et al. 1964; Friedman and Podolny 1992). Derived from agency theory, Kesner and Shapiro (1994) have suggested that economic incentives play a key role in brokering mergers. Thirdly, there is a scarcity of empirical literature that looks at the processes that determine brokering activities. The only exception seems to be Hargadon and Sutton's study (1997), which provides a detailed account of how a product design company provides innovative solutions through firm-level knowledge brokering. Hargadon (2002) further argues that the knowledge brokering process involves bridging multiple domains, learning about the resources within those domains, and linking that knowledge to new situations. As such, the nature of the processes behind brokerage remains to be precisely understood (Murray 2004).

We explore in this chapter two themes to shed light on these questions. The first is the role of social structure in creating the legitimacy for successful interactions. Such legitimacy can come about from the structure of the network or the close tie between the broker and the immediate institutional context of the broker. The legitimacy could also arise from the personal knowledge of the broker and the way that he or she is introduced into the company, perhaps via the board of directors.

The social network literature emphasizes that it is the social structure that renders broker advantages. Social structure has many aspects. In a very general sense, the term includes 'groups, institutions, laws, population characteristics and sets of social relations that form the environment of the organization' (Stinchcombe 1965). In short, social structure can be seen as a network residue to social history; a network in which individuals are variably connected to one another as a function of prior contact, exchange, and attendant emotions (Burt 2005). Building upon the notion of the strength of weak ties (Granovetter 1973), Burt (1992) argued that social capital is a function of spanning structural holes, which separate non-redundant sources of information in a network. Since people on either side of a structural hole circulate in different flows of information, spanning structural holes gives actor advantages including broad and early access to the information as well as having good ideas or visions otherwise unseen.

Most of the literature on networks implicitly assumes that the 'network structure' determines the behaviour of brokers. Although coming from the same origins, the institutional literature takes a different line, focusing on a key dimension of the structure, namely the principal institution involved in the broker's network. According to these theorists, these institutions are all powerful and generate overwhelming isomorphic tendencies. Mimetic isomorphism is a process by which, in ambiguous and uncertain situations, organizational changes are imitated in order to gain legitimacy (DiMaggio and Powell 1983). Mimetic isomorphism (or 'mimicry') provides legitimacy and is more likely to happen when managers face ambiguous situations with unclear solutions (Cyert and March 1963), since in those situations legitimacy becomes crucial for organizational survival (Deephouse 1996; Meyer and Rowan 1977; Scott 1987; Singh, Tucker, and House 1986; Westphal, Gulati, and Shortell 1997). Past writers have adopted a variety of approaches to identify the process of selection that identifies who imitates whom. Hybels (1995) and Deephouse (1996) identified regulators and media. Barreto and Baden-Fuller (2006) argue for legitimacy-based groupings as the basis of choice. These groups are not selected on the basis of the firm's own choice, but on what others in a position of authority say. 'Legitimacy is a generalized perception or assumption that the actions of an entity are desirable, proper, or appropriate within some socially constructed system of norms, values, beliefs, and definitions' (Suchman 1995: 574). This rightly emphasizes the dependence of organizations on collective observers, the legitimacy providers, i.e. those who assess the conformity of firm behaviour to a specific standard in order to provide legitimacy. It is not necessary to probe in depth how legitimacy providers come up with their categorizations; rather, it is important to note that these legitimacy providers typically judge the organizations' behaviour against these benchmarks to assess conformity (Meyer and Rowan 1977), and that managers use such categorization as long as it serves as a gauge against which their actions are evaluated and justified (Dutton and Dukerich 1991). In summary, we argue that when mimetic behavioural pressures are strong, firms will follow the actions of those signalled as legitimate by outside legitimacy providers.

Theory Question One: Will brokering activities be driven by the network structure of the brokers or will institutional labels carry weight in the process?

The second theme is that of incentives. Transferring knowledge is a deeply personal activity and requires high levels of personal motivation. We explore what kinds of mainly non-monetary motivation is involved and why there needs to be positive motivation on both sides for effective transfer. The extant literature lacks a process view of brokering activities as most studies rely on quantitative data to examine brokering advantage. For example, Burt (2005: 47) drove the structure-based argument home by suggesting that 'the structure around a person indicates the kind of person he or she is, so motivation does not have to be measured once one has a measure of network structure'. Likewise, the institutional view is that mimetic pressures will drive performance and that individual motivation will be largely irrelevant. On the other hand, empirical evidence in the extant brokering literature seems to suggest that social structure alone does not determine brokering behaviour; rather, managerial choice plays a key role in the process of brokerage. Tushman and Scanlan (1981) reported that well-connected extensive internal and external communications are each necessary but not sufficient conditions for informational boundary-spanning activities. In the meantime, other scholars have also suggested that brokerage is strongly affected by a broker's cognitive dexterity, which is largely a function of the amount, quality, and diversity of the actor's knowledge stock (Hargadon and Sutton 1997; Rodan and Galunic 2004). More recently, Finlay and Coverdill (2000) pointed out, not all structural holes are equivalent and equally attractive; and it is a broker's job to respond to these variations by configuring a deal network. Following this line of inquiry, Pollock, Porac, and Wade (2004) studied the brokering role of investment bankers in the context of the US IPO market and reviewed a large amount of descriptive accounts of brokerage in various mediated markets. They argue, in a convincing manner, that both social and economic motivations mutually shape a broker's role as a network 'architect' who intentionally designs, builds, and maintains network configurations. Their study makes a significant contribution towards theorizing the proactive and network-building role of brokers. However, the study is mainly focused on the brokering role of constructing transaction networks in mediated markets and the published study lacks data.

Theory Question Two: What is the role of motivation in driving brokering behaviour? And how does this motivation link to the network's structure?

We draw upon 229 instances of brokering activity in twelve high-tech start-up companies in the United Kingdom over a thirty-eight-month period of time. In our data we carefully distinguish between the resources that brokers have and the use of them. Using this distinction we explore the gaps between what brokers know and what they do.

Context for the research

The high-tech start-up process typically involves various development stages in response to a set of dominant problems that a new venture faces at sequential times (Kanzanjian 1988). In this study, our research scope focuses on three very early stages of high-tech start-up process in the United Kingdom from pre-founding to achieving A-Round funding, a critical milestone for high-tech start-up survival. At T0, original founders generate innovative ideas that are often based on scientific research in academic institutions. Such an idea can be patented, but it takes a business model to value intellectual property (IP) (Chesbrough 2003). Often, at the end of T0 or beginning of T1, a start-up was incorporated. At T1, the main challenge is to achieve proof of concept, which typically consists of feasibility studies that convert academic research into an initial business plan. This stage is primarily funded by government agencies such as University Challenge Funds, Scottish Enterprise, and so on. The funds available are often up to £250,000. At T2, the main task is to achieve A-Round commercial funding, which ranges from £250,000 to £5 million. This stage can be funded by venture capital as well as early Initial Public Offerings (IPOs).

The high-tech start-up process differs from many other company foundations because of the liability of newness coupled with significant technical and financial risks (Nicolaou and Birley 2003; Lam 1991). Here the ambition of the founders is often very great; the level of intellectual property is high, but the founders typically have no serious commercial experience and few connections. To be successful commercially, start-ups have to construct social networks in order to access money and technical, scientific, and managerial knowledge beyond that provided by the original founders. However, developing knowledge costs money and takes time to accumulate, and start-ups can rarely afford to buy into the firm all the knowledge that they need. Therefore, they need to use brokers to access knowledge.

Brokers differ in the knowledge and social capital that they have, both of which can be seen as a function of their prior experience and social structure (Coleman 1988). From our discussions with the companies involved in this industry, we identified two kinds of brokers and related knowledge that seemed critical in the start-up process: *functional brokers* and *entrepreneurial brokers*.

Functional brokers have knowledge about a particular field within a venture development stage. For example, start-ups need legal advice. The first need is for assistance with filing start-up papers and employee contracts to set up the business. There are other needs for a lawyer in the early stages that include filing for patents and drafting partnership or alliances agreements. At stage T2, start-up companies need a lawyer to deal with issues relating to funding and even mergers and acquisitions. What is noticeable about high-tech start-ups is that a general lawyer cannot help with all these issues. For instance, an IP lawyer needs to be very specialized and very skilled, and typically knows little about other issues such as those related to fund-raising. Although a law firm may provide a full range of services in-house, the start-up still needs to deal with different lawyers as it grows, and many high-tech start-ups avoid general practice lawyers because they need to access highly specialized skills. Accordingly, functional brokers often bring in highly specialized knowledge assets and networks that are not similar to other brokers.

Entrepreneurial brokers are rather different from functional brokers (although a few were once such brokers: some having been academics or even lawyers). Entrepreneurial brokers typically know about venturing in general, have experience and knowledge across venture development stages, and have prior experience of setting up and growing a business. Entrepreneurial brokers are valued not so much for what they know, but more because they have a sense of what types of knowledge are required at different points of time in the new venture creation process. They are also highly valued because they typically know about functional brokers and can access them and evaluate their qualities. By definition, entrepreneurial brokers have built a large network spanning structural holes across various domains, including academic research, finance, and industry communities. Also, it is obvious that entrepreneurial brokers sometimes are able to give quite specialized advice in domains that are normally reserved to functional experts on account of their access and prior experience.

Our distinction between functional and entrepreneurial brokers has some similarity to the notion of 'architectural and component knowledge' in the product innovation literature (Henderson and Clark 1990).

Our separation of functional and entrepreneurial brokerage is not the same as that discussed in the venturing literature or even by the industry. The literature and the industry (Bozeman 2003; Wright, Robbie, and Ennew 1997; Mason and Harrison 1995) talk about the broker's institutional affiliation (including venture capitalist, technology transfer officer, independent adviser, academic researcher, and professional adviser) or the broker's formal role in the start-up (such as executive and non-executive board director). We therefore expand our first research question to ask what is the connection between our classification of *functional* and *entrepreneurial* brokering and the classifications of the literature:

Our first research question is expanded and concerns the connections between brokering activities and the institutional affiliation of the broker and his or her status in the firm.

We also note that there are important issues of motivation. Most start-up companies in the high-tech sphere are short of cash. Brokers cannot be rewarded with cash, but they can be rewarded with promises and shares of companies. Alternatively, they can be rewarded by the intrinsic excitement of being part of the venture. What motivates brokers to be active, and does this motivation influence the way in which knowledge is transferred?

Our second research question is expanded and looks at the factors that influence a broker's involvement with a firm. What are the motivations and constraints, and how do they influence brokering performance?

Empirical study

Methods and data

As our research questions concerned what do brokers do and what factors influence their behaviours, we utilized an in-depth micro-study of individuals and firms involved in the high-tech start-up process in the UK high-tech industry. Our research is the result of a real-time longitudinal project lasting thirty-eight months from October 2003 to December 2006 involving twelve case companies, their boards, and their advisers. During the preliminary data collection period, we identified three individuals who seemed institutionally different and were actively involved in this process; namely, a university technology transfer officer (TTO), a venture capitalist, and an independent adviser. Using snowballing strategy, we identified twelve companies with which the three brokers were closely involved. We then conducted semi-structured interviews with all twelve company founders and current CEOs and at least two brokers who were often board members and gave advice and help with the new venture creation process at early stages, as suggested by founders or CEOs. To add further insight, we became fully immersed in two of our company cases, where one of the authors sat in the board meetings and traced the actors' behaviours and thinking processes. The other author drew on the experience of being on the board of one of the studied companies and seeing how behind the scenes engagement really works. Fifty semi-structured interviews and board meetings were tape recorded and transcribed. Secondary data sources included confidential corporate documents as well as public data sources (e.g. company website, FAME, Perfect Filing database, and so on). An interview protocol was designed and used systematically.

Our sample, consisting of ten university spin-outs and two non-university spin-outs, is described in Table 6.1. It should be noted that the year of incorporation is not the year of founding, but rather it is typically the end of T0 and the start of T1. We also show the size of the company at the end of T2, at the time of A-Round funding (or close to it), and the size of the board of directors. Like many fast-growth high-technology companies, the boards of these companies are large and strongly independent. This is quite different from the situation in low-technology firms.

Table 6.1. *A summary of case characteristics*

Case company	Industry	Year of legal formation (T1)	Number of board directors (T2)	Number of executive directors (T2)	Number of full-time employees (T2)
AUV	Life science	1996	4	2	12
MED	Life science	1999	6	4	35
ID	Medical devices	2001	7	4	9
AIR	Medical devices	2001	5	1	6
PHY	Life science	2002	8	3	4
CAP	Life science	2002	8	3	7
PROX	Life science	2003	5	2	11
NOVA	Life science	2004	9	3	12
PHONO	Physical science	2004	6	3	0
CYTO	Life science	2005	5	1	1
BLUE	Software	2005	4	1	0
AOX	Life science	2005	6	2	1

One of our companies was not a university spin-out and its founders were not scientists. We used this company as a reference point to non-high-technology start-ups. This company, PHY, is a UK-based company started with a business idea of commercializing medical knowledge accumulated in China over the past 2,000 years. The founding team has business knowledge instead of scientific or technological knowledge.

Our unit of analysis was the brokering activity during each development stage in each case. We made 229 such observations. In every case, we identified the individual brokering activity with a firm and were therefore able to link events across levels of data. We used Atlas.ti software to manage and search our database and to compare the knowledge and social capital that each broker had and his or her use of them within and across our 229 cases.

Findings

KNOWLEDGE BROKERING GROWS IN IMPORTANCE AS THE FIRM DEVELOPS

Comparing our data on brokers and what they do at the stages of development, we are able to confirm that brokering plays a key role in facilitating the flow of knowledge into young firms. The new venture creation process requires finding and integrating different types of knowledge for the different stages, and it is highly inefficient for a firm to acquire the wide array of specialized knowledge that it needs (Grant and Baden-Fuller 2004). This is where brokers can help.

Our data set of 229 brokering activities is a close approximation to a complete catalogue of all the brokering activities of our twelve firms. Table 6.2 provides a summary of our data on the types of brokering by each firm and each time period, with summary totals at the bottom of the table. We

Table 6.2. *Number of observations of brokering activities (N = 229)*

	Use of entrepreneurial knowledge and social capital	Use of functional knowledge and social capital	Sub-total
T0	1	23	24
T1	13	59	72
T2	33	100	133
Total No.	47	182	229
Total %	21%	79%	100%

were not surprised that only 21% of the total observations were captured by the entrepreneurial broker. According to industry sources, these kinds of brokers are quite rare because their knowledge spans many stages of development and is multifunctional.

Our data shows that firms initially start with quite small networks, and that these grow as the time passes and as the firm progresses. The growth occurs in both functional and entrepreneurial knowledge. If we focus on the functional brokers (typically those with very specific knowledge), we see that their activities increase from 23 at T0 to 100 at T2. What is not shown in the tables is the fact that the range of functional knowledge also grows over time. As the firm develops, it needs more knowledge of different types, and the firms typically adopt a just-in-time approach to knowledge acquisition. This suggests that, as start-ups grow, the size, the amount, and the type of knowledge flows into the firm are increasing. This finding highlights the key characteristics of the high-tech start-up processes:

Finding: In high-technology start-ups, different types of knowledge need to be integrated at different stages, and the amount and diversity of knowledge required increases sharply as the firm develops.

BROKERING BEHAVIOURS AND INSTITUTIONAL TYPES

Our initial theorizing asked how the effectiveness of knowledge is linked to institutional factors. Our data clearly shows that brokers are not always consistent in their behaviour when classed either by network structure or by institutional type.

Our data suggest that brokers in general behave according to their positions in the network, but that there are exceptions. While most functional brokers do not have entrepreneurial knowledge and so cannot act as such, the opposite is not true for the entrepreneurial broker. Standing in the middle of a dense network of contacts that spans functions as well as other kinds of integrative knowledge, there is an opportunity for these brokers to lend knowledge in a narrow as well as a rich format. Out of forty-seven observations of entrepreneurial brokering activities, there are two occasions where entrepreneurial brokers 'withheld' some knowledge acting only as functional spanners. We view these exceptions as important, and we probe them further.

Table 6.3 probes the institutional affiliation of our brokers, and we find that brokers do not behave by their institutional affiliation. We observe that venture capitalists, independent advisers, professional advisers, and

Table 6.3. *Institutional affiliation and brokering*

Broker's institutional affiliation	Use of entrepreneurial knowledge and social capital		Use of functional knowledge and social capital		Total	
	Number of observations	Number of brokers	Number of observations	Number of brokers	Number of observations	Number of brokers
Venture capitalist (VC)	4	4	7	3	11	7
Technology transfer officer (TTO)	0	0	17	7	17	7
Independent adviser	35	7	52	32	87	39
Academic researcher	0	0	64	31	64	31
Professional adviser	5	4	38	21	43	25
Government agent	1	1	6	5	7	6
Total	45	16	184	99	229	115

government agents could all carry on both entrepreneurial and functional brokering activities. There are some positives and some negatives. Contrary to conventional wisdom, several professional advisers seem to be able to act well beyond their functional knowledge. This is an important finding because it indicates that institutional affiliation does not hinder the offer of more complex knowledge or the possibility that the recipient organization can accept that knowledge. Such observations strongly counter the notion that venturing is subject to normative rules typically found in mature industries.

We also found that many brokers who carry an institutional label are not capable or willing to perform the function often ascribed to them. We found few people in government agencies with entrepreneurial knowledge despite their claim that they had such skill. Likewise, we found that few university technology transfer officers (TTOs) had entrepreneurial knowledge. Indeed, several firms noted the level of value-added that is provided by TTOs varies significantly.

One of the frustrations was the quality of advice that you could find in the university technology transfer offices. . . . Some of it was good, some of it was bad. . . . For instance, when we had to do the Unilever contracting, they were extremely helpful in educating us about IP, and how we could structure the agreement. However, most TTOs don't really have any business experience, so their contributions to start-ups are often limited as we grow.

George (a TTO) obviously has more business experience. His background is in business and marketing. He pays much attention to financial details, budget and legal contracts. He always goes with us to presentations. . . . He does not really have a science background, but he is a very bright chap; he has a very good idea of how things work.

The fact that entrepreneurial brokers appear in many forms and types suggests that they feel themselves to be free of institutional constraints. This observation is further reinforced when we see that they do not behave by their formal roles in the start-up rather they take on board positions to gain credibility.

Our data suggest that brokers' behaviours neither conform to their institutional affiliations nor to their formal roles in the start-up. As such, institutionally driven mimetic behavioural pressures are not very strong in an entrepreneurial setting. There are two possible reasons for this. First, in comparison to the United States, start-ups in technology-related industries are less developed in the United Kingdom. The overall status of university technology transfer offices and the high-tech venture capital sector is less well developed. (In contrast, the UK venture capital sector is well developed for management buy-outs, see for instance Wright, Thompson, and Robbie 1992.) Another explanation could be that institutional forces are generally very weak during the very early stages of high-tech start-up process because there is far less institutional pressure to conform in entrepreneurial settings.

Our findings help explain the mixed results in the extant literature on the value-added of different types of actors, often defined by their institutional types, such as venture capitalist, TTO, and so on (Rosenstein et al. 1993; Busenitz, Fiet, and Moesel 2004; Ensley and Hmieleski 2005). Scholars have found inconsistent results on venture capitalists' value-added to start-ups as knowledge 'coaches' or 'scouts' (Baum and Silverman 2003). In both our own fieldwork and the literature, we find that start-ups have mixed opinions towards TTOs' value-added, which is often associated with the TTO's institutional role as safeguarding the university's interests.

Finding: The role of institutional legitimization for a broker is weak in the entrepreneurial setting. Legitimacy is not assured by association with strong types.

Institutional theory will not allow us to bypass the question of what is the factor that gives a broker legitimacy if it is not the institutional affiliation. In Table 6.4, we see how the instances of brokering that are used by a company are associated with either the top management team (TMT) or with the status of being on the board. Forty instances of entrepreneurial brokering (by fifteen people) are associated with members of the board, whereas only six instances occurred outside the board. In the case of functional brokering, ninety-two instances were undertaken by forty board members, twenty-eight were initiated by the top management

Table 6.4. *Formal roles and brokering*

Broker's formal role in start-ups		Use of entrepreneurial knowledge and social capital		Use of functional knowledge and social capital		Total	
		Number of observations	Number of brokers	Number of observations	Number of brokers	Number of observations	Number of brokers
Board of directors	Non-executive	32	7	32	18	64	25
	Executive	8	8	60	22	68	30
Top management team (TMT)		0	0	28	19	28	19
Outside adviser		6	3	63	38	69	41
Total		46	18	183	97	229	115

teams, and sixty-three instances were related to thirty-eight brokers that were outside the board. It can be clearly seen that the majority, but by no means all brokering instances are undertaken by board members.

Not shown in our data is the role of board members in legitimating brokers who are not board members. We observe that outside advisers become brokers who are accepted and used by the company either because they are known to the top management team or more often they are recommended by other brokers (typically the entrepreneurial ones) who are on board. This process, rather than institutional names, creates legitimacy in the eyes of the company. Indeed, board members often recommend advisers based on their prior working experience together. Moreover, entrepreneurial brokers on the board are often aware of the danger of choosing advisers by their institutional affiliations.

When you are going to professional advisers, who are very important in this process (the start-up process), it is very important to keep a balance. For instance, I will not choose XYZ, who acts as an institution rather than purely accountancy. They are accountants! Rather, if you go to accountancy or lawyers, you want expertise rather than institutional arrogance. And on no gain no fee bases. Also, a city broker made a good point to me once, 'Why does a small entity need such a big accountancy firm?'

Our data fills an important gap in our knowledge about how the brokering process actually takes place and is legitimized. Writers have often speculated that the process is one where brokers introduce other people, but few have observed this activity. Within a closed network, norms and trust exercise a major influence on information and knowledge flow (Granovetter 1985; Coleman 1988).

Finding: Board members play a critical role in legitimizing outside advisers' brokerage.

BROKERING BEHAVIOURS AND MOTIVATION

The above section on the dynamics of brokering invites us to probe deeper into the process. For each instance of brokering, we asked at least two people in each company: 'How did the broker help the company? What did the broker do?' We further triangulated the data from our observations from board meetings and informal socialization activities. From these data, we classified a broker as 'actively' using his or her knowledge and social capital when the broker actively seeks new contacts for the start-up. In contrast, we infer a broker as 'passive' in using his or her knowledge and social capital when the broker has neither brought in new contacts to the start-up nor actively searched for contacts.

We categorized each of our 229 instances of brokering into 136 active and 93 passive instances. This classification allowed us to further probe motivation issues. We return once again to the observation that brokers do not always behave as to type, and in particular entrepreneurial brokers may act differently in different situations.

It is obvious that context will influence the way in which brokers contribute their knowledge. Context has multi-levels, including firm specific, industry specific, and geography specific. Sometimes, brokers may not be able to transfer their existing knowledge and social capital to another context. In one case, we observed that an entrepreneurial broker's behaviour seemed to be related to lack of specific industry experience, so he withdrew his entrepreneurial knowledge and only contributed his functional knowledge as a legal expert. In the other case, we observed that an entrepreneurial broker's contribution to the start-ups was very limited despite the fact that he had over twenty years of experience in the pharmaceutical and biotech industry, including successfully setting up his own companies, and he has built up a large network spanning structural holes across industry, academic research, and finance communities. However, most of this knowledge is related to the United States and not the United Kingdom.

We also found that similar brokers may behave differently in different cases. For example, John, an entrepreneurial broker, is typically a non-executive chairman. In most cases, he contributes and utilizes his existing knowledge and social capital, and seldom goes beyond his existing social network to search for new contacts. But there are two exceptions, one where he was more personally involved, another where he unusually withdrew his entrepreneurial knowledge. Our data also shows instances where brokers reject opportunities to become involved with companies. Probing suggests that motivation explains the differences.

Overall, all these observations lend support to the contentions of Finlay and Coverdill (2000) and Pollock, Porac, and Wade (2004) that motivations play a key role in brokering activities. Our data suggest that there is a high degree of variation among brokers' perceived opportunities of a technological idea, which is largely a function of the broker's prior experience and knowledge (Shane 2000). In the meantime, our data suggests that brokers 'cannot' always use their knowledge and social capital as they wish even when they have the motivation and the ability to do so. This can be seen as what Pollock, Porac, and Wade (2004) call a contextual factor or deal condition, which also significantly affects a broker's motivation.

Finding: Brokers' motivation plays a key role in their brokering activities.

Discussion

The existing literature does not distinguish between the human and social capital that an actor has and the use of them. This assumption may be the cause of many inconsistent results on the causal relationship between human and social capital and entrepreneurial performance. Gimeno et al. (1997) found that human capital increases venture performance but not persistence. Davidsson and Honig (2003) also found a weak relationship between human capital and successful venture performance. In the social capital literature, most studies focus on how different types of network and network relationship affect venture performance; and the results vary (Uzzi 1996; Singh et al. 1999; McEvily and Zaheer 1999).

Our research provides an alternative explanation of the mixed findings in the literature, suggesting a shift of research focus from actor's resources to the combination of the resource and the actual use of actor's resources. Our finding supports Pollock et al.'s contentions that motivations play a key role in brokering activities and that these are largely driven by a broker's perception of future opportunities. This finding stresses the importance of managerial cognition and intent; it is a view that echoes findings elsewhere, such as considerations of rejuvenation (Baden-Fuller and Stopford 1994), maintaining momentum in successful organizations (Balogun and Johnson 2004), and entrepreneurial orientation in opportunity exploitation process (Lumpkin and Dess 1996).

Our findings also form a bridge between the work on boards and the work on brokering. Most of the literature on boards has stressed their role as monitors of managerial actions. Yet, the behaviour of boards flies in the face of such assumptions, for boards spend relatively little time and effort monitoring. Our research provides new insights, suggesting that the board is indeed monitoring, but it is not managerial laxity that is at stake. Rather, a key issue is the assessment and monitoring of the brokering relationships between the firm and its environment. Here, we suggest the board plays a key role in adding value for the young company.

Thirdly, and most importantly, this study provides a dynamic view of the brokering process. That is, a broker's value-added could still be limited even when the broker lacks neither motivation nor capabilities. We emphasize the importance of the interaction between social structure and motivation, which drives the network formation process. The emergent structuration of a network influences firm behaviour (Giddens 1984). Therefore, brokers, including original founders, at an aggregate level drive the process of discovering and exploiting entrepreneurial opportunities by searching and recombining the existing resources (Schumpeter 1934). This study also contributes to the network literature by suggesting a link between the social capital of structural hole and network closure.

The key managerial implication is that, by linking the young firm to knowledgeable brokers, the firm can in effect acquire years of experience at a single stroke and so increase its chances of survival by fast-track aging and avoiding the worst liabilities of 'newness'. However, there is a challenge, since similar brokers may behave differently in different situations. Therefore, it is not enough for a start-up to connect to knowledgeable brokers; it must know how to distinguish, motivate, and leverage a broker's knowledge and social capital in knowledge exploitation. In this respect, our distinction between entrepreneurial and technical brokers is important, and the company needs to take its entrepreneurial brokers very seriously.

Finally, we remind the reader that we are cautious. Although our findings are based on our unique real-time longitudinal research design, we have only a small sample of 12 cases and only 115 brokers. We are also aware that our research context limits the generalizability of our findings to all brokering activities in young firms in more mature settings.

Conclusions

In a book that is dedicated to examining the contributions of knowledge to the economy, we unpick some of the important dynamics of knowledge building in young firms. We note that young high-tech firms in the United Kingdom have to develop sources of knowledge quickly and efficiently, and that they use broker networks to achieve this end. We build on Pollock, Porac, and Wade's (2004) theory of brokering in a mediated market and develop a dynamic view of brokering that takes account of motivations as well as capabilities. Considering the importance of social networks in knowledge management, studying the brokering role in this manner helps to fill some of the missing puzzle of how to construct a network to facilitate effective and efficient knowledge integration. This study also contributes to the process view of the firm. Future studies may focus on linking individual brokering and firm-level network formation outcomes.

Acknowledgements

We gratefully acknowledge the support of the UK's ESRC under the Evolution of Business Knowledge (EBK) programme, award no: RES 334-25-0016 and the guidance of Professor Harry Scarbrough. We also acknowledge helpful comments from our colleagues at Cass and the participants of the Cass International Workshops during 2005 and 2006; the Wharton Entrepreneurship Workshop Series, February 2007; and the 23rd European Groups of Organizational Studies Colloquium, July 2007.

References

Aldrich, H., and Herker, D. (1977). 'Boundary Spanning Roles and Organization Structure'. *Academy of Management Review*, 2: 217–30.

Allen, T. J. (1977). *Managing the Flow of Technology: Technology Transfer and the Dissemination of Technological Information within the R&D Organization.* Cambridge, Mass.: MIT Press.

Baden-Fuller, C., and Stopford, J. M. (1994). *Rejuvenating the Mature Business.* Boston: Harvard Business School Press.

Balogun, J., and Johnson, G. (2004). 'Organizational Restructuring and Middle Manager Sensemaking'. *Academy of Management Journal*, 44/4: 523–50.

Barreto, I., and Baden-Fuller, C. (2006). 'To Conform or to Perform: Mimetic Behavior, Legitimacy-Based Groups and Performance Consequences'. *Journal of Management Studies*, 437: 1559–81.

Baum, J. A. C., and Silverman, B. S. (2004). 'Picking Winners or Building Them? Alliance, Intellectual, and Human Capital as Selection Criteria in Venture Financing and Performance of Biotechnology Startups'. *Journal of Business Venturing*, 19/3: 411–36.

Bielby, W. T., and Bielby, D. D. (1999). 'Organizational Mediation of Project-Based Labor Market: Talent Agencies and the Careers of Screenwriters'. *American Sociological Review*, 64/1: 64–85.

Bozeman, B. (2003). 'Technology Transfer and Public Policy: A Review of Research and Theory'. *Research Policy*, 29: 627–55.

Burt, R. S. (1992). *Structural Holes: The Social Structure of Competition*. Cambridge, Mass.: Harvard University Press.

—— (2004). 'Structural Holes and Good Ideas'. *American Journal of Sociology*, 110/2: 349–99.

—— (2005). *Brokerage and Closure: An Introduction to Social Capital*. Oxford: Oxford University Press.

Busenitz, L. W., Fiet, J. O., and Moesel, D. D. (2004). 'Reconsidering the Venture Capitalist' "Value Added" Proposition: An Interorganizational Learning Perspective'. *Journal of Business Venturing*, 19: 787–807.

Chesbrough, H. (2003). *Open Innovation: The New Imperative for Creating and Profiting from Technology*. Boston: Harvard Business School Press.

Coleman, J. S. (1988). 'Social Capital in the Creation of Human Capital'. *American Journal of Sociology*, 94: S95–S120.

Cooper, A. C. J., Gimeno-Gascon, F. J., and Woo, C. Y. (1994). 'Initial Human and Financial Capital as Predictors of New Venture Performances'. *Journal of Business Venturing*, 9: 371–95.

Cyert, R., and March, J. (1963). *A Behavioral Theory of the Firm*. Englewood Cliffs: Prentice-Hall.

Dacin, M. T., Goodstein, J., and Scott, W. R. (2002). 'Institutional Theory and Institutional Change'. *Academy of Management Journal*, 45/1: 45–57.

Davidsson, P., and Honig, B. (2003). 'The Role of Social and Human Capital among Nascent Entrepreneurs'. *Journal of Business Venturing*, 18: 301–31.

Deephouse, D. L. (1996). 'Does Isomorphism Legitimate?' *Academy of Management Journal*, 39: 1024–39.

DiMaggio, P. J. (1992). 'Nadel's Paradox Revisited: Relational and Cultural Aspects of Organizational Structure', in N. Nohria and R. Eccels (eds.), *Networks and Organizations*. Boston: Harvard Business School Press.

—— and Powell, W. W. (1983). 'The Iron Cage Revisited: Institutional Isomorphism and Collective Rationality in Organizational Fields'. *American Sociological Review*, 48: 147–60.

Dutton, J. E., and Dukerich, J. M. (1991). 'Keeping an Eye on the Mirror: Image and Identity in Organizational Adaptation'. *Academy of Management Journal*, 34/3: 517–54.

Eisenhardt, K. M. (1989). 'Building Theory from Case Study Research'. *Academy of Management Review*, 14/4: 532–50.

Ensley, M. D., and Hmieleski, K. M. (2005). 'A Comparative Study of New Venture Top Management Team Composition, Dynamics and Performance between University-Based and Independent Start-Ups'. *Research Policy*, 34: 1091–105.

Felin, T., and Foss, N. (2006). 'Individuals and Organizations: Thoughts on a Micro-foundations Project for Strategic Management and Organizational Analysis'. Paper presented at Druid conference, January.

Finlay, W., and Coverdill, J. E. (2000). 'Risk, Opportunism and Structural Holes: How Headhunters Manage Clients and Earn Fees'. *Work and Occupations*, 27: 377–405.

Friedman, R. A., and Podolny, J. (1992). 'Differentiation of Boundary Spanning Roles: Labor Negotiations and Implications for Role Conflict'. *Administrative Science Quarterly*, 37: 28–47.

Giddens, A. (1984). *The Constitution of Society*. Cambridge: Polity Press.

Gimeno, J., Folta, T. B., Cooper, A. C., and Woo, C. Y. (1997). 'Survival of the Fittest? Entrepreneurial Human Capital and the Persistence of Underperforming Firms'. *Administrative Science Quarterly*, 42: 750–83.

Granovetter, M. (1973). 'The Strength of Weak Ties'. *American Journal of Sociology*, 78 (May): 1360–80.

——(1985). 'Economic Action and Social Structure: The Problem of Embeddedness'. *American Journal of Sociology*, 91 (November): 481–510.

Grant, R. M. (1996). 'Toward a Knowledge-Based Theory of the Firm'. *Strategic Management Journal*, 17 (Special issue): 109–22.

——and Baden-Fuller, C. (2004). 'A Knowledge Accessing Theory of Strategic Alliances'. *Journal of Management Studies*, 41/1: 61–84.

Hargadon, A. (2002). 'Brokering Knowledge: Linking Learning and Innovation'. *Research in Organizational Behavior*, 24: 41–85.

——and Sutton, R. I. (1997). 'Technology Brokering and Innovation in a Product Development Firm'. *Administrative Science Quarterly*, 42: 716–49.

Henderson, R. M., and Clark, K. B. (1990). 'Architectural Innovation: The Reconfiguration of Existing Product Technologies and the Failure of Established Firms'. *Administrative Science Quarterly*, 35: 9–30.

Hybels, R. C. (1995). 'On Legitimacy, Legitimation, and Organizations: A Critical Review and Integrative Theoretical Model', in D. P. Moore (ed.), *Academy of Management Best Proceedings*, 241–5.

Inkpen, A. C., and Tsang, E. W. K. (2005). 'Social Capital, Networks and Knowledge Transfer'. *Academy of Management Review*, 30/1: 146–65.

Kahn, R. H., Wolfe, D. M., Quinn, R., and Snoek, J. D. (1964). *Organization Stress: Studies in Role Conflict and Ambiguity*. New York: Wiley.

Kanzanjian, R. K. (1988). 'Relation of Dominant Problems to Stages of Growth in Technology-Based New Ventures'. *Academy of Management Journal*, 31/2: 257–78.

Katz, J., and Gartner, W. B. (1988). 'Properties of Emerging Organizations'. *Academy of Management Review*, 13/3: 429–41.

Kesner, I. F., and Shapiro, D. L. (1994). 'Brokering Mergers: An Agency Theory Perspective on the Role of Representatives'. *Academy of Management Journal*, 37/3: 703–21.

Kogut, B., and Zander, U. (1992). 'Knowledge of the Firm, Combinative Capabilities and the Replication of Technology'. *Organization Science*, 3/3: 383–97.

Lam, S. (1991). 'Venture Capital Financing: A Conceptual Framework'. *Journal of Business Finance and Accounting*, 18/2: 137–49.

Leonard, D., and Swap, W. (2004). 'Deep Smarts'. *Harvard Business Review*, 82/9: 88–97.

Lorenzoni, G., and Baden-Fuller, C. (1995). 'Creating a Strategic Centre to Manage a Web of Partners'. *California Management Review*, 37/3: 146–63.

Lumpkin, G. T., and Dess, G. G. (1996). 'Clarifying the Entrepreneurial Orientation Construct and Linking It to Performance'. *Academy of Management Review*, 21/1: 135–72.

Mason, C. M., and Harrison, R. (1995). 'Closing the Regional Equity Capital Gap: The Role of Informal Venture Capital'. *Small Business Economics*, 7/2: 153–72.

McEvily, B., and Zaheer, A. (1999). 'Bridging Ties: A Source of Firm Heterogeneity in Competitive Capabilities'. *Strategic Management Journal*, 20: 1133–56.

Meyer, J. W., and Rowan, B. (1977). 'Institutional Organizations: Formal Structure as Myth and Ceremony'. *American Journal of Sociology*, 83: 340–63.

Murray, F. (2004). 'The Role of Academic Inventors in the Entrepreneurial Firms: Sharing the Laboratory Life'. *Research Policy*, 33: 643–59.

Nahapiet, J., and Ghoshal, S. (1998). 'Social Capital, Intellectual Capital, and the Organizational Advantage'. *Academy of Management Review*, 23/2: 242–66.

Nelson, R. R., and Winter, S. G. (1982). *An Evolutionary Theory of Economic Change*. Cambridge, Mass.: Harvard University Press.

Nicolaou, N., and Birley, S. (2003). 'Academic Networks in a Trichotomous Categorisation of University Spinouts'. *Journal of Business Venturing*, 18: 333–59.

Polanyi, M. (1966). *The Tacit Dimension*. New York: Anchor Day Books.

Pollock, T. G., Porac, J. F., and Wade, J. B. (2004). 'Constructing Deal Networks: Brokers as Network "Architects" in the U.S. IPO Market and Other Examples'. *Academy of Management Review*, 29/1: 50–72.

Rodan, S., and Galunic, C. (2004). 'More than Network Structure: How Knowledge Heterogeneity Influences Managerial Performance and Innovativeness'. *Strategic Management Journal*, 25: 541–62.

Rosenstein, J., Bruno, A. V., Bygrave, W. D., and Taylor, N. T. (1993). 'The CEO, Venture Capitalists and the Board'. *Journal of Business Venturing*, 8: 99–113.

Schumpeter, J. A. (1934). *The Theory of Economic Development*, tr. Redvers Opie. Cambridge, Mass.: Harvard University Press.

Scott, W. R. (1987). 'The Adolescence of Institutional Theory'. *Administrative Science Quarterly*, 32: 493–511.

Shane, S. (2000). 'Prior Knowledge and the Discovery of Entrepreneurial Opportunities'. *Organization Science*, 11/4: 448–70.

Singh, J. V., Tucker, D. J., and House, R. J. (1986). 'Organizational Legitimacy and the Liability of Newness'. *Administrative Science Quarterly*, 31: 171–93.

Singh, R. P., Hills, G. E., Lumpkin, G. T., and Hybels, R. C. (1999). 'The Entrepreneurial Opportunity Recognition Process: Examining the Role of Self-Perceived Alertness and Social Networks'. Paper presented at the 1999 Academy of Management Meeting, Chicago.

Stinchcombe, A. (1965). 'Social Structure and Organizations', in J. March (ed.), *Handbook of Organizations*. Chicago: Rand McNally.

Suchman, M. (1995). 'Managing Legitimacy: Strategic and Institutional Approaches'. *Academy of Management Review*, 20/3: 571–610.

Tushman, M. L., and Scanlan, T. J. (1981). 'Boundary Spanning Individuals: Their Role in Information Transfer and their Antecedents'. *Academy of Management Journal*, 24/2: 289–305.

Uzzi, B. (1996). 'The Sources and Consequence of Embeddedness for the Economic Performance of Organizations: The Network Effect'. *American Sociological Review*, 61: 674–98.

Weick, K. (1979). *The Social Psychology of Organizing*. Reading, Mass.: Addison-Wesley.

Westphal, J. D., Gulati, R., and Shortell, S. M. (1997). 'Customization or Conformity: An Institutional and Network Perspective on the Content and Consequences of TQM Adoption'. *Administrative Science Quarterly*, 42: 161–83.

Wright, M., Robbie, K., and Ennew, C. (1997). 'Venture Capitalists and Serial Entrepreneurs'. *Journal of Business Venturing*, 12: 227–49.

—— Thompson, S., and Robbie, K. (1992). 'Venture Capital and Management-Led Leveraged Buy-Outs: European Evidence'. *Journal of Business Venturing*, 7/1: 47–71.

Yin, R. K. (2003). *Case Study Research: Design and Methods* (3rd edn.). Thousand Oaks, Calif.: Sage Publications.

7

Knowledge Integration and Resource Selection in the UK Film Industry

Joseph Lampel and Pushkar Jha

Introduction

The production of knowledge from other knowledge is a complex and uncertain business. It is complex because the production of knowledge often depends on the integration of disparate bodies of knowledge, and it is uncertain because under most circumstances knowledge cannot be separated from the human beings and the social settings in which it is embedded.

The problem of knowledge integration has therefore two facets. There is the need to identify, acquire, and use different types of knowledge to achieve an outcome (see Collins 1993; Blackler 1995), and then there are the different individuals who must be selected and organized in order for knowledge integration to be successfully accomplished (Liebeskind et al. 1996; O'Mahony and Bechky 2006). A persistent theme in research on organizations is the importance of context in mobilizing both knowledge and the individuals who participate in knowledge integration (Andreu and Sieber 2005). A key distinction is made between internal and external contexts of knowledge integration, which usually means between knowledge integration that takes place within firm boundaries, as opposed to knowledge integration that takes place largely outside the firm (Ancona and Caldwell 1992; Galunic and Rodan 1998).

Until recently, the literature on knowledge integration focused primarily on internal contexts. As part of the EBK programme, however, we set out to explore how knowledge integration takes place in an external context, specifically in projects that are external to the organization. Our research site is the UK film industry, which is almost purely project-based: skills and talent are not attached to any specific organization but are recruited and organized into teams for each film project. Financing, marketing, distribution, and promotion are allocated on a film-by-film basis rather than as continuous support.

An indispensable condition for effective knowledge integration in these settings is the selection of the right people, not only for specific tasks but also for team compatibility and project mission (Faraj and Sproull 2000). This means judging whether potential team members have the right mix of knowledge types for the project and selecting a team leader who will perform the role of 'knowledge integrator'—coordinating the various types of knowledge and ensuring that group interaction facilitates the process of knowledge integration.

The dilemma confronting project-based organizations when it comes to recruiting team members and team leaders is therefore itself a knowledge problem. What kind of knowledge do you use to select the right individuals for the project? There are essentially two models that project-based organizations use to address this problem: the 'garden model' and the 'market model'. In the garden model, organizations recruit on the basis of *direct* knowledge of the capabilities and performance of potential candidates, which in project-based industries usually means knowledge that derives from past project collaborations. The advantage of the garden model is that knowledge of individuals is rich in detail, but the drawback is that it confines selection to a relatively small group with the inevitable restriction that this puts on exploration and innovation. The 'market model', by contrast, bases selection on *indirect* knowledge of the capabilities and performance of potential candidates, which in project-based industries (as in most other industries) usually means relying on market reputation. The advantage of this model is that selection can be made from a far larger group of potential candidates, and assessment is also less vulnerable to personal bias and the accidents of past collaboration. The disadvantage is the informational imperfections of markets: there is often a gap between market reputation and the actual skills and capabilities of the individuals involved.

This chapter is an exploration of both models. When it comes to resource selection, decision makers have a choice between the 'garden model' and 'market model' of recruitment. We discuss both models generally and then turn our attention to discussing and analyzing how these models operate in the context of the UK film industry.

Context of the research

Models of resource selection

Knowledge integration that is externally focused is much in evidence in industries where firms are unable or unwilling to retain within organizational boundaries the highly specialized resources necessary to undertake their primary production activity. This is especially the case in industries where specialized knowledge cannot be attached to the organization on a permanent basis, either because it is very costly (e.g. acoustic experts needed to build a concert hall) or because anticipating the demand for the specialized resource is next to impossible (e.g. a sailing ship for a film on the British navy during the Napoleonic wars). Prime examples of such industries are engineering construction, large information systems, and film—the industry on which this chapter focuses.

A response to the challenge of external resource integration has been the rise of projects—temporary focal task structures that are externally situated. The advantage of external projects is that they allow firms to attach resources to an entity with a finite life without having to incur the risk and expense of retaining these resources indefinitely. The disadvantage is the mirror image of the advantage: recruiting resources externally comes with significantly higher selection risk than mobilizing resources internally. It is much easier to make mistakes when recruiting external resources and much harder to correct for mistakes once the project is 'green lighted'.

The main challenge confronting external integration of knowledge in project-based industries is therefore not only to acquire the different types of knowledge necessary to accomplish the task but also to ensure that one has identified and recruited the individuals who can provide this knowledge. When it comes to recruiting human expertise, project-based organizing relies heavily on occupational structures and professional categories to identify the skills and knowledge needed to perform the designated tasks (Hines 1998). This, however, takes the knowledge problem to another level: not only identifying the person with the right professional and occupational qualifications but also ensuring that this person is best for the job. Because the transformation of knowledge into performance is essentially uncertain, there is always selection risk during recruitment. Organizations can mitigate this risk in two ways. First, they either display a preference for working with the individuals about whom they have direct knowledge, usually from previous projects (the 'garden model'). Second, they can rely on indirect knowledge of the individuals they propose to recruit, where this indirect knowledge comes from industry reputation (the 'market model').

THE GARDEN MODEL OF RESOURCE SELECTION

The garden model of resource selection is based on recruiting individuals with whom one has had previous dealings. Organizations see their immediate resource environment as a garden that they tend with care—developing relationships and alliances by awarding projects and exchanging favours. In a sense, organizations gather the fruits of their previous collaborations and then use them to develop new projects. Relationships and alliances are crucial for intimate evaluation of the capabilities and idiosyncrasies of individuals, and exchanging information and favours is important to improve motivation and decrease opportunism.

THE MARKET MODEL OF RESOURCE SELECTION

The market model of resource selection is based on interpreting the reputation and past track record of individuals in a market context. Organizations are more interested in the generic capabilities that contribute to performance and less interested in the idiosyncratic or subtle aspects that facilitate or hinder knowledge integration. As a result, the dynamics of reputation in a particular market play a very important role in determining the selection process.

Research site: the UK film industry

The UK film industry employs about 33,000 individuals in production and support services. British-made films generate about a billion pounds in sales, of which half comes from overseas receipts (Gray 1996). About 100 films are made each year. While many are small budgets and are not widely distributed outside the United Kingdom, a significant number are distributed globally and are widely recognized for quality. British films often capture top awards in film festivals, and since 1997 have received forty-six Oscar nominations (Lennon 1998).

The UK film industry has always lacked the economies of scale and the distribution reach to match the power of the US film industry. The UK film industry, however, has shown little willingness to settle for the 'auteur'-driven art cinema strategy that is pursued elsewhere in continental Europe. Instead, a strategy of high-quality films with commercial appeal has emerged as the consistent focus of the industry. In evolutionary terms, the UK film industry has developed institutions, networks, and communities of practice that serve to integrate creative and commercial knowledge.

In a highly decentralized and dispersed field of activity such as the film industry, knowledge integration depends on collaborative compatibilities. The UK film industry, like film industries in other countries, is project-based. This means that films are developed and produced as separate projects with the required resources recruited for each project. Resource integration begins during film development, but at this stage it involves primarily script development and discussion among writers, producers, potential directors, and marketing and distribution specialists. The tempo and intensity of resource integration increases as the project moves from development to production primarily because resources have to be committed to the project, or to use the terminology of the film industry, they must be 'attached' to the film. Even small films require the attachment of a wide variety of technical and creative skills. The individuals involved are then assembled for principal photography. Principal photography takes place under very stringent time constraints, and it calls for collaborative teamwork among individuals with diverse skills and background.

The film director, who also acts as team leader, takes charge of the process shortly before principal photography begins and maintains total control until it is completed. The involvement of the director, however, is not confined to principal photography. The director carries the main creative responsibility for the film (Proferes 2001). He or she has a strong, if not dominant, influence in the hiring of key production personnel and is often also an active participant in the casting process. From the point of view of knowledge integration, therefore, the director can be viewed as the 'knowledge integrator': the person concerned with identifying the skills and talents needed to execute specific tasks, and then making sure that they are combined effectively to achieve the best results possible.

Project performance in this context depends on recruiting the individuals who have the right skills and the right attitudes. Most of the decisions about which actors, cinematographers, make-up artists, design specialists, etc. to select are made in the transition between development and production stages of the film project. The decisive juncture is the so-called 'green lighting': the point at which there is commitment in principle to proceed with the project. Key production personnel become attached to the project either before or shortly after this point in the project process.

Their selection is crucial for both the implementation of the project and its success. The main responsibility for the selection resides with the producer. The producer oversees script writing, obtains financing, hires the director and other key production personnel, monitors the production—ensuring that the film is on time and budget, and negotiates terms with distribution companies (Prigg 2004). If the director can be viewed as a 'knowledge integrator', the producer, whether he or she works alone or in conjunction with other producers, is essentially a 'resource mobilizer' (Lampel and Shamsie 2003; Lampel 2006). In this respect, the producer has final responsibility for authorizing recruitment of key production personnel, including the director.

Producers are particularly concerned with selection of the director because of the crucial role that directors play as knowledge integrators. A film project brings together a variety of professional and occupational specialists. The director must not only have a precise understanding of how each expertise fits into the project, but he or she must be able to motivate and direct the contribution of each individual in the team. Ultimately, the challenge confronting the film director is to transform the crew from a group of disparate individuals into a team, ensuring that individuals give each other the requisite support and enabling the production process to move towards a successful conclusion—on time and on budget.

THE GARDEN MODEL OF RESOURCE SELECTION IN THE UK FILM INDUSTRY

The complex and ambiguous creative process that is film making inclines film makers to work with individuals they trust and feel comfortable with. For example, there is a long tradition in the film industry of directors working repeatedly with the same cinematographers (Bergman with Gunnar Fischer), or directors with set designers (Fellini with Dante Ferretti), or directors with composers (Steven Spielberg and John Williams).

Past collaboration is one of the best ways for film directors to know how individuals will perform in the future. The advantages of seeking out and recruiting highly skilled individuals from past film projects are strong: a considerable amount of tacit learning is generated in projects. Members of the team do not have to replicate the familiarization and socialization process. They are aware of the preferences and eccentricities of different team members and can adjust accordingly. Finally, there is a strong bonding and willingness to contribute that result from the intense production process.

The obvious advantages of the garden model would suggest that direct-ors should display a strong preference for repeat collaboration as a way of ensuring the best resource integration outcome. There is however a caveat: repeat collaboration delivers primarily efficiency advantages (see Corman and Jerome 1989; Grant 1996). Selecting past collaborators in preference to new collaborators favours efficiency over variation as the primary driver for performance. In the creative industries an opposite view holds that film makers should strive for exploration and experimentation as much as possible, and that one way of increasing the outcome of both is to collab-orate with new skills and talent. Repeat collaboration has the potential of entrenching past ideas and reducing openness to alternative approaches. The counter argument, therefore, holds that film makers should avoid repeat collaboration if they seek creativity as opposed to trying to ensure the smooth functioning of the project. The two perspectives represent alternative views of the trade-offs between efficiency and creativity as illustrated in Figure 7.1. The director can seek repeat collaboration to attain efficiency, and thus improve the probability of completing principal photography on time and on budget with certain quality expectations in mind, or he or she can recruit outside past collaboration via the market

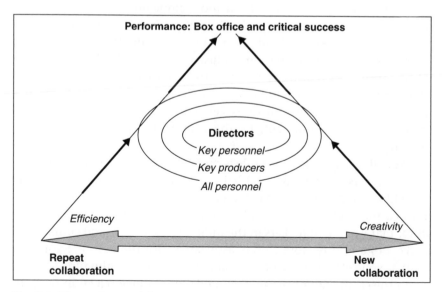

Fig. 7.1. The garden model

with less attention to efficiency and more interest in exploration and innovation.

THE MARKET MODEL OF RESOURCE SELECTION IN THE UK FILM INDUSTRY

By contrast to the garden model, which relies primarily on project-specific personal knowledge of individuals and their skills, the market model of resource selection relies on past project performance, where this performance is encoded and filtered by impersonal institutional and market mechanisms. The market model of resource selection is therefore less vulnerable to personal bias and less subject to the accidents of collaboration. The main assumption of the market model is that the capabilities of an individual resource are captured by their market reputation. Such reputation is a proxy for attractiveness of the resource. It informs decisions to recruit or to associate with the resource when it comes to shaping a collaborative arrangement. In industries where the relationship between capabilities and performance is relatively unambiguous, reputation is closely aligned with expertise. For instance, surgeons' reputations are largely based on their medical degrees, the hospitals in which they were residents, the number of years they have practiced, and surgical procedures they innovated.

In the creative industries, by contrast, the relationship between capabilities and performance is far more ambiguous. Books, films, and music are credence goods: it is difficult to know what makes them successful both before and after their consumption (Duleck and Kerschbamer 2006). In the film industry, there is added ambiguity by virtue of the fact that films are collective endeavours. Thus, if tracking the contribution that individual knowledge makes to performance is difficult in creative industries generally, in the film industry this is made even more difficult by the team-based nature of knowledge integration.

The main exception to this rule is the film director. As we noted earlier, film directors are widely regarded as the knowledge integrators—the individuals most responsible for ensuring that skills and talents are melded together into high-quality output. In the public's mind, as well as for many decision makers in the industry, the critical and commercial success of a film is more closely associated with the film director than with anyone else. Thus, when it comes to recruiting a film director for a film project, the use of the market model of resource selection tends to dominate. Producers will search for directors who are associated with successful films, even when their track record is short and their reliability is uncertain. What is even more remarkable is the willingness of film production firms to recruit and give relatively untested directors films with large budgets. Perhaps the most famous example of this kind of risk taking was the decision by RKO's president George Schaefer to offer Orson Welles a two-picture deal with total artistic control, including script, cast, final cut, and crew on the basis of no more than the ground-breaking radio broadcast 'War of the Worlds'. The first film *Citizen Kane* is regarded as a masterpiece, though it did not make much money when first released. The second *The Magnificent Ambersons* failed both critically and commercially (Heylin 2005). On the other hand, the more recent example of Robert Rodriguez suggests that a reputation based on a single film may be a robust signal of reliable performance. Rodriguez made the critically acclaimed and commercially successful *El Mariachi* for around $7,000. Based on this film, he was recruited for big-budget Hollywood productions that have enjoyed remarkable commercial success (Lyman 2002).

Director reputation is therefore a crucial signal of future performance. In a market model, this signal becomes important not only to film producers but also to members of the team. For the latter, joining a team led by a strong director increases the probability of being associated with a commercially and critically successful film. Such an association increases their own reputation, which in turn improves their market position. Therefore, having a director with a strong reputation makes it easier for a producer to recruit high-quality resources that are likely to improve the chances of commercial and critical success.

Thus, because the market model relies heavily on reputation to identify and recruit resources, resource owners have an interest in managing their reputation. In the film industry, performance is composed of two key indicators. The first is the box office performance of the film: the more commercially successful the film, the greater the reputation of the director. The second is the critical success of the film: the more the film wins prizes and awards, not to mention the plaudits of the critics, the greater the reputation of the film director. The correlation between critical acclaim and commercial success is relatively low. Thus, when it comes to managing their reputation, directors must effectively deal with each one separately. As a crucial signalling attribute, directorial reputation is thus positioned by performance feedback to inform recruitment decisions, as illustrated in Figure 7.2.

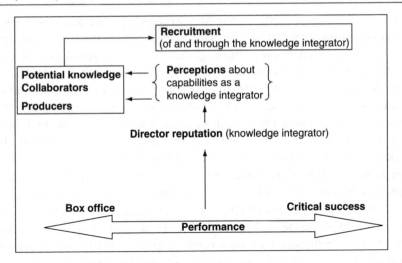

Fig. 7.2. The market model

Empirical study

Data and variables

DATA

We use two sets of data in this empirical study to examine the garden and market model in the context of knowledge integration in the UK film industry. The first one is to examine the impact of repeat collaboration on box office performance and critical success at film festivals. This comprises a sample of 300 UK films accounted for by 87 directors over the period 1969–2004. The number of movies in analysis as UK releases is 241, and 265 movies are UK films with a US release. The samples overlap to a great extent with most of the movies being released in both places. The data is informed by archival sources and uses information on personnel involved in the movie projects, box office and awards-nominations statistics, and information on the directors' movie projects portfolio.

The second data set is used to examine the relationship between directorial reputation and film performance. Directorial reputation is a combination of essentially two aspects: the formal and informal esteem of peers (i.e. awards and word-of-mouth), and the brand visibility with audiences. We focused on the position of the director on movie posters and the way in which the name of the director is used as a way of operationalizing these two components of directorial reputation, for the following reasons. First, the

146

position of the director's name is an important subject of negotiations between the director and the film distributor. For directors, their position relative to other key participants in the film, for example, whether they are grouped together with the actors at the bottom of the poster or listed separately above, or their position relative to the title of the film, specifically whether they are listed above or below the title, is an important indication of their reputation in the film industry. The stronger their reputation, the more likely they are to gain the right to be listed separately and above the title; and likewise, the lesser their reputation, the less likely they are to obtain this right. By the same token, distributors are likely to go along with these wishes if a director has a strong brand visibility with audiences based on associations with popular or controversial hits, or if the director has a long track record that is likely to bring more people into the cinema.

We use poster data for 38 directors for 76 UK film releases and for 35 directors for 70 UK films *also* released in the United States. We also use information from archival sources for information on box office, award-nominations statistics, and characteristics that profile a director's movie portfolio.

In the following section, we discuss how this information has been used to shape variables and measures for testing hypotheses using multiple regression analysis.

VARIABLES AND MEASURES

Examining movie performance as a function of collaboration

Dependent variable. Performance as the dependent variable is coded as:

1. Box office performance of the movie given by revenue/budget of the movies made by the director
2. Critical success based on nominations received by the feature films made by the director

We conduct separate sets of analysis, first using box office performance and then critical success as movie performance.

Independent variable. Collaboration as the independent variable is coded based on the extent and nature of collaboration that a director carries from film to film. We code this at three levels:

1. Extent of collaboration between director and all personnel [C1]
2. Extent of collaboration between director and key producers [C2]
3. Extent of collaboration between director and key personnel like writer, editor, composer, cinematographer, and production designer [C3]

We control for commercial performance of the movies over which collaboration is coded when the dependent variable in analysis is critical success. Alternatively, we control for critical success when the dependent variable in the analysis is commercial performance. In both sets of analysis, we control for the number of prior features that have been made by the director and years since the director made the preceding movie.

Reputation as a function of movie performance

Dependent variable. Change in reputation of a director is the dependent variable. This is proxied by change in mention and prominence of a director in movie posters over successive movie projects. The reputation quotient has been pegged at four levels:

0 for no director named on the poster
1 for director named
2 for Possessory below title
3 for Possessory above title

The difference in this score over the compared movie posters has been coded as change in reputation.

Figure 7.3 illustrates the coding. The two posters are from the movies *Trainspotting* and *The Beach*, respectively. Both movies have Danny Boyle as their director. *Trainspotting* was a controversial film in its own right because of the way drug use content has been portrayed. It also came into the limelight because it was nominated for an Academy award and labelled as one of the best ever British films.

Of course, Danny Boyle got an opportunity in Hollywood thereafter (incidentally most of the controversy related to the film was in the United States) and in Figure 7.3 is mentioned on the *The Beach* poster more prominently.

Independent variables. Change in performance as the independent variable is examined both for movies released in the United States and for releases in the United Kingdom. We take into account the critical success attributed to a movie by film festivals in United States and by those outside the United States. The independent variables are coded for both commercial and critical success as:

1. Change in commercial success as measured by difference in revenue/budget ratio over the two movies for a director [S1]
2. Change in critical success in film festivals outside the United States is measured by the change in awards/nominations ratio over the two movies for a director at these festivals [S2]

Fig. 7.3. Coding of poster data for change in directorial reputation

3. Change in critical success in film festivals in the United States is measured by the change in awards/nominations ratio over the two movies at
these festivals [S3]

We control for change in productivity of a director, which is measured by
the change in rate at which films are made. This is based on:

- How far back in time were each of the pair of movies (over which
reputation change is being measured) from the preceding feature made

- Time in years between the two movies over which reputation change is
being measured

For example, if director X took three years from the last feature to come
out with movie A and two years to come out with movie B and, the time
between movie A and movie B was five years the change in productivity
would be: 1/5. In other words, director X took five years to reduce the time
between movies by one year.

All other things remaining the same, if director Y was to also reduce the
time by one year but the reference movies for the director were ten years
apart, the productivity measure then would be 1/10.

149

Findings

COLLABORATION AND PERFORMANCE

Correlations (Tables 7.1 and 7.2) suggest a strong positive association between collaborations and critical acclaim as a measure of performance. There is also some degree of association of commercial performance with critical acclaim. The difference between UK and US releases for the UK films in this case is that commercial performance is negatively associated with critical acclaim in the case of the former and positively in the case of the latter. This suggests an interesting split in how a movie is seen in both cultures: as a creative product whose quality is compromised by commercial intentions in the United Kingdom and as a creative product with commercial expectations in the United States.

Regression analysis (Tables 7.3 and 7.4) indicates that an increase in collaboration with key producers and with key personnel (collaborations of type C2 and C3), respectively, will lead to an increase in critical acclaim both in the case of films released in the United Kingdom and those

Table 7.1. *Collaboration and performance: correlations for UK releases*

Correlations—UK	1	2	3	4	5	6	7	8
1. Performance (cr/cb)	1	—	—	—	—	—	—	—
2. Movie number	−0.12	1	—	—	—	—	—	—
3. Nominations	−0.18[*]	0.19	1	—	—	—	—	—
4. Last movie's revenue/£m-budget	0.22	−0.13	0.04	1	—	—	—	—
5. Years since last movie	−0.08	−0.01	−0.08	0.048	1	—	—	—
6. Collaboration: C1	−0.00	0.49	0.35	−0.04	−0.211	1	—	—
7. Collaboration: C2	−0.03	0.50	0.61	−0.04	−0.16	0.78	1	—
8. Collaboration: C3	−0.03	0.51	0.56	−0.05	−0.16	0.82	0.96	1

N = 241, correlations of 0.13 or higher are significant at the 0.05 level

Table 7.2. *Collaboration and performance: correlations for US releases*

Correlations—US	1	2	3	4	5	6	7	8
1. Performance (cr/cb)	1	—	—	—	—	—	—	—
2. Movie number	0.015	1	—	—	—	—	—	—
3. Nominations	0.16	0.21	1	—	—	—	—	—
4. Last movie's revenue/£m-budget	0.12	0.03	0.17	1	—	—	—	—
5. Years since last movie	−0.14	−0.14	−0.11	−0.039	1	—	—	—
6. Collaboration: C1	0.08	0.58	0.33	0.17	−0.23	1	—	—
7. Collaboration: C2	0.08	0.55	0.57	0.15	−0.17	0.77	1	—
8. Collaboration: C3	0.07	0.56	0.56	0.14	−0.18	0.80	0.96	1

N = 265, correlations of 0.12 or higher are significant at the 0.05 level

Table 7.3. *Dependent variable: critical success (nominations) for posters of UK releases*

Variables	UK	Model 1	Model 2	Model 3	Model 4
Control	Movie number	0.26	0.27	−0.30	−0.42
	This movie's revenue/budget	−0.84	−0.84	−0.69	−0.72
	Last movie's revenue/£m-budget	1.52^+	1.52^+	0.90	0.81
	Years since last movie	−1.02	−1.02	−0.75	−0.40
Independent	Collaboration: C1	—	0.01	—	—
	Collaboration: C2	—	—	0.21^{**}	—
	Collaboration: C3	—	—	—	0.36^*
	Adjusted R^2	0.14	0.09	0.49	0.43
	Change in adjusted R^2	—	0.05	0.35	0.28
	F	1.98	1.56	4.74^{**}	3.94^*

$+p < 0.1, \, ^*p < 0.05, \, ^{**}p < 0.01, \, ^{***}p < 0.005$

Table 7.4. *Dependent variable: critical success (nominations) for posters of US releases*

Variables	US	Model 1	Model 2	Model 3	Model 4
Control	Movie number	0.04	−0.01	−0.13	−0.14
	This movie's revenue/budget	0.15	0.20	0.17	0.22
	Last movie's revenue/£m-budget	0.16	0.14	0.05	0.08
	Years since last movie	−0.88	−0.69	−0.57	−0.47
Independent	Collaboration: C1	—	0.02	—	—
	Collaboration: C2	—	—	0.15^{***}	—
	Collaboration: C3	—	—	—	0.24^{***}
	Adjusted R^2	0.02	0.03	0.31	0.34
	Change in adjusted R^2	—	0.01	0.28	0.33
	F	1.08	1.04	3.59^*	3.96^{**}

$+p < 0.1, \, ^*p < 0.05, \, ^{**}p < 0.01, \, ^{***}p < 0.005$

Table 7.5. *Dependent variable: commercial success as box office performance (revenue/budget) for UK releases*

Variables	UK	Model 1	Model 2	Model 3	Model 4
Control	Movie number	0.12	0.17	0.20	0.21
	Critical success (award nominations)	$−0.62^+$	−0.55	−0.40	−0.40
	Last movie's revenue/£m-budget	1.11	0.92	0.90	0.81
	Years since last movie	−0.42	−0.41	−0.49	−0.44
Independent	Collaboration: C1	—	0.08	—	—
	Collaboration: C2	—	—	0.13	—
	Collaboration: C3	—	—	—	0.21
	Adjusted R^2	0.08	0.04	0.04	0.06
	Change in adjusted R^2	—	0.04	0.04	0.03
	F	1.40	1.10	1.10	1.18

$+p < 0.1, \, ^*p < 0.05, \, ^{**}p < 0.01, \, ^{***}p < 0.005$

Table 7.6. *Dependent variable: commercial success as box office performance (revenue/ budget) for US releases*

Variables	US	Model 1	Model 2	Model 3	Model 4
Control	Movie number	0.10	0.10	0.11	0.12
	Critical success (award nominations)	0.09	0.20	0.17	0.22
	Last movie's revenue/ £m-budget	−0.16	−0.14	0.05	0.08
	Years since last movie	−0.18[+]	−0.20[+]	−0.20	−0.20
Independent	Collaboration: C1	—	−0.02	—	—
	Collaboration: C2	—	—	0.12	—
	Collaboration: C3	—	—	—	0.12
	Adjusted R^2	0.11	0.11	0.08	0.07
	Change in adjusted R^2	—	0.00	0.03	0.01
	F	1.78	1.80	1.08	1.05

$+p < 0.1$, $^*p < 0.05$, $^{**}p < 0.01$, $^{***}p < 0.005$

Table 7.7. *Performance and reputation: correlations—directors based on posters of UK releases*

	1	2	3	4	5
1. Change in reputation	1	—	—	—	—
2. Change in productivity	0.035	1	—	—	—
3. Change r/b	−0.14	0.12	1	—	—
4. Change critical success (non-US)	0.27	−0.06	−0.06	1	—
4. Change critical success (US)	0.38	−0.07	−0.02	0.32	1

N = 76, correlations = > 0.25 are significant at the 0.05 level or higher

released in the United States. This indicates that repeat collaboration is a factor influencing movie performance.

We did not find any significant explanations offered by collaboration when we used box office performance as the dependent variable (Tables 7.5 and 7.6). Thus, it is only performance in terms of critical acclaim that increases as a function of collaboration; box office performance is not affected by collaboration.

PERFORMANCE AND REPUTATION

For the UK sample of directors, correlations indicate that success at both non-US film festivals and at US film festivals are associated with an increase in the director's reputation (Table 7.7). The correlations also indicate that for the US sample (Table 7.8) productivity is positively associated with a change in reputation and commercial success. This suggests that for the US-based directors: the higher the market visibility and better the proof of ability to finish and deliver a resource-intensive product, the higher is the reputation.

Table 7.8. *Performance and reputation: correlations—directors based on posters of US releases*

	1	2	3	4	5
1. Change in reputation	1	—	—	—	—
2. Change in productivity	0.38	1	—	—	—
3. Change r/b	0.07	0.31	1	—	—
4. Change critical success (non-US)	0.06	0.003	−0.14	1	—
4. Change critical success (US)	0.04	−0.026	−0.07	0.31	1

N = 70, correlations > 0.25 are significant at the 0.05 level or higher

Table 7.9. *Dependent variable: change in directors' reputation based on posters of UK releases*

	Model 1	Model 2	Model 3	Model 4	Model 5	Model 6
Control						
Change in productivity	0.08	0.13	0.16	0.20	0.11	0.22
Independents						
S1. Change in commercial success (r/b)	—	−0.13	−0.12	−0.12	−0.07	−0.06
S2. Change in critical success outside US (aw/nom)	—	—	0.58*	0.36	0.50	0.12
S3. Change in critical success in the US (aw/nom)	—	—	—	0.62**	0.33	0.70**
S1*S2	—	—	—	—	−0.91	—
S1*S2	—	—	—	—	—	−0.44*
R^2	0.001	0.02	0.09	0.20	0.24	0.26
Change in R^2		0.019	0.07	0.11	0.04	0.02
F value	0.04	0.4	1.26*	2.07*	2.06*	2.4**

$^* p < 0.1$, $^{**}p < 0.05$

Regression analysis to explain director's reputation from poster data for UK releases (Table 7.9) indicates that an increase in critical success of the movie leads to an increase in the reputation of the movie's director. The results also indicate that an increase in critical success of the movie in the United States is more influential in increasing the reputation of the director than an increase in critical success outside the United States. Furthermore, commercial success and critical acclaim of a movie interact negatively indicating that commercial success in tandem with critical

Table 7.10. *Dependent variable: change in directors' reputation based on posters of US releases*

Dependent change in reputation of a director	Model 1	Model 2	Model 3	Model 4	Model 5	Model 6
Control						
Change in productivity	6.4**	6.73**	6.74**	6.64**	6.13	7.09**
Independents						
S1. Change in commercial success (r/b)	—	0.34***	0.32***	0.33*	0.33**	0.33**
S2. Change in critical success outside US (aw/nom)	—	—	−0.72	−0.66	−0.63	−0.65
S3. Change in critical success in the US (aw/nom)	—	—	—	0.50	0.65	0.46
S1*S2	—	—	—	—	−0.13	—
S1*S2	—	—	—	—	—	0.33
R2	0.15	0.39	0.40	0.40	0.40	0.41
Change in R2		0.24	0.01	0.00	0.00	
F value	4.98*	8.9***	5.8***	4.21***	3.2**	3.34**

$* p < 0.1, ** p < 0.05, *** p < 0.01$

success may diminish reputational gains from critical success in the UK market.

In contrast to results for the UK releases, regression analysis for US releases (Table 7.10) indicates that an increase in commercial success of the movie leads to an increase in the reputation of a movie's director. There is also an indication that productivity of a director leads to an increase in reputation of the director. The results provide support to the assertion that ability to churn out movies at regular intervals, and actual delivery of the movie to earn money instead of being part finished with great promise, matters for directorial reputation in the US market.

Discussion

The garden and market models

Our results suggest that the garden model and market model of resource selection work differently in different contexts. The key to the difference is how the industry interprets the relationship between resource inputs and project performance.

The relationship between resource inputs and project performance in the film industry is widely regarded as complex and ambiguous. There are many factors that influence the quality of the film and its performance in the box office. But of the two dimensions of performance—critical and commercial success—the latter is more ambiguously linked to inputs than the former.

To be successful in the box office, films must appeal to a wide audience. Public tastes, however, are fickle. Successful themes and bankable stars are no guarantee of future success. In addition, box office success often depends on effective marketing and distribution decisions. While the industry has one hundred years of experience when it comes to marketing and distributing films, the process is still more an art than a science. It is easy to make the wrong marketing and distribution decisions. An additional source of uncertainty is competition from other films that are often aggressively marketed and pushed into exhibition. Competition for scarce exhibition space further curtails the box office potential of films. The impact of competition on a film's revenue potential is uncertain, since films must be released relatively soon after they are produced, often against stiff and unpredictable competition.

Critical success, on the other hand, is relatively less uncertain when it comes to interpreting causal factors. It is less uncertain in part because the individuals that judge the merit of films form a relatively small and exclusive group. The tastes of these evaluative elites are less diverse than the public as a whole, and hence more easily linked to key characteristics of the film. In addition, these evaluative elites are also prone to bandwagon effects—enthusiastically endorsing films that others in their circles have also endorsed.

The results show a clear relationship between collaboration and success is significant only for critical success. This has interesting implications for the garden model of resource selection.

The garden model of resource selection points to repeat collaborations as the best way of assessing the value and fit of knowledge resources. Using the garden model of resource selection, as opposed to the market model, will clearly be influenced by performance. The better the performance that results from relying on past collaborations, the more likely is the garden model to be used; and vice versa, the poorer the performance, the less likely is the garden model to be used and by implication the more likely are film makers to use the market model.

The results show that repeat collaborations have no impact on commercial success, but do have an impact on critical success. The results raise the possibility that directors seek past collaborators with an eye on critical acclaim rather than box office success. This may be due to the fact that directors like everybody else realizes that box office success is so uncertain that relying on past collaboration to improve box office success may not be worthwhile. To use our terms, they do not have confidence in the garden model when it comes to selecting resources with box office success in mind.

An additional motivation, however, may be that directors are more interested in creating critical reputation than box office reputation. The reasons for this may be found in the dynamics of reputation in the film industry. With the exception of record-breaking box office performance, reasonable commercial success is rarely attributed to the director. By contrast, long-standing tradition tends to attribute critical success to the director. This suggests that when it comes to selecting resources directors will prefer the garden model and will use their influence as much as possible to make other decision makers in the project use the garden model as well.

This takes us to the results on reputational dynamics of directors. As indicated earlier, reliance on reputations is the hallmark of the market model. Directors are crucial knowledge integrators. They are recruited on the basis of their reputation because of their role and because their track record is based on relatively few projects. The market model applies strongly here, for film producers and investors seeking to attach directors, and for directors seeking to increase the value of their career assets.

Reputational dynamics in the UK and US markets

The UK film industry is strongly dependent on the US market for revenues and potential financing. Success in the US market is generally seen in the United Kingdom as key to financing and distributing future film projects (see Puttnam 1987). For this reason, there is intense focus on the commercial success and critical reception of UK films in the United States. The two markets, however, are different culturally and commercially. These differences throw a light on how the market model works in the United Kingdom as opposed to the United States, and in the process also reveal certain features of the market model more generally.

The main difference between reputational dynamics in the UK and US systems is the impact of commercial performance on reputations as opposed to the impact of critical performance. If we bear in mind that these results are based on UK versus US posters for the *same films*, then what we have here is a revealing picture of how the two systems deal with reputation. Thus, commercial performance has no significant relationship with a director's reputation in the United Kingdom, whereas it is significant in the United States. When it comes to critical success, we find the exact opposite: critical success has a strong significant relationship with reputation in the United Kingdom but not in the United States. What is also interesting is that directors' reputation for films released in United Kingdom will be significantly impacted by critical recognition in the United States. The same is not the case for the impact of UK critical recognition on posters that announce US releases.

An additional intriguing insight is provided by the role of productivity. Productivity has no impact on directorial reputation in the United Kingdom, but it is strongly significant in the United States. This suggests that reputation is far more stable in the United Kingdom than the United States. Once directors achieve prominence in the United Kingdom, they tend to retain their reputation for a long time. This is due in part to the relatively small size of the UK film community—relatively few top directors monopolize public attention—and partly because British cultural elites have a stronger role in allocating recognition and resources than in the United States. In the United States, by contrast, reputations are more perishable. The adage 'you are as good as your last movie' may be an exaggeration, but it is not entirely so: US directors must keep producing to keep their profile alive in the public's eye. The system is far more competitive and far less forgiving when it comes to getting and retaining attention—from the public as well as from the industry.

It is also clear from this data that to be successful in a market model of resource selection, UK film directors have to play a dual game. They must take advantage of the dynamics of reputation in the United Kingdom, while at the same time paying heed to how reputations are managed in the US market. Because the UK system retains reputations longer, it is easy for directors to rest on their laurels. But in reality, given the importance of the US market for film performance and hence resource recruitment, doing this may drive directors out of the market model into the garden model. Unfortunately, the garden model in the UK context usually means reliance on a small network of powerful resource providers with the government playing a preponderant role.

Conclusions

The integration of disparate knowledge inputs is increasingly crucial to effective organizational performance (Connor and Prahalad 1996; Spender

157

and Grant 1996). However, the key problem that organizations face when it comes to selecting and then transforming resources into high-quality products and services is the ambiguous relationship that exists between performance and the knowledge integration process (Swan and Scarbrough 2005).

If there is one role that stands out in our study, it is that of the film director as knowledge integrator. The knowledge integrator is the person most directly charged with transforming knowledge inputs into an integrated quality output. His or her judgement is crucial for interpreting past performance, selecting skills and talent to suit the task, and ensuring that the individuals concerned function together as a team (Doz 1996; Lumpkin and Dess 1996; Kogut 1988).

The centrality of the knowledge integrator in the knowledge integration process often goes hand-in-hand with a preference for the garden model, which in turn points to repeat collaboration. However, the ability of knowledge integrators to exercise influence on the resource selection process is dependent on their reputation: the greater their reputation for achieving high performance, the greater will be their influence when it comes to selecting resource inputs.

The link between reputation and performance has been a persistent theme in management research. Specifically, researchers have explored the reliability of past performance signals when it comes to making decisions about future investments (Wilson 1985; Weigelt and Camerer 1988). While reputation has been examined as an intangible factor that impacts organizational performance (Rao 1994), the impact of collaboration-performance on reputation has not been dealt with explicitly in literature.

Scientific, managerial, and artistic-creative knowledge systems are characterized by increasing intricacies of performance legitimization as we move from low to high reliance on collaboration. Greater reliance on collaboration leads to reputational signals becoming increasingly ambiguous. In addition, as reliance on collaboration increases we witness increasing complexity in reasoning about partner capabilities and fit in collaborations.

When a knowledge system is project-based, the complexity associated with making choices for repeat collaboration is further amplified as each contributor's capabilities, fit in a working team, and past performance are evaluated against requirements of a new project.

In examining the movie industry in this chapter, we take on a research site that is at one extreme of the continuum: a creative milieu and characterized by collaborations that deliver movie projects. Our results are therefore limited in generalizability in as far as the film industry has some relatively unique features. Further research is clearly needed to examine how the same models of resource selection and recruitment operate in industries that are less fragmented and more resource rich than the UK film industry.

References

Ancona, D. G., and Caldwell, D. F. (1992). 'Bridging the Boundary: External Process and Performance in Organizational Teams'. *Administrative Science Quarterly*, 37/4: 634–65.

Andreu, R., and Sieber, S. (2005). 'Knowledge Integration across Organizations: How Different Types of Knowledge Suggest Different "Integration Trajectories"'. *Knowledge and Process Management*, 12/3: 153–60.

Blackler, F. (1995). 'Knowledge, Knowledge Work and Organizations: An Overview and Interpretation'. *Organization Studies*, 16/6: 1021–46.

Collins, H. M. (1993). 'The Structure of Knowledge'. *Social Research*, 60/1: 95–116.

Connor, K. R., and Prahalad, C. K. (1996). 'A Resource-Based Theory of the Firm: Knowledge versus Opportunism'. *Organization Science*, 7: 477–501.

Corman, R., and Jerome, J. (1989). *How I Made a Hundred Movies in Hollywood and Never Lost a Dime*. New York: Random House.

Doz, Y. (1996). 'The Evolution of Cooperation in Strategic Alliances: Initial Conditions or Learning Processes?' *Strategic Management Journal*, 17: 55–83.

Duleck, U., and Kerschbamer, R. (2006). 'On Doctors, Mechanics, and Computer Specialists: The Economics of Credence Goods'. *Journal of Economic Literature*, 44/1: 5–42.

Faraj, S., and Sproull, L. (2000). 'Coordinating Expertise in Software Development Teams'. *Management Science*, 46/12: 1554–68.

Galunic, C. D., and Rodan, S. (1998). 'Resource Combination in the Firm: Knowledge Structures and the Potential for Schumpeterian Innovation'. *Strategic Management Journal*, 19/12: 1193–201.

Grant, R. M. (1996). 'Prospering in Dynamically-Competitive Environments: Organizational Capability as Knowledge Integration'. *Organization Science*, 7/4: 375–87.

Gray, R. (1996). *Cinemas in Britain*. Hampshire: Lund Humphries.

Heylin, C. (2005). *Despite the System: Orson Welles vs the Hollywood Studios*. Edinburgh: Canongate Books.

Hines, W. E. (1998). *Job Descriptions for Film, Video and CGI (Computer Generated Imagery): Responsibilities and Duties for the Cinematic Craft Categories and Classifications*, 5th edn. London: Samuel French.

Kogut, B. (1988). 'Joint Ventures: Theoretical and Empirical Perspectives'. *Strategic Management Journal*, 9/4: 319–32.

Lampel, J. (2006). 'The Genius behind the System: The Emergence of the Central Producer System in the Hollywood Motion Picture Industry', in J. Lampel, J. Shamsie, and T. Lant (eds.), *The Business of Culture: Emerging Perspectives in Media*. Mahwah, NJ: Lawrence Erlbaum.

—— and Shamsie, J. (2003). 'Capabilities in Motion: New Organizational Forms and the Reshaping of the Hollywood Movie Industry'. *Journal of Management Studies*, 40/3: 2189–210.

Lennon, D. (1998). 'London: Boom Times for UK Films'. *Europe*, September/379: 38–9.

Liebeskind, J. P., Oliver, A. L., Zucker, L., and Brewer, M. (1996). 'Social Networks, Learning, and Flexibility: Sourcing Scientific Knowledge in New Biotechnology Firms'. *Organization Science*, 7/4: 428–44.

Lumpkin, G. T., and Dess, G. G. (1996). 'Clarifying the Entrepreneurial Orientation Construct and Linking it to Performance'. *Academy of Management Review*, 21: 135–72.

Lyman, R. (2002). 'A Can-Do Dude in a Texas Castle, Making Movies'. *New York Times*, 28 July: 11.

O'Mahony, S., and Bechky, B. (2006). 'Stretchwork: Managing the Career Progression Paradox in External Labor Markets'. *Academy of Management Journal*, 49/5: 918–41.

Prigg, Steven (ed.) (2004). *Movie Moguls: Interviews with Top Film Producers*. Jefferson, N.C.: McFarland.

Proferes, N. (2001). *Film Directing Fundamentals: From Script to Screen*. Oxford: Focal Press.

Puttnam, D. (1987). *Movies and Money*. New York: Alfred A. Knopf.

Rao, H. (1994). 'The Social Construction of Reputation: Certification Contests, Legitimation and the Survival of Organizations'. *Strategic Management Journal*, 15: 29–44.

Spender, J. C., and Grant, R. M. (1996). 'Knowledge and the Firm: Overview'. *Strategic Management Journal*, 17: 5–9.

Swan, J., and Scarbrough, H. (2005). 'The Politics of Networked Innovation'. *Human Relations*, 58/7: 913–43.

Weigelt, K., and Camerer, C. (1988). 'Reputation and Corporate Strategy: A Review of Recent Theory and Applications'. *Strategic Management Journal*, 9/5: 443–54.

Wilson, R. (1985). 'Reputations in Games and Markets', in A. E. Roth (ed.), *Game Theoretic Models of Bargaining*. New York: Cambridge University Press.

8

The Evolution of Biomedical Knowledge: Interactive Innovation in the United Kingdom and United States

Jacky Swan, Mike Bresnen, Sue Newell, Maxine Robertson, Anna Goussevskaia, and Ademola Obembe

Introduction

Biomedical innovation, particularly radical innovation, typically relies on diverse sources of knowledge (scientific, business, commercial, clinical, and regulatory) being brought together through collaborative work arrangements across many different types of organizations (e.g. public research organizations, commercial firms, clinical research organizations, hospitals, regulatory agencies, and patient groups). Tissue engineering, for example, encompasses disciplines as diverse as molecular biology, chemistry, informatics, and engineering, and it has a wide range of medical applications (e.g. bone and organ growth, wound and cartilage repair). In our research, we studied a leading tissue engineering research centre in the United Kingdom. This research centre, which is based at a university hospital, had managed to develop a spin-out company, NewTissueCo, to combine new forms of materially engineered technologies ('scaffolds'), on which stem cells grow, with advances in basic research in stem cells and molecular biology, ultimately aiming to advance products for bone and organ growth.

The challenges were enormous—scientists across disciplines needed to work collaboratively; regulation surrounding product development and clinical trials (e.g. on the use of stem cells) was fluid; the market for products was not well established; venture capitalists were little interested in such high-risk, long-term investments; the underpinning science and technologies were still formative; clinicians—whose skills were required to use and develop the technology—needed to be convinced that such techniques were advantageous for patients so that trials could be carried out; preclinical 'basic science' had to be redone in the light of new evidence from the development process, and so forth. In short, the quality of the scientific knowledge did not 'speak for itself'. In NewTissueCo, then, the founding academic 'Star Scientists' (one also being a practising clinician) had to rely heavily on their reputations and 'social capital' to cultivate interest among the scientific and clinical communities that needed to be involved and to negotiate commercial partnerships, both with their own universities and with downstream biotechnology firms, in order to develop a more robust funding model. They also needed to take crucial decisions about current financial contracts and preclinical work based on 'best guesses' about a highly uncertain future.

This example demonstrates the highly interactive, iterative nature of the biomedical innovation process. The ability to integrate diverse forms of knowledge by moving back and forth between basic science and clinical development (referred to as 'integrative capabilities') and the ability to collaborate with diverse organizations ('relational capabilities') are particularly crucial, especially where knowledge and resources are highly distributed. Other work suggests, further, that different national contexts may be more or less supportive of these kinds of capabilities (the United States being more supportive than Europe, for example, see Owen-Smith et al. 2002). However, little is known about how these macro-level capabilities impact different kinds of innovation processes at the micro (project) level, or about crucial socio-political processes that facilitate or impede the evolution of knowledge 'at the interstices' of diverse groups and organizations (Powell, Koput, and Smith-Doerr 1996). Our research study, then, was a multilevel analysis of biomedical innovation, comparing innovation projects in the UK and the US contexts in order to identify those mechanisms and processes, at institutional and project levels, that appeared important in driving (or precluding) interactive innovation.

Context for the research

The challenges of biomedical innovation

Innovation in the pharmaceutical and biotechnology sectors is a major source of economic advantage (ABPI 2006). However, despite an increasing

162

number of breakthroughs (e.g. in stem cells) that have the potential to radically change healthcare, the challenges of translating new knowledge into improved clinical practices continue, as shown by the increasing time and costs involved in drug development (CMR International 2006). Even where scientific knowledge is validated through, for example, lengthy and costly clinical trials, many promising discoveries fail to be used in practice, with a significant number of failures occurring in early development phases of innovation (Dopson 2005).

Biomedical innovations—especially more 'radical' innovations—are particularly challenging because, like other complex innovation processes (e.g. in construction, film, and large engineering projects), they cut across professional, occupational, and organizational boundaries and threaten to disrupt established medical practices (Christensen 2000). The knowledge production process involved relies, then, on the combination and integration of diverse forms of knowledge (scientific, technological, commercial, clinical, and regulatory) across a distributed array of professional groups, commercial organizations, public research organizations (PROs), and health organizations (Coombs, Harvey, and Tether 2003; Dodgson, Gann, and Salter 2004). The innovation process is, therefore, non-linear, complex, highly uncertain, and high risk, relying on iterative cycles of knowledge integration that take place through collaborative networking relationships (Powell, Koput, and Smith-Doerr 1996; Dodgson, Gann, and Salter 2004). As Powell, Koput, and Smith-Doerr (1996: 116) note: 'When the knowledge base of an industry is both complex and expanding and sources of expertise are widely dispersed, the locus of innovation will be found in networks of learning, rather than in individual firms.' We refer to this kind of innovation process as 'interactive innovation'—innovation encompassing the integration of knowledge across diverse scientific, professional, and organizational groups (cf. Rothwell 1994; Massey, Quintas, and Wield 1992).

It is also the case that outcomes of collaboration and the potential applications of scientific discovery are, at best, unknown and, at worst, unknowable at the outset of the innovation process (Pisano 2006; Dougherty 2007). Moreover, the heterogeneous groups involved in biomedical innovation maintain distinctive professional and epistemic practices surrounding the production of knowledge (Knorr-Cetina 1999). Chemists, engineers, and molecular biologists, for example, are seen to create, evaluate, and warrant knowledge in characteristically different ways (Knorr-Cetina 1999). As Carlile (2004) notes, 'knowledge boundaries'—boundaries that arise from specialization and distributed practice—create both opportunities and constraints for the integration of knowledge across specialist groups coming together to work on novel projects. The key, it is argued, is to provide an environment in which collaborations can flourish, with an expectation that these collaborations are likely to require ongoing, rather than short-term, commitment and resources (Pisano 2006).

Understanding interactive innovation processes demands new approaches and models that take seriously issues of process, such as the organization of networks, the role of boundary spanning, the mediating role of trust and legitimacy, professional power and influence, and combinations of different forms of expertise (Swan and Scarbrough 2005). It also demands attention to the institutional context in which innovation unfolds (Owen-Smith et al. 2002), bringing into question the adequacy of the existing structure or 'anatomy' of the biopharmaceutical sector in supporting innovation and commercialization (Pisano 2006). Our research aimed, then, to understand the processes underlying the evolution of knowledge for biomedical innovation in the institutional contexts provided by the United Kingdom and United States, and in areas where breakthroughs in science had the potential to lead to radical innovation in medical treatments and services.

Theoretical approach

Our theoretical approach was to treat knowledge as dialectical—i.e. as situated in social and organizational practices and relationships that are themselves embedded in wider institutional contexts (Tsoukas and Vladimirou 2001; Lam 1997). Thus, biomedical innovation was defined as the *process* of creating and applying scientific and technological knowledge to improve the delivery of human healthcare and the treatment of disease (this includes new drugs, diagnostics, and drug delivery regimes for human use, but excludes animal, agricultural, and natural resource biotechnology applications) (Rasmussen 2005). This pointed to a critical focus on networks of relationships and work practices through which knowledge was being constructed (Brown and Duguid 2001) and on the distribution of knowledge and power across organizational, occupational, and professional groupings (Lam 1997). The broad theoretical lens of social constructivism (e.g. Tsoukas and Vladimirou 2001) and related frameworks deriving from practice-based theorizing (e.g. Brown and Duguid 2001; Carlile 2002) were applied as appropriate. These literatures are linked by their premiss that knowledge claims co-exist with political interests and institutionally embedded network relationships and structures. Power was thus treated, not as a property of a particular individual or group, but as embedded in networks of interaction (Swan and Scarbrough 2005; Hardy, Phillips, and Lawrence 2003). What counted as valid knowledge at any moment in time was contested, as more or less powerful, medical professionals and scientists with particular vested interests sought to sustain control over their own work practices (Abbott 1988; Drazin 1990).

Multilevel analysis in the United Kingdom and United States

Against this backdrop, our research attempted a multilevel, contextually sensitive analysis of the social and political processes surrounding the production and evolution of biomedical knowledge. As Gittell and Weiss (2004: 148) suggest, 'Frameworks for analyzing organizational phenomena must be responsive to the dynamic and complex characteristics and inter-relationships between multiple levels of analysis that "real life" situations reflect.' The UK and US contexts offered useful points of comparison for our study. Previous research has highlighted that, from a 'Varieties of Capitalism' perspective, they are both 'liberal market economies' that should excel in developing the necessary competencies to innovate in industries dominated by rapidly emerging health technologies (Whitley 2000). In both the United Kingdom and United States, national systems of innovation are largely supportive of biomedical industry (Casper and Kettler 2001). Both nations also accommodate entrepreneurial patterns of business and have developed active local markets, as well as a supply of technology, scientists, clinical expertise, and 'know-how' in the biomedical domain. The United States is a world leader in terms of the number of biotech companies, with 1,830 companies in 2003, 1,089 of those related to healthcare technologies (DTI 2005). The United Kingdom is second in Europe, with around 455 biotechnology companies in total, 239 being healthcare-related, following Germany (recognizing that the figures change regularly).

The United Kingdom and United States are also broadly similar in other respects. For example, the development of the UK biotechnology industry has also been closely modelled on regulatory frameworks, strategies, and structures for institutional support developed in the United States (Casper and Kettler 2001). The distribution of specialist expertise is also similar across contexts and both have strongly established powerful, professional bodies in health. Managerial predispositions and, of course, language, also tend to be similar across the United Kingdom and United States (Clark 2000).

Recognizing similarities, there are also critical differences that make the United Kingdom and United States useful points of contrast for informing theory, for example, in the financing and organization of healthcare, and in the impact of professional and educational institutions on the legitimization of knowledge and new technology (Aldrich 2000). Hence, the way that knowledge is deployed is likely to reflect nationally distinctive innovation systems and distinctive cultural repertoires or 'styles of thinking' among managers in the United Kingdom and United States (Clark 1987). Clark (1987), for example, notes how the appropriation of knowledge across the United Kingdom and United States generates 'pivotal modifications' in innovation design, such that it is possible to identify 'typical variety' across contexts. Thus, by comparing the UK and the US systems, which are relatively similar but also distinctive, particular influences on biomedical innovation at the institutional level might be isolated and understood.

A feature in our analysis, then, was to try to unravel the development and impact of macro-level mechanisms linking scientific research to commercial and clinical development at the meso and micro levels (Swan et al. 2007a). Important macro-level mechanisms have been referred to by Owen-Smith et al. (2002) as 'integrative' and 'relational' capabilities. These refer, respectively, to the ability of scientists to combine and integrate knowledge by moving back and forth between basic science and clinical development; and to the ability of organizations within an innovation system to collaborate with other, diverse organizations. In keeping with 'national innovation systems' approaches, Owen-Smith et al.'s earlier work has suggested that these capabilities stem from macro-level institutional differences in the structure, operation, and density of network ties and, thus, differ across nations—being better developed in the United States than in Europe (Carlsson 2002; Nelson 1993). Our major findings, outlined below, focus, in particular, on explaining how these macro-level capabilities shape actual processes of managing and organizing innovation at the meso and micro levels.

Clearly our research project was large (probably too large!) in scope, scale, and ambition. It is also fair to say that, at the outset, we significantly underemphasized the enormous complexity of biomedical innovation. The 'ecology' of the field (as Grabher 2002 would put it), the intricacies and uncertainties of knowledge flows, and interdependencies among actors involved, are hugely complex (see Newell et al. 2007). As a result, our journal papers and articles have, by necessity, focused narrowly on specific sections of the empirical work as relevant to particular theoretical purposes (e.g. modes of organizing biomedical innovation and the role of integrative and relational capabilities, Swan et al. 2007a; the implications of policy aimed at translating science through interactive innovation, Robertson 2007; the role of objects in boundary work, Swan et al. 2004; national institutional differences between the United States and United Kingdom, Swan et al. 2007b; the dynamics of project organization in complex ecologies, Newell et al. 2007; the influence of professional practices and power, Bresnen et al. 2006; the dynamics of commercialization, Goussevskaia et al. 2007). In contrast, we take this opportunity to 'paint the bigger picture' by providing an overview of our major research findings and giving a flavour of the key theoretical and practical concerns they address.

Empirical study

The empirical research involved a three-year study of biomedical innovation in the United Kingdom and the United States aimed at collecting primary and secondary data on:

- Macro-level institutional influences on biomedical innovation and key differences between the United Kingdom and United States
- Meso-level relationships among project stakeholders, including networks within and between organizations and the 'boundary-spanning' activities involved
- Micro-level organization and management of biomedical innovation in specific project settings and the role of individual actors in the innovation process

Clearly, in our relatively short duration project, it was impossible to trace an entire biomedical innovation process from discovery to market. We therefore selected radical innovation projects (i.e. that had the potential to change existing clinical practices) and those in early development (i.e. at the point of moving from proof of concept into clinical trials). This was because: (1) radical innovation is high risk but potentially yields the highest returns and improvements in health; and (2) early development is a point at which many biomedical innovation projects fail. These kinds of project pose major challenges in terms of collaboration across diverse organizations, professional groups, and scientific disciplines.

The study was conducted in two linked phases. Phase 1 involved a systematic literature review—following the methodology deployed by Pittaway et al. (2004)—and an interview-based survey of ninety-seven stakeholders (44 in the United Kingdom, 53 in the United States) with significant experience of working in interactive innovation projects. Interviewees were initially identified via our Scientific Advisory Board (SAB) that had been set up (in the spirit of interactive innovation) to guide the research. Additional interviewees were identified using a 'snowballing' technique. This kind of non-probability convenience sampling can be extremely useful when the research is exploratory and population parameters are unknown (Saunders et al. 2000). In addition, twenty-two meetings were held to discuss the research and further participation (17 in the United Kingdom; 5 in the United States). Interviewees included: 'entrepreneurial' academic researchers; scientists and managers in biotechnology and pharmaceutical firms; venture capitalists (VCs); technology transfer officers; and members of biomedical support organizations such as governmental agencies and charities. Recognizing regional variations, fieldwork focused on the Boston area in the United States, which has a concentration of such institutions (including Harvard, Massachusetts Institute of Technology (MIT) and Massachusetts General Hospital, for example) and densely connected networks between them. In the United Kingdom, we concentrated on the Oxford–Cambridge–London triangle, which is also recognized for its high level of activity and reputation for innovation in the biomedical area.

Phase 2 comprised detailed longitudinal case studies of innovation projects (six in the United States and four in the United Kingdom), identified from the first phase interviews as offering exemplars of different ways of organizing biomedical innovation. Thus, the research deployed collective case studies to facilitate interpretation (Alvesson and Skoldberg 2000) by comparing the similarities and differences provided by multiple settings. While access was negotiated via focal organizations and/or individuals, the unit of analysis was the innovation process, not a specific firm, so interviewees spanned different organizations involved. The cases were selected on the basis of, first, the choice of research topics and questions being posed (Stake 1995), and, second, the possibility of capturing both historic and 'live' processes to inform the longitudinal analysis (Pettigrew 1990). Thus, in all cases, activity relating to the innovation process had been going on for at least two years and was still projected to be ongoing during the research period.

The cases were traced over 30 months with a minimum of four fieldwork visits and an average of fourteen interviews per case. Interviews were complemented with extensive documentary data (including companies' reports, inter-partner correspondence, contracts, and meeting minutes) and observation (including non-participant observation of project team meetings where access permitted). Data from both phases were transcribed and coded using NVivo software and Phase 1 data was analysed using the 'memoing' technique (Miles and Huberman 1994). Due to the complexity of the Phase 2 cases, each was investigated by two researchers. On completion of fieldwork, detailed case descriptions were produced (average 10,000 words) containing primary data (quotes from interviews, inserts from documents, etc.) and structured thematically. All case descriptions were content-analysed by the entire team in order to establish inter-rater agreement. The data were further validated through presentations and discussions at five SAB meetings and through written case reports to participating companies.

Discussion

The analysis is outlined below in three main sections. The first draws from Phase 1 data to present, in broad terms, macro-level institutional differences in the United Kingdom and United States. The second outlines a new framework summarizing different modes of organizing biomedical innovation. We call this 'meso-level' because modes of organizing biomedical innovation characteristically span organizations, meaning that the single firm—emphasized in previous work on innovation—is not an appropriate unit of analysis. This framework, developed from Phase 1, was used to select Phase 2 cases and progressively modified as a result. By relating modes of organizing to macro-level differences, an exploratory account of the relative importance of macro-level capabilities for different kinds of innovation project is developed. The third section identifies particular mechanisms at the micro project level that appeared to play an important role in influencing interactive innovation and relates these to integrative and relational capabilities.

Macro level: national institutional differences

In broad terms, our research reinforced earlier work that suggests that the UK context is less supportive of the capabilities needed for interactive biomedical innovation than the US context (Owen-Smith et al. 2002). More specifically, we identified a number of institutional mechanisms that appeared to play an important role in shaping integrative and relational capabilities and in explaining differences between the UK and US contexts. These are outlined next (labelled after Casper and Kettler 2001).

ACCESS TO HUMAN RESOURCES

Career and incentive systems proved more of a barrier to biomedical innovation in the United Kingdom than in the United States (cf. Mallon, Duberley, and Cohen 2005). Career paths are more fluid in the United States, allowing scientists and clinicians to move back and forth between public and commercial activity without detriment to their careers or status (Owen-Smith 2003). For example, in the United States it was considered quite acceptable to pursue medical and business training simultaneously, with 24 of the 27 'Research 1' universities offering dual degree programmes (as compared to only one such programme in the United Kingdom). Such career movements are important in generating 'knowledge spillovers' through overlapping, but distinctive, scientific, clinical, and industry networks at the institutional level (Zucker, Darby, and Brewer 1998; Murray 2002).

These findings echo Clark's (1987) observations of greater 'conflict with capital' in UK educational and career systems, and a more pragmatic orientation towards applied, or 'how to', knowledge in the United States. This, he argues, generates a stronger polarization in the United Kingdom between 'academic thinking, which is often regarded as unnecessary and impossible to digest and the rule of thumb empiricism which seems to have a firm grip in many sectors' (Clark 1987: 223). In our study, combining basic science and clinical research with commercial objectives appeared to be a more widely accepted goal in the US context, generating a 'natural' advantage in terms of being able to exploit scientific knowledge for clinical development. In contrast, boundaries between basic research, commercial, and clinical professions were more strongly entrenched in the United Kingdom, with participants seeing a move from one domain to another as a career choice from which there would be little opportunity to return. These findings concur with Mallon, Duberley, and Cohen (2005), who found that the majority of UK scientists working in PROs had an overriding sense that naked commercial ambition was not quite acceptable within public sector science and so did not incorporate this into their career planning. Only one-third of their sample—described somewhat cynically by peers as 'strategic opportunists'—were prepared to consider a move from 'the bench' to a commercial career, but most of this group had become aware of the opportunities because they had previous experience of working outside the public sector. Thus, while Nowotny, Scott, and Gibbons (2001) note the increased blurring of boundaries between knowledge traditionally produced in university, government, and private sector research organizations, we found that this 'blurring' is also deeply politicized and strongly shaped by the national innovation system. Taken together, these findings led us to conclude that:

Problems in the supply and coordination of personnel, and differences in career and incentive systems and the availability of multidisciplinary training, may militate against the development of integrative and relational capabilities needed to support interactive innovation in the United Kingdom as compared to the United States.

ACCESS TO TECHNOLOGY

Access to technology concerns access to high-quality basic science, coupled with appropriate regulatory policies and institutions for technology transfer to effectively exploit and commercialize the science base (Casper and Kettler 2001). Given that universities (or hospitals) were rarely in a position to develop commercial markets on their own, other resources and incentives were needed to encourage innovation. These included, for example, licensing protocols, supportive intellectual property (IP) laws and incentives, rules governing the transfer of research between the public and private sectors, technology transfer offices in universities, consulting resources, and spin-off technology firms, technology parks, and so forth. Our findings suggest further that these resources are, in general, more widely available in the United States than in the United Kingdom. For example, US universities often benefit from large private endowments that allow them to exploit IP by taking basic research into development, and a greater share of the profits usually goes to the individual scientist/ entrepreneurs. The United States also makes larger investments in basic research through public institutions such as the National Science Foundation (NSF) and the National Institute of Health (NIH). Yet, despite this, the UK biomedical science base compares favourably. For example, the United Kingdom ranks second in the world (second only to the United States) in terms of citations and the number of citations per researcher is around twice those to US researchers.

In terms of regulation, the United Kingdom has to some extent emulated the 'Bayh-Doyle Act' in the United States for intellectual property (IP). However, our findings suggest that it still lags behind the United States in its overall approach to technology transfer. One reason is the lack of clarity of ownership of IP in early development, particularly in collaborations involving joint university–industry funding. While UK universities produce roughly equivalent numbers of patents and licensing agreements per-unit research fund, these generate significantly lower income. UK technology transfer offices usually demand a larger equity share and universities tend to view IP as a way of making money, which lowers incentives for entrepreneurship. In contrast, leading US universities (such as MIT) take a more 'hands-off' approach and view entrepreneurial activity as 'reputation enhancing' rather than income-generating, so accepting failure as an inevitable part of their technology transfer activity. That said regulation in some areas (stem cells, for example) has been much more restrictive in the United States. Taken together, these observations led us to conclude that:

The development of biomedical innovation will be influenced by differences in institutional arrangements governing access to technology, which, in general, are more supportive in the United States than in the United Kingdom, although this depends on the particular nature of the science.

ACCESS TO HIGH-RISK FINANCE

Access to high-risk finance for early development is influenced by national financial institutions (especially venture capital) and general market confidence. Significantly, there were differences between the major sources of finance in the UK and US biotechnology sectors, in terms of size, composition, and characteristics of investment decisions (Robertson et al. 2006). For example, venture capital financing, specifically of the high technology sector (of which the biomedical sector is a major constituent), in 2000 in the United States was £45 billion as compared to £1.6 billion in the UK (NVCA 2002)—a gap which has continued to date. In both the United States and United Kingdom, however, there was a major gap in early stage financing to support projects reaching proof of concept and just entering clinical development (e.g. between 2003 and 2004, this decreased in the United Kingdom by 30%). However, philanthropy played a more significant role in filling this gap in the US context as compared with the UK context.

Interviewees also noted important differences in the profile of investors. Thus, US 'business angels' tend to be individuals who combine high levels of expertise and experience within high-technology industries with financial and business acumen. They are, therefore, well placed to invest in high-risk, early stage opportunities in the high-technology sector (cf. Tylecote 1999; Manigart et al. 2000). In contrast, UK business angels typically have less specialist backgrounds and so a far greater proportion of investments (75% in 1999) are made in high-technology management buyouts (Lockett et al. 2002), which are considered to be less risky.

In the period of our project, large pharmaceutical firms were increasingly looking to partner with projects that had already entered clinical trials in order to reduce their own risk, so placing additional financial burden on smaller biotechnology firms. Moreover, smaller biotechnology firms in both the United Kingdom and the United States often lacked necessary expertise in clinical trials and relevant networks with clinical and regulatory groups. As a result, they were heavily dependent on collaboration with increasingly large and powerful clinical research organizations over which they often had little influence. Taken together, these observations suggested that:

The greater availability and access to high-risk (early stage) finance in the United States promotes the development of interactive innovation in the biomedical sector to a greater extent than in the United Kingdom.

HEALTHCARE SYSTEMS

The healthcare system in the United States is typically referred to as the 'medical-industrial complex' (Relman 1980), reflecting not only the dense interaction between public and private institutions but also including the American Medical Association (AMA), insurance companies, Health Maintenance Organizations (HMOs), the Department of Health and Welfare, and politicians. Crucially, it is this medical-industrial complex, rather than state or federal government, that largely determines public health issues. As Nester (1997: 194) highlights, 'Representatives of the medical industrial complex have fought and usually defeated every substantial reform bill to appear in Congress while successfully pushing through bills that serve their own interests.' In contrast, the UK NHS is regarded as a major global source of innovation, providing, for example, the world's largest accessible population of patients for clinical trials. Yet, conflicts between public and private sector values, incentives, interests, and funding limit innovation in the NHS. In addition, unlike the United States, clinical research in UK hospitals was widely seen as being in decline or as increasingly without incentives, leading to a significant gap in translating innovations into practice.

On first reflection, then, it might be concluded that the major difference between the United Kingdom and the United States is the largely self-regulated nature of the healthcare system in the United States compared to the highly regulated, centralized healthcare policy system in the

United Kingdom. However, in terms of state intervention, there are at least two important exceptions in the United States. The first is tighter state control over stem cells in the United States. The second is the congressionally mandated Federal Agency for Health Care Policy and Research (AHCPR), launched in 1986, whose remit was to enhance the quality, appropriateness, and effectiveness of healthcare services through the application of evidence-based medicine. This agency suffered a series of setbacks during the mid-1990s (Harrison, Moran, and Wood 2002) when its budget was progressively cut in the face of powerful opposition from the AMA, whose interests reflected institutionally based assumptions of private-sector supremacy. However, the AHCPR was supported by Health Maintenance Organizations—an intermediary group representing the interests of health insurance companies. The ensuing conflict between two of the most powerful players within the medical-industrial complex resulted in the battle being won by the federal government.

In contrast, policy was introduced promoting the use of evidence-based medicine in the United Kingdom thirteen years after the United States when the UK Government established the National Institute of Clinical Excellence (NICE) as part of the National Health Service (NHS) Quality Framework. Monitoring of standards is achieved centrally through the Commission for Health Improvement and assessed against the National Performance Framework and the National Patient and User Survey. It is too early to assess the long-term success or otherwise of the move towards evidence-based medicine in the United Kingdom and the United States. What is apparent, however, is that while policy has emerged in very different ways, ultimately there has been policy convergence, despite what appears to be very different healthcare systems. Thus our research suggested that:

The largely self-regulated US medical-industrial complex promotes the development of interactive biomedical innovation, where it is in the interests of powerful stakeholders such as pharmaceutical firms, health insurance companies, etc. However, increasing government intervention in important new fields (such as stem cells and evidence-based medicine) may ulimately pose contraints, particularly on radical innovation, even in the United States.

Meso level: modes of organizing interactive innovation

Recognizing the differences in the national contexts, it is also clear that there are wide variations in the ways in which interactive innovation processes are organized (e.g. as university start-ups, as development projects in biotechnology firms, as R&D in global pharmaceuticals). Our research has found that these variations mediate, significantly, the effects (and also emergence) of a nation's integrative and relational capabilities. In order to understand these influences, we generated an analytical framework that mapped typical variation in modes of organizing biomedical innovation projects at the meso level. Importantly, our research revealed two broad dimensions, along which biomedical innovation projects could be characterized.

Organizational coupling refers to the governance, organization, and management of the innovation process and the pattern of collaboration among partners (Alter and Hage 1993). Variation along this dimension ranged from networked/loosely coupled modes to hierarchical/tightly coupled modes. In the former, innovation projects were pursued within a loosely coupled network of organizations, with work being conducted across several organizations. Management was decentralized and vertical dependency on centralized resources was low (Alter and Hage 1993). Where formal contracts existed, these focused on mutual obligations and the allocation of future gains (e.g. revenues generated through patents). In contrast, in tightly coupled modes, most activity was carried out within a large focal firm and managed centrally, but with identified parts (e.g. manufacturing) being formally subcontracted.

Knowledge boundaries relates to knowledge flows across the different knowledge domains involved and can be considered as ranging from high to low. Most innovation projects were multidisciplinary. The important issue, then, was whether or not projects required new ways of working across these disciplines and/or disrupted existing knowledge/practice boundaries (cf. Carlile 2004), in which case they were classified as having high knowledge boundaries. These arose in situations where there was greater novelty, where medical need was uncertain or contested, and where implications for medical practice were difficult to forecast. Therefore, significant efforts were made to enlist clinicians and integrate their expertise into early design. These kinds of situation engendered 'pragmatic boundaries' (Carlile 2004), meaning that alignment of professional interests and development of shared expectations among stakeholders was crucial.

Combining these two dimensions provided a new framework for classifying different modes of organizing interactive innovation projects. This is shown in Figure 8.1, with case studies (using pseudonyms) located in it.

Quadrant I was typically populated by small early stage spin-off companies founded by academic entrepreneurs. There was high dependency on the parent university and multiple sources of funding were sought for facilities and specialist expertise. The development process required relatively low

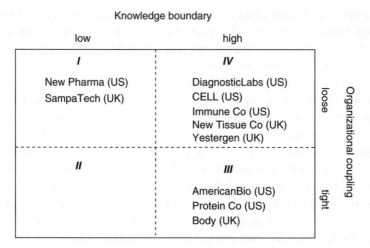

Fig. 8.1. Modes of organizing biomedical innovation and selected cases

levels of knowledge integration and low knowledge boundaries. Innovations here might result in significant improvements in treatment but were less disruptive to existing modes of treatment delivery.

Case Vignette Quadrant I: SampaTech is a small company developing novel therapeutics for hepatitis. It was founded by two scientists from a leading UK university, who developed the basic technology in collaboration with a large pharmaceutical firm (that subsequently withdrew from the project) and another university. By early 2005, the company had acquired two rounds of seed funding: one from one of the universities and another from a donation. The intention was to develop the lead project, out-license it, and use the royalties for further developments. SampaTech had a loosely coupled management structure, relying on a number of part-time executives and administrative personnel, coordinated by one of the two founding scientists (who continued her academic activities at the university). Although the academic director had a history of interaction with industry, via involvement on the advisory boards of biotechnology companies, the company still relied heavily on the technology transfer office of the university, which provided access to biotech companies and the venture capital community. SampaTech's first CEO had formerly worked as a manager in a large pharmaceutical firm but was later considered to lack the scientific background required to secure further venture capital funding. With the help of the technology transfer office, a new CEO, who had 'the right' profile, was appointed. She had previously started several biotechnology companies, thereby developing a reputation as a 'serial entrepreneurial scientist'. This change of CEO resulted in a major refocusing of the organization strategy. It was initially geared towards the development of three technology platforms, which required extensive funding. By reassessing the strategy, the new CEO narrowed the area of development to therapeutics, thereby generating external pharmaceutical interests in licensing the lead product.

Quadrant II and *III* projects were typically led by larger companies. Quadrant II was not central to our study, as projects here were usually aimed at incremental improvement of existing therapeutics, with technology being either developed in-house, acquired, or licensed. Quadrant III, on the other hand, describes cases where the companies ventured into highly innovative areas, where the development of breakthrough technologies placed demands on the organization to collaborate with basic researchers, and where constant interaction with end users (health professionals) and regulators was required. Interorganizational relationships in Quadrants II and III were tightly controlled by the focal organization and usually based on formal contractual agreements.

Case Vignette Quadrant III: AmericanBio is a US biotechnology company developing ELBOW—a product for cartilage repair based on tissue engineering technology. The ELBOW project was conducted by a multifunctional core team. AmericanBio had a strong internal regulatory group responsible for interaction with the FDA—regulatory expertise that was crucial because initially there was no regulatory framework and AmericanBio was able to shape the regulations to secure approval for their first-generation product. Besides the challenges of regulation, sales and marketing had also proven costly and complex as the product disrupted established ways in which orthopedic surgeons (the main users) practised. Thus, development required a significant degree of interaction with the user community. Currently, AmericanBio is developing a new generation of ELBOW. Setbacks with its internal development prompted the decision to search for external technology that could help 'leapfrog' the project through early stage clinical trials. The company had a special interest in EU companies because the lack of regulation of tissue-engineered products in Europe meant that patient data on the technology was available that might help ease the progression to clinical trials in the United States (interestingly, while AmericanBio had played a major role in shaping US regulation, which made it difficult for competitors to enter the market, they now had to face those same regulatory barriers to develop their own new generation product). AmericanBio identified and acquired a company in Europe that had the technology needed and initial clinical data. One important criterion in their selection was a match in terms of organizational cultures. AmericanBio had earlier carried out diligence on another company but decided not to acquire it because of 'significant organizational differences'. Following the acquisition, meeting timelines in product development proved difficult, one of the reasons being that the clinical data was not as ready for FDA approval as expected, despite the fact that AmericanBio had conducted very a thorough due diligence process and, according to one respondent, 'knew where to look for dead bodies'.

Quadrant IV also contained highly novel projects but resources and management were decentralized. The novelty of the technology, or combination of technologies, generated an informal inter-organizational 'web' of smaller companies and collaborating PROs. These 'sexy technologies' created an aura of attraction that drove interest and collaboration. These projects depended on highly networked individuals to orchestrate loosely coupled, decentralized projects.

> *Case Vignette Quadrant IV: DiagnosticLabs* is a small US company specializing in diagnostic assays that initiated a development project to transform them into a 'theragnostic' company, combining diagnostic and therapeutic products. The logic was that availability of a targeted drug would increase the market for their diagnostic and vice versa. This project was championed by their recently appointed CEO, who had a reputation for managing successful biotech companies. The specific disease chosen was an area of acute medical concern, with a high mortality rate and no approved treatment. The project built upon an existing diagnostics kit for this disease, which was being developed by DiagnosticLabs through collaboration with academic partners. DiagnosticLabs lacked clinical trials and regulatory expertise and so, via the CEO's personal networks, formed an alliance with Bioclinical, a company specializing in clinical trials consulting and services, which provided a dedicated team to lead the clinical trials. The CEO used her personal connections to identify a company TherapeuticCo that held IP for the matching therapeutic. She originally believed that this IP was supported by sufficient preclinical data to allow the project to go straight into clinical trials. Bioclinical conducted a due diligence assessment of TherapeuticCo's IP on a 'good will' basis and concluded that the preclinical data available would not be sufficient to gain FDA approval for clinical trials and to convince venture capitalists to provide the investment needed. TherapeuticCo was not interested in making additional investments in a non-core area and a newly appointed CEO at the company did not want to dedicate further time to the project. In addition, DiagnosticLabs's owner decided to sell the company, so halting new investment. On top of this, there was a breakdown in the relationship between the CEOs of DiagnosticLabs and Bioclinical, as the Bioclinical team realized that DiagnosticLabs was pushing for venture capital for themselves and not for the project alliance. As a result, the development project was abandoned.

Micro level: project processes for developing biomedical innovation

Cross-project analyses identified eight processes, or mechanisms, at the project level that were crucial in influencing the ways in which knowledge evolved in interactive innovation. These are summarized in Table 8.1 and are seen as both linking to integrative and relational capabilities at the macro level (see Swan et al. 2007a, for a detailed discussion of these links)

Table 8.1. *Critical mechanisms influencing biomedical innovation projects*

Mechanisms linked to integrative capabilities	Illustrative case examples
1. Access to people working at interstices of networks to acquire knowledge and reproduce skills base	• Reliance on tech transfer office network to establish commercial contacts (SampaTech)
2. Establishing scientific and commercial credibility in project team in order to ensure funding through partnering, venture capital, or research funds	• Importance of scientific founders, host university, and CEO with prior start-up experience in providing credibility (NewTissueCo; Diagnostic Labs)
3. Symbolic figureheads	• Leading scientist's personal vision and commitment to commercialization (NewTissueCo)
4. Career perceptions and professional values in relation to motivation to engage with innovation commercialization activity	• Scientists and clinicians placing scientific/altruistic reasoning in opposition to commercial objectives, thus constraining commercial activity (SampaTech)
Mechanisms linked to relational capabilities	Illustrative case examples
1. Alignment of interests and expectations across partner organizations	• Employing 'cultural matching' and two-way 'due diligence' with potential partners (AmericanBio; Body). One-way due diligence insufficient (Diagnostic Labs)
2. Building upon existing networks to generate resources and sustain more risky and long-term projects	• Using existing networks of clinicians to promote product by publishing results and increasing the community of experience and patients (AmericanBio)
3. Using networks to shape regulations and ensure approval	• Regulatory group in-house dedicated to interaction with FDA able to shape the regulatory framework for the first-generation product. Next generation product approval is also being developed through interaction with FDA (AmericanBio)
4. Product 'magnets'	• 'Revolutionary' nature of the work provides a focus for research, but at the same time hampers commercialization efforts (NewTissueCo)

Conclusions

Our study has focused on identifying processes influencing the evolution of knowledge for biomedical innovation at different levels of analysis. More importantly, it has allowed us to explore the linkages between national level integrative and relational capabilities—found to be important in earlier research (Owen-Smith et al. 2002)—and processes of organizing biomedical innovation and integrating knowledge at the meso and micro levels (depicted in Figure 8.2). This builds from earlier research that has shown how institutions governing labour, finance, and product markets affect innovation activities and the performance of sectors and nations (Nelson 1993; Hall and Solskice 2001; Clark 1987).

A first contribution has been to explore contingencies between macro capabilities and characteristically different ways of organizing innovation projects at the meso level. Thus, the influence of institutionalized capabilities on innovation at the micro level appeared to be systematically related to different modes of organizing innovation processes, with integrative capabilities being more crucial in the case of start-ups (Quadrant I) and relational capabilities in the case of strategic alliances centred on focal biotech companies (Quadrant III). Most significantly, Quadrant IV projects relied heavily on both integrative and relational capabilities. Success here was, therefore, relatively more difficult to achieve in the UK context (see Swan et al. 2007a).

The second contribution has been to identify and unpack the mechanisms that both relate to, and moderate, the effects (positive and negative) of macro-level capabilities on micro-level innovation projects. Thus, micro-level mechanisms (Table 8.1) were important in moderating the impact of macro integrative and relational level capabilities and allowing projects to 'succeed' (or fail), despite being in a relatively unsupportive (or supportive) national context. This helps to address a central critique of comparative institutional studies concerning, as Casper and Murray

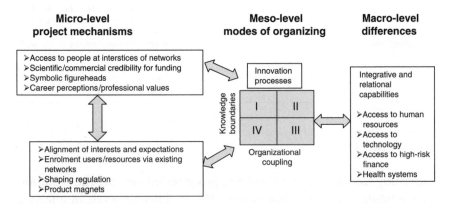

Fig. 8.2. Multilevel framework: processes influencing biomedical innovation

(2005: 56) put it (in relation to labour market institutions), 'the limited connection made between macro-institutions and the micro-dynamics (of individual careers) through which these institutional differences are manifested'. This kind of analysis also leads us to recognize the limitations of generic statements about relative national advantage in biomedical innovation. Whether a particular institutional context will be advantageous or not depends both on the kind of project and on the combination of mechanisms deployed at project, firm, or sector levels (Casper and van Waarden 2005). Moreover, attempts to replicate US policy are unlikely to be fully effective in the UK context. It also suggests a need for national policy aimed at improving biomedical innovation to be sensitive to the different ways of organizing innovation identified here.

While our findings echoed previous work in suggesting that the UK context is generally less supportive of interactive biomedical innovation (Owen-Smith et al. 2002), they indicated further that US advantage is derived mainly from superior integrative capabilities. Broadly speaking, multidisciplinary training, career development, and opportunities for career mobility available in the United States—especially within biotechnology-intensive regions such as Boston—could be said to result in the 'bonding' of different professional and occupational practices and 'hybridization' of knowledge domains, while in the United Kingdom the demarcation of professional and occupational practices remain strongly entrenched. Since knowledge sticks at boundaries of practice (Carlile 2004), this would make interactive innovation—especially of the kind seen in Quadrant IV—particularly challenging in the UK context and, therefore, places more emphasis on developing, at project level, mechanisms of the kind found in our research (Table 8.1).

Where previous work has focused on knowledge flows and knowledge transfer in relation to interactive innovation and network building (e.g. Owen-Smith and Powell 2004), our study suggests that political and normative concerns were equally, if not more, important in terms of mobilizing interactive innovation. Such mechanisms as developing credibility (e.g. with investors), aligning interests, symbolic figureheads, and product magnets are arguably more concerned with mobilizing commitment, engagement, and identity than with 'transferring knowledge' per se (at least, if 'knowledge' is treated as extant from social relationships). Assessments of the validity of knowledge (e.g. for investment) were frequently based on these mechanisms as proxy indicators, rather than on the science itself (Zider 1998). Yet, most policy initiatives aimed at encouraging interactive innovation (e.g. technology transfer, network initiatives, joint patenting, etc.) focus on knowledge flows/knowledge transfer between public and private organizations. In the UK life sciences these include, for example, dedicated programmes and 'centres of excellence' for research in biomedical science and genomics; regional development initiatives aimed at fostering biotechnology clusters; incentives for biotechnology start-ups; activities for university technology transfer; collaborative projects (e.g. EU framework funding); and life science networks (e.g. industry, academic, and clinical networks). Many of these initiatives are premised on the idea that providing mechanisms to bridge academic science, industry, and clinical practice will speed the transfer of new discoveries, produced in academe, into commercially viable and clinically accepted products and treatments.

Our study suggests, however, that the effects of these initiatives may be limited if attention is not also given to the normative mechanisms highlighted. In the UK context—where scientific, clinical, and commercial interests, and careers and work practices are more clearly demarcated—these latter, normative concerns become even more central than in the United States, where the 'bonding' of scientific, clinical, and commercial values is more acceptable. To use a construction metaphor, in the United Kingdom, building bridges to promote knowledge flows between academic, commercial, and clinical organizations is difficult because the ends of the bridge are substantively different.

Our research has highlighted, further, potentially perverse effects of, supposedly supportive, policy initiatives for knowledge transfer (Robertson 2007). For example, the UK Genetics Knowledge Parks—also a central case in our study—was a major policy initiative in the United Kingdom specifically aimed at interactive innovation by funding six regionally based 'Parks' where local hospitals, universities, and industries would collaborate in research and translational activity. This case highlighted the unintended effects of such policy, for example, in the disruption it caused to existing, largely informal, collaborations in the genetics community and the encouragement of 'knowledge protectionism' via competition for funding and the regional basing of the initiative (Robertson 2007). Moreover, while government rhetoric behind the initiative was, at least outwardly, centred on the 'Knowledge Economy' and a 'Mode 2' ideology (Nowotny, Scott, and Gibbons 2001), the heavily politicized practices of policy makers, and the government departments involved in managing the initiative (the Department of Health and the Department of Trade and Industry), were underpinned by a characteristically 'Mode 1' approach and traditional linear thinking on the separation between research, on the one hand, and commercial/clinical application, on the other. Government policies aimed at helping academic scientists to switch to industry careers (e.g. by starting up businesses) or university policies that allow academics to engage in a specified number of days' consultancy 'outside' of their academic work, similarly, may perversely serve to reinforce the fundamental gap between academic and commercial values and career interests. More important in the UK context might be to develop initiatives and incentives (e.g. scientific advisory boards, Ph.D. secondments) that allow scientists to remain in their institutions doing the science but which encourage 'strategic opportunism' to become a legitimate part of academic practice (Mallon, Duberley, and Cohen 2005).

Finally, our cases provided insights into processes of project organization and management of interactive innovation (see Newell et al. 2007). Thus, early development biomedical innovation projects typically entail a portfolio of subprojects (e.g. for clinical trials, manufacturing, and business planning) where outcomes are unknown and, to a large extent, unknowable (Dougherty 2007). In this context, traditional project management techniques (focusing on single projects with plans and goals relatively well known in advance) are not all that helpful. Rather, closer attention needs to be paid to the development of, what might be termed, network capabilities—i.e. to manage interdependencies across projects, and to develop reciprocal collaborative relationships, across projects distributed in terms of organizations, timeframes, and geographical location, and to find ways of overcoming the 'knowledge protectionism' reinforced by the IP regime within the sector as whole.

Acknowledgements

We would like to acknowledge Miriam Mendes and Dr Markus Perkmann for their contributions to the early phases of this research. This research was jointly funded by the Economic and Social Research Council and the Engineering and Physical Sciences Research Council (under the Warwick Innovative Manufacturing Research Centre).

References

Abbott, A. (1988). *The System of Professions*. Chicago: University of Chicago Press.
ABPI (2006). 'Contribution of the Pharma-Related Business Activity to the Scottish Economy'. *APBI* Scotland, July.
Aldrich, H. (2000). *Organizations Evolving*. London: Sage.

Alter, C., and Hage, J. (1993). *Organizations Working Together*. Newbury Park, Calif.: Sage.

Alvesson, M., and Skoldberg, K. (2000). *Reflexive Methodology: New Vistas for Qualitative Research*. London: Sage Publications.

Bresnen, M., Goussevskaia, A., Newell, S., Obembe, A., Robertson, M., and Swan, J. (2006). 'Bonding or Bridging for New Knowledge Production? Exploring Practices, Organization and Institutionalization in Biomedical Innovation', 22nd European Group on Organization Studies Colloquium, University of Bergen, Norway, 4–6 July.

Brown, J. S., and Duguid, P. (2001). 'Knowledge and Organization: A Social-Practice Perspective'. *Organization Science*, 12/2: 198–213.

Carlile, P. (2002). 'A Pragmatic View of Knowledge and Boundaries: Boundary Objects in New Product Development'. *Organization Science*, 13: 442–55.

—— (2004). 'Transferring, Translating, and Transforming: An Integrative Framework for Managing Knowledge across Boundaries'. *Organization Science*, 5/5: 555–68.

Carlsson, B. (ed.) (2002). *Technological Systems in the Bio Industries: An International Study*. Boston: Kluwer Academic Publishers.

Casper, S., and Kettler, H. (2001). 'National Institutional Frameworks and the Hybridization of Entrepreneurial Business Models: The German and UK Biotechnology Sectors'. *Industry and Innovation*, 8: 5–30.

—— and Murray, F. (2005). 'Exchange under Conflicting Institutional Logics: Commerce and Science in the World of Population Genetics'. Unpublished manuscript.

—— and van Waarden, F. (eds.) (2005). *Innovation and Institutions: A Multidisciplinary Review of the Study of Innovation Systems*. New Horizons of the Economics of Innovation Series. Cheltenham: Edward Elgar Publishing.

Christensen, C. M. (2000). *The Innovator's Dilemma*. New York: Harper Business.

Clark, P. (1987). *Anglo-American Innovation*. New York: De Gruyter.

—— (2000). *Organizations in Action: Competition between Contexts*. London: Routledge.

CMR International (2006). *Centre for Medical Research International R&D Compendium*.

Coombs, R., Harvey, M., and Tether, B. S. (2003). 'Analyzing Distributed Processes of Provision and Innovation'. *Industrial and Corporate Change*, 12/6: 1125–55.

Dodgson, M., Gann, D., and Salter, A. (2004). 'Innovation Technology: Exploring the Impact of Simulations on the Innovation Process'. DRUID Summer Conference. Industrial Dynamics, Innovation and Development, Helsingore, Denmark.

Dopson, S. (2005). 'The Diffusion of Medical Innovations: Can Configurational Sociology Contribute?' *Organization Studies*, 26/8: 1125–44.

Dougherty, D. (2007). 'Trapped in the 20th Century? Why Models of Organizational Learning, Knowledge, and Capabilities Do Not Fit Bio-Pharmaceuticals, and What to Do About That'. *Management Learning* (in press).

Drazin, R. (1990). 'Professionals and Innovation: Structural-Functional Versus Radical-Structural Perspectives'. *Journal of Management Studies*, 27/3: 245–63.

DTI (2005). *Comparative Statistics for the UK, European and US Biotechnology Sectors.* UK Department of Trade and Industry.

Gittell, J. H., and Weiss, L. (2004). 'Coordination Networks within and across Organizations: A Multi-Level Framework'. *Journal of Management Studies,* 41/1: 127–53.

Goussevskaia, A., Newell, S., Swan, J., and Bresnen, M. (2007). 'Commmercialisation of Breakthrough Biomedical Innovation: The Emergence of the Structural Tissue Engineering Sector'. Working paper, IKON, University of Warwick.

Grabher, G. (2002). 'The Project Ecology of Advertising: Tasks, Talents and Teams'. *Regional Studies,* 36/3: 245–62.

Hall, P. A., and Solskice, D. (eds.) (2001). *Varieties of Capitalism: The Institutional Foundations of Comparative Advantage.* Oxford: Oxford University Press.

Hardy, C., Phillips, N., and Lawrence, T. (2003). 'Resources, Knowledge and Influence: The Organizational Effects of Interorganizational Collaboration'. *Journal of Management Studies,* 40/2: 321–46.

Harrison, S., Moran, M., and Wood, B. (2002). 'Policy Emergence and Policy Convergance: The Case of "Scientific-Bureaucratic Medicine" in the United Sates and United Kingdom'. *British Journal of Politics and International Relations,* 4/1: 1–24.

Knorr-Cetina, K. (1999). *Epistemic Cultures: How the Sciences Make Knowledge.* Cambridge, Mass.: Harvard University Press.

Lam, A. (1997). 'Embedded Firms, Embedded Knowledge: Problems of Collaboration and Knowledge Transfer in Global Cooperative Ventures'. *Organization Studies,* 18/6: 973–96.

Lockett, A., Murray, G., and Wright, M. (2002). 'Do UK Venture Capitalists *Still* Have a Bias against Investment in New Technology Firms?'. *Research Policy,* 31: 1009–30.

McMillan, G. S., Narin, F., and Deeds, D. (2000). 'An Analysis of the Critical Role of Public Science in Innovation: The Case of Biotechnology'. *Research Policy,* 29: 1–8.

Mallon, M., Duberley, J., and Cohen, L. (2005). 'Careers in Public Sector Science: Orientations and Implications'. *R&D Management,* 35/4: 395–407.

Manigart, S., De Waele, K., Wright, M., Robbie, K., Desbrieres, P., Sapienza, H., and Beekman, A. (2000). 'Venture Capitalists, Investment Appraisal and Accounting Information: A Comparative Study of the USA, UK, France, Belgium and Holland'. *European Financial Management,* 6/3: 389–403.

Massey, D., Quintas, P., and Wield, D. (1992). *High Tech Fantasies: Science Parks in Society, Science and Space.* London: Routledge.

Miles, M. B., and Huberman, A. M. (1994). *Qualitative Data Analysis.* Cambridge: Cambridge University Press.

Murray, F. (2002). 'Innovation as Co-Evolution of Scientific and Technological Networks: Exploring Tissue Engineering' *Research Policy,* 31: 1389–403.

Nelson, R. (ed.) (1993). *National Innovation Systems: A Comparative Analysis.* New York: Oxford University Press.

Nester, W. (1997). *American Industrial Policy: Free or Managed Markets*. London: Macmillan.

Newell, S., Goussevskaia, A., Swan, J., Robertson, M., Bresnen, M., and Obembe, A. (2007). 'Managing Interdependencies in Interactive Project Contexts: The Case of Biomedical Innovation'. Working paper, IKON, University of Warwick.

Nowotny, H., Scott, P., and Gibbons, M. (2001). *Re-Thinking Science: Knowledge and the Public in an Age of Uncertainty*. Cambridge: Polity.

NVCA (2002). National Venture Capital Association / PricewaterhouseCoopers MoneyTree Survey.

Owen-Smith, J. (2003). 'From Separate Systems to a Hybrid Order: Accumulative Advantage across Public and Private Science at Research One Universities'. *Research Policy*, 32: 1081–104.

—— and Powell, W. W. (2004). 'Knowledge Networks as Channels and Conduits: The Effects of Spillovers in the Boston Biotechnology Community'. *Organization Science*, 15/1: 5–22.

—— Riccaboni, M., Pammolli, F., and Powell, W. (2002). 'A Comparison of US and European University–Industry Relations in the Life Sciences'. *Management Science*, 48/1: 24–43.

Pettigrew, A. M. (1990). 'Longitudinal Field Research on Change: Theory and Practice'. *Organization Science*, 1/3: 267–92.

Pisano, G. (2006). 'Can Science Be a Business? Lessons from Biotech'. *Harvard Business Review*, October: 114–25.

Pittaway, L., Robertson, M., Munir, K., Denyer, D., and Neely, A. (2004). 'Networking and Innovation: A Systematic Review of the Evidence'. *International Journal of Management Reviews*, 5–6/3–4: 137–69.

Powell, W., Koput, W., and Smith-Doerr, L. (1996). 'Interorganizational Collaboration and the Locus of Innovation: Networks of Learning in Biotechnology'. *Administrative Science Quarterly*, 41/1: 116–30.

Rasmussen, B. (2005). 'Pharmaceutical Industry Project'. Working Paper Series, Centre for Strategic Economic Studies, Victoria University of Technology, February.

Relman, S. (1980). 'The New Medical Industrial Complex'. *New England Journal of Medicine*, 303: 963–70.

Robertson, M. (2007). 'Translating Breakthroughs in Genetics into Biomedical Innovation: The Case of UK Genetic Knowledge Parks'. *Technology Analysis and Strategic Management* (forthcoming).

—— Goussevskaia, A., Swan, J., Obembe, A., and Bresnen, M. (2006). 'The Triple Helix Unravelled: The Development of Biomedical Innovations in the US and UK'. Academy of Management Conference, Atlanta.

Rothwell, R. (1994). 'Towards the Fifth Generation Innovation Process'. *International Marketing Review*, 11: 7–31.

Saunders, M., Lewis, P., and Thornhill, A. (2000). *Research Methods for Business Students*. Harlow: FT Prentice Hall.

Stake, R. E. (1995). 'Case Studies', in N. K. Denzin and Y. S. Lincoln (eds.), *Handbook of Qualitative Research*. Thousand Oaks, Calif.: Sage.

Swan, J., and Scarbrough, H. (2005). 'The Politics of Networked Innovation'. *Human Relations*, 58/7: 913–43.

—— Bresnen, M., Newell, S., and Robertson, M. (2004). 'The Object of Knowledge: The Role of Objects in Interactive Innovation'. European Group on Organization Studies Colloquium, Lubliana, July.

—— Goussevskaia, A., Newell, S., Robertson, M., Bresnen, M., and Obembe, A. (2007a). 'Modes of Organizing Biomedical Innovation in the UK and US and the Role of Integrative and Relational Capabilities'. *Research Policy*, 36/4 (forthcoming).

—— Newell, S., Robertson, M., Goussevskaia, A., and Bresnen, M. (2007b). 'The Role of Institutional Differences in Biomedical Innovation Processes: A Comparison of the UK and US'. *International Journal of Healthcare Technology and Management*, 8/3: 333–53.

Tsoukas, H., and Vladimirou, E. (2001). 'What Is Organizational Knowledge?' *Journal of Management Studies*, 38/7: 973–93.

Tylecote, A. (1999). *Corporate Governance and Product Innovation: A Critical Review of the Literature*. EU Commission Report SOE1-CT98-1113.

Whitley, R. (2000). 'The Institutional Structuring of Innovation Strategies: Business Systems, Firm Types and Patterns of Technical Change in Different Market Economies'. *Organization Studies*, 21/5: 855–86.

Zider, B. (1998). 'How Venture Capital Works'. *Harvard Business Review*, 76/6: 131–9.

Zucker, L., Darby, M., and Brewer, M. (1998). 'Intellectual Capital and the Birth of US Biotechnology Enterprises'. *American Economic Review*, 88: 290–306.

9

Managing Knowledge Representation in Design

Jennifer Whyte, Boris Ewenstein, Mike Hales, and Joe Tidd

Introduction

Today's companies have extensive data sets at their fingertips, but face problems making sense of and using them in their knowledge work. In board rooms, executives are seen wracking their memories and jotting fragmented ideas on whiteboards. Yet in much of the literature, knowledge is seen as something that organizations can capture, codify, and transfer. From the perspective taken in this literature, digital and physical archives are seen as good and sufficient mechanisms for collecting, storing, and accessing knowledge within organizations. The limitation to such a perspective is highlighted both by empirical observations of practice in organizations and by theoretical work on organizational knowledge and learning. Knowledge can never be fully codified within organizations: there are both tacit and codified aspects to all knowledge (Tsoukas 1996).

Thus, from a 'practice-based' perspective, knowledge is understood as emergent; it is developed through interactions between people and objects (Knorr Cetina 1999; Gherardi and Nicolini 2000). Our work builds on this practice-based perspective, focusing on the role of a particular class of objects—visual representations. These have particular characteristics as objects, as they are made to convey meaning. According to Henderson (1999), they provide a 'holding ground' for different types of practitioner knowledge and are often changed and evolved as knowledge develops. Yet we know relatively little about the practices with and around visual materials in organizations.

In particular, questions remain about the role that interactions with visual representations play in the evolution of business knowledge. How are pictures and other images used in knowledge work within firms? How are they shared and changed as knowledge evolves? What motivates their use in the evolution of knowledge? In other fields of research, patterns of interactions with visual representations have been studied. For example, in psychology, drawing has been studied in relation to childhood development and learning (e.g. Van Sommers 1984); and in sociology, visual languages are discussed in relation to the norms of professional groups (e.g. Goodwin 2000). However, management and organization scholars tend to prioritize analysis of linguistic discourses, and so there is much work to be done to understand non-verbal and aesthetic modes of reasoning in organizations.

Design is an area of business in which knowledge is deliberately evolved, and hence it provides an interesting context in which to explore questions about knowledge work that involves interactions with objects. The working methods of designers were the focus of a classic study of professionals' modes of reflective practice. Schön (1982, 1983) describes the 'conversation with materials' that occurs when an architectural student and her tutor interact around a sketch. However, a limitation of the case that Schön analyses is its location in a university design studio. The findings are extrapolated to, rather than grounded in, professional practice. Subsequent work has extensively explored design activities in relatively artificial contexts, such as the laboratory or university design studio. This work has advantages in terms of isolating particular phenomena and in providing useful hypotheses to guide empirical research, but it has limitations in terms of developing an understanding of knowledge work through design activities within organizations.

We conducted a detailed study of visual practices in two contrasting design settings: an architectural practice and a high-tech equipment manufacturer. The study found and explored different rhythms of visual practice in each of the settings (Whyte et al. 2007). In this chapter we extend our analysis to explore *why* visual materials were used in the dynamic business processes associated with knowledge work. We draw on the existing work in organizational knowledge and learning and on the wider literatures across psychology, management, sociology, and design. Through ongoing review of the literatures relating to visual representation and learning, we developed a conceptual model that guided the empirical study and data analysis. It is shown schematically in Figure 9.1. The literature suggests three different motivations for dynamically changing and updating visual representations in the evolution of business

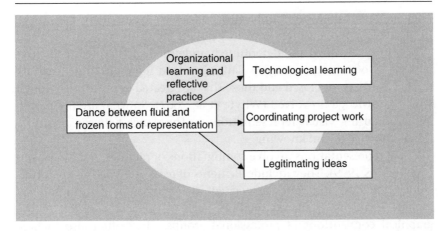

Fig. 9.1. Motivations for using visual representations in the evolution of business knowledge

knowledge: (1) to learn about new technology; (2) to coordinate the work of project teams; and (3) to legitimate new ideas across wider stakeholder groups. In the model we propose that all of these motivations are important in the evolution of business knowledge.

Context for the research

From the practice-based perspective, from which we start, the context in which knowledge is produced is seen as important. All knowledge is understood to have aspects that are tacitly understood as well as aspects that are codified (Tsoukas 1996). These tacit aspects, which were discussed at length by Polanyi (1967 [1983]), include the ability to decode and interpret visual and verbal discourses. Where tacit knowledge is missing, particular discourses become incomprehensible. The metaphor of a dance is used to convey the movement between knowledge and knowing that generates new ideas (Cook and Brown 1999). We have used and extended this metaphor in our work, which also explores the dance between frozen and unfrozen representations in knowledge work. This metaphor of a dance draws attention to the ways in which uncertainty, ignorance, and ambiguity coexist with knowledge within firms.

What is known and what is left uncertain are understood as evolving together. Austin and Darsø (2006) explicate the concept of 'closure', describing it as a point of convergence that happens once or repeatedly.

They suggest that closure can be either a forced closure or crystallization. In the evolution of business knowledge, there are shifts between open and closed, undetermined and determined, undefined and defined. These can be seen as occurring through a dance between representations that are treated as frozen or closed and those that are treated as unfrozen through which knowledge is evolved (Whyte et al. 2007). So what are the motivations for using visual representations in the dance between organizational knowledge and knowing.

Visual representations involve combinations of pictures, notations, and texts (Elkins 1999). They include elements of *pictures* involving the forms, colours, shades, and tones associated with photos or paintings. They include *notations* or shared symbols, such as musical notation or the graphical conventions of professional groups. They often also include *writing* or the representation of a spoken language. Elements of pictures, notations, and writing are never isolated or pure but always in combination. In work on maps and plans, processes of representation and interpretation have been described variously as acts of knowledge construction (Macheachren 1995) or as complex forms of reasoning (Bosselmann 1999). But what might this mean? How might this work? In the following subsections, we explore the motivations for the use of visual materials that we derived from our analysis of the literatures.

Technological learning

Visual representations can be useful tools for problem solving. Herbert Simon argues that: 'solving a problem simply means representing it so as to make the solution transparent' (Simon 1969: 132). A good representation is parsimonious, focusing attention on the overall structure of the task it is being used for (Scaife and Rogers 1996), rather than seeking to replicate the product or process in all its aspects. The process of visual representation directs attention, making certain information explicit at the expense of information that is pushed into the background and may be quite hard to recover (Marr 1982: 21). Hence the act of visual representation is seen to play a critical role in decomposing and analysing problems and revealing solutions.

At the most basic level, there is substantial evidence in the literatures to suggest that visual representation is important as a tool in individual learning. It reduces the amount that needs to be held in short-term or working memory to accomplish problem-solving tasks (Larkin and Simon 1987; Scaife and Rogers 1996). When people try to solve complex and unfamiliar problems in their heads, they may find themselves forgetting things that are relevant to the task. External representations provide a 'holding ground' (Henderson 1999) for this information. They have been described as 'disciplining' the mind (Latour 1986, 1987; Lynch and Woolgar 1990) and can be considered as tools for thinking.

Designers and engineers are found to make extensive use of visual representations in practice (Ferguson 1993; Bucciarelli 1994; Henderson 1999). Ideas are often generated and then developed through the use of visual media. Henderson (1999) argues that they support non-verbal reasoning, individual inquiry and problem solving, interactive communication, and group thinking as a form of distributed cognition. However, recent research on design challenges ideas of design as problem solving (e.g. Hatchuel 2002). Thus, we may see visual representations used in problem finding as well as problem solving (e.g. Oxman 2002). Particular types of media and representations allow for different types of thinking, thus Goel (2000) argues that sketching supports design cognition in ways that more finite and precise representations cannot. Such representations allow rapid transitions between focused reasoning and free association (McCullough 1998: 109).

Based on the understandings in these literatures, we approached our data with interest in uses of visual representations in the evolution of business knowledge informed by research on problem finding and problem solving.

Coordinating project teams

The literatures suggest that visual representations also play a role in knowledge development and problem solving across a wider project team. The development of a shared frame of reference to coordinate work across a team has been described in organizational theory, social psychology, and sociology literatures, through concepts such as *collective mind* (Weick and Roberts 1993), *inter-work* (Millar et al. 1997), and *communities of practice* (Brown and Duguid 1991; Lave and Wenger 1990). In these studies, a social formation such as a project team, a functional division, or a face-to-face community of practitioners develops a shared frame of reference. This comprises shared norms and values, perspectives, methodologies, and goals.

At the most general level, distinctive modes of visual representation shape common methods of depiction as well as ways of seeing. Goodwin (1994) describes the development of shared visual practice as the crystallization of 'professional vision'. This is part and parcel of the formation of a *professional habitus* (Bourdieu 1990); for example, that of engineers, with its distinct norms, values, heuristics, myths, aesthetics, and visual culture.

In the context of projects, working with a shared set of visual representations also helps to establish a somewhat unified view across the team. In the context of scientific practice, Latour (1986) has conceptualized circulating visual representations as 'inscription devices'. Distributed to different actors, the inscription establishes a normative vision and thereby a preferred understanding of the object of knowledge—be it a scientific proposition or a product in development. Different stakeholders are then themselves *inscribed* into a shared frame of reference. Motivating different actors to subscribe to a dominant vision involves the exercise of power. We will discuss the relationship between visual representation and power in the next section. Suffice it to note at this stage that visual representations in circulation can serve to establish shared understanding, but this can be a process of negotiation that involves struggle and resistance as well as buy-in and support.

Visual representations allow for bridges to be built across functional or disciplinary boundaries because they can be interpreted in a tightly focused way by specialists, while being simultaneously readable by generalists. Thus, a single representation can be interpreted by different stakeholders in different ways. Meanings are not fixed but shifting (Barthes 1975; Eco 1984). The term *boundary object* draws attention to the role of objects such as visual representations in mediating boundaries. It was originally introduced by Star and Griesemer (1989) to describe the various repositories, ideal types, coincident boundaries, and standardized forms that assist communication in museum work and has been used widely since then to look at the integration of cross-disciplinary knowledge in new product development through interactions with software (D'Adderio 2001, 2003) and project management tools and timelines (Yakura 2002; Sapsed and Salter 2004). Our understanding of visual representations as distinct boundary objects has been developed in particular in the area of computer-supported collaborative work (Eckert and Boujut 2003; Schmidt and Wagner 2003). Sketches, diagrams, plans, and sections can involve different implications for beholders, depending on their position and agenda. Ambiguous signs are interpreted differently as the beholder must complete the meaning of the image, and multiple layers of signification carry different implications for different actors. In multi-functional teams, elements of visual representations are differently pertinent to different actors (Prieto 1975). The input of a number of actors can thus be mobilized or conscripted through the representation (Henderson 1999). Consequently, it becomes a holding ground for multiple forms of knowledge.

Thus, visual representations focus different forms of expertise upon certain aspects of a developing design. In very practical terms, then, the use and exchange of visual materials is a key mechanism through which collaboration in innovation is managed. As noted above, this process can involve struggle and resistance, wherein boundary objects appear not just as 'bridges and anchors' but also as 'barriers and mazes' (Oswick and Robertson 2005).

Legitimating new ideas

As visual representations are used within the wider networks associated with developing new technologies, the literatures suggest that they become important in the struggles and resistances around developing the legitimacy of new ideas. Technological change is enmeshed in the emergence of new fields and the transformation of existing fields (DiMaggio 1991) and the reputation and ultimately innovative success of a firm is linked to its ability to establish its legitimacy in the field (Rao 1994).

At the micro-sociological level, practices of visual representation are important in this process of aligning a wider network of stakeholders and interest groups and enlisting support. There are many examples of the use of visual representations in industrial contexts—to establish legitimacy with regulators, end users, stakeholder groups, standards organizations, and so on. For example, Dodgson et al. (forthcoming) point to the importance of a visual simulation of crowds exiting in case of fire. The visualization of a workable idea played a key part in convincing regulators to accept a design solution that is outside the established regulations and rules. New ideas are thus literally legitimated.

Latour describes such legitimation processes and highlights the role of visual representations, which are characterized by a number of distinct properties: they are seen to be mobile, immutable, flat, at a scale that is modifiable, reproducible, can be recombined, superimposed, integrated with other texts, and merged with geometry. Both writing and imaging are seen as particularly important, as they can muster on the spot well-aligned and faithful allies. Latour describes the importance of images and inscriptions as:

The unique advantage they give in the rhetorical or polemical situation. 'You doubt of what I say? I'll show you.' And, without moving more than a few inches, I unfold in front of your eyes figures, diagrams, plates, texts, silhouettes and then and there present things that are far away and with which some sort of two way connection has now been established. (1986: 14)

Latour's work (1986) allows us to see the relationship between visual representation and the negotiation of power within industrial contexts. Dominant ways of seeing can be constructed through the circulation of representations across different contexts. Representation is never a neutral process of depicting. How new technologies are visualized influences decision makers and end users and by extension those involved in the design process. As Henderson (1999) reminds us, visual representations are not only devices for communal sharing of ideas but are also a ground for design conflict and company politics, precisely because they facilitate the social organization of workers, the work process, and the concepts that workers develop to produce a collective product.

Visual representations in circulation can serve to establish dominant ideas about the object of design. With increased circulation, the content depicted can become standardized and thereby legitimated. Social and material reality is constructed through the processes of making certain ideas visible at the expense of others which are effaced. More specifically, this process works through directing and shaping the gaze. Power is exercised by shaping what to look at and how to see (Fyfe and Law 1988). Goodwin describes professional vision as 'socially organized ways of seeing and understanding events that are answerable to the distinctive interests of a particular group' (1994: 606). In technology development, sketches, plans, and 3D models constrain the way new products are viewed and understood, de facto exercising power.

Empirical study

We conducted an in-depth empirical study of the evolution of knowledge through interaction with visual representations within two industrial settings—'HighTech' the design department of a major capital goods equipment manufacturer and Edward Cullinan Architects (ECA), a professional services firm offering architectural design services.

Research setting

The settings for our study were chosen for theoretical reasons: they provide good test-beds for developing understandings of organizational knowledge and knowing. They are both contexts in which designers, engineers, and managers work to evolve knowledge. There are profound differences between the two settings, allowing us to compare and contrast the findings and seek more fundamental patterns.

Edward Cullinan Architects is a professional service firm that offers architectural design services in the construction sector. Since its foundation in 1965, it has been a major contributor to the development of post-war British architecture. As such, the practice constitutes a productive context for the exploration of knowledge work. There is a well-established culture within ECA that puts value on the collective. Unusually for a commercial organization, it is a partnership in which every member of staff acts as a partner. The collective ethos of the practice is manifest in its office building, which is housed in an old warehouse in North London. While the ground floor of the building houses the meeting rooms and a kitchen, there is a single, open, office space upstairs in which all members of staff work. Bays within this space provide a home for the various project teams.

'HighTech' is the pseudonym that we use for an international equipment supplier. It operates in an intensely competitive global market making process plant for semiconductor manufacture, based on sophisticated capabilities in applied physics. It has a constantly evolving base of process-technology products, advanced, proprietary knowledges in applied physics and engineering, and ongoing relationships with primary customers. The average in-service life of new products is nine months. Our study in HighTech examines work practice associated with new product development in one division of this firm. It covers activities that may be seen as contained within 'conceptual design', and thus spans the transition from exploratory research and market feedback, through engineering and product conceptualization, to commitment of assets for prototype manufacture and release of beta-status products.

Data collection and data analysis

In ECA, fieldwork began with pilot work in February 2004, with the most intensive work taking place between June and October 2004. In HighTech, initial work was in April 2004, with the most intensive fieldwork between September 2004 and January 2005. Our main forms of engagements within the two industrial settings included:

1. *Group meetings*: Within both organizations, we had set-up, interim review, and feedback meetings. These involved a range of stakeholders

including project designers, managers, and others. At each of these meetings we had at least three researchers present, making them key events in terms of our data collection at each site. They lasted two hours and provided opportunities for us to develop and share an overview of how work is coordinated across the organizations and, as the research progressed, to discuss our emerging understandings.

2. *Tracking design projects*: In each site we tracked progress on two design projects over a six-month period through non-participant observation. In both instances, one project became a major focus during the field-work. Through the observational work at the sites, the data collection exercise collated:

   - *Photographs*: Overall we took 1,392 digital photographs of activities across the two sites. These include photographs of project and client meetings, and of individual work with visual materials.

   - *Field notebooks*: Each researcher kept a diary of their time in the field, jotting down observations alongside the date and time. At times engineers and designers took the notebooks and drew directly into them.

   - *Transcripts*: Overall we had thirty-four hours of taped materials, which ranged from eight-minute ad-hoc conversations during fieldwork to two-hour transcripts of team meetings and semi-structured interviews.

   - *Collected documents*: We collected documents in digital and hard-copy formats. At HighTech we had full access to the server and were able to browse all digital documents related to the new product development project.

3. *Attending project and client meetings and company events*: We attended a number of project meetings on each project, and at ECA we were also present at client meetings.

4. *Semi-structured interviews and informal discussions*: Both in the office and at the local pub, we had a number of semi-structured interviews and informal discussions with the research participants, either one-to-one and in small groups.

5. *Materials about the organizations*: Where appropriate, we gathered additional information about the projects studied using the Internet and other published materials. At ECA, detailed information was available as work is frequently described in the architectural press and has been written up in a number of monographs (Edward Cullinan Architects 1984; Powell 1995; Hale 2005).

Each researcher separately coded data, and we compared and contrasted the coding categories used and our emerging findings. Text-based data from both sites was entered into a software analysis package so that it could be compared and contrasted. When key analytic topics—such as the open and closed nature of representations—emerged, then we returned to the data and wrote narratives about these in each setting, to facilitate comparison across the settings and to allow all of the researchers to engage in the interpretation and analysis across the sites. During the analysis phase, we found the digital photographs particularly useful as these were powerful reminders of organizational life in the settings and they allowed us to compare and contrast visual practices across the two sites. We continued to read the existing literatures while analysing our data, and where we felt unable to explain our observations adequately, we returned to the site and had further conversations with participants. As much of the work that we observed is nonverbal, expert knowledge work, the interviews and discussions were also extremely important in giving us access to the thought processes of participants and allowing us to interpret what we had seen correctly.

Findings

Overall, our data support the conceptual model and suggest ways in which technological learning, coordinating project work, and legitimating ideas motivate and shape the visual practices associated with the evolution of business knowledge in these two settings. These motivations are evident in the conversations and interactions with and around various forms of visual materials, through which engineers and designers hold stable or change what is known within the organization. In each setting there is a distinctive aesthetic culture, with different norms of practice, and the degree and nature of empirical support for each of the motivations varies across the two settings. In Table 9.1 we summarize illustrative data from the field notes, interview transcripts, and documentation collected in the field. This is interpreted in the following sections, alongside photographs of representations and practices.

TECHNOLOGICAL LEARNING

In both ECA and HighTech, we observe how visual practices were used to evolve the understanding of, and change the design of, the things that are represented. Representations are used in the synthesis of old and new, incorporating learning from previous projects and from manufacturing and use. In ECA the focus of representation is the physical and spatial

Table 9.1. *Illustrative evidence from field notes, interviews, and documents supporting the three motivations for the use of visual representations*

	Edward Cullinan Architects	HighTech
Technological learning: Synthesis of old and new, through the incorporation of learning from previous projects; from manufacturing and use	'You can't draw up all the parameters and use that as your solution, you have to start with a whole proposition . . . you can't just look at a site and say, oh, that's so big, you actually have to draw it, and walk it and get to know it, in order to understand what sort-of building you can put in it.' (Architect, interview, 10 December 2004) 'Or vacate a lot of this stuff and put it in here and move that into there [pointing to drawing]. I mean all of that is quite easy for us to produce figures on, and then they [the client] can look at it.' (Project architect, design team meeting, 22 June 2004) 'So during Stage C the work of the feasibility stage was expanded upon, but refinement of the broad brush moves began in parallel. A critical refinement has been to develop the footprint and zoning diagrams of the east wing into a set of architectural plans . . .' (ECA Stage C report, 2004, p. 5)	'I'll send you what there is [drawings], it's not set in stone by any stretch of the imagination. But, you know, it's halfway drawn, so we could make it wider as well, we could do whatever we want.' (Teleconference transcript, 8 September 2004) 'What it [the marketing requirement specification] does is it draws a line in the sand for the engineers . . . and until you have that line in the sand, everything's variable . . . so at the moment, I mean, we basically do the best we can, and that changes weekly, so someone will come up with a new idea and we'll test it out, and then . . . ' (Interview, Materials manager, 3 February 2005) 'Now we're trying to change that, I mean you talk about tools, this came off the white board yesterday . . . we got one of their customer representatives in and, you know, if we're successful in selling their product, this is the plan. So if we can win this business, there's four systems here . . . and you know, there's gonna' be more business coming to us there . . . ' (Interview, Business Development director, 13 January 2005)
Coordinating project work: Development of a shared frame of reference; and/or coordination of diverse knowledge sets	'We're kind of playing a chess game as well. Well we have to be careful what we draw, we don't want spend too long doing work that isn't adding any value to the communication of the building. So if we start drawing big pieces of electrical wiring in great detail which are actually being built on someone else's drawing . . . ' (Interview, Project architect, 12 August 2004) *Consultation/ for specific actors' information. However, overall,*	*There is relatively little data from transcripts to support this category, as engineers at 'HighTech' tend to talk about the engineering issues, rather than their representation in drawings.* *Extensive use of project process charts to coordinate timing.*

the stage report is to be agreed and thus can be negotiated. It is thus at least somewhat unfrozen and the distinction between un/frozen is a matter of degree and situated judgement. (researcher's notes)

Circulating detailed design information to allow the work of other consultants to proceed. Example: ECA to circulate B10 balcony design for ARUP to then develop the structural engineering. (researcher's notes)

One example is the detailed work going on in B10: Manor, the kitchen manufacturers, are to update their drawings following ECA 'comment', and reissue for sign-off by the client. ECA will then produce elevation drawings showing tiling and fixing blockings. Colston, the mechanical and services engineers will then finalize service points. (researcher's notes)

Drawing reviews (of one consultant by another) are phenomena in which frozen drawings are red-lined and marked up, thereby becoming unfrozen. (researcher's notes)

Legitimating ideas: Development of reputation; negotiation of power

'A visual exploration of a potential building west of the existing buildings was used to articulate a design option that was not the main focus of previous discussions with the client-side project manager, yet which needed to be delicately raised with other senior actors on the client side.' (field notes, 8 July 2004)

The beta tool is a prototype machine, installed in full operating condition in a customer's manufacturing environment, for evaluation. As a prototype, the beta tool's job is proof of concept. Some of the major issues of product conceptualization—and also some of the most visible and significant work done by visual representations—were handled in the process of defining and achieving 'cut-in' for the beta tool, within a pre-existing setting of activities and commitments. (researcher's notes)

Projection of images for input. Digitally encoded representations are ubiquitous in HighTech. The prime example of a digitally encoded visual representation in the HighTech design setting is their CAD model; but other prominent examples include the spreadsheet model, the PowerPoint slide and a variety of alphanumeric databases. These are handled at computer workstations where normally a single person has access, and where the technique of manipulation may be esoteric (again, the CAD model is a prime example: fluency at the CAD terminal is a highly developed specialist skill). The use of digital projectors and wall projection screens opens the view of such representations to larger numbers of people; and touching and pointing are available as ways of interacting with the image. However, making marks on a screen image or a wall-projected image is not. (researcher's notes)

Managing aspirations within the organization. 'I think that chart is extremely optimistic, and really doesn't capture any like the number of tasks we've got, you know, it doesn't speak to the risk, it doesn't address the problems, it just, it doesn't assume any facts, like we've got lead times in the supply chain, apart from anything else. It doesn't, what it is, is a "What the business needs" type chart, and that's good.' (Interview, Materials manager, 3 February 2005, HighTech)

(continued)

Table 9.1. (continued)

Edward Cullinan Architects	HighTech
Eliciting buy-in and getting sign-off—Purpose of meeting: to agree content of Stage AB report with the director with a focus on the following key issues: review options for change of use to existing wings; review car park access options; review wider sites issues including impact of car park and future western extension. (field notes, 15 July 2004)	At the formal initiation of a product development programme within HighTech, the scale and scope of the eventual assessment are formally defined, key actors are identified and codified. (Observation, HighTech)
Comment, input and modification—In one episode, a stage report (A/B) is tabled by ECA so as to present different options to the director of the client organization. Around the 'frozen' representation, a narrative unfolds about possible scenarios for the site. To this the director responds and his feedback is considered and embodied in following generations of drawings. (ECA)	A lot of this activity has gone on for the last fifteen years in this business, and what we've captured now in PDP is a way of cleaning it up, and making sure that we don't send half-finished, incomplete, inadequately tested, and inadequately programme managed products out into the field and then fix them in the field to our customers dissatisfaction and to our cost. Business Development director, 13 January 2005.

Fig. 9.2. Technological learning: snapshots of everyday representations and practices in Edward Cullinan Architects

aspects of the proposed building. In HighTech the focus is predominantly on the gross margins, costs, business risks, and processes.

Figure 9.2 shows how drawings and models are particularly salient at ECA. Here the exploration of technological design problems and solutions is ubiquitous, in individual work on on-screen CAD drawings and in the work of design teams, which is characterized by sketching. Designers deliberately 'unfreeze' representations to problematize and understand the rationale behind decisions taken and to explore alternative solutions. At many of the meetings we observed, designers held tracing paper over existing drawings and sketched onto it. Through this use of tracing paper they maintain the frozen status of certain representations while at once supporting their learning and exploration of technological solutions. In one of the interviews a designer explained that 'you can't draw up all the parameters and use that as your solution, you have to start with a whole proposition.'

Figure 9.3 shows how whiteboard annotations and process maps are particularly salient in HighTech. Representations are used widely to define conceptual design problems and explore solutions with relation to gross margin and cost issues, business risk issues, and issues of legitimate process and outcome. There is also some use of representations of the physical object, but these play a minor role. Engineers share an understanding of the basic dimensions of the machine as the design family is relatively stable, and previous versions of the machine are accessible downstairs from where the designers are working. The work with representations of the physical machine takes place in small groups in the cubicles of the open plan offices as well as in solo work: zooming, sectioning, reshaping, comparing, assembling/disassembling, and otherwise manipulating 3D-CAD models on screen displays or interacting with printouts, while in conversation. The CAD designer who owns the version of the model is the hands-on operator in virtual space. When particular issues arise, printed versions of a drawing

Fig. 9.3. Technological learning: snapshots of everyday representations and practices in HighTech

may become the focus of shared learning. Figure 9.3 shows a distance being measured on a full-scale printout of a CAD drawing.

Comparing our data from across the two sites, we find that technological learning motivates the representation of design problems, with a focus on areas where knowledge is absent, ambiguous, or uncertain. Hence, the visual representations used are usually treated as fluid. They are changed, altered, and updated as the design evolves. In ECA tracing paper is used to allow for this exploration of new ideas while retaining a memory of what has gone before. Within HighTech hard copies of multiple, concurrently stored, exploratory CAD-model versions are used alongside live interaction with a model at the CAD terminal.

COORDINATING PROJECT TEAMS

Representations are also used to coordinate the work across project teams. In the early stages of design at ECA, coordination work often occurs in parallel with technological learning—project team meetings with a number of specialists may be conducted around evolving sketches and annotations on tracing paper. In HighTech the weekly project meetings are the main focus of coordination work, and actions are agreed at this meeting to be implemented later by the actors that 'own' particular issues and their related representations. Hence, at both sites representations are exchanged between participants from different epistemic communities and act as 'boundary objects' that play a role in mediating the developing knowledge. They are used in the development of a shared frame of reference; and/or coordination of diverse knowledge sets. However, the representations used and patterns of interaction are markedly different in the two sites.

Figure 9.4 shows how representations are used by ECA to coordinate work with other professionals in the project team and to discuss it with their clients. Detailed design information is circulated to allow the work of

Fig. 9.4. Coordinating project work: snapshots of everyday representations and practices in Edward Cullinan Architects

other consultants to proceed. For example in the detailed design stage of a project at ECA, the details of a balcony design were given to the engineer so that they could work on the structural engineering design. In the same project, getting shop drawings from the manufacturers of windows, kitchens, elevators, and so on allowed detail design to proceed. Freezing drawings, and the associated actions and responsibilities, is essential to move construction projects forward, and meetings with such detail drawings and at the stage of construction consist primarily in clarifying, updating, accounting for, coordinating, agreeing, negotiating, changing, and deciding actions. Even production information can become the focus of coordination work, for example, when a fax received from the civil engineer showed conflicting locations for manholes in a revision to a drainage drawing.

Figure 9.5 shows how representations are used to coordinate project work in HighTech. Though processes are more formalized at HighTech than they are at ECA, work is shared informally, as a matter of workgroup practice, with the filing of documents on the workgroup N-drive, under an ad hoc classification system. Coordination largely takes place through discussion around visual representations and other documentation in project-convened, cross-function team meetings that are scheduled weekly. As well as whiteboard sketches of timelines, PowerPoint presentations of ongoing work are projected and discussed as are images of timelines, drawn up in Microsoft Project Gantt charts.

Across the two sites, the coordination of project teams focuses the use of representations on establishing what is known and unknown across the team. Some of the representations that are used to coordinate project teams remain frozen, while others are annotated or altered as part of this

Fig. 9.5. Coordinating project work: snapshots of everyday representations and practices in HighTech

coordination process. Immutable representations are used to create shared vision for projects. For example, in ECA, a drawing of the entire site and development idea by Edward Cullinan was used to give people a shared vision and timelines are used to shape a shared sense of how the project will unfold across time.

LEGITIMATING NEW IDEAS

Another motivation for using visual representations is to legitimate new ideas. Here frozen representations are used to manage meaning and project narrative. These are used in the development of reputation, the negotiation of power, and the provision of a vision to inform and drive development. They also are used in accounting and keeping a record of the work.

In ECA, representations play a key role in legitimating new ideas. Figure 9.6 shows two images taken from stage reports. Representations mediate a complex and subtly, yet politically imbued relation with the client and other stakeholders by controlling what is and is not shown and when. In construction projects there are usually multiple stakeholders with interests in the outcome of the design work—one of the projects we studied involved planners from the council, English Heritage, local action groups, and others. These all have to be carefully managed and involved in the design process. Visual representations in a stage report are largely treated as frozen once the report is issued. Stage reports are used to establish the details of the design to date and to have a reasonably firm basis of work that can be signed off and treated as a deliverable to clients. Drafts are circulated to the director of the client organization and his input is considered before the report is finalized.

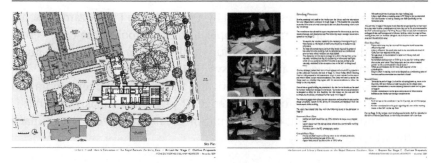

Fig. 9.6. Legitimating ideas: snapshots of everyday representations and practices in Edward Cullinan Architects

We observed a meeting to agree the content of the Stage A/B report with the director. It focused on key issues such as a review of car park access options and the impact of a car park and future western extension.

Figure 9.7 shows how HighTech representations also play a key role in legitimating new ideas. However, there is less emphasis on this than there is at ECA, and they are used in this role across functions internally within the organization, rather than with the client. They are used extensively in accounting and keeping a record of the work, and these processes are more formalized and codified than in ECA. In the final meeting of a cross-functional team to sign-off the beta release, a template is used (a Lotus Notes database and workflow model) to provide standard pro formas for documentation, and a hierarchical workflow for sign-off actions on assessment tasks. In the run-up to beta release, the PDP handbook provides references to mandatory standard metrical algorithms for product quality and to sign-off criteria (which typically

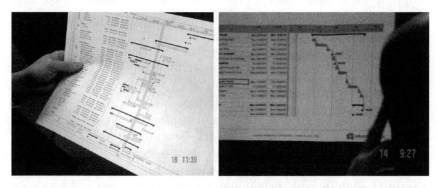

Fig. 9.7. Legitimating ideas: snapshots of everyday representations and practices in HighTech

are tied to numeric indices generated by a metric). The PDP wizard (or some other software application, for example, a software tool in the engineering domain or the manufacturing operations MRP domain) implements many of these as parameterized, computable, symbolic representations.

The legitimation of new ideas motivates the use of visual representation in the evolution of business knowledge. It puts an emphasis on what is known, and frozen forms of representation are used to give this legitimacy in the wider community.

Discussion

The use of visual representations in design highlights one type of aesthetic knowledge that comes from practitioners' sense of sight and explores the types of understandings that derive from the look of things. Other studies have explored how a range of aesthetic forms of knowledge, deriving from the look, feel, smell, taste, and sound of things play an under-recognized role in organizations (Gagliardi 1996; Strati 1999; Hancock 2005). In our work we have explored the aesthetic nature of the knowledge used in ECA and shown how practitioners subscribe to and draw on a shared aesthetic knowledge base in their everyday work, making their own aesthetic judgements in relation to it (Ewenstein and Whyte, forthcoming). This chapter focuses on the motivations for using visual materials in the evolution of business knowledge. It further contributes to our understandings of aesthetic knowledge and knowing by comparing and contrasting how aesthetic judgements are made in two design settings. Two areas that our study opens up for discussion are the relationships between visual and verbal discourses in organizations, and the contribution of visual practices to strategic decision making within organizations.

In the lived-in experiences of practitioners, visual and verbal discourses unfolded together. Although we did not set out to study the verbal discourses of the organization, they were intertwined with the visual discourse. For example, in the project-convened, cross-function team meetings at HighTech, PowerPoint displays dominated and became the focus for storytelling about the work. Other recent work has begun to explore the verbal discourses around visual materials used in designer–client interactions (Luck 2007), and we see the findings of our study contributing to this debate and highlighting its importance.

A key question for discussion is the degree to which visual practices are involved in the tactical and strategic operations of the organization. Our data suggests that visual materials and aesthetic modes of interaction may play a bigger role in strategic decision making than is usually recognized. This question is beginning to be explored in a number of strands of the literature and could be of interest to scholars who are considering managing as a form of designing (Boland and Collopy 2004), as well as to scholars interested in the aesthetic practices of the boardroom. Again this is a significant area of further research.

Conclusions

Visual materials play a role in the evolution of business knowledge. Based on the literatures, we build a theoretical model of the motivations for using visual materials and we then examine its empirical basis. We find that motivations for the use of visual representations include technological learning (where the focus is on resolving uncertainties), coordination of project work (where the focus is on establishing what is known and what is not known across the team), and legitimation of ideas (where the focus is on establishing what is known in wider networks).

This work suggests that knowledge becomes seen not so much as something that can be codified, but as something that can be *represented*, in ways that are to varying degrees ambiguous, contingent, partial, and indeterminate. Visual representations play a particular role in this dance between what is known and what is not known and are used alongside conversations and texts. Used in combination, fragments of pictures, notation, and writing allow for ambiguities in knowledge to be exposed.

This research has practical implications. As visual practices are motivated by technological learning, coordination of project work, and legitimizations of ideas, managers can evaluate whether the materials they use for these purposes are suitable. As visual materials are grossly observable, an analysis of the focus of representation can be a useful diagnostic tool for managers. Where business knowledge has not evolved at the expected pace or in the direction anticipated, it may be that the wrong drawings and images are being used to address the problems. We believe that all managers have much to learn from designers, who routinely use pictures and drawings to visualize complex sets of information.

Acknowledgements

The collaborations with both firms, Edward Cullinan Architects and HighTech, were absolutely invaluable to this research—and the authors gratefully acknowledge their contribution. In particular, we owe thanks to the professionals working on the projects studied, and to those who generously devoted their time to challenging our emerging understandings, and to explaining, clarifying, and discussing their work with us, both in formal interviews and in more informal settings over lunch and drinks.

The authors gratefully acknowledge the support of the UK's ESRC under the Evolution of Business Knowledge (EBK) programme, award no. RES-334-25-0007, and also the support of the UK's EPSRC through the Innovative Manufacturing Research Centre, BEIC, held at the Tanaka Business School, Imperial College London.

As a co-author of the original research proposal, Dr Jane Millar also contributed substantially to the genesis and early development of ideas. Professor David Gann was also an investigator on the research project and provided strategic input, particularly through his involvement in set-up and feedback meetings with Edward Cullinan Architects. We are grateful for and keen to acknowledge both of their contributions.

References

Austin, R., and Darsø, L. (2006). *A Framework for Examining the Concept of Closure in Innovation Process*. Art of Management and Organization, Krakow, 5–8 September.

Barthes, R. (1975). *S/Z*. London: Cape.

Boland, R. J., and Collopy, F. (2004). *Managing as Designing*. Stanford, Calif.: Stanford University Press.

Bosselmann, P. (1999). *Representation of Places: Reality and Realism in City Design*. Berkeley: University of California Press.

Bourdieu, P. (1990). *The Logic of Practice*. Cambridge: Polity Press.

Brown, J. S., and Duguid, P. (1991). 'Organizational Learning and Communities-of-Practice: Toward a Unified View of Working, Learning, and Innovation'. *Organizational Science*, 2/1: 40–57.

Bucciarelli, L. L. (1994). *Designing Engineers*. Cambridge, Mass.: MIT Press.

Cook, S. D. N., and Brown, J. S. (1999). 'Bridging Epistemologies: The Generative Dance between Organizational Knowledge and Organizational Knowing'. *Organization Science*, 10/4: 381–400.

D'Adderio, L. (2001). 'Crafting the Virtual Prototype: How Firms Integrate Knowledge and Capabilities across Organisational Boundaries'. *Research Policy*, 30/9: 1409–24.

D'Adderio, L. (2003). 'Configuring Software, Reconfiguring Memories: The Influence of Integrated Systems on the Reproduction of Knowledge and Routines'. *Industrial and Corporate Change*, 12/2: 321–50.

DiMaggio, P. J. (1991). 'Constructing an Organizational Field', in W. W. Powell and P. J. DiMaggio (eds.), *The New Institutionalism in Organizational Analysis*. Chicago: University of Chicago Press.

Dodgson, M., Gann, D. M., and Salter, A. (forthcoming). ' "In Case of Fire, Please Use the Elevator": Simulation Technology and Organization in Fire Engineering'. *Organization Science*.

Eckert, C., and Boujut, J.-F. (2003). 'The Role of Objects in Design Co-operation: Communication through Physical or Virtual Objects'. *Computer Supported Co-operative Work*, 12/2: 145–51.

Eco, U. (1984). *Semiotics and the Philosophy of Language*. London: Macmillan.

Edward Cullinan Architects (1984). *Edward Cullinan Architects*. London: RIBA Publications Limited.

Elkins, J. (1999). *The Domain of Images*. Ithaca, NY: Cornell University Press.

Ewenstein, B., and Whyte, J. K. (forthcoming). 'Beyond Words: Aesthetic Knowledge and Knowing in Organizational Contexts'. *Organisation Studies*.

Ferguson, E. S. (1993). *Engineering and the Mind's Eye*. Cambridge, Mass.: MIT Press.

Fyfe, G., and Law, J. (eds.) (1988). *Picturing Power: Visual Depiction and Social Relations*. London: Routledge.

Gagliardi, P. (1996). 'Exploring the Aesthetic Side of Organizational Life', in S. Clegg, C. Hardy, and W. Nord (eds.), *Handbook of Organization Studies*. London: Sage.

Gherardi, S., and Nicolini, D. (2000). 'To Transfer is to Transform: The Circulation of Safety Knowledge'. *Organization*, 7/2: 329–48.

Goel, V. (2000). 'Dissociation of Design Knowledge', in C. Eastman and W. C. Newstetter (eds.), *Knowing and Learning to Design: Cognitive Perspectives in Design Education*. Oxford: Elsevier.

Goodwin, C. (1994). 'Professional Vision'. *American Anthropologist*, 96/3: 606–33.

——(2000). 'Practices of Seeing: Visual Analysis: An Ethnomethodological Approach', in T. van Leeuwen and C. Jewitt (eds.), *Handbook of Visual Analysis*. London: Sage Publications.

Hale, J. (2005). *Ends, Middles, Beginnings*. London: Blackdog Publishing.

Hancock, P. (2005). 'Uncovering the Semiotic in Organizational Aesthetics'. *Organization*, 12/1: 29–50.

Hatchuel, A. (2002). 'Toward Design Theory and Expandable Rationality: The Unfinished Programme of Herbert Simon'. *Journal of Management and Governance*, 5/3: 260–73.

Henderson, K. (1999). *On Line and On Paper: Visual Representations, Visual Culture and Computer Graphics in Design Engineering*. Cambridge, Mass.: MIT Press.

Knorr Cetina, K. (1999). *Epistemic Cultures: How the Sciences Make Knowledge*. Cambridge, Mass.: Harvard University Press.

Larkin, J. H., and Simon, H. A. (1987). 'Why a Diagram Is (Sometimes) Worth 10,000 Words'. *Cognitive Science*, 11: 65–100.

Latour, B. (1986). 'Visualization and Cognition: Thinking with Eyes and Hands'. *Knowledge and Society: Studies in the Sociology of Culture Past and Present*, 6: 1–40.

——(1987). *Science in Action: How to Follow Scientists and Engineers through Society.* Cambridge, Mass.: Harvard University Press.

Lave, J., and Wenger, E. (1990). *Situated Learning: Legitimate Peripheral Participation.* Cambridge: Cambridge University Press.

Luck, R. (2007). 'Using Artifacts to Mediate Understanding in Design Conversations'. *Building Research and Information,* 35/1: 28–41.

Lynch, M., and Woolgar, S. (1990). *Representation in Scientific Practice.* Boston: MIT Press.

Macheachren, A. M. (1995). *How Maps Work: Representation, Visualisation and Design.* New York: Guilford Press.

Marr, D. (1982). *Vision: A Computational Investigation into the Human Representation and Processing of Visual Information.* San Francisco: Freeman.

McCullough, M. (1998). *Abstracting Craft: The Practiced Digital Hand.* Cambridge, Mass.: MIT Press.

Millar, J., Demaid, A., and Quintas, P. (1997). 'Trans-Organizational Innovation: A Framework for Research'. *Technology Analysis and Strategic Management*, 9/4: 399–418.

Oswick, C., and Robertson, M. (2005). *Boundary Objects Reconsidered: From Bridges and Anchors to Barricades and Mazes.* European Group for Organizational Studies Conference (EGOS), Berlin, 1–3 July.

Oxman, R. (2002). 'The Thinking Eye: Visual Re-cognition in Design Emergence'. *Design Studies*, 23/2: 135–64.

Polanyi, M. (1967 [1983]). *The Tacit Dimension.* New York: Doubleday.

Powell, K. (1995). *Edward Cullinan Architects.* London: Academy Editions.

Prieto, L. (1975). *Pertinence et pratique: Essai de sémiologie.* Paris: Minuit.

Rao, H. (1994). 'The Social Construction of Reputation: Certification Contests, Legitimation and the Survival of Organizations in the American Automobile Industry: 1985–1912'. *Strategic Management Journal*, 15: 29–44.

Sapsed, J., and Salter, A. J. (2004). 'Postcards from the Edge: Local Communities, Global Programs and Boundary Objects'. *Organization Studies*, 25: 1515–34.

Scaife, M., and Rogers, Y. (1996). 'External Cognition: How Do Graphical Representations Work?' *International Journal of Human-Computer Studies*, 45: 185–213.

Schmidt, K., and Wagner, I. (2003). *Ordering Practices: Coordinative Artifacts in Architectural Design and Planning.* GROUP'03: International Conference on Supporting Group Work, Sanibel Island, Florida, 9–12 November, ACM Press.

Schön, D. A. (1983). *The Reflective Practitioner: How Professionals Think in Action.* Aldershot: Basic Books.

——and Wiggins, G. (1982). 'Kinds of Seeing and their Functions in Designing'. *Design Studies*, 13/2: 135–56.

Simon, H. A. (1969). *The Sciences of the Artificial*. Cambridge, Mass.: MIT Press.

Star, S. L., and Griesemer, J. R. (1989). 'Institutional Ecology, "Translations," and Boundary Objects: Amateurs and Professionals in Berkeley's Museum of Vertebrate Zoology, 1907–1939'. *Social Studies of Science*, 19: 387–420.

Strati, A. (1999). *Organization and Aesthetics*. London: Sage.

Tsoukas, H. (1996). 'The Firm as a Distributed Knowledge System: A Constructionist Approach'. *Strategic Management Journal*, 17: 11–25.

Van Sommers, P. (1984). *Drawing and Cognition: Descriptive and Experimental Studies of Graphic Production Processes*. Cambridge: Cambridge University Press.

Weick, K. E., and Roberts, K. H. (1993). 'Collective Mind in Organizations: Heedful Interrelating on Flight Decks'. *Administrative Science Quarterly*, 38/3: 357–81.

Whyte, J. K., Ewenstein, B., Hales, M., and Tidd, J. (2007). 'Visual Practices and the Objects of Design'. *Building Research and Information*, 35/1: 18–27.

Yakura, E. K. (2002). 'Charting Time: Timelines as Temporary Boundary Objects'. *Academy of Management Journal*, 45/5: 956–70.

10

Evaluation Practices in the Commercialization of Early Stage Technology: The Role of Trust

Harry Scarbrough and Kenneth Amaeshi

Introduction

The drive for innovation is a crucial part of the evolution of business knowledge. Innovation is seen as an imperative for successful businesses, and there are many useful accounts of the way in which innovation processes can be best designed and managed (e.g. Tidd, Bessant, and Pavitt 2007). As with previous chapters, however, the distinctive contribution of the EBK perspective is to view innovation not as a discrete activity in its own right but as a process that emerges from, and is constrained by, the embedding and disembedding of knowledge within and between firms. This perspective leads us to emphasize two important features of the innovation process. First, we view that process as centring on activities and interactions that enable the exchange and integration of knowledge between different groups, some of which are located outside the focal firm. This view of innovation can be contrasted with the classic linear view of innovation, which was based on the experience of R&D product development in manufacturing. Secondly, we emphasize the interplay between the process of innovation and its surrounding social and organizational context. If we focus only on the innovation process itself, that interplay is too easily glossed over. However, it is crucial to understanding the ways in which innovation processes are both a medium for, and an outcome of, the embedding and disembedding of knowledge.

These themes are developed further in this chapter through a study of the evaluation practices that different groups apply to the exchange and integration of knowledge. Evaluation—i.e. systematic approaches to determining potential or actual value—is an especially difficult task when it comes to the novel or emergent forms of knowledge that are central to innovation processes. Put simply, it is difficult to establish whether a particular idea or a form of knowledge has any value until it is fully realized as a product or process in the marketplace. This is partly because the ultimate market for half-formed ideas is uncertain and may require significant development resources to secure. Equally, it also reflects what economists term 'appropriation risk'—that is, the risk that disclosing an idea to enable collaboration will actually allow unscrupulous individuals to steal that idea. This inhibits communication between the very groups who most need to communicate.

In reviewing the kinds of evaluation practices that have been developed to deal with these problems—ranging from so-called 'stage-gate' methods within firms to the finely honed judgements made by venture capitalists—we were keen to see, first, how such practices contributed to the exchange and integration of knowledge between groups, and, secondly, how this interacted in turn with the social and organizational context in terms of embedding and disembedding knowledge.

Context for the research

A number of recent studies have argued that innovation processes increasingly depend upon collaboration among a wide variety of groups, both inside and outside the innovating organization (Hardy et al. 2003; Powell et al. 1996). This is seen as a consequence of a number of different factors in the business environment, including the new possibilities for interorganizational collaboration created by the Internet and IT systems, together with the need for ever greater specialization in technological fields (Coombs 2003; Pittaway et al. 2004). When played out against the backcloth of globalization, these factors mean that it is neither possible nor necessary for the individual firm to retain exclusive control of the different sources of knowledge deployed within the innovation process (Walsh 2002). This has led to the rejection of the traditional R&D-centred model of innovation in favour of new models that highlight 'networked' or 'open' forms of innovation (Swan and Scarbrough 2005; Tether 2003).

Chesbrough (2003), for example, claims that firms are moving towards a more open mode of innovation, which involves a new emphasis on the acquisition of external knowledge, the greater role of users, and a more collaborative (licensing, joint ventures, etc.) approach to the management of intellectual property. These models of open innovation have been enthusiastically adopted by governments, and the UK government in particular, as a way of overcoming what are seen as entrenched barriers to the exploitation of the science base provided by public sector R&D institutions (Lambert 2003).

The particular merits of these new models of innovation are not the focus of this chapter, though clearly there is some debate as to whether they are actually describing a qualitatively new phenomenon or simply repackaging what have long been important features of the innovation process (Freeman 1991). More relevant, however, is what is often missing from these new models: this is some account of the difficulties that organizations experience when they try to evaluate and select nascent ideas and early stage technologies. While the new rhetoric of openness and collaboration is hard to resist, rhetoric alone cannot help companies overcome this challenge. Yet, if firms really are to rely more on inter-organizational collaboration to develop their innovations, they need to address some tough questions, such as: How do we identify the people with the right ideas and technologies to help us develop this innovation? How do we know that what they have to offer is worth backing? Ultimately, how can we tell that these groups will actually deliver what they promise?

In the face of questions like these, the warm words of greater openness can easily go cold. This is because the traditional approach to innovation, whatever boundaries it created to external collaboration, did provide powerful support for internal collaboration, including an established set of incentives, greater transparency in information flows, and unified control of the process. Now, the challenge of evaluating ideas is a feature of any innovation process, however it is conducted. But, once firms move towards more open processes of innovation, the evaluation challenge becomes correspondingly more acute. This is partly because of the increasing volume, novelty, and diversity of ideas available, and partly because established evaluation criteria, based on previous experience, are much less helpful to decision makers. The implications of this shift and the contrasting methods available to address the resulting evaluation challenge are outlined in the description of our empirical study below.

Empirical study

The research was carried out in two distinct strands. The first strand sought to develop an overview of the challenges of evaluating ideas posed by different institutional and organizational settings, including R&D and product development functions, venture capital investors, and technology transfer offices. Work in this phase included a major literature review of the field, theoretical development, and initial empirical study. This strand also identified appropriate arenas for more intensive research. The second strand focused more narrowly on understanding the evaluation practices applied in the commercialization of early stage science and technology by venture capitalists and business angels.

Our methodological approach was adapted to each strand of the study. In the first strand, our methods focused on the conceptualization of the research problem through comparative work across different settings (Glaser 1967, 1998). A total of thirty-four 'grand tour' interviews were conducted with experienced practitioners in different fields (Spradley 1979), including technology transfer office staff, corporate venture and R&D staff within firms, and entrepreneurial groups, including venture capitalists, entrepreneurs, and lawyers. The aim of these interviews (average 90 minutes) was to identify the evaluation practices used in each setting and the contextual factors that influenced their use. All interviews were recorded, transcribed, and analyzed. The data were subsequently coded and analysed with the support of NVivo software.

For the second strand, we developed a semi-structured interview template (Kahn and Cannell 1957) that relied on the critical incident technique (Flanagan 1954) to address the sharing and assessing of highly novel ideas. A total of thirty-four respondents were identified through a variety of means including 'snowball sampling' (Watters and Biernacki 1989) but with an emphasis on identifying experienced practitioners in each domain. Unlike our earlier interviews, these interviews were developed to primarily gather comparative data (Spradley 1979) comparing ideas that were evaluated quickly with those that involved significant investments of time. Here, we were particularly concerned to understand the way in which investors and innovators coped with the added challenges associated with the arms' length relationships of the market for ideas. Typically, we collected two successful high-investment incidents, one unsuccessful high-investment incident, and several low-investment incidents. For each of these incidents, we attempted to identify the relationship between the actors, artefacts, and actions involved with each incident.

The focus on evaluation practices offers a new perspective on the dynamics of open innovation, complementing and extending previous work in this field. The initial strand of our study found that the practices used to evaluate early stage innovations seemed to be linked to the context in which evaluation was taking place. Here, a useful contrast can be drawn between conventional innovation processes within firms—what Chesbrough (2003) terms 'closed innovation'—and the encounters between innovators and investors in the market for ideas. As outlined in Figure 10.1, evaluation practices are important in both of these settings. For a given population of ideas or projects, the question of whether and how to allocate resources is a crucial one. The way that question is posed, however, and the means by which answers are supplied differs radically between these settings.

Within the organizational boundaries of the firm, evaluators are faced with a much narrower range of ideas and projects to assess. They are also better able to manage the way in which such ideas are processed. The firms in our sample had adopted what are termed stage-gate methods (Cooper 1993) to evaluate and select projects. Such methods require that innovators submit their ideas to a highly structured process in which evaluation takes place at a number of discrete points (stage-gates) to determine whether a project is to proceed further and be supported with additional resources. A key factor in this setting has to do with the specification of corporate goals for the innovation process. Where such goals are fixed by the need to support a particular business strategy, or to integrate within an existing product architecture, then both the variety of possible ideas and the range of desired outcomes are much more constrained. In these circumstances, the process exerts a strong pull on those involved, such that it is sometimes presented as a pipeline or a funnel. This contrasts with what has been termed the 'market for ideas' (Stevens and Burley 1997) where entrepreneurs and venture capitalists operate. Here, there are no organizational boundaries on the supply of ideas, and fewer, if any, constraints on the possible market outcomes. The allocation of resources is thus based on the pursuit of maximum gain not on supporting a particular business strategy.

The comparison in the initial phase of work between a range of settings, including corporate innovation processes and the wider market for ideas, suggested that evaluation practices could be broadly characterized in terms of two important dimensions of context (see Figure 10.2). These dimensions were identified as the 'selection environment' (the relationship between a particular idea and the overall number of ideas being

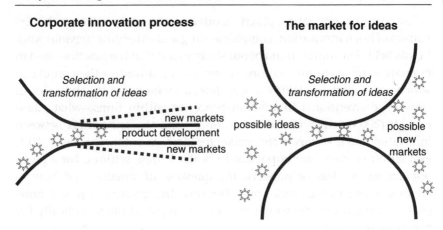

Corporate innovation process

The market for ideas

Fig. 10.1. Different contexts for evaluation

evaluated within that context), and the 'transformation environment' (the relationship between the original idea and its ultimate outcome within a particular context).

Here, we observed that venture capitalists (VCs) work in a high attrition, high transformation environment. Very few of the ideas they consider ever get funded, but those few are then given a high level of development to achieve commercialization and marketing (Gompers and Lerner 2005). Conversely, corporate venturing groups, for instance, were typically evaluating a more constrained set of ideas and were less interested in the transformation of the idea but rather sought to act as brokers between their company and external purchasers of technology and licences. We also observed that in terms of the supply of ideas, business angels were receptive to a wide range of innovative ideas from many different sources, but tended to rely more upon personal networks than VCs. They were also conscious of a wide range of demand opportunities but had less awareness of other sectors than VCs who were more able to pool sectoral knowledge. Their capabilities were more idiosyncratic, being based on personal experience of business success, and their goals were more personal, being influenced by ethical as well as economic considerations.

The focus of the next strand of the research was on one of the extreme arenas highlighted by this analysis. This is the role of VCs and innovators in the commercialization of early stage technology. As indicated above, this arena is much more challenging because it combines a high potential for the transformation of an idea with extremely high levels of attrition. In terms the existing literature, much less is known about how people

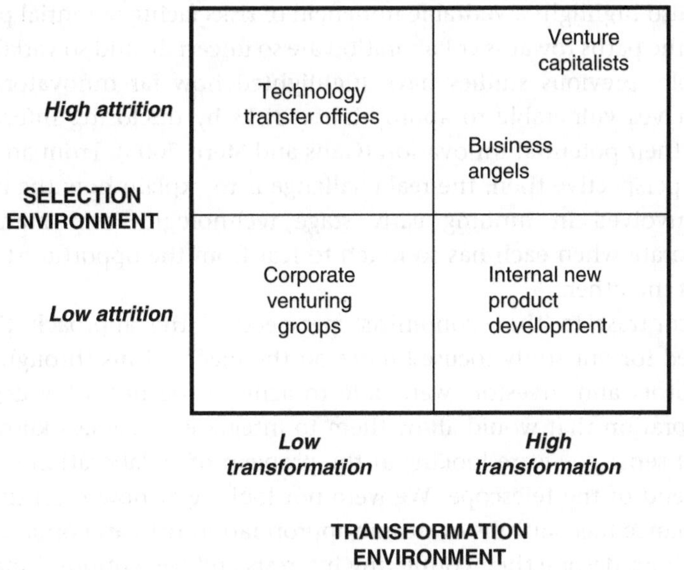

	Low transformation	High transformation
High attrition	Technology transfer offices	Venture capitalists Business angels
Low attrition	Corporate venturing groups	Internal new product development

SELECTION ENVIRONMENT

Low transformation   High transformation

TRANSFORMATION ENVIRONMENT

Fig. 10.2. Evaluation practices across contexts

assess and exchange knowledge in this arena compared to, say, the arena of product development within firms (Carlile and Rebentisch 2003). In the latter case, hierarchical settings provide a relatively structured environment in which relationships, incentives, technological requirements, and even customers are already to a large extent pre-defined. In contrast, the commercialization of early stage technologies is an arena where relationships are emergent, incentives undefined, and technologies or customers relatively unknown. The goal of this phase of the research, therefore, was to understand how different actors (e.g. scientific entrepreneurs, investors, lawyers, technology transfer offices, etc.) involved in the commercialization process collaborated to select and advance ideas around early stage science and technology.

Theoretical framework

There is not enough space in this chapter to outline the wide range of different theoretical perspectives that have been applied to the development of collaboration between innovators and investors. Much existing work in this area is based on economic frameworks and theories of entrepreneurship. These approaches tend to frame such collaboration in terms of the relevance of particular incentives and governance mechanisms.

They also highlight a veritable minefield of risks facing potential partners when the paths towards collaboration are so uncertain and so variable. For example, previous studies have highlighted how far innovators make themselves vulnerable to appropriation risks by disclosing information about their potential innovation (Gans and Stern 2003). From an economist's perspective then, the real challenge is to explain how the individuals involved in funding early stage technologies ever manage to collaborate when each has so much to fear from the opportunist behaviour of the other.

In contrast to the economists' perspective, the approach that we adopted for our study focused more on the mechanisms through which innovators and investors were able to achieve the necessary degree of collaboration that would allow them to integrate and assess knowledge. In that sense, we were looking at the problem of collaboration from the other end of the telescope. We were not looking at how incentives and governance mechanisms overcame appropriation risks and opportunism, but at how, despite their conflicting interests and perceptions, innovators and investors ultimately became embedded in social relationships capable of supporting the evaluation and integration of knowledge between them.

From this standpoint, the fundamental problem is not opportunism, but the lack of shared understandings, relations, or history that comes from collaborating in a market context. In our study, moreover, two particular features of that context stood out as barriers to any kind of meaningful collaboration. The first of these is termed 'information asymmetry' in the existing literature. This has to do with the investor's lack of knowledge and information about the innovator's intentions and competences, as well as the potential problems and opportunities posed by the innovation itself. The second feature is caused by the massively disproportionate ratio between the number of opportunities in the market for ideas and the funding available. Stevens and Burley note in their US study that it takes up to 3,000 ideas to produce one successful commercial outcome (Stevens and Burley 1997). And Mason and Harrison (1994) found that between 93% and 97% of investment proposals received by business angels in the United Kingdom are rejected. The challenge here then derives from the 'information overload' confronting investors as they seek to identify the one in 3,000 ideas worthy of their investments in time and money (Edmunds and Morris 2000; O'Reilly 1980).

In seeking an explanation of how innovators and investors come to collaborate, we sought to identify the boot-strapping mechanisms that enabled the embedding of knowledge in collaborative relationships in the face of both information asymmetry and information overload. We use the term 'boot-strapping' because such mechanisms allow the groups involved to pull themselves up 'by their boot-straps', i.e. with no support initially. One such mechanism, already recognized in the literature, is through a phased approach to evaluation and collaboration. A phased approach offers investors an efficient way to overcome information overload by aligning the effort involved in eliciting information with the perceived potential of an idea. Thus, in each phase, innovators' proposals are evaluated and filtered, with more intensive scrutiny only being applied to those that come through this filter. This phased process from idea identification to commercialization has generally been characterized in terms of three main phases: (1) early phase, (2) mid-phase, and (3) late or deal-making phase (Harrison et al. 1997).

With respect to this phasing mechanism, our study broadly confirmed the analysis of previous studies. Thus, we found that the early phase of the path towards innovator–investor collaboration typically comprises deal origination and the screening of ideas. In this phase, potential investment opportunities come to investors' attention, and investors reach initial decisions to further investigate these investment opportunities (or not). This is normally not an in-depth assessment and is usually swift, as investors are constrained by limited resources (including time) and seek to economize on them efficiently. It may involve a cursory glance at some artefacts such as business plans and patent applications and a quick check of sources of ideas. Given that investors are literally bombarded by many ideas at this phase, research has found that their primary strategy is usually to spend less time on ideas and focus more on rejecting than accepting them (Harrison, Dibben, and Mason 1997; Mason and Rogers 1997). Few ideas survive this first phase.

The next phase involves a much more detailed analysis of opportunities, including the assessment of concepts, people, and returns. It sometimes involves due diligence, which is an extended phase of the evaluation step, if warranted, and may include formal market studies, reference checks, consultation with third parties, and so on. Ideas that make the second phase are finally progressed to the deal-making phase, where investors and entrepreneurs iron out the framework for a deal. This may involve the drawing up of formal contracts and timesheets and formalizing the commercialized idea. This phase is resource and time-intensive. The deal closes once the parameters are acceptable to both parties.

As we note later, phasing was an important mechanism in enabling collaboration. However, phasing in itself, while allowing the better alignment of time and effort to the evaluation task, does relatively little to overcome some of the key challenges of evaluation, particularly the problems of selecting ideas in the face of information overload and evaluating them under conditions of information asymmetry. We now turn, therefore, to a second mechanism, which provided the major focus of our study. This is the role of trust in enabling collaboration.

The concept of trust has received increasing attention in the literature on early stage technology investments. Shane and Cable (2002), for example, suggest that economic mechanisms are insufficient to overcome the information asymmetry involved in such investments, and that trust is more important than previously recognized. One of the problems of unpacking the role of trust in this context, however, is that much previous work has focused on trust as a feature of interpersonal relations. This cannot explain trust's boot-strapping function in early stage technology, since the lack of interpersonal relations between investors and innovators is actually central to the problem that needs to be overcome. It follows that in exploring the role of trust, we needed to develop a multifaceted framework that would encompass all the different phases of collaboration, from initial phases when there are no direct relationships between innovator and investor to the final phase when relations are personal and intense.

In developing such a framework, we turned first to the influential work of Lynne Zucker (1986). Zucker's work is especially relevant here because it allows for trust to be produced in a number of different contexts, and she does not limit her focus to interpersonal contexts alone. Thus, Zucker traces the production of trust to three main sources. The first, termed 'process-based trust', arises from reciprocal or recurring interactions between individuals or organizations. The second, 'characteristic-based trust', is produced through the social similarities linking actors, for example, family background, gender, or nationality. Finally, Zucker highlights 'institution-based trust', which is a source of trust not based on previous exchanges or personal characteristics. Such trust derives from societal institutions, including the education and legal systems, government regulation, and widespread societal norms and expectations. In adapting Zucker's approach for the purposes of our research, we incorporated the findings from other more recent studies to develop a framework capable of encompassing the shifting role of trust across the different phases of collaboration identified above. This framework identifies three major sources of trust—institution-based, network-based, and interpersonal trust—as outlined below.

INSTITUTION-BASED TRUST

Following Zucker's account, 'institution-based trust' is defined here in terms of the expectations embedded in societal norms and structures. A focus on this source of trust draws attention to the effect of institutional practices, which, as Neu puts it, 'are accepted as "social facts" and not often questioned' (Neu 1991: 248). This source of trust is thus signalled less by the immediate features of a particular idea or project than by the wider context in which this project is set. Luhmann (1979) gives an example of the role that such trust plays even in the most fundamental of economic exchanges, by highlighting the codified, institution-based trust associated with money artefacts. Important producers of institution-based trust for our study were the institutions of science, including university systems, professional associations (Coleman 1990; Pixley 1999), and the intellectual property rights created by governmental institutions.

NETWORK-BASED TRUST

This highlights, in particular, the importance of the social networks in which individuals are embedded as a possible source of trust (Uzzi 1997). Such networks are widely seen as supportive of socio-economic exchange (Granovetter 1985; Uzzi 1996). Professional groups, for instance, are often presented as classic examples of network-based trust (Coleman 1990; Pixley 1999). More broadly, Shane and Cable (2002) found that direct ties and indirect ties, mediated by trust, have a positive influence on entrepreneurs securing funding from investors. Relevant sources of network-based trust for our study included university–industry relations (Owen-Smith et al. 2002) and a range of informal social networks. In the informal venture capital market, for instance, network-based trust is especially important due to the importance of referrals from personal contacts (Harrison, Dibben, and Mason 1997).

INTERPERSONAL TRUST

Personal relationships are infused with values (Ring and Van de Ven 1994) and bring with them norms of fairness and reciprocity (Uzzi 1997). The trust associated with such embedded relationships has also been identified as a productive feature of socio-economic exchanges, since it decreases opportunistic behaviour (Uzzi 1996), reduces monitoring costs, enables cooperation (Coleman 1988), and facilitates information transfer (Larson 1992; Uzzi 1997) and knowledge sharing (Zahra, Yavuz, and Ucbasaran

2006). However, this form of trust is also the costliest and requires time and devotion to build. Thus, its development is 'subject to time compression diseconomies because it cannot be developed quickly, nor can it be bought or sold in the marketplace' (Dyer and Singh 1998: 672).

THE ORGANIZING ROLE OF TRUST

The different sources of trust outlined above are important because they enable the evaluation and exchange of knowledge to be embedded within collaborative relationships. Trust has a particular contribution to make here because it is seen as offering an important resource for organizing such relationships. Previous studies have highlighted multiple facets of this organizing role. Thus, trust is seen as allowing actors to conserve cognitive resources, economize on information processing, and safeguard behaviours (Uzzi 1997). As McEvily et al. note, 'When knowledge is received from a trusted source, the receiver is less likely to verify the knowledge for accuracy and is more inclined to accept the knowledge at face value. . . . Without trust, receivers would have to expend time and effort verifying the accuracy and validity of knowledge received, rather than immediately using and refining the knowledge' (McEvily, Perrone, and Zaheer 2003: 97).

At the same time, our appreciation of trust's organizing role needs to be balanced by consideration of the possible pitfalls of an over-reliance on trust. One problem area arises, for example, when a certain level of trust is not available to decision makers. In some countries, for example, institution-based trust is scarce due to societal distrust and weak public institutions such as police systems and market mechanisms (Nooteboom and Six 2003). If this means that socio-economic exchanges become over-reliant on network-based or interpersonal trust, the result is likely to be less effective and more inefficient decision making and overall higher transaction costs (DiMaggio and Louch 1998). Even where trust is available from multiple sources within a particular context, the individual actor's ability to access it may be limited by their embeddedness within interpersonal relationships and social networks. Thus, the trust gained from close personal relationships may lead to 'over-embeddedness', which limits the flow of people and information into and out of an existing set of exchanges (Uzzi 1997). Likewise, previous studies have suggested that social networks based on strong rather than weak ties are more prone to becoming closed networks, and hence more likely to constrain access to other levels of trust (Edelman et al. 2004; Chakravorti 2004).

Research findings

Our study found ample evidence of the organizing role of trust in supporting collaboration between innovators and investors. Thus, we found that investor groups such as venture capitalists not only adopted a phased approach to dealing with the ideas they received from innovators, but were also highly efficient in evaluating such ideas. This meant that they drew differentially on various sources of trust according to the phase of the deal-making process.

Analysing the interactions between innovators and investors in early phases of the deal-making, we found that institution-based trust is signalled relatively easily and is key to addressing concerns about the protectability of the novel idea (e.g. intellectual property and contract regimes) and the nature of the market (e.g. competition, national business systems). We found that investors were especially reliant on this source of trust in these early exchanges. Ideas that were not able to signal institution-based trust in key areas of concern could be quickly screened out. Commenting on the source and ownership of intellectual property rights, for example, one of our respondents said:

First of all, it's got to be free to be commercialized. So, a lot of research that's paid for by an industrial partner isn't free because the industrial partner will take the research back itself. It's got to have some intellectual property position . . . so, either a strong patent or the ability to file a strong patent or some very strong know-how that means this is novel and special and different and protectable.

Another example of this kind of comment came from one of our interviewees who was involved in the initial phase of decision making for an early stage electronics venture:

It's a new invention which could have an application in the electronics industry in sort of the next ten years' time frame. So, when I saw that, I was immediately quite impressed with not just the technology but also the possible applications for it. . . . When we were satisfied that there was nothing directly competing with the idea, then we got a patent agent involved to draft up the patent, and the patent was then drafted, and we applied for a patent in the United Kingdom, which is the normal first step.

Revealingly, this comment shows that the investor's decision making is based on impersonal factors that are independent of interpersonal relationships. The institutional factors are easily visible and relatively cheap to assess. The source of the science is traceable and the quality of the science can be easily linked to the institution from which it originates.

Turning to the role of network-based trust, we found that this was also important in screening out ideas at a relatively early phase in the process. Its role here is exemplified by the following comment from one of our interviewees:

If you know your markets well...you know what a real problem for them to deal with is. And if you don't know what the real problems are, then you ask, and that's one of the critical steps. Or you ask your colleagues...you would ring up your network acquaintances...and say, 'Yeah, hello, Joe. We've got this guy, and he's got this, and this is particularly relevant in your sector. Is this a real problem for you? If we could solve X by doing Y, is that valuable to you?' And so, then, if you discover the answer to that question is 'Yes, wow! I'd pay anything!' you know you're onto a winner. If they say, 'Well, actually, the way it is at the moment is like this, and it's a bit of a pain, but frankly, if it was going to cost us a lot of time, effort, capital equipment, training, whatever...if there's a huge barrier to adopting the new technology...it might do it a bit quicker or a bit cheaper, but frankly, the cost is going to be too high for us to make the switch,' then you think, 'probably let that one go.' And that's kind of early stage checking of the market before you go into it in that much depth—making the decisions which ones you want to take forward to the next step.

This screening applies as much to the people involved as to the ideas they are promoting. One respondent commented quite simply that 'we only initiate discussions with entrepreneurs from people we know'.

Most investors also relied on their colleagues as internal networks. Most of the time, these networks are informal. However, we also found that some of these networks had become formalized. This was much more prevalent among academic/research-related investors (e.g. funds specifically targeting innovations from universities and research institutes). The implications of reliance on this kind of network-based trust are expressed in the interviewee comment below:

So, we don't do anything that hasn't come through the university Technology Transfer Department. They screen out the people who are frankly mad; they screen out the things that are not eligible; they screen out things that shouldn't be formed into companies but maybe should just be licensed or sold, and they just do a sort of general feasibility check around it, and our relationship now is very much...they will phone up and say, 'We've got a project that looks like this, and it's sort of this shape in a stage. What do you think?' And if we say, 'Well, sounds quite interesting,' then they'll start working.... So, it is very unlikely that someone could come from outside.

Network-based trust was seen as requiring less time and resource commitment than more person-based sources. Thus, in discussing the referrals they make, one of our lawyers said:

The first thing is that if they're to get a recommendation, they need to have credibility as it were, because the venture capitalists are more likely to consider it if it's recommended by somebody who is a contact of theirs, whom they rely on. So, one has to be comfortable with that . . . level of trust in the relationship because otherwise, the recommendation becomes rather pointless.

We also found that network-based trust was most heavily relied on where institutional-based trust was weak or less visible. One of our interviewees gave an example where his firm was in the process of investing in a foreign country with weak institutions. In this situation, they found that for the screening and evaluation of the investment, they had to rely on networks established with a local firm in that country.

The role of institutional and network-based trust in the earlier phases of the deal-making process contrasted markedly with the role of interpersonal trust. Institutional and network-based trust generally offered a quick and effective means of evaluating a large number of ideas and thus of overcoming the evaluation challenge posed by information overload. Ideas that failed to signal such trust could be speedily filtered out, allowing effort to be concentrated on the surviving few ideas that merited more attention. It was primarily at this later phase in the process that interpersonal trust became significant. Such trust is more difficult to access because it depends on longer and closer contacts with the innovator and their ideas. Like the other sources of trust, it ultimately provides a way of selecting ideas—if interpersonal trust does not develop, it is difficult to finalize. Equally important in our research, however, was the role that interpersonal trust played in overcoming information asymmetry—enabling innovator and investor to exchange knowledge about the idea and about themselves on a more assured basis, without too great an apprehension of the risks involved. This is especially important in the later phases of deal-making, since it is at this point that real resource commitments are being made; commitments that demand a much finer appreciation of what is being offered both in terms of the novel idea and the capabilities of the individuals involved. Commenting on these issues, one of our respondents said:

The other things we look for . . . we've got to have the scientist who's committed and enthusiastic. If they see this as just a way of getting more grant funding, we're not going to take it further forward. So, the scientist has got to be able to explain his or her science clearly at any level ... very high level for a non-scientist or in detail. They've got to *want* to commercialize it, and they've got to have a bit of a commercial view about what's happening in the market. ... If we have to work together for the next five years, it's good that we actually get on, which sounds silly, but it's actually pretty important. If a scientist and me hate each other on sight, it's probably not going to work.

When interpersonal trust does not emerge, it becomes very difficult to make the leap of faith required to finalize a deal. Commenting on a deal that went sour, one of our interviewees said:

We weren't comfortable doing business with them. They aren't a partner; that's the point. They weren't prepared to be a partner and that's OK. We were looking for a partner; they were looking to buy something in. It was just a wrong expectation. Neither of those is wrong. There are things that companies can do, where they can buy in a new piece of equipment or they can find some new ingredients and they improve their business. Good luck to them. Well done. But we were looking for someone who could be a partner with us, and they weren't it. Other people are much more prepared to be a partner with us, or we found a way that there is some value to both parties.

Where the early and middle phases are dominated by institution and network-based trust, interpersonal relations really emerged as a dominant frame of reference in the final, deal-making phase. Most of our interviewees emphasized the importance of interpersonal trust in the deal-making phase and beyond. For example, one investor commented as follows:

I think that in order for a venture capitalist to invest, usually there will have to be a level of trust, which connects absolutely, immediately. It will be either a slightly strange or an extremely masochistic venture capitalist who invested in circumstances where that were not the case. ... It does depend on, obviously, what level of interest the venture capitalist is seeking to put into it. I mean, if they want to be involved in the business ... then they need to have that level of trust.

Discussion

In summary, our interview data suggests that trust is an important organizing mechanism that enables collaboration among the entrepreneurial actors involved in technology commercialization. These actors draw on different sources of trust at appropriate phases of the deal-making process. This allows them to evaluate people and ideas more effectively and

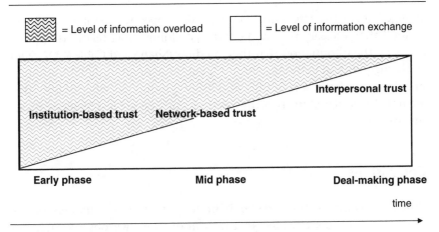

Fig. **10.3.** The role of trust in the deal-making process for technology commercialization

efficiently, overcoming the problems of information overload and asymmetry, which otherwise tend to inhibit collaboration. As outlined in Figure 10.3, the organizing benefits of trust also depend crucially on the availability and sequencing of different sources of trust. Relying on interpersonal or network-based trust too early in the process risks short-circuiting the evaluation practices needed to select and support innovations.

Although many aspects of the activity have been studied from an economic perspective, our work overall contributes to a growing body of literature that emphasizes the social aspects of the commercialization of early stage ventures. In particular, in the second strand of our study, we were concerned to address the role of trust not only in overcoming the challenges of particular decision phases, but as a crucial mechanism through which actors were able to navigate through the deal-making process as a whole, from the uncertainties of the initial phase to striking a deal in the final phase. We found that different sources of trust are introduced, represented, and assessed at different phases. Institution-based trust tends to be used very early in the process. This ranges from concerns about the protectability of the novel idea (e.g. intellectual property and contract regimes), to the source and ownership of intellectual property rights (Sine, Shane, and Di Gregorio 2003). Ideas that are not able to signal trust in one or more of these areas of concern are very likely to be screened out. Network-based trust tends to figure at early and middle phases, and draws upon the investor and innovator's embeddedness in social networks, exploiting the reputational effects arising from such embeddedness (Uzzi 1997). Interpersonal trust tends to emerge later as the actors involved have developed sufficient assurance to commit the necessary time and effort to building closer relationships and assessing the information that they produce (Shane and Cable 2002). Our study suggests that early stage ideas that are consistent in signalling appropriate trust across these levels are most likely to be funded, whereas ideas that are not able to signal trustworthiness in the process are less likely to attract investments.

Conclusions

When we compare these research findings to the new models of the innovation process outlined in the Introduction, we observe that our study has highlighted the critical role that evaluation practices play in enabling different groups to collaborate effectively. The exchange and integration of disparate sources of knowledge is central to these new models, but they do not always recognize the evaluation challenge that arises when groups with different interests, and possessing different levels of knowledge about each other, seek to collaborate. If this challenge is not overcome, the attractions of a more open approach to innovation will remain a matter of rhetoric more than reality for the firms involved.

These difficulties of achieving the knowledge integration needed to support innovation bring us back to the wider EBK perspective outlined in the Introduction to this book. In particular, the findings from the present study provide us with some insights into the way in which innovation is linked to the embedding and disembedding of knowledge from social contexts. As we observed, the market for ideas lacks the necessary shared understandings and social relations that would support collaboration between disparate groups of entrepreneurial actors. Yet abandoning the market in favour of existing social networks and interpersonal ties is likely to limit the free flow of ideas needed to spark effective collaboration. The answer to this dilemma, as we discovered from our research, is to apply trust as both a disembedding and embedding force in relation to existing social relations. Trust supports the disembedding of knowledge within the market for ideas by helping to overcome the problems of information overload and asymmetry that beset the deal-making process for new ventures. At the same time, the organizing role of trust also facilitates the development of the new collaborative relationships required to underpin the innovation process. It does this by enabling key actors, such as venture capitalists, to simultaneously select and advance those relationships in an economical way; not sacrificing their openness to new people and ideas, but not inhibiting the development of closer ties where the attractiveness of the venture justifies it.

Importantly, however, our study not only explores the socially embedded nature of early stage commercialization but also highlights the way in which the trust derived from social and institutional contexts guides actors navigating through the economic and technical uncertainties of a complex decision-making process. It thus points the way towards further work in this field. This might include research that relates the role of trust to the efficiency and outcome quality of the decision-making process for early stage ventures. This would be able to advance our understanding of the way in which the interplay between different levels of trust may both enable and constrain deal-making, by relating this more systematically to different features of the social and institutional context.

References

Carlile, P. R., and Rebentisch, E. S. (2003). 'Into the Black Box: The Knowledge Transformation Cycle'. *Management Science*, 49/9: 1180–95.

Chakravorti, B. (2004). 'The New Rules for Bringing Innovations to Market'. *Harvard Business Review*, 82/3: 59–67.

Chesbrough, H. W. (2003).'The Era of Open Innovation'. *MIT Sloan Management Review*, 44/3: 35–41.

Coleman, J. (1988). 'Social Capital in the Creation of Human Capital'. *American Journal of Sociology*, 94: 95–120.

——(1990). *Foundations of Social Theory*. Cambridge, Mass.: Harvard University Press.

Coombs, R. (2003). 'Analysing Distributed Processes of Provision and Innovation'. *Industrial and Corporate Change*, 12/6: 1125–55.

Cooper, R. G. (1993). 'Stage-Gate Systems: A New Tool for Managing New Products'. *Business Horizons*, 33/3: 44–54.

DiMaggio, P., and Louch, H. (1998). 'Socially Embedded Consumer Transactions: For What Kinds of Purchases Do People Most Often Use Networks?' *American Sociological Review*, 63/5: 619–37.

Dyer, J. H., and Singh, H. (1998). 'The Relational View: Cooperative Strategy and Sources of Interorganizational Competitive Advantage'. *Academy of Management Review*, 23/4: 660–79.

Edelman, L. F., Bresnen, M., Newell, S., Scarbrough, H., and Swan, J. (2004). 'The Benefits and Pitfalls of Social Capital: Empirical Evidence from Two Organizations in the United Kingdom'. *British Journal of Management*, 15/S1: S59–S69.

Edmunds, A., and Morris, A. (2000). 'The Problem of Information Overload in Business Organisations: A Review of the Literature'. *International Journal of Information Management*, 20/1: 17–28.

Flanagan, J. C. (1954). 'The Critical Incident Technique'. *Psychol Bulletin*, 51/4: 327–58.

Freeman, C. (1991). 'Networks of Innovators: A Synthesis of Research Issues'. *Research Policy*, 20/5: 499–514.

Gans, J. S., and Stern, S. (2003). 'The Product Market and the Market for "Ideas": Commercialization Strategies for Technology Entrepreneurs'. *Research Policy*, 32/2: 333–50.

Glaser, B. (1967). *The Discovery of Grounded Theory: Strategies for Qualitative Research*. Berlin: Aldine de Gruyter.

——(1998). *Doing Grounded Theory: Issues and Discussions*. Mill Valley, Calif.: Sociology Press.

Gompers, P., and Lerner, J. (2005). *The Venture Capital Cycle*. Boston: MIT Press.

Granovetter, M. (1985). 'Economic Action and Social Structure: The Problem of Embeddedness'. *American Journal of Sociology*, 91/3: 481–510.

Hardy, C., Phillips, N., and Lawrence, T. B. (2003). 'Resources, Knowledge and Influence: The Organizational Effects of Interorganizational Collaboration'. *Journal of Management Studies*, 40/2: 321–47.

Harrison, R., Dibben, M., and Mason, C. (1997).'The Role of Trust in the Informal Investor's Investment Decision: An Exploratory Analysis'. *Entrepreneurship: Theory and Practice*, 21/4: 54–68.

Kahn, R., and Cannell, C. (1957). *The Dynamics of Interviewing*. New York: Wiley.

Lambert, R. (2003). *Lambert Review of Business–University Collaboration*. London: HMSO.

Larson, A. (1992). 'Network Dyads in Entrepreneurial Settings: A Study of the Governance of Exchange Relationships'. *Administrative Science Quarterly*, 37/1: 76–104.

Luhmann, N. (1979). *Trust and Power: Two Works*. New York: Wiley.

McEvily, B., Perrone, V., and Zaheer, A. (2003). 'Trust as an Organizing Principle'. *Organization Science*, 14/1: 91–103.

Mason, C. M., and Harrison, R. T. (1994). 'The Informal Venture Capital Market in the U.K.', in A. Hughes and D. J. Storey (eds.), *Financing Small Firms*. London: Routledge.

——and Rogers, A. (1997). 'The Business Angel's Investment Decision: An Exploratory Analysis', in D. Deakins, P. Jennings, and C. Mason (eds.), *Small Firms: Entrepreneurship in the 1990s*. London: Paul Chapman.

Neu, D. (1991). 'Trust, Contracting and the Prospectus Process'. *Accounting, Organizations and Society*, 16/3: 243–56.

Newell, S., and Swan, J. (2000). 'Trust and Inter-Organizational Networking'. *Human Relations*, 53/10: 1287–328.

Nooteboom, B., and Six, F. (2003). *The Trust Process in Organizations: Empirical Studies of the Determinants and the Process of Trust Development*. Cheltenham: Edward Elgar Publishing.

O'Reilly, C. A. (1980). 'Individuals and Information Overload in Organizations: Is More Necessarily Better?' *Academy of Management Journal*, 23/4: 684–96.

Owen-Smith, J., Riccaboni, M., Pammolli, F., and Powell, W. W. (2002). 'A Comparison of US and European University–Industry Relations in the Life Sciences'. *Management Science*, 48/1: 24–43.

Pittaway, L., Robertson, M., Munir, K., Denyer, D., and Neely, A. (2004). 'Networking and Innovation: A Systematic Review of the Evidence'. *International Journal of Management Reviews*, 5/3–4: 137–68.

Pixley, J. (1999). 'Impersonal Trust in Global Mediating Organizations'. *Sociological Perspectives*, 42/4: 647–71.

Powell, W.W., Koput, K. W., and Smith-Doerr, L. (1996). 'Interorganizational Collaboration and the Locus of Innovation: Networks of Learning in Biotechnology'. *Administrative Science Quarterly*, 41/1: 116–45.

Ring, P., and van de Ven, A. (1994). 'Developmental Processes of Cooperative Interorganizational Relationships'. *Academy of Management Review*, 19/1: 90–118.

Shane, S., and Cable, D. (2002). 'Network Ties, Reputation, and the Financing of New Ventures'. *Management Science*, 48/3: 364–81.

Sine, W. D., Shane, S., and Di Gregorio, D. (2003). 'The Halo Effect and Technology Licensing: The Influence of Institutional Prestige on the Licensing of University Inventions'. *Management Science*, 49/4: 478–96.

Spradley, J. (1979). *The Ethnographic Interview*. Austin, Tex.: Holt, Rinehart and Winston.

Stevens, G., and Burley, J. (1997). '3,000 Raw Ideas Equals 1 Commercial Success!' *Research Technology Management*, 40/3: 16–27.

Swan, J., and Scarbrough, H. (2005). 'The Politics of Networked Innovation'. *Human Relations*, 58/7: 913–43.

Tether, B. (2003). 'The Sources and Aims of Innovation in Services: Variety between and within Sectors'. *Economics of Innovation and New Technology*, 12/6: 481–505.

Tidd, J., Bessant, J., and Pavitt, K. (2007). *Managing Innovation: Integrating Technological, Market and Organizational Change*. New York: Wiley.

Uzzi, B. (1996). 'The Sources and Consequences of Embeddedness for the Economic Performance of Organizations: The Network Effect'. *American Sociological Review*, 61: 674–98.

—— (1997). 'Social Structure and Competition in Interfirm Networks: The Paradox of Embeddedness'. *Administrative Science Quarterly*, 42: 35–67.

Walsh, V. (2002). 'Technological and Organizational Innovation in Chemicals and Related Products'. *Technology Analysis and Strategic Management*, 14/3: 273–98.

Watters, J. K., and Biernacki, P. (1989). 'Targeted Sampling: Options for the Study of Hidden Populations'. *Social Problems*, 36/4: 416–30.

Zahra, S., Yavuz, R., and Ucbasaran, D. (2006). 'How Much Do You Trust Me? The Dark Side of Relational Trust in New Business Creation in Established Companies'. *Entrepreneurship Theory and Practice*, 30/4: 541–59.

Zucker, L. (1986). 'Production of Trust: Institutional Sources of Economic Structure, 1840–1920'. *Research in Organizational Behavior*, 8: 53–111.

Part III

Inter-Organizational Relationships

11

Rethinking the Role of Management Consultants as Disseminators of Business Knowledge

Knowledge Flows, Directions, and Conditions in Consulting Projects

Andrew Sturdy, Karen Handley, Timothy Clark, and Robin Fincham

Introduction

Consultants are seen as core agents in the dissemination of business knowledge through their relative expertise and/or rhetorical and knowledge management practices. However, relatively few studies focus specifically on their role in projects with client organizations. This chapter examines knowledge flow in consultancy projects from longitudinal observation and interview research as well as a survey of clients and consultants working together. Our analysis suggests that the conventional view of consultants as disseminators of new management ideas to clients is, at best, exaggerated and certainly misrepresents their role in project work. First, it tends to occur by default rather than by design. More importantly, however, learning is often concerned with project processes or management more than the knowledge domain of the particular project and occurs in multiple, sometimes unexpected, directions. Furthermore, a range of enabling and constraining conditions for knowledge flow are identified—not in a deterministic sense, but as a loose or partial structuring of knowledge in practice.

The chapter is organized in the following way. After introducing the relevant literature, we briefly outline our research design before setting out our findings in terms of knowledge flow domains, directions, and conditions. We conclude with a brief discussion of the implications of our analysis for understanding consultancy, project working, and the evolution of business knowledge more generally.

Context for the research

There is now a substantial and continuing literature on the economic importance of knowledge to organizations and societies (e.g. see Argote, McEvily, and Reagans 2003). Much of this emphasizes the role of those involved in bringing new knowledge into organizations from the outside either as some form of knowledge transfer or as part of the process of helping firms to (co-)create new knowledge (Menon and Pfeffer 2003; Haas 2006). A whole range of actors and activities are seen to perform this role, but external management consultants are often at the forefront, not least because of the scale, profile, and growth of their activities in many western economies in recent years (Suddaby and Greenwood 2001; Engwall and Kipping 2002). For example, in a recent historical study of consultants, McKenna describes them as 'pre-eminent knowledge brokers' on the basis of their status as expert outsiders (2006). More generally, consultants are seen as core agents in the dissemination of business knowledge in the form of ideas, tools, and practices, and a huge amount of literature is devoted to documenting their rhetorical (Clark 1995; Fincham 2002; Sturdy 1997) and knowledge management practices and strategies (Alvesson 2004; Werr and Stjernberg 2003; Bogenrieder and Nooteboom 2004; Heusinkveld and Benders 2005). However, relatively few studies focus specifically on their role in knowledge flow in projects with client organizations. Rather, it seems to be assumed that because consultants actively promote new management approaches and appear to be widely used, they do indeed perform this role.

Those studies which do examine knowledge flow through consultancy are largely consistent in reproducing this conventional and common sense view of consultants. For example, Antal and Krebsbach-Gnath (2001) see consultants' outsider status, their 'marginality', as the *necessary* contribution they bring to organizational learning in terms of new knowledge (see also Clegg, Kornberger, and Rhodes 2004; Sorge and Van Witteloostuijn 2004; Anand, Glick, and Manz 2002). More specifically, in this view, consultants are seen to bring distinctive and unfamiliar knowledge to assignments such as that associated with management and technological change methods and tools (see Werr, Stjernberg, and Docherty 1997; Kieser 2002). For example, Gammelsaeter (2002: 222) suggests that 'consultants as carriers of knowledge are generally embedded in contexts that are external to the organization, whereas the management they interact with is embedded in internal organization'.

Clients, then, are seen as being mostly concerned with 'operational' knowledge directed towards 'regulating' day to day activities of their organization (Armbruster and Kipping 2002). But this is seen to present a problem for knowledge flow. Kipping and Armbruster (2002), for example, describe the 'burden of otherness' faced by consultants such that contrasting knowledge bases are seen as 'primary' in explaining the consultants' failure to communicate meaningfully with clients and effect lasting change (Kipping and Armbruster 2002: 221; Armbruster and Kipping 2002: 108; see also Schon 1983: 296; Engwall and Kipping 2002; Ginsberg and Abrahamson 1991).

Despite its persistence, this conventional view of consultants as outsiders bringing alien knowledge to clients is highly problematic. Not only does it not hold as a generalization about consultancy, but, as we shall argue, it is especially unhelpful at the empirical level of consultancy project work and as a conceptual framing of knowledge flow. While the traditional or 'expert' view persists in most studies of knowledge flow in consultancy, the wider consultancy literature (as well as that on professional services generally) suggests that client–consultant relations are more complex and varied. First, the expert view does not take into account the long traditions of process consultancy (Schein 1969), although even here, new knowledge or expertise is assumed in the form of process skills. Second, the growth of management consultancy may be the result not only of consultants' successful persuasive practices with clients (i.e. bringing new knowledge) but also their roles in confirming or legitimating senior clients' knowledge and preferences (i.e. 'rubber-stamping' or re-assurance) (Sturdy et al. 2004; McKenna 2006). Third, as a result of various developments, such as the growth of management discourse in the media and formal education (e.g. MBAs), clients are more familiar with some of the types of knowledge and tools typically associated with consultants; they are more 'sophisticated' (Sturdy 1997; Kennedy Information 2004; Hislop 2002; Kitay and Wright 2004).

Fourth, and importantly for our focus, in professional services, consultants are seen as learning from their clients, especially the more innovative ones. For example, consultants are often involved with their clients, as partners or even 'partial employees', in product development (Fosstenlokken, Lowendahl, and Revang 2003; Mills and Morris 1986; Werr and Styhre 2003). This draws attention to the importance of specifying more precisely the actors and dynamics or stages of consultancy, which offers a fifth challenge to the dominant view. While some clients may indeed be introduced to, and persuaded of the value of, a new management approach by consultants wielding their rhetorical armoury (Sturdy 2004), once the project has begun, this activity lessens in significance, especially for the project team members. Here, one can see a new knowledge boundary emerging between the project team and their respective organizations—a liminal or transitional and often segregated space (Czarniawska and Mazza 2003; Sturdy et al. 2006). Team members are perhaps more likely to share expertise in the project domain, and certainly come to do so, and therefore, exchange this on a more equal and participative basis than the 'expert' view of consultancy suggests. Indeed, knowledge flow processes are more likely to match those associated with project working than the traditional view of external consultants as carriers of alien knowledge to clients. Here, the key challenge has come to be seen as the flow of knowledge from the project to other parts of the members' organizations or networks (Tempest and Starkey 2004) as much as between members themselves (Scarbrough et al. 2004; Sydow, Lindkvist, and DeFillippi 2004). However, this can suggest a particular view of knowledge which itself can be seen as problematic and to which we now briefly turn before examining our research in more detail.

The conventional view of consultants described above, as disseminators of new or expert knowledge, implicitly assumes a traditional view of knowledge as a pseudo-object that can be transmitted or, more commonly, transferred. This idea of knowledge transfer or diffusion continues to pervade consultancy discourse more generally. However, within academic discourses of knowledge and innovation, the term 'diffusion' has been subject to considerable criticism, notably from the perspective of the sociology of translation or actor network theory, where the term 'translation' is preferred. Essentially, diffusion is seen to imply that ideas have an initial inertia and that their subsequent transformation or obstruction is a problem to be explained. By contrast, the term 'translation' recognizes that the spread of ideas in time and space 'is in the hands of people' with interests and it is 'faithful transmission' that most needs to be explained (see Latour 1987: 266–7). While such criticism is sometimes misdirected in that classic studies of the 'diffusion of innovations' do in fact recognize the inevitable transformation or 'reinvention' of innovations (e.g. Rogers 1995; Clark 1987), it remains important.

There is not the scope to discuss this debate more fully here. However, it is important to set out briefly the position we adopt in the following analysis. First, in terms of business knowledge, we are generally concerned with the mobilization of a range of knowledges in business contexts rather than specific and separate knowledge forms. In recognition of the non-object-like character of knowledge, we prefer the term 'knowledge flow' and overall are concerned with practices, processes, and conditions (Czarniawska and Joerges 1996) and how they relate to identity and power (Lave and Wenger 1991). The term 'flow' highlights a sense of movement as well as range of actors. At the same time, however, there is a need to focus and to try to retain a connection with how different actors experience knowledge and learning. In this way, in order not to reduce everything to knowledge, we adopt specific but broad-ranging forms of knowledge and learning. For example, we are concerned with both 'knowledge of' and 'knowledge how' (e.g. with respect to concepts, frameworks, consultancy interactions), but as a process and, in particular, in context/s. Thus, we are concerned with conventional issues of communication as well as meaning or understanding and the politics of knowledge and its transformation associated both with actors' senses of interests or motivations (cf. Carlile 2004).

Overall, however, in this chapter, our main concern is more modest and empirical, for as Tagliaventi and Mattarelli recently noted, 'one particularly important topic which has as yet to be explored empirically is knowledge flow between the heterogeneous communities and networks that cut across an organisation' (2006: 292). In particular, we examine knowledge flow in consultancy projects based primarily on the findings of a longitudinal research project of clients and consultants working together in four different consultancy projects. In particular, over fifty coded instances of apparent or claimed knowledge flow (and/or its failure) and their associated contexts are explored. This data is supplemented by that from a survey conducted among paired clients and consultants reporting on their learning from joint projects. Overall, our analysis suggests that the conventional view of consultants as disseminators of new management ideas to clients is, at best, exaggerated and certainly misrepresents their role in project work. First, it tends to occur by default rather than by design. More importantly, however, learning is often concerned with project processes or management more than the knowledge domain of the particular project and occurs in multiple, sometimes unexpected, directions. Furthermore, a range of enabling and constraining conditions for knowledge flow are identified—not in a deterministic sense, but as a loose or partial structuring of knowledge in practice.

Empirical study

A research design was required to allow a focus on *client–consultant relationships* and *processes of knowledge flow* as units of analysis. Therefore, it incorporated observation of interactions and accounts of them and of their broader contexts. Four project case studies were selected to maximize the degree of difference (Table 11.1). In addition, as a secondary part of the research, we conducted a survey of participants in the 2003/4 and 2004/5 Management Consultancies Association (MCA) Awards for Best Management Practice.

A case study approach enabled us to examine the processual and relational aspects of relationships and knowledge flow. Our principal methods of data collection were observation (35 formal meetings), semi-structured interviews (81), and documentary research. For observation, the 'observer as participant' (i.e. 'sitting in') approach was selected with the main focus on formal project meetings and tracking developments in relationships

Table 11.1. *The project case studies*

	Project organizations (type/sector)	Project type (% UK market, 2005)	Length	Management consultants
Case 1	Global (private, multinational) StratCo (strategy house)	Strategy analysis and advice (5%)	9 months	9
Case 2	Prison (public) Network (two management consultants in a network of associates)	Project management advice and quality assurance (11%)	4 months	2
Case 3	Imperial (private, retail financial services) Techno (IT consultancy)	IT development and implementation (11%)	17 months	5
Case 4	Borough (public, local authority) OpsCo (IT/general consultancy)	Operations advice (e-procurement) (5%)[*]	2 years (mini project 4 months)	4

[*] Market figures from MCA 2006.

and indications of knowledge flow. We identified the types of events, activities, actors, interactions, and emotional behaviours that might reveal insights into the phenomena of interest. In addition to taking fieldnotes, most meetings were recorded. Interviews were semi-structured, recorded, and lasted between 45 and 90 minutes. Choice of questions was informed by an interview schedule developed from a number of exploratory research questions (Sturdy et al. 2006a).

Two postal questionnaires were conducted of all clients (and consultants in 2003/4) who submitted entries to the MCA awards (in 2003/4 and 2004/5). Questions focused on the perceived factors influencing project success, characteristics of a successful client–consultant relationship, and the nature of 'learning'. For the 2004/5 awards, the short-listed clients were also interviewed by telephone to explore perceptions on relationships in greater depth (Table 11.2) (Handley et al. 2006).

In terms of data collection, we developed a conceptual framework informed by situated learning theory (Lave and Wenger 1991) and a practice-based view of knowledge (Orlikowski 2002), where learning is viewed as the development of *practices* and *identity* through different forms of *participation* within communities and networks of practice (Brown and Duguid 2001) (Figure 11.1). This informed later data analysis, such as development of qualitative codes and is discussed in more detail elsewhere (Handley et al. 2004, forthcoming).

Given the above theoretical parameters and the otherwise exploratory nature of our research, we used inductive qualitative techniques of '*condensing*' and '*categorizing/coding*' (Kvale 1996) to analyse data at a microlevel of interaction allowing for some openness to unexpected insights. Also, the transcribed form of the data allowed further analysis using different lenses, such as knowledge flow.

'Condensing' involved summarizing entire texts (e.g. interviews, observation fieldnotes, or project meeting transcripts), keeping intact some quotations and a narrative thread. The condensed versions of our data were accumulated in the form of comprehensive 'case packs' containing

Table 11.2. *MCA's annual awards survey and interviews*

	Survey responses	Response rate	Interviews	Response rate
2003/4	37 (paired)	100%	N/A	N/A
2004/5	67 (client only)	84%	39	100%

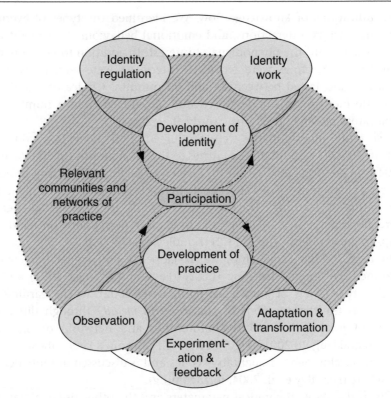

Fig. 11.1. Situated learning in the context of communities and networks of practice

documentation required for an understanding of the background, events, personalities, and narratives of each case. 'Categorizing' involved coding discrete segments of interview text and observation fieldnotes using open coding techniques and then comparing and contrasting those segments to reveal nuances of meaning. To validate initial coding, our research adopted a number of strategies, including the development of a 'code-book'; the use of NVivo software to manage and facilitate re-analysis; and regular team discussions. The code-book followed established practice and included, for each of the main codes, three elements: code name (i.e. the descriptive label); definition or guidance on how to know when the code occurs, plus description of any qualifications or exclusions; and examples (Boyatzis 1998). The code-book fully documented 79 of the 160 codes developed during analysis and provided a comprehensive resource. The following is based on 55 coded instances of 'knowledge flow' or its failure from the case studies. These were selected from reviews of the data and are not intended to be exhaustive of knowledge flows, but representative of the case study and their contexts. In addition, survey data were content analysed and are drawn upon below, mostly from open questions around learning. The analysis presented here reflects an overview rather than rich case material, which is discussed in detail elsewhere (e.g. Handley et al. forthcoming).

Discussion

Knowledge domains

In keeping with the conventional view of the role of consultants as disseminators of business knowledge, there was indeed some evidence of knowledge flow (or 'transfer') in the form of clients acquiring new or increased knowledge from their interactions with expert consultants in the formal knowledge domain of the project. For example, concepts, frameworks, processes/options, tools, skills, and languages associated with procurement, systems design and management, and strategic portfolio analysis were developed. This happened as much by default as design. Client learning was not always an explicit or contractual element in projects, and even where it was, it was not always pursued or achieved, especially beyond the project group context. As we shall discuss below, among other factors, a focus on achieving project objectives in limited time appeared to inhibit any knowledge transfer aspirations on the part of clients and/or consultants.

There was some evidence of the continued use of knowledge that arose from participation in projects. However, this was mostly limited, perhaps in keeping with its low formal priority in the projects themselves, and the knowledge was often in a highly partial, selective, and translated form. The exception was the IT project where practices designed into the system were adopted/translated by users and specialists. However, these findings are derived from our post-project interviews only. In addition, some clients felt that they learned from a more amorphous notion of the consultants' 'external' (from the organization) view, from the consultants' knowledge of the client sector, and from the reflection arising simply from having commissioned consultants.

As indicated earlier, the case studies reflect different forms of contemporary consulting, although in-depth case study research cannot claim representativeness. Many of the dynamics observed reflect themes noted, but not fully explored, in the consulting literature (e.g. interactional style, power, and dependency relations). However, the low priority formally attributed to conventional knowledge transfer has not been evident in prior research. Nevertheless, it was reflected in the results of our survey. In the 2005 survey and interviews of clients, for example, from an open question, 'What have you personally learned through your involvement in this project?', only ten (from 110 entries) referred to learning about the specific content of the project (e.g. culture). A few also mentioned the value of external expertise and the specific issue of knowledge transfer, but only three respondents reported instances of more personal reflections suggesting that they gained a more strategic view from working with consultants or a greater sense of confidence.

Overall then, both from the cases and survey, the findings contradict the dominant view of consultancy or, at best, suggest that such a perspective exaggerates and distorts the role of consultancy in practice. Where learning was far more evident from the accounts of actors at least was in the domain of *project practices and processes* more generally. This was especially evident in the direct survey question on personal learning, where the remaining 100 of the 110 entries were concerned with project (32) and change management (29), either generally or in terms of the importance of clear and shared goals, communication, planning, securing stakeholder involvement/buy-in, and teamwork processes. In addition, respondents learned about working with and managing consultants in projects (39). Here, the importance of close, professional or partnership relations is highlighted (7) as well as that of careful selection (6). In addition, general (negative) preconceptions of consultancy were dispelled (5) along with more specific ones such as how consultancy cannot be cost-effective and learning the value of specific firms or firm types. These issues were also evident in the case studies. Likewise, case study and survey data matched in terms of gaining specific skills (such as how to prepare a business case or how to select and measure consulting) and in terms of tactics (such as the importance of responding quickly to consultant feedback and of getting senior support for the use of consultants).

Directions and actors

In addition to identifying the dominant domain of learning claimed from consulting projects as being that of project processes rather than what might be expected from the conventional view of consultancy as the clients' experts, other significant yet largely neglected, knowledge flow channels and directions were evident.

FROM CONSULTANTS TO CLIENTS

Aside from what might be expected in terms of consultants bringing project domain and sector knowledge to projects, in the StratCo case, they also provided internal organizational knowledge in the form of client procedures, personnel, and strategic data, for example. This was derived from databases and ongoing documentation (e.g. CDs) from previous and other projects in the client firm, as well as the knowledge of the consultancy–client relationship manager who had worked with the client longer than many of the client employees. In this way, the consultants can be seen to be acting as an organizational library or memory.

FROM CLIENTS TO CONSULTANTS

Although it is acknowledged in some of the literature, especially that of professional services in general, we found that consultants gained or appropriated client organization and sector (contextual) knowledge, especially from project participation in contextualizing their analyses and prescriptions as well as in seeking to identify future business opportunities such as through managing off-line interactions with leading questions to senior prospective client managers.

AMONG CONSULTANTS AND CLIENTS

Knowledge flows occur not only from consultants to clients and vice versa but also among clients themselves and among the consultants who are working with them. As we have seen, general and consultancy project management knowledge and responsibility were claimed to have been gained by clients; this is also the case for many of the consultants involved as well.

The very act of commissioning consultants, dedicating financial and other resources to it, prompted reflection *among clients* and a search for other sources of information such as elsewhere in their particular sector.

The familiar internal knowledge management processes of consulting firms were largely beyond the scope of this research. However, learning was evident *among consultants* in terms of incidental observation and coaching with respect to client, process and project domain knowledge, and testing and using tools and frameworks.

Enabling (and constraining) channels, practices, and orientations

The case study research revealed a range of (pre-)conditions, practices, orientations, actors, and channels which appeared to enable and, in their absence, impede knowledge flows in their various forms, directions, and outcomes (e.g. transfer, translation, and application). Some of these relate to more generalized checklists from learning and consultancy literatures (e.g. tailored consultancy styles, commitment, and joint working), but their range and complexity reflects the more contextualized nature of this aspect of our research.

- Time, physical space, motivation, and planning for joint client–consultant activity and/or observation (operational proximity) and reflection as well as other communication channels (i.e. access to clients and consultants).

- Interactional styles of questioning and challenge towards clients that are appropriate to the individual clients, project phase, and context overall (e.g. combined humour and politeness [emotional restraint] in creating space for communication).

- Development of individual client–consultant relationships such as an emerging mutual (behavioural) commitment to project goals and individuals, perhaps beyond initial expectations (importance of reciprocation and trust regarding motives) (including time for this to develop, if necessary). Initial or emergent consultant credibility (trust regarding ability) and likeability.

- Consultant able/allowed to acquire and use contextual (e.g. project and organizational) knowledge early in project (in order to translate and communicate/teach).

- Legitimation of a new knowledge/approach from (extra-)organizationally powerful sources, both explicitly and in terms of being conducive to individual and organizational career/business interests.

- (Emerging) client confidence in new knowledge domain/language combined with some openness or low attachment to other or competing knowledge (but conflicting knowledges can be held).

- Boundary objects or tools/frameworks/systems and access to them (e.g. documentation).

- Formal (planned and practised) and informal learning networks, meetings, and processes (including documentation).

- In/formal networks/links beyond project team; role and engagement of intermediaries/translators such as client operational managers, primary clients, and internal consultants or boundary spanners and (IT) user groups.

More generally, combined with the absence of the enablers listed above, the following appeared to hinder knowledge flow:

- Consultants' lack of: contextualized (e.g. organizational/sector) knowledge or capacity/access to acquire it; conceptual (or other relevant) skills compared to competitor firms; attractiveness as a personality to the client; ability to translate client concerns over prescriptions/suggestions.

- Parties': 'tiredness' or low investment in relationship and/or future trajectory of project (implementation); excessive cognitive/work load (not enough time, energy, motivation) for engaging with/reflecting on new knowledge; failure to work jointly and closely (operational proximity); conflicting objectives/orientations (e.g. client desire for focus vs. consultant desire for thoroughness; client sees consultants as idea suppliers vs. collaborators; competing over [cf. sharing] sector knowledge or solutions/recommendations); failure to anticipate knowledge transfer or include it explicitly into contract or project plan.

- Clients': negative prior/early perceptions of consultant/firm (e.g. credibility) leading to lack of engagement (cf. push back) and failure to create space for communication; failure to provide full client team (and relevant operational managers) access to consultants; inability/unwillingness to move discussion forward (i.e. solutions in context); lack of time (or anticipation/motivation) for coaching (cf. prescription), reflection, preparation of client team and consultants, and documentation/observation; existing knowledge (or identity as expert) in project domain area (competing knowledge or power issue).

Conclusions

We began this chapter with an account of how studies of knowledge flow through consultancy persist with the traditional view of expert consultants disseminating alien knowledge to clients and how this brings with it both a strength ('weak ties') and burden ('otherness'). We then saw how wider literature on consultancy as well as that from professional services has begun to challenge this generalized view by pointing to variations between consulting projects as well as how the legitimizing role of consultants, greater client 'sophistication' (e.g. education), and joint activity and product development in teams results in a boundary shift. The traditional concern with the boundary between *organizations* moves to one between the project team and both client and consulting organizations. Thus, at this level of activity, a concern with persuasive consulting rhetoric and clients' responses to it, which has long been a focus in the literature, becomes less salient. Knowledge boundaries or 'cognitive distance' (Nooteboom 2004) are lessened between consultants and their clients. At the same time, the traditional view was challenged for its more or less explicit adoption of a diffusion perspective rather than giving greater recognition to more processual and practice-based views of knowledge and learning in context— 'knowledge flows'. Here too we set out a broad conception of business knowledge, beyond that associated with formal and relatively explicit management concepts and techniques.

After introducing our research design and methods, we set out an overview of some of the findings with respect to the domains, directions, and conditions of knowledge flows from that which was reported by survey and case study participants as well as that deduced from our observations and analysis. Here, we found that, although some knowledge flow following a traditional route from consultants to clients was evident in the formal knowledge domains of the projects (e.g. strategy), this was not always evident, especially to the actors concerned (e.g. the survey participants). Also, it seemed to occur as much by default as by design. Rather, emphasis was placed on gaining knowledge of project processes such as project, consultancy, and change management. Why might this be the case and what are the implications for our understanding of consultancy and knowledge flow and research?

First, and most straightforwardly, the apparent, relative absence of conventional knowledge flow might stem from the fact that it was not a formal or primary objective in the case study projects and where it was formally incorporated into objectives, it soon gave way to other more concrete or operational objectives as resources became stretched and priorities shifted. The latter was certainly evident in the prison case but might also be relevant more widely and would at least account for why case study and survey participants did not report such learning or its failure so readily. Second, client participants might have had other reasons for not perceiving or reporting the acquisition of project domain knowledge from their consultants. As suggested earlier, at the level of the project, clients are more likely than their peers already to have a sense of expertise in the project domain. Indeed, in each of the case studies, client team members, especially less junior ones, were familiar and even highly experienced in their project domain, often indistinguishable from the consultant team members in terms of experience for example (i.e. low cognitive distance). This would suggest that the emphasis on consulting rhetoric in much of the literature is not appropriate at the level of the consulting project. More generally it reflects how the dominant view of knowledge flow in consultancy can often, if not typically, overestimate the degree of 'otherness' and the weakness of ties with consultants and therefore their 'strength' for developing new knowledge (Sturdy et al. 2006b).

Third, some caution is required here at the methodological level. It is important to recognize what participants in such circumstances might be expected to reveal and conceal and what they might perceive, regardless of what longer-term learning outcomes might be. In particular, if client participants are seen to be within a particular functional specialism—procurement, IT, strategy, and so on—they may well be reluctant to admit, or perceive, themselves as 'sub-expert' in relation to consultants (see also Whittle 2006). On this basis, we might assume, therefore, that they were less attached, existentially, to the domain of project processes for this is more freely asserted, especially in the survey.

However, here, there is another, fourth, possible interpretation. If learning is wholly or at least partly, based in practices, especially those shared through participation in joint activity, then it is hardly surprising that those involved in project practices, including its management, report this domain as significant in terms of their learning—it is what they were doing. By contrast, if we were to have focused the research on those prospective clients attending consultants' (pre)sales presentations or on client employees faced with the implementation of a new management approach or technique, we would expect different results. Indeed, for example, for those in the prison case study for whom the project domain was both novel and non-threatening in terms of their identity, high levels of felt learning were evident with only little consultant input.

The emphasis on practices combined with a broad conceptualization of business knowledge places different activities, actors, and interaction in view and brings us to the different and sometimes unexpected directions of knowledge flow observed and reported in the case studies. Here, we saw knowledge flow from consultants to clients (in terms of providing an organizational memory or 'database') and from clients to consultants in various ways, as well as learning among clients, consultants, or both parties. However, we should not place too much emphasis on explicit interaction and observable practices just because this fits with current perspectives on learning. It was also clear that more classically cognitive processes were important such as reflection and, at the most basic level, 'writing things down' and other forms and outcomes of documenting activities.

In setting out knowledge domains, directions, and actors in consulting projects, our account had been largely decontextualized and static. We then set out a whole host of (pre-)conditions, practices, orientations, and dynamics relating to the different actors and channels which appeared, from our observations and analysis, to enable/constrain knowledge flows in their various forms, directions, and outcomes. There was not the scope to explore these in any detail. Rather, the aim was to highlight the importance of context. Some of these factors build on other studies of learning and are familiar, obvious even (e.g. motivation; resources such as time, space, and personnel; materials; documenting; optimum cognitive distance; planned and informal learning activities; and associated dynamics), while others are more case/context specific. Indeed, the process of detailing contexts revealed a complexity that is rarely evident in generalized checklists of conditions seen to facilitate knowledge flow. While such lists are useful, they not only simplify (which is inevitable), but neglect interconnections or dependencies between conditions and, importantly, a dynamic component to such activities. For example, trust or motivation may develop or decline over time and new directions emerge from interaction, reflection, and unforeseen/changing conditions. Furthermore, conditions, such as space for joint working, can be experienced differently. They are not generalizable to all actors or situations.

This means that checklists of ideal contexts are insufficient as a reliable guide to predicting knowledge flow outcomes. None are necessarily essential conditions. It is their combination in context which is important such that any framework for client–consultant relations needs to allow for situational specificity, human agency, and relationship dynamics—to account for the interactive way in which relationships (and knowledge) are negotiated. In other words, the conditions outlined, among others, might be seen as a loose or partial structuring for knowledge flow. However, some caution is required as structuring itself varies according to context. Thus, in the case of implementing the new IT system at Imperial, for example, employees effectively had little choice but to adopt new practices. This suggests that besides conventional and interaction-based views of conditions for knowledge flow, more attention should be given to motivation, but in the sense of conditions of power and control (see also Handley et al. 2006), such as those associated with the employment relationship or labour process—some structures are looser than others.

Overall then, we have argued that at the level of consulting projects explored over time and, in part, from the perspectives of the actors involved, the conventional and still dominant view of consultants as disseminators of new management practices and approaches is partial and misleading. This not only derives from the conceptual difficulties posed by a 'diffusion' or 'transfer' view of innovation and a limited view of what constitutes business knowledge, but from the positions and practices of the actors concerned. Rather, other, sometimes surprising, knowledge domains and directions of knowledge flow are evident, particularly those associated with project, consultancy, and change management or practices. Furthermore, we identified a range of more or less loosely structured conditions and dynamics of knowledge flow that challenge more conventional checklist approaches to knowledge management and point to the importance of interactively produced and negotiated outcomes and therefore to research with such a focus.

Acknowledgements

We acknowledge the financial support of the ESRC for the project titled 'Knowledge Evolution in Action: Consultancy–Client Relationships' (RES-334-25-0004), under the auspices of the Evolution of Business Knowledge Research Programme, without which this research could not have been undertaken.

References

Alvesson, M. (2004). *Knowledge Work and Knowledge Intensive Firms*. Oxford: Oxford University Press.

Anand, V., Glick, W. H., and Manz, C. C. (2002). 'Thriving on the Knowledge of Outsiders: Tapping Organizational Social Capital'. *Academy of Management Executive*, 16/1: 87–101.

Antal, A. B., and Krebsbach-Gnath, C. (2001). 'Consultants as Agents of Organizational Learning', in M. Dierkes, A. Berthoin, J. Child, and I. Nonaka (eds.), *Handbook of Organizational Learning and Knowledge*. Oxford: Oxford University Press.

Argote, L., McEvily, B., and Reagans, R. (2003). 'Managing Knowledge in Organizations: An Integrative Framework and Review of Emerging Themes'. *Management Science*, 49/4: 571–82.

Armbruster, T., and Kipping, M. (2002). 'Types of Knowledge and the Client–Consultant Interaction', in K. Sahlin-Andersson and L. Engwall (eds.), *The Expansion of Management Knowledge—Carriers, Flows, and Sources.* Stanford, Calif.: Stanford University Press.

Bogenrieder, I., and Nooteboom, B. (2004). 'Learning Groups: What Types Are There? A Theoretical Analysis and an Empirical Study in a Consultancy Firm'. *Organization Studies*, 25/2: 287–313.

Boyatzis, R. E. (1998). *Transforming Qualitative Data: Thematic Analysis and Code Development.* Thousand Oaks, Calif.: Sage.

Brown, J. S., and Duguid, P. (2001). 'Knowledge and Organization: A Social-Practice Perspective'. *Organization Science*, 12/2: 198–213.

Carlile, P. R. (2004). 'Transferring, Translating and Transforming: An Integrative Framework for Managing Knowledge across Boundaries'. *Organization Science*, 15/5: 555–68.

Clark, P. A. (1987). *Anglo-American Innovation.* New York: De Gruyter.

Clark, T. (1995). *Managing Consultants: Consultancy as the Management of Impressions.* Buckingham: Open University Press.

Clegg, S. R., Kornberger, M., and Rhodes, C. (2004). 'Noise, Parasites and Translation: Theory and Practice in Management Consulting'. *Management Learning*, 35/1: 31–44.

Czarniawska, B., and Joerges, B. (1996). 'Travels of Ideas', in B. Czarniawska and G. Sevon (eds.), *Translating Organizational Change.* Berlin: De Gruyter.

——and Mazza, C. (2003). 'Consulting as Liminal Space'. *Human Relations*, 56/3: 267–90.

Engwall, L., and Kipping, M. (2002). 'Introduction: Management Consulting as a Knowledge Industry', in M. Kipping and L. Engwall (eds.), *Management Consulting: Emergence and Dynamics of a Knowledge Industry.* Oxford: Oxford University Press.

Fincham, R. (2002). 'Charisma v Technique: Differentiating the Expertise of Management Gurus and Management Consultants', in T. Clark and R. Fincham (eds.), *Critical Consulting.* Oxford: Blackwell.

Fosstenlokken, S. M., Lowendahl, B. R., and Revang, O. (2003). 'Knowledge Development through Client Interaction: A Comparative Study'. *Organizational Studies*, 24/6: 859–80.

Gammelsaeter, H. (2002). 'Managers and Consultants as Embedded Actors: Evidence from Norway', in M. Kipping and L. Engwall (eds.), *Management Consulting: Emergence and Dynamics of a Knowledge Industry.* Oxford: Oxford University Press.

Ginsberg, A., and Abrahamson, E. (1991). 'Champions of Change and Strategic Shifts—The Role of Internal and External Change Advocates'. *Journal of Management Studies*, 28/2: 173–90.

Haas, M. R. (2006). 'Acquiring and Applying Knowledge in Transnational Teams—The Roles of Cosmopolitans and Locals'. *Organization Science*, 17/3: 367–84.

Handley, K., Sturdy, A. J., Clark, T., and Fincham, R. (2004). 'Have Ideas, Will Travel?' *Spectra: Journal of the Management Consultancies Association*, Winter 2004: 42–4.

Handley, K., Sturdy, A. J., Clark, T., and Fincham, R. (2006). 'Within and Beyond Communities of Practice: Making Sense of Learning through Participation, Identity and Practice'. *Journal of Management Studies*, 43/3: 641–55.

—————— (forthcoming). 'Researching Situated Learning: Participation, Identity and Practices in Client–Management Consultant Relationships'. *Management Learning*.

Heusinkveld, S., and Benders, J. (2005). 'Contested Commodification: Consultancies and their Struggle with New Concept Development'. *Human Relations*, 58/2: 283–310.

Hislop, D. (2002). 'The Client Role in Consultancy Relations during the Appropriation of Technological Innovations'. *Research Policy*, 31: 657–71.

Kennedy Information (2004). *The Global Consulting Marketplace 2004–2006: Key Data, Trends and Forecasts*. Peterborough, NH: Kennedy Information.

Kieser, A. (2002). 'On Communication Barriers between Management Science, Consultancies and Business Organizations', in T. Clark and R. Fincham (eds.), *Critical Consulting*. Oxford: Blackwell.

Kipping, M., and Armbruster, T. (2002). 'The Burden of Otherness—Limits of Consultancy Interventions in Historical Case Studies', in M. Kipping and L. Engwall (eds.), *Management Consulting: Emergence and Dynamics of a Knowledge Industry*. Oxford: Oxford University Press.

Kitay, J., and Wright, C. (2004). 'Take the Money and Run? Organisational Boundaries and Consultants' Roles'. *Service Industries Journal*, 24/3: 1–19.

Kvale, S. (1996). *Interviews: An Introduction to Qualitative Research Interviewing*. Thousand Oaks, Calif.: Sage.

Latour, B. (1987). *Science in Action*. Cambridge, Mass.: Harvard University Press.

Lave, J., and Wenger, E. (1991). *Situated Learning: Legitimate Peripheral Participation*. Cambridge: Cambridge University Press.

MCA (2006). *The UK Consulting Industry, 2005/6*. London: Management Consultancies Association.

McKenna, C. (2006). *The World's Newest Profession*. Cambridge: Cambridge University Press.

Menon, T., and Pfeffer, J. (2003). 'Valuing Internal vs. External Knowledge: Explaining the Preference for Outsiders'. *Management Science*, 49/4: 497–513.

Mills, P. K., and Morris, M. (1986). 'Clients as Partial Employees of Service Organizations: Role Development in Client Participation'. *Academy of Management Review*, 11/4: 726–35.

Nooteboom, B. (2004). *Inter-Firm Collaboration, Learning and Networks: An Integrated Approach*. London: Routledge.

Orlikowski, W. (2002). 'Knowing in Practice: Enacting a Collective Capability in Distributed Organizing'. *Organization Science*, 13/3: 249–73.

Rogers, E. M. (1995). *Diffusion of Innovations*, 4th edn. New York: Free Press.

Scarbrough, H., Bresnen, M., Edelman, L., Laurent, S., Newell S. L., and Swan, J. (2004). 'The Processes of Project-Based Learning: An Exploratory Study'. *Management Learning*, 35/4: 491–506.

Schein, E. (1969). *Process Consultation: Its Role in Organization Development*. Reading, Mass.: Addison-Wesley.

Schon, D. (1983). *The Reflective Practitioner: How Professionals Think in Action*. New York: Basic Books.

Sorge, A., and Van Witteloostuijn, D. (2004). 'The (Non)sense of Organizational Change'. *Organization Studies*, 25/7: 1205–31.

Sturdy, A. J. (1997). 'The Consultancy Process—An Insecure Business?' *Journal of Management Studies*, 34/3: 389–413.

—— (2004). 'The Adoption of Management Ideas and Practices'. *Management Learning*, 35/2: 155–79.

Sturdy, A. J., Schwarz, M., and Spicer, A. (2006). 'Guess Who's Coming to Dinner? Structures and Uses of Liminality in Strategic Management Consultancy'. *Human Relations*, 59/7: 929–60.

Sturdy, A. J., Clark, T., Fincham, R., and Handley, K. (2004). 'Silence, Procrustes and Colonisation'. *Management Learning*, 35/3: 337–40.

—— —— —— —— (2006a). 'Knowledge Evolution in Action—Consultancy–Client Relationships'. Final report to ESRC, project number RES-334-25-0004, September.

—— —— —— —— (2006b). 'Boundary Complexity in Management Consultancy—Re-thinking Potentials for Knowledge Flow'. Working paper, University of Warwick.

Suddaby, R., and Greenwood, R. (2001). 'Colonizing Knowledge—Commodification as a Dynamic of Jurisdictional Expansion in Professional Service Firms'. *Human Relations*, 54/7: 933–53.

Sydow, J., Lindkvist, L., and DeFillippi, R. (2004). 'Project-Based Organizations, Embeddedness and Repositories of Knowledge: Editorial'. *Organization Studies*, 25/9: 1475–90.

Tagliaventi, M. R., and Mattarelli, E. (2006). 'The Role of Networks of Practice, Value Sharing, and Operational Proximity in Knowledge Flows between Professional Groups'. *Human Relations*, 59/3: 291–319.

Tempest, S., and Starkey, K. (2004). 'The Effects of Liminality on Individual and Organizational Learning'. *Organization Studies*, 25/4: 507–27.

Werr, A., and Stjernberg, T. (2003). 'Exploring Management Consulting Firms as Knowledge Systems'. *Organization Studies*, 24/6: 881–908.

—— and Styhre, A. (2003). 'Management Consultants—Friend or Foe? Understanding the Ambiguous Client–Consultant Relationship'. *International Studies of Management and Organization*, 32/4: 43–66.

—— Stjernberg, T., and Docherty, P. (1997). 'The Functions of Methods of Change in Management Consulting'. *Journal of Organizational Change Management*, 10/4: 288–307.

Whittle, A. (2006). 'Preaching and Practising "Flexibility": Implications for Theories of Subjectivity at Work'. *Human Relations*, 58/10: 1301–22.

12

Antagonism, Knowledge, and Innovation: Organizations and Corporate Social Responsibility

Gerard Hanlon

Introduction

Corporate Social Responsibility (CSR) has grown as a strategically import-ant area for business over the past twenty years. Most recently, the *Economist* and *Harvard Business Review* (2003) ran special issues on CSR, and increasing numbers of academic papers are being written on CSR. On top of this, in the 'real' world, corporations such as British Nuclear Fuels Ltd and Shell have embarked upon ongoing dialogues with stakeholders over a number of years in bids to become what Shell called 'the world's most admired company' (Fombrum and Rindova 2000) through a process of engagement and transparency. All of this suggests that CSR is an increas-ing area of strategic concern for corporations. However, such a phenom-enon is relatively recent, for example, Nichols's (1969) work on managers suggested that it was a non-issue in the United Kingdom.

Much of the debate concerning CSR attempts to establish what it is (Carroll 1979), the ethical framework within which it should or should not operate (Carroll 1998), its link to corporate citizenship (Matten and Crane 2005), and whether or not there is a business case for it (Donaldson and Preston 1995). These debates would lead one to assume that CSR is a challenge to business and that it is perhaps intent on limiting the corporation's entrepreneurial essence. Certainly in some ways CSR is a challenge to senior management's right to manage because it entails stakeholders questioning corporate behaviour. However, this chapter will simultaneously question this view while acknowledging that this questioning highlights the increasing porosity of the organization and it is this very porosity that makes CSR a difficult area to define or study. There is no adequate definition of CSR (Matten and Crane 2005), and this lack of definition reflects the innovation and fluidity I am attempting to describe in this chapter. I will not attempt to define CSR because I believe the antagonism, opposition, and resistance it reflects is necessarily open-ended and is bound up with its capacity to transform and innovate in terms of issues—in short, to grow, contract, and mutate. As with the human sciences more generally, to categorize CSR is to render it un-dynamic—to fossilize it in some sense (Hacking 2006). In this chapter, I want to put issues of definition to one side and instead examine how CSR fits into a world of opposition, knowledge, and innovation and hence how it has enabled corporations to respond to challenge by deepening capitalist social relations.

Context for the research

Contestation and organization—legitimacy and porosity

The nature of knowledge, our engagement with it, the role of expertise, the understanding of risk, and so on have all become areas of governmental, corporate, and academic concern (Beck 1992; Lyotard 1984; Power 2004; Lloyd 2001; Giddens 1999; Jones, Parker, and Ten Bos 2005). From a variety of different perspectives, various theorists have suggested that in late industrial society we face a crisis of knowledge. In this chapter, I cannot examine all of these viewpoints; however, I will comment briefly on the issues of legitimacy and struggle in the study of knowledge. Given that CSR, as a knowledge form, is seen to represent a questioning (often-times unsuccessful) of senior management and the corporation's right to manage the use and distribution of resources, these issues of legitimacy and struggle will help to inform the analysis that follows.

Giddens (1984, 1994, 1999) argues that today individuals are more reflexive than in the past and as such organizations of all descriptions are challenged in ways that are new. In short, 'everyday life is becoming opened up from the hold of tradition' (Giddens 1999), while simultaneously tradition is resurgent in many forms. Both prospects present organizations with new difficulties. For example, the biotechnology industry is confronted by a radically new science and the 'traditional' knowledge of religious groups. In a similar vein, Ulrich Beck (1992) suggests that today we live in a risk society because (Western) humanity has overcome the vagaries of the natural world and replaced these with human-made risks such as financial instability, nuclear explosion, pollution, and so on. The development of industrial society—what Beck calls 'simple modernity'—solved many of our material difficulties, but in doing so it led to a de-traditionalizing society wherein knowledge became subject to interrogation from both lay people and experts. Today in 'reflexive modernity' expertise and knowledge are contested because of this increased reflexivity. This reflexivity takes two forms: (1) systemic self-monitoring wherein social institutions and organizations attempt to reflexively monitor themselves and the risks they are creating; and (2) individual self-monitoring wherein individuals attempt to shape their path through an ever more complex social existence that is less bound by tradition and institutions. These twin processes mean that knowledge fields are both contested and open (Beck 1999: 125).

For Beck, one of the most obvious examples of this is the conflict that emerges between the lay public (many of whom are themselves experts in another field, e.g. accountants can have lay person views on chemicals) and experts. He suggests that lay people operate on a 'social rationality' principle, whereas experts use a 'scientific rationality' (Beck 1992: 51–90). Essentially, a scientific rationality is based on causality and something akin to Popper's falsification thesis, whereas the lay public's social rationality tends towards correlation. This, combined with an increasing range of competing expert voices, means that 'facts' are interpreted thereby setting up a conflict between the two rationalities. In light of this conflict, knowledge becomes more open-ended, trust in institutions is weakened, and risk is heightened—we enter a realm of confusion and a crisis of legitimacy in expertise and knowledge (Beck 1996: 33). In short, today risk is an organizing principle (Power 2004) and at its heart is the fact that the organization and its expertise is increasingly open-ended and inter-penetrated with the 'social' world, that is, porosity is a central feature of organizational life.

The legitimacy of knowledge has also been challenged by postmodernism, and Jean-François Lyotard (1984) is often cited in this light. However, another way of reading Lyotard is to question whether he is actually declaring the death of meta-narratives or is encouraging us to be incredulous of them (Jones 2003: 509). What he is centrally engaged in is the examination of the legitimation of knowledge (Jones 2003: 508; Jameson 1984: viii; Lyotard 1984). His key questions concern how 'science' and

261

'knowledge' are legitimated and why are they undergoing a crisis of legitimation today? This is not a rejoicing of postmodernism or a plurality of voices. Rather, as Jones (2003) describes, this plurality needs always to be viewed through the lens of capitalist efficiency. As such, all can be heard but only the 'efficient' can be enacted—science and knowledge replace traditional knowledge and end up in the service of the wealthy. To quote Lyotard (1984: 45): 'No money, no proof—and that means no verification of statements and no truth. The games of scientific language become the games of the rich, in which whosoever is the wealthiest has the best chance of being right. An equation between wealth, efficiency and truth is thus established.'

In this world, idealism gives way to the creation and verification of a 'reality' that requires resources. Knowledge is about mapping this reality; for example, are GM foods safe?, is modern animal husbandry repugnant?, how best can rights over indigenous knowledge be patented?, and so on become important scientific questions, whereas the moral questions concerning our right to engage in these processes become secondary. Idealism gives way to functionalism, performativity, and input–output ratios. The condition Lyotard maps out is a complex one. It is one where power—especially corporate and state power—is prevalent and knowledge is bent to this power. At the same time, he rejects the idea of consensus because (1) the language games of knowledge and science do not necessarily end in agreement; and (2) science is based on parology—'someone always comes along to disturb the order of "reason"' (Lyotard 1984: 61). For Lyotard, there is no synthesis here, no linear improvement—antagonism not agreement is at the heart of critical thinking and knowledge.

The centrality of power and antagonism as knowledge is further emphasized by the Marxist autonomist movement based primarily, but not exclusively, in Italy. This viewpoint suggests that Marx's *Grundrisse* (especially the 'Fragment on Machines' section, 1976: 706–8) holds one of the keys to the role of knowledge in modern capitalism. In this work, knowledge is seen as a source of struggle and transformation. The environment is shaped by many determinations and factors; it is both plural and a totality and its struggles and transformations are never linear (Negri 1991: 41–59; Marx 1976: 81–111). Important here is also the notion of immaterial labour. Immaterial labour is made up of two forms of content. First, it is comprised of informational content. And second, it is derived from aspects of life that have not traditionally been considered 'work'—taste, aesthetics, fashion, and politics. This new form of work and knowledge is based on what Virno (2006) calls transindividuality (historically captured knowledge based on a pre-individuality—our historic embedded knowledge and ways of living) and inter-individuality (knowledge derived from the bringing together of existing individuals to produce products and services). The renewed coming together of these two forms in post-Fordism has given rise to a new type of work that is embedded in all areas of social practice and knowledge even (or especially) those not traditionally part of work and organization. As Virno puts it (2006: 38),

post-fordist labour has absorbed into itself the transindividuality of the collective as well: so much so that many productive operations seem like political actions, in that they demand the presence of others, and must contend with the possible and the unexpected. For all these reasons it seems that labour expands infinitely, to the point of comprehending that which, in terms of political economy, is not labour: passions, affects, language games, and so on.

At the core of this new work is the interface (Virno 2004, 2006). Workers increasingly interface between work teams, customers, hierarchies, functions, technology, and so on. Again, the rise of this new type of work—immaterial labour—makes interfacing, exchange, porosity of organizational boundaries, politics, trust, and so on central because our understanding of the concrete—of reality—comes from daily practice in all its collective forms. The use of knowledge is therefore to transform collective life (Negri 1991: 47). For example, should we create a market in order to provide babies to childless couples is a question answered by our understanding of the issues concerning markets, childlessness, power, the developing world, globalization, poverty, and so on. This collective knowledge then transforms reality. Again, in this world antagonism is the key. Antagonism, power, struggle, alternatives, these are the motor of change. Difference and the conflict that it engenders drive forward 'progress' because these oppositions create innovation (Negri 1991: 44).

From the perspective of organization studies, the above suggests that contestation and porosity are at the heart of innovation. The battle for ideas and alternative ways of organizing social life or wealth need to be examined as sites of much innovation, alongside those of more traditional organization studies. Corporate Social Responsibility provides us with a test case of how this antagonism may lead to innovation. Thus, instead of seeing NGOs, civil society, environmentalism, and so on as a challenge to capital, we can perhaps see them as another mechanism for capital to capitalize on the challenges provided by these alternative knowledge sources and life forms.

Empirical study

The methods and data for the study were based on postal surveys, in-depth interviews, dialogue focus groups, and case studies.

Postal surveys

Using two different questionnaires, 150 companies and 85 NGOs were surveyed to ask about their engagement with CSR, how they organized their CSR activities, why they engaged in it, how many staff worked on CSR, and so on. The response rate for both surveys was roughly 40%. Participant observation was carried out at the Business in the Community (BiTC) open dialogue events. These events took place over eighteen months and entailed monthly dialogues and discussions around emerging themes.

In-depth interviews and dialogue focus groups

The research team carried out twenty-five interviews with NGO personnel, company, and facilitators (professionals who chair stakeholder dialogues) to develop data about what CSR means, how typologies of CSR are developed, what differences exist between different actors in the field, how CSR is implemented within corporations, and so on. The data emanating from these interviews were then used to inform four focus groups. These focus groups were devised along the following lines.

The first two focus groups were made up of NGO and company personnel, respectively. Each group discussed the topics that emerged as the most important from our interviews: developing trust between participants, measuring outcomes and success, and the changing nature of relationships between NGOs and companies. Focus group three brought both groups together to discuss the themes that had emerged from the previous sessions in order to track overlap, difference, argument, and so on. The final focus group did the same thing but with a set of regional rather than London-based actors. The purpose was to weaken a London-based bias.

Case studies

Two company case studies were carried out focusing on how the lessons, experiences, and knowledge gained from CSR dialogue processes fed into company strategy and activity. In both cases, companies provided documentation, members of the CSR management groups were inter-viewed, and a focus group was carried out in each company to access this data.

Discussion

Unsurprisingly, CSR appears to be based on the differing world-views of businesses and the groups that could loosely be said to represent civil society. Often these contestants attempt to engage in a process of dialogue from a basis of mutual suspicion. In this realm, companies are perceived as cynically opportunistic and driven by PR concerns (often called Green-wash) (see Christian Aid 2004). As one interviewee so trenchantly put it,

It's good PR if they can persuade us to mention in a corporate magazine that they are talking to Friends of the Earth and they've had meetings. It is good for middle managers or the senior executives just to report to the Board—'oh yes we've met these people, there's a lot of common ground between us'. And they were doing it, they were saying it on radio interviews, on television interviews—'oh yes we've had long discussions with Friends of the Earth and we think there is an awful lot of common ground between us.' And sod it, you know, no way, no way are we going to have these sort of. You know essentially there is a real danger that CSR could be used by the big companies in order to present themselves in a better way. And if you read some of the stuff coming out in the States, some of the books that are being written about what is happening there and what has happened here, you will see that advertising agencies are advising their customers, their big corporate clients, to involve NGOs like Friends of the Earth in dialogue as a way of managing the big environmental impact they have. And it is a complete con.

Meanwhile, the NGOs are perceived as being too radical or too unrealistic. However, in an economy increasingly dominated by globalization, brands, and reputation (Klein 2000), and one where NGOs are increasingly capable of damaging companies through their use of the media (Lloyd 2001), engagement with the outside world is becoming a real strategic concern for large corporations.

Traditionally, the call for social responsibility has been either greeted sceptically and viewed as an unwarranted challenge to the corporation's historic mission (Friedman 1962), or it has been viewed from a range of ethical and/or economic arguments to suggest that behaving 'well' (how-ever that may be defined) is either morally necessary and/or good for business (Carroll 1979; Donaldson and Preston 1995). However, another view of CSR is also possible. This one suggests that CSR represents a deepening of capitalist social relations rather than a challenge to them (Hanlon, forthcoming). Furthermore, the interaction between these contested forms of knowledge about how life should be organized is increasingly important in helping corporations to innovate and to develop new markets and processes—although such contested knowledge is not the only form of knowledge within the firm. This is not merely about corporations being aware of the market or close to the consumer. Nor is it a straightforward marketing task based on a perceived co-joining of interests, for example, the creation and satisfaction of a need or desire. Rather, antagonism is a key tendency in this relationship. CSR represents the naming of a tendency towards the social factory—where 'all of society becomes a medium for accumulation' (Ryan 1991b: 208). The 'social factory' is a term used to describe an environment where more and more areas of social life are commodified and are also at the heart of wealth creation and the regeneration of capitalism, for example, our genetic make-up has evolved outside of capitalist relations but today this 'wealth' will be increasingly commoditized to give rise to a new industry (Davis 2005). Other examples are:

1. *Environmental movement.* The environmental movement's ongoing struggles with corporations and its often outright hostility to them have given rise to new forms of knowledge (itself a product of struggle) and hence to new forms of products and processes (note the large-scale investment by firms in 'green' fuels). For example, in 2006 Ford UK invested £1 billion in cutting carbon emissions (Milne 2006). Similarly environmentalist highlighting of the pressure on global forests has been instrumental in the Forestry Commission's development of a sustainable development timber industry in the United Kingdom (where 40% of all timber coming from UK sawmills is now certified) (Forestry Commission 2006). Lastly, the challenge of Greenpeace to corporations has led to the development of many 'environmentally friendly' products that Greenpeace now encourages its members to buy via their monthly newsletters in certain states. In short, antagonism and resistance have given rise to innovation, to new products, and new industries.

2. *Biodiversity.* The claims of corporations to rights over biodiversity have proved controversial in late capitalism (O'Neill 1998). Biodiversity has provided companies with opportunities For example, RiceTec Ltd. recently labelled one of its rice products as 'basmati' after it had modified a strain of its rice to take on basmati characteristics. However,

266

biodiversity has also proved problematic, RiceTec's actions and its approach to the US Patent Office have been likened to colonialism and construed as stealing away the generational knowledge, history, and culture that developed this rice strain in the first place and made the brand 'basmati' valuable (Shiva 2000). The label 'basmati' has come to be valuable over time, but it is claimed to be a product of the social factory, that is, outside of traditional capitalist organization. Other examples of conflicted knowledge and organizational strategy concern genetically modified food. Monsanto famously withdrew from this arena in the European Union after the storm of protest around its plans to introduce genetically modified soya into the European food chain. Such processes have led to calls for greater labelling of foodstuffs in Europe and have led to food stores such as Tesco innovating to propose banning all GM foods from their shelves in 1999 (Tesco 2006). Two things are noticeable about the debates on biodiversity. First, they are conflictual. Where value has already been created, for example, by the development over centuries of the basmati 'brand' in northeast India and the surrounding countries or the human gene pool, its enclosing by corporations is resisted. And, second (but related), there is an increasing resistance to the claims to legitimacy made by corporations through their use of science. To return to Lyotard, the power behind the science is recognized and challenged. Yet again, as with the environmental movement (although perhaps more negatively from a corporate perspective), antagonism is central to corporate innovation.

3. *New technologies*. Other areas of life that are also leading to innovation outside the corporation are things such as city living and new technologies. For example, Harvey (2002) suggests that urban entrepreneurship is regularly developed on the distinctiveness of places and cities such as Barcelona. This distinction is often built by groups acting in opposition to capital, which capital then seeks to exploit and extract monopoly rents from thereby leading to the destruction of this very uniqueness. Likewise, new technologies (especially the Internet) have enabled people to develop new forms of social relations via sites such as YouTube, MySpace, and/or open-source software that has challenged traditional organizational and social forms (e.g. Microsoft). Yet these relations have also enabled corporations such as Google or News Corporation to turn these social relations into capital relations through the enclosing of these activities in a market dominated by advertising rights (Coté and Pybus, forthcoming).

267

These examples suggest that 'resistance' via the alternative activities of the social factory that Negri and Virno describe is changing our reality. Our collective knowledge is transforming the corporate world—creating innovation via antagonism. These processes are simultaneously generating mechanisms of enclosure, commons, innovation, and change.

However, in case we emphasize resistance too much, I do not want to suggest that the development of alternative ways of living is somehow pre-planned or all-encompassing. Resistance is more organic than that and can take many forms and may often be unnoticed or unconscious. For example, I can defend free health and support university fees simultaneously, but does this make me a supporter or a resistor of 'capitalism'? I would, however, like to suggest that corporations are also aware of the value to be unlocked from these sources within the social factory. For example, *The McKinsey Quarterly* has suggested that the next big markets for corporations are based in opening up the developing world, developing new technologies (especially biotechnologies), and privatizing the welfare states of the major economies (Davis 2005; Cogman and Oppenheim 2002). The language they use is different, but what they are suggesting is the commoditization of these aspects of social life. That is, the espousal of the view or the knowledge that a privatizing logic will lead to progress over and above one that seeks to leave these arenas and others outside of the market. In short, Marxists and management consultants meet—the value of the 'social factory' or the non-market, the traditional is to be either enclosed or unlocked (depending on your politics) via capital's ability to respond/innovate and capture these fields.

Capital needs to respond to labour's first move and to the issues of knowledge, legitimacy, and the world-views being used to transform reality. Davis (2005) argues very strongly that to do so requires corporate social responsibility. He suggests that 'from a defensive point of view, companies that ignore public sentiment make themselves vulnerable to attack' (Davis 2005: 1). But Davis then goes further, seeing this unease with capitalism not as a threat but a market opportunity. He comments, 'Social pressures often indicate the existence of unmet social needs or consumer preferences. Businesses can gain advantage by spotting and supplying these before their competitors do' (ibid: 2.). To be innovative, to be strategic and spot these opportunities, corporations increasingly need to engage with their interlocutors. They need more porosity and engagement with those who are antagonistic. They may need CSR to unlock new markets and value.

This desire for the exchange of world-views—of knowledge—has encouraged corporations to develop a variety of dialogue processes. As suggested at the beginning, Royal Dutch Shell and British Nuclear Fuels Ltd have both used the Environmental Council to engage in dialogues that have lasted for a number of years. However, these processes have led NGOs to suggest that the learning is largely one way. As one interviewee expressed it:

One of the weaknesses of the model is that it is tending to lead to a lot more learning on one side than on the other and I think that is one of the reasons why the NGO's, certainly the campaigning NGO's are very sceptical of stakeholder engagement and there are cases rightly so...in a lot of instances it is used as green wash and it is just to like extend conversations so you don't have to do anything. All that is true in certain instances, but it is not always true. But yes I think the fact that there is far more involvement on one side than the other side the stakeholder side tends to lead to asymmetrical learning.

Even if learning is one-way and takes the form of a hoped for understanding of future controversies, of alternative views that can then be accommodated, embraced, or subsumed, or of a knowledge of issues surrounding industries, supply chains, and so on, there are still real difficulties with CSR and the corporation. In particular, CSR is resisted internally because of issues concerning measurement and value.

Conclusions

One of the most taxing issues for CSR proponents (with and beyond the corporation) is the issue of measuring its contribution to the corporate and social good. A frequent criticism is that it damages the bottom line (most famously, see Friedman 1962); although CSR proponents often rather weakly suggest that it contributes to corporate profitability albeit in the 'long run' (Carroll 1998, for example). Now, as it was when Nichols interviewed managers in 1969, the need for profitability remains unquestioned. Profitability requires measurement and notions of value, and CSR as a field exhibits difficulty in demonstrating this value. As one interviewee who regularly organized CSR dialogues between corporations and their 'stakeholders' that sometimes spanned years expressed it,

Honestly no (we have no mechanisms for measuring impact). We would love to have them. The three or four evaluations that we've run or had run on the dialogues . . . have all highlighted that the, the impact or effectiveness of the dialogue like this is so hard to evaluate and quantify rather. You can only ever quantify by using proxy indicators and never actually saying, this has changed, that has changed. I mean just sometimes you can if someone is willing to go on the record to say 'We never would have taken that decision if it hadn't been . . . of dialogue' but that is pretty rare to be honest, just because of the nature in which decisions are made you have a whole load of information, inputs and opinions and then the decision is taken, and the dialogue is normally only ever one input into that. Mechanisms that we have tried to use to improve that transfer ability have, I think have been twofold, one is that in the ground rules for the operation of larger dialogues anyway there is a ground ruling that stakeholders all own and sign up to, that says, not only are they responsible for feeding back their organization's view into the dialogue but also they are responsible for feeding the dialogue's process and opinion back to the organization so our stakeholders are actually stakeholder representatives in quite a formal way and they are obliged to follow this cycle of feedback.

Such an admission hampers the 'reforming' cause of CSR because, returning to Lyotard again, its knowledge is not seen as functional or as efficient by many within management. It comes to be seen as a talking shop—this is true both for corporations and for NGOs. Bennett (2004) suggests, 'All too often CSR professionals are obsessed with the means rather than the ends, the dialogue rather than the delivery.' This issue often relegates CSR to the operational level—managing the process of stakeholder engagement rather than strategy.

However, such a view may misunderstand CSR. It may be that for important new markets CSR is the necessary tactic for capturing or enclosing this value—in short, for developing these forms as markets. CSR may be unmeasurable because for many future strategic corporate markets it is a necessary input for the commodification of these areas in the first place, in other words, it is the legitimizing knowledge that enables the corporation to turn social relations into capital relations. How do you 'value' something that is as yet unknown in scale and/or is not commodified—hence the ongoing difficulties of corporations and their ever-growing entanglements with CSR. At the heart of CSR seems to be the issue of legitimacy. Here knowledge is transformation. It is struggle because it changes the environment both for the corporation and more generally. This view of knowledge gives us openness, its 'horizon is always plural, variated, mobile: the knowledge one has of it possesses the vivacity and the passion of struggle' (Negri 1991: 56). The interface of this struggle for the firm is increasingly with the social factory and the politics, aesthetics, and taste of knowledge. For the corporation, this is both a challenge and an opportunity. For the individual, it is both a moment of exploitation and socialization (Negri 1991).

Acknowledgements

This chapter forms part of the work from the ESRC-funded project entitled 'Shaping Knowledge through Dialogue' (ESRC grant number Res-334-25-0011). This is one project in a series of projects from the Evolution of Business Knowledge Programme. The author would like to thank his colleagues on the project Theodora Asimakou, Pavan Athwal, Jon Burchell, and Joanna Cook.

References

Beck, U. (1992). *Risk Society: Towards a New Modernity*. London: Sage Publications.
—— (1996). 'Risk Society and the Provident State', in S. Lash, B. Szersznski, and B. Wynne (eds.), *Risk, Environment and Modernity: Towards a New Ecology*. London: Sage Publications.
—— (1999). *World Risk Society*. Cambridge: Polity Press.
Bennett, C. (2004). 'A Little Less Conversation, a Little More Action'. *Elements 21 February*.
Carroll, A. B. (1979). 'The Three Dimensional Conceptual Model of Corporate Performance'. *Academy of Management Review*, 4/4: 497–505.
—— (1998). 'The Four Faces of Corporate Citizenship'. *Business and Society Review*, 100/101: 1–7.
Christian Aid (2004). *Behind the Mask: The Real Face of Corporate Social Responsibility*. London: Christian Aid.
Cogman, D., and Oppenheim, J. M. (2002). 'Controversy Incorporated'. *McKinsey Quarterly*, No. 4.
Coté, M., and Pybus, J. (forthcoming). 'Learning to Immaterial Labour 2.0; MySpace and Social Networks'. *Ephemera: Theory and Politics in Organization*.
Davis, I. (2005). 'What is the Business of Business?' *McKinsey Quarterly*, No. 3.
Donaldson, T., and Preston, L. E. (1995). 'The Stakeholder Theory of the Corporation: Concepts, Evidence and Implications'. *Academy of Management Review*, 20/1: 65–91.
Fombrum, C. J., and Rindova, V. P. (2000). 'The Road to Transparency: Reputation Management at Royal Dutch Shell', in M. Schutz et al. (eds.), *The Expressive Organization*. Oxford: Oxford University Press.
Forestry Commission (2006). 'Certification'. <http://www.forestry.gov.uk/forestry/hcou-4u4jgl>.

Friedman, M. (1962). *Capitalism and Freedom*. Chicago: University of Chicago Press.

Giddens, A. (1984). *The Constitution of Society*. Cambridge: Polity Press.

—— (1994). *Beyond Left and Right: The Future of Radical Politics*. Cambridge: Polity Press.

—— (1999). *Runaway World*. Reith Lectures, BBC, London.

Hacking, I. (2006). 'Making Up People'. *London Review of Books*, 28/16 (17 August): 23–6.

Hanlon, G. (forthcoming). 'Re-Thinking Corporate Social Responsibility and the Role of the Firm—On the Denial of Politics', in A. Crane et al. (eds.), *The Oxford Handbook of Corporate Social Responsibility*. Oxford: Oxford University Press.

Harvey, D. (2002). 'The Art of Rent: Globalization, Monopoly and the Commodification of Culture'. *Socialist Register*.

Jameson, F. (1984). *Marxism and Form*. Princeton: Princeton University Press.

Jones, C. (2003). 'Theory after the Postmodern Condition'. *Organization*, 10/3: 503–25.

—— Parker, M., and Ten Bos, R. (2005). *For Business Ethics*. London: Routledge.

Klein, N. (2000). *No Logo*. London: Flamingo.

Lloyd, J. (2001). *The Protest Ethic*. London: Demos.

Lyotard, J.-F. (1984). *The Postmodern Condition: A Report on Knowledge*. Minneapolis: University of Minnesota Press.

Marx, K. (1976). *Grundrisse*. Harmondsworth: Penguin.

Matten, D., and Crane, A. (2005). 'Corporate Citizenship: Toward an Extended Theoretical Conceptualization'. *Academy of Management Review*, 30/1: 166–79.

Milne, M. (2006). 'Ford Puts £1bn behind UK Research in Drive to Cut Carbon Emissions'. *Guardian*, <http://environment.guardian.co.uk/travel/story/0,,1850817,00.html>.

Negri, A. (1991). *Marx Beyond Marx: Lessons on the Grundrisse*. New York: Autonomedia.

Nichols, T. (1969). *Ownership, Control and Ideology: An Enquiry into Certain Aspects of Modern Business Ideology*. London: George Allen & Unwin.

O'Neill, J. (1998). *The Market: Ethics, Knowledge and Politics*. London: Routledge.

Power, M. (2004). *The Risk Management of Everything: Rethinking the Politics of Uncertainty*. London: Demos.

Ryan, M. (1991a). 'Translators' Introduction', in A. Negri, *Marx Beyond Marx: Lessons on the Grundrisse*. New York: Autonomedia.

—— (1991b). 'Epilogue', in A. Negri, *Marx Beyond Marx: Lessons on the Grundrisse*. New York: Autonomedia.

Shiva, V. (2000). 'Poverty and Globalisation', <http://www.bbc.co.uk/radio4/reith2000/lecture5.shtml>.

Tesco (2006). <http://www.tescocorporate.com/page.aspx?pointerid=6A750D771B FE4E98A3F0741AA32E5489>.

Virno, P. (2004). *The Grammar of the Multitude*. New York: Semiotext(e).

—— (2006). 'Reading Gilbert Simondon: Transindividuality, Technical Activity and Reification'. *Radical Philosophy*, 136: 34–43.

13

Screenworlds: Information Technology and the Performance of Business Knowledge

Hannah Knox, Damian O'Doherty, Theo Vurdubakis, and Chris Westrup

Introduction

As noted in the Introduction to this volume, the problematic of 'business knowledge' tends to be articulated in terms of two contrasting perspectives: that of knowledge conceived as a (more or less) manageable, biddable *resource* versus that of knowledge conceived as the generation of *meaning* as (ultimately *un*manageable) sense-making. We argue in this chapter that to understand how these two dimensions of business knowledge have come to have prominence in contemporary business organization, we must pay attention to how they are mutually created, enacted, and codified in business settings. In practice, this means that we must turn our focus from narrations and abstractions of knowledge and its effects, to look at its instantiation in concrete forms of action and specifically, we suggest, in the creation and use of Information and Communications Technologies (ICTs). We argue that ICTs are central to the ways in which the conceptualization and use of knowledge has become reconfigured in recent years, with striking implications for work and organization.

Context for the research

If on a winter's evening a passer-by were to glance through an office window, all she or he would be likely to see of the 'knowledge economy' at work would be people gazing intently at computer screens, seemingly oblivious to their surroundings. So generic and widespread as to be almost invisible, the VDU is a central medium through which contemporary business organizations 'know themselves'. Few knowledge practices exist that are not these days mediated through the hidden capacities of networks, local hardware, and diverse software packages. Yet we often talk about knowledge as if it exists apart from the information technological devices that permeate all levels of business organization. In this chapter we illustrate how it is that ICTs have been central to the emergence and reproduction of a dominant view of organization by turning our attention to the way in which ICTs are implicated in the reproduction of the two dimensions of knowledge as a *resource* and as *meaning*. Traditionally ICTs have been seen as ways of managing knowledge as a resource (e.g. Galliers and Newell 2000; Newell et al. 2002; Tsoukas 2005), but we argue that much of what is termed 'knowledge work' that uses ICTs, is valued precisely because it requires a *mediation* between these contrasting understandings of knowledge.

The centrality of ICTs to the knowledge economy is recognized by businesses, which have invested heavily in the development and maintenance of IT infrastructures. ICTs hold the promise of organization, transparency, efficiency, management, and the control of knowledge production. Over the last decade or so organizations have moved away from 'building' their own systems to 'buying' packaged software applications. This trend is most clearly exemplified by the ubiquity of 'Enterprise Resource Planning' (ERP) systems in contemporary corporate settings. Mostly supplied by a small handful of global providers, ERP systems currently comprise the dominant commercial infrastructure in most large 'first world' companies and are making rapid inroads elsewhere (Gattiker and Goodhue 2005; Fitzgerald 2005), thus giving rise to talk of an 'ERP revolution' (e.g. Kumar and Van Hillegersberg 2000; Ross and Vitale 2000). ERP systems (a term coined in the 1990s by the Gartner Group) have emerged out of Material Requirements Planning (MRP) systems through the addition of layers of 'knowledge-based functionality' (Mohamed 2002) to the MRP nucleus. The shift from MRP to ERP is said to reflect the shift in emphasis from *tangible* assets (late 1970s) to *'intangible* or knowledge-based assets' (late 1990s) (ibid.). The current phase of ERP evolution has seen the integration of new sub-domains (including

Customer Relationship Management and Supply Chain Management) to form Enterprise Systems. Nearly all large Western organizations are using ERP or Enterprise Systems, and it may not be too far-fetched to suggest that in the near future most medium-sized companies will be using similar integrated suites of ICT applications for most of their activities.

Enterprise Systems promise to facilitate ways of knowing 'the organization' that break out of a perceived sclerosis of functional 'silos' to bridge the gap between what were once deemed business support functions and wider business strategy and organization management. It is here that we see a dominant model of organization emerging in ICT design. This model of organization is reiterated in the process of ICT implementations where struggles for control over the ways in which ICT can change the role of knowledge in an organization are played out between ICT vendors, consultants, and user organizations. Here we find an emergent promise that Enterprise Systems will be able to deliver integration through standardization across diverse international sites. Moreover, they hold the potential to make new kinds of knowledge available and new objects of knowledge to appear. In their study of market traders, Knorr-Cetina and Bruegger (2002: 163) describe how the introduction of integrated dealing systems meant that the formerly abstract 'market became fully available...for the first time....The market on screen is a "whole" market and a global presence.' Before the present era of integrated screens, they note, traders had to invest considerable time and effort 'locating the market' in a maze of networks and institutional spaces such as banks and other financial institutions. Similarly, organizations that in the past had to locate the organization in a maze of departments and subdivisions are now able to see the organization as a regional, national, or global whole. In this view, Enterprise Systems might be understood as productive of new kinds of electronically mediated *presence*. Widely used, it is possible to see Enterprise Systems as instantiations and enactments of a broadly embedded and widely accepted model of twenty-first-century organization.

Empirical study

Our research was conducted over a two-year period in four organizations (including overseas sites): (1) 'BigRed Plc', a manufacturer located in the north-west of England; (2) 'WizSys', an information systems software manufacturer/vendor in Germany; (3) 'Indigo', a privatized UK utilities company; and (4) 'Westwich Airport', a major UK international airport. This chapter draws directly upon empirical material from research conducted at BigRed Plc and WizSys, but it is also informed by broader findings from the other two sites. We designed and completed a series of open-ended and semi-structured interviews that amounted to some 200 hours of recorded interviews. The majority (80%) of interviews were carried out with two or more members of the research team present and additional notes were taken to capture the broader social context of the interviews themselves. Documents were also collected and time was spent observing the use of the technologies that we were studying in practice.

A key feature of the methodology was our efforts to see/hear interviews not simply as an exercise in information retrieval, but rather to engage with the interview as an occasion of 'practical reasoning' in which organization (as a verb rather than a noun) was being variously represented and 'accomplished' by its members and users. We tried to keep in focus the ways in which our own discourse with its concepts and categories helped to shape and co-create the reality of organization (Silverman 1993). If we shifted from the specialized and recognizable discourse of 'Information Systems' into another discursive register, for example, or indeed simply changed the tone in which we asked our questions, we were able to elicit quite different understandings of organization and the way in which ICTs operate. By attending to the interview as a component within the wider socially 'negotiated' construction of reality (Berger and Luckmann 1967), we began to work within the more processual dimensions of organization where organization exists in a more contingent and unpredictable disposition. Finally, it is worth noting that what we were often only able to 'hear', so to speak, after the interview, to attend to that which appeared marginal or insignificant in the doing of the interview but later became vested with greater importance.

We also developed and exercised a more ethnographic style of research that on occasion allowed us to take on the role of participant observation. We attended a number of workshops and group meetings and in total calculate that some 150 hours of time was spent in our organizations in addition to the interviews. We learned to attend to organization as it was happening in the corner-of-the-eye—in the seemingly trivial and marginal, those asides and the routine, the often unremarkable, everyday. These methods proved crucial in uncovering the ways in which ICT-based applications to business processes rely upon knowledge in organization that is always evolving, but also tacit, implicit, and highly skilful in its improvisational qualities.

Discussion

A long-standing concern in the Social Study of Technology has been to reveal the ways in which the design of particular technologies has been 'shaped' by its social, cultural, and organizational 'contexts'. Technologies constitute the means through which particular social values and cultural expectations (e.g. pertaining to what constitutes good order and organization) are given artefactual form. That is to say, ICT applications tend to give material expression to dominant ideals of organization. In turn, the kind of ICT applications with which contemporary businesses are furnished are, so to speak, used 'to think with' (Douglas and Isherwood 1980; Lévi-Strauss 1962) and thus help (re)shape the prevalent understandings of organization. In contemporary organizations then, we might expect to see 'the evolution of business knowledge' *as,* as well as *through*, a succession of technological applications. The implementation of Enterprise Systems over the past two decades is one of the most widespread instantiations of technological development that large organizations have faced. In this discussion section, we look at three dimensions of this implementation process to better understand the 'evolution of business knowledge' and its relationship to ICTs. The first section examines the social values and cultural expectations about knowledge that form and are given form by Enterprise Systems. The second section considers the social processes through which these cultural expectations are (re)produced, and the final section suggests some of the implications of our findings for contemporary business organization.

Knowledge claims and the informationalization of work

We turn first to vendors of Enterprise Systems to consider what they see to be the benefits of Enterprise Systems for their customers. Although clearly a form of sales discourse, the way in which the benefits of Enterprise Systems are articulated by vendors provides a useful starting point for beginning to understand the cultural and social commitments that Enterprise Systems mobilize. Enterprise System vendors such as WizSys are primarily concerned to demonstrate their systems' ability to embody 'state of the art' knowledge concerning good organization, including 'best industry practice'. The 'legacy' systems of previous eras are now viewed as representing the unwitting reifications of 'local' (i.e. of past times and different places) organizational cultures and practices (Williams

2000), with the development of Enterprise System packages predicated upon a series of assumptions about what constitutes generic/abstract organization.

First, Enterprise Systems create visibilities and, as a consequence, raise expectations of increased management knowledge and an extended scope of application, decision making, and control. This is achieved through a process of mirroring, whereby Enterprise Systems embody what practitioners term 'information blueprints' of organizations. These blueprints are either defined specifically by the user organization, or, more commonly, are based on generic 'best industry practices', models designed into the Enterprise System. User companies are compelled to align their business processes and work practices to this blueprint if they are to avoid the high costs associated with customized systems.

Importantly, these blueprints define an organization in terms of the interconnectivity of different parts of the business, focusing on organizational processes as opposed to the functional activities of traditional departments such as accounting, human resources, manufacturing, warehouses, sales, and so on. The rise of ERP systems was in part linked to programs of Business Process Reengineering, which called for the streamlining of businesses along new processual rather than institutional lines. In this way, these systems were a means of exemplifying the ways in which good organization should be accomplished through the installation of effective business processes and day-to-day work routines. The effect of enacting this reengineering through the implementation of ERP systems was to posit the production of information and knowledge as the main benefits of this realignment. Davenport (2000), for instance, describes the 'promise of Enterprise Systems' in the following terms: 'ES represent the opportunity to achieve "true connectivity" by enabling data to be shared internally and externally "in real-time". Supply and demand can be effectively co-ordinated. ES means that managers can now understand "every aspect of a company's operations and performance with the click of the mouse" ' (HBS 2000). The emergence of Enterprise Systems was therefore part of a programme of desired control by management, which it was believed could be achieved through the capturing, collation, and analysis of previously dispersed pockets of information.

An example from BigGreen Plc, a WizSys user, serves to illustrate the particular cultural expectations concerning useful knowledge and good organization—like those articulated by Davenport above—that become invested in ICT design. BigGreen Plc is a major European food-processing multinational (further details are to be found in Newman and Westrup

2005). WizSys was chosen by the head office as the ERP supplier in 1998 and the roll out in the United Kingdom took place in 1999 and 2000. A large well-known consulting firm was employed to oversee the implementation of the system. Consultants went around BigGreen's UK operation requesting those in charge of various functional areas to complete forms that listed their information requirements. When these were completed, any perceived ambiguities were discussed and clarified, and the consultants then configured the company's WizSys system accordingly. For those working in particular sections, their next encounter with '*the* WizSys', as the system came to be commonly known, came when they were being trained in its use and in the associated discussions on how information currently held on BigGreen's legacy systems would migrate to the new system. In this phase, the consultants performed considerable amount of work in order to effect the alignment of the ERP with the organization by configuring the WizSys, to better fit the information requirements of the potential users. Exactly how this should be done was not subject to extensive debate and, in retrospect, the consultants' own knowledge of WizSys was taken very much for granted. The nature of this alignment remained invisible, except that is on occasions when system and organization would become misaligned and 'drift' from one another. For example, it was decided early on that each BigGreen site would have its own server, which would replicate much of the data held on other servers in the United Kingdom. This configuration was supposed to be very robust so that if one server went down, service could be maintained from other sites. It was rapidly realized that this arrangement led to a very slow and complex system as the different servers were frequently engaged in keeping up to date with each other. The expectation of 'real-time' knowledge of 'every aspect of a company's operations and performance with the click of the mouse' was therefore disappointed.

We suggest that the initial phase was telling for the way in which it forced BigGreen's employees to think explicitly about their jobs in terms of their informational output. As noted in the introduction, the ubiquity of information technologies often renders them somewhat invisible in their role as mediators of information generation. But this stage in the process of implementation of ERP required that the mediating role of ICTs was made very clear. In the packing warehouse, employees were asked to write down the precise movements of food products and to note down how changes that occurred to the product at each stage of the production process were recorded. The consultants explained that possible problems arose for the ERP system where there were informational 'gaps' where non-computational mediators (for example, employees themselves) did the work of information transfer (for example, they carried goods from one part of the production line to the other, an act based on knowledge of the production process and not an instruction from a system). As far as the system was concerned, the effect of this employee action would be the temporary disappearance of the product from the system, with potentially unfortunate consequences.

Although the labour of standardization and informationalization is customarily seen as diminishing ambiguity and increasing control, the 'clearing away' of confusion and overcoming of disorder, it could equally be presented as introducing a new lack of flexibility. Here the mapping was focused on definitions of terminologies for units of calculation. Terms such as 'cost-centre', 'warehouses', 'expenses' had always been contentious and a point of debate and difference between different regions and different countries. Now, in the process of ERP implementation, the meaning of these terms was to be debated for the last time in order to be universally agreed upon and fixed. Not only were employees actions having to be thought of as informationally constituted but the formerly descriptive terms upon which organization was premised were now transformed into rigid operators of universal comparison.

This process of standardization was ostensibly driven by the need to fit the universal system to the idiosyncrasies of the organization in a discursive and complementary way. The aim was to increase visibility of the organization and its processes through information; however, this process of alignment often had the opposite effect, making visibilities that the Enterprise System did not value or had not considered very difficult to achieve. In BigGreen, the ERP database that was used by managers to measure sales performance was organized by product, which reflected normal and established practice. Within a year however, the marketing group wanted to change how sales were measured from products to product channels such as shops at petrol stations. This move, they argued, would give better knowledge concerning the best ways that their food products could be sold and sold at the highest margins. They found however, that the ERP system could not provide this information in the form required and that the system itself was going to have to be reorganized if they were going to achieve this perspective on their sales data. As a management accountant explained in an interview: '[s]o we have some fundamental work to do on how the data is held in the WizSys... before we can even get the reporting [of the financial information]'. Debates that would have previously been a matter of analytical preference were now framed in terms of what the Enterprise System did and did not allow and how that system might or might not be tinkered with in order to yield certain desired information. More than simply being a new context for organizational representation, based on a stabilization of representational qualities, the Enterprise System in fact inhabits a more active role as a new organizational actor. The ERP had become an important site for struggles over what constituted useful knowledge and the possibilities of achieving that knowledge. On the one hand, the implementation process had been concerned with making sure that the ERP could be a comprehensive source of interconnected data, but how to transform that data into meaningful knowledge emerged and re-emerged as a continuing source of friction and debate.

The notion that organization could be mirrored in an informational form was necessary to the realization of the management dream of control of the organization through access to information and the subsequent knowledge that would result. In practice, the nature of this alignment often remained invisible to employees, and the act of informationalization was treated as a merely descriptive exercise rather than a more political process where the very nature of *what* and *how* it was possible to know was being redefined. This political dimension became particularly apparent when managers started to question how they managed when they 'discovered' that there had been, and despite the implementation of an ERP system still were, several ways used to represent (ostensibly) the same items in the company. As the UK financial director put it to us:

[O]ne of those frightening things [is] that you suddenly realize that you don't know how you're running your business. It's awful to say but when you actually have to accumulate your master data you have to put down exactly what you should do and what's happening you suddenly realize you have three bills of materials for each product. One held by the factory, one is held by the laboratory, one is held by the accountant. You think they are the same thing but they aren't and maybe on the factory floor they are doing something quite different as well—that's the scary one.

The informationalizing logic of ERP as a means of managing meant managers were being required to reconsider the basis upon which their management knowledge was constituted. Information was emerging as the dominant means through which management could be successfully achieved—more information meaning more knowledge, and more knowledge meaning better management. But the same process of informationalization simultaneously revealed the limitations of the current capture of information, with the subsequent drive for more standardization and more informationalization to close the gaps.

A final dimension of the Enterprise System's logic that we detect here is the way in which knowledge as an informationally defined resource has come to effect a powerful separation between the benefits of universalization vs. the needs of locality and specificity. As we have seen, attempts to standardize 'organization' as the logic of Enterprise Systems demands involves a complex negotiation between an ideal of best practice and prior existing practices. Tensions thus emerge between the standardizable versus the idiosyncratic, the generic versus the particular (Pollock, Williams, and Procter 2003). Against this backdrop, an Enterprise System implementation institutes a distinction between those elements of the package in question that are configurable and those which are 'core' and thus not amenable to further 'localization'. As regards the latter, organizational processes and practices have to be redesigned to achieve a 'fit' with the requirements of the reference models and templates out of which the package has been designed. Managers and employees find themselves coming to evaluate their own participation in organizational processes and the participation of others, on the basis of this situated distinction between a universal ideal and a local necessity that we see as inextricably tied to the informationalizing logic of these systems. The following section considers some of the ways in which this shift has occurred and the role that different actors and practices have played in the move to the informationalization of work.

The productions of an information logic?

Much of the extant literature on ERPs has focused on the enumeration of the success factors, and the impacts and pitfalls of Enterprise Systems and their implementation processes. Such evaluations rest upon an assumption that the ideals of Enterprise Systems that we have seen imposed by IT vendors are legitimate, apolitical, and correct, and that when failures occur it is because these ideals have become corrupted, distorted, and altered in the process of implementation in a user organization. On this basis, the Enterprise System is considered to be a carrier of ideas and a logic of organization that needs to be adopted unproblematically by organizations. Mackenzie (1992), however, has argued that technological trajectories should not be understood as an unfolding product of an intrinsic techno-logic. Instead technologies are better understood as institutionalizations of particular sets of (self-fulfilling) cultural expectations. In this section we aim to show that the reproduction of the informationalizing logic of the Enterprise Systems that we explored in the previous section is far from the outcome of either a clearly conceptualized design on the part of vendors, or a smooth and successful implementation on the part of user organizations. Rather we suggest that the informationalization of work and the shifts this has produced for knowledge and organization are necessarily political, both in the sense of being related to the political economy of market forces, and the complex relational politics of organizational actors.

We start again, with the vendor's narrative and the idea of the pure or ideal system in the shifts in knowledge and organization that we are claiming have occurred. As we noted initially, vendors such as WizSys produce narratives about the benefits of Enterprise Systems that cannot be divorced from the sales orientation of their business. Even in non-commercially directed conversations such as those which we engaged in during interviews, the description of Enterprise Systems that was available for re-articulation by interviewees was a repetition of a sales-oriented narrative. Within WizSys all our informants agreed that the industry-specific 'solutions' they market have '90%' of the necessary business processes that provide a 'blueprint' for companies. Their message to prospective clients is that 'we understand your business'. This 'understanding' is developed, and 'best practice' templates constructed, through a complex process that involves WizSys consultants working intensively with selected companies to formulate aspects of an 'industry solution' (see also Pollock, Williams, and Procter 2003).

Vendors treat Enterprise Systems as a commodity-type product and typically produce a succession of new versions of their Enterprise Systems. Contracts for systems also involve incremental upgrades over a predetermined period within the software version that is bought. Upgrades to a new version of the system (rather than upgrades within packages) are usually charged at an additional rate. These upgrades are considered improvements upon 'best practice'. Improving upon 'best practice' in WizSys occurred in three ways. First, ongoing developments in the technical infrastructure involve changes to system architectures and the incorporation of new technological capabilities (such as RFID) leading to new releases. Second, changes are made by adding new industry solutions (such as financial services or education) or creating additional modules such as CRM to existing ones. In WizSys, this process is described as putting more pieces of 'Lego' together, which users can then 'plug and play'. The incorporation of new features appeared to be of both functional and symbolic value: 'to give out the message', we were told, 'that WizSys is

efficient and forward looking'. At the same time they were wary of producing products that are 'over-engineered' and 'ahead of the market'. Third,
an important market development for WizSys was to introduce products
for smaller companies.

This cycle of production of new releases every few years and the opening
out into new commercial markets can be seen simultaneously as a corporate strategy and as an enactment of a cultural notion of technological
progress. Each version provides new features and sometimes requires
changes in hardware or systems software configuration. From the moment
when they sign up to the Enterprise System contract, user companies
are made aware that they will have to upgrade their Enterprise System at
some point in the future. The maintenance and support contracts that the
Enterprise System vendor provides are based upon an agreement to maintain an up-to-date version of the system over time. Vendors claim that
upgrades ensure that companies are working with systems that are compatible with modern computer hardware and that they are getting the best
from their ICT investment. It is, of course, possible to see the provision of
continuous upgrades as also providing an ongoing revenue stream for
Enterprise System vendors, through long-term tie-ins that make it very
difficult for organizations to change their choice of Enterprise System after
they have installed an initial version from a particular vendor.

Clearly then, the production of Enterprise Systems and the informationalization of knowledge work is as much a commercial venture for the
vendor corporations as it is a commitment to an abstract techno-logic. The
people we interviewed in our case study companies clearly recognized that
competition and economic success were a driving concern for Enterprise
System vendors and were often sceptical of new versions of Enterprise
System products: 'new gadgets' was one description; another said, 'if
I was cynical I would say it was a licence to print money' and told us his
concerns about the time (up to six months) needed to implement them.
Nonetheless, this commercial imperative can be seen to build upon and to
be part of a more general desire for management control and a cultural
expectation that information is the means through which control will be
able to be achieved.

There is a long-established and influential intellectual tradition, which
sees in each new generation of ICTs the solutions to the application of
knowledge to problems of organization. In Euro-American societies 'management' is routinely understood as predominantly concerned with the
ordering and manipulation of representations: representations of objects,
people, and events. For management, therefore, ICTs represent the ability

to engage in a more efficient, one might say frictionless, traffic in representations/inscriptions and to make them combinable in new ways. Against this backdrop, our informants as a rule did not explicitly question the logic of, or the desirability for, Enterprise Systems, despite recognizing its entanglement with commercial ends. They accepted the large amounts of money consumed by complex system implementations as the price to pay for better organization and an increased understanding of the company's operations. As one of our informants in BigRed Plc put it: 'The benefit of [a] WizSys [system] is, if you follow it and you try to go with that standard logic ... it forces you to be more logical. And it flushes out those old systems when you start to impose that on the organization. And to me that is the biggest benefit.' At the same time our informants would (as already mentioned with regard to the reception of new Enterprise System versions) often temper such claims with various degrees of 'healthy' scepticism about the ability of systems to fully deliver the promised benefits, to produce accurate knowledge, or ensure effective control.

Unsurprisingly, the imposition of such disciplinary systems did not occur without some local unease, anxiety, and resistance on the part of user organizations and their employees. We suggest that the effective functioning of standardized packages cannot be adequately understood without taking into account the position they occupy in what we might call 'local ecologies' of work-around practices and applications—which in turn may enjoy varying degrees of (in)formality, (in)visibility, and (il)legitimacy. The unease and tension that we showed in the last section to be produced in implementation processes that depended upon fixing terms and definitions is, we argue, an important aspect in the informationalization of work and the shifts for knowledge that it has effected. Discussion, arguments, frustration, and the creation of work-arounds should not be seen as a straightforward resistance to changes in information and its place in knowledge practices, even if they appear to be a resistance to the technology, which seems to instantiate so clearly this technological-informational logic.

However successful the implementation was deemed to be in user organizations (and in all our case study organizations the implementation had ultimately been judged a success), tensions were an unavoidable feature of Enterprise System implementations. These tensions revolved primarily around the problem of the blueprint and its fixity in determining business practice, which was felt to compromise employees' ability to solve problems or take ad hoc action. Employees responded to the constraints that the Enterprise System imposed by finding alternative ways of organizing themselves and information in order to circumvent the system's limitations.

In BigRed, for instance, there was widespread perception of the unsuitability of the 'business warehouse' module of the Enterprise System—a reporting module whose role was to collate information gathered from other parts of the information system. The decision to add a 'bolt-on' of Business Warehouse (BW) to the main structure of the system which would be better at providing summaries of data was justified in terms of the needs of 'The Board' and the limitations of the 'standard WizSys' to give them what they desired.

[WizSys] has a transactional structure and is not built to produce high-level reports. However this kind of reporting is one of the potential benefits of the collection of all this data which is held by the WizSys system. This is where BW comes in, as it is able to transform data into high-level reports. BW extracts information and transforms it. This is possible as it gets rid of much of the detail contained within WizSys. BW presents data in a way that senior management can understand.

However, employees had considerable difficulty extracting useful reports from this module, a situation that led to the (relatively) informal deployment and use of alternative packages into which relevant data were imported from the Enterprise System for analysis. Similarly, in the area of sales, we found that valued customers in certain markets had become accustomed to discounts with the result that prices could not to be fixed until after the products had been delivered. Clearly, this is not a notion of business practice that the system intended or supported given its emphasis on uniformity and universality. To deal with this variability of pricing then, staff found a way in which they could enter sales order data only *after* payment was received and then subsequently create an invoice that satisfied the Enterprise System. Company accountants, in other words, were 'working around' the steps laid out in the system in order to preserve established practice. In the organizational studies literature (with few exceptions, e.g. Pollock 2005), such violations of the governing logic of Enterprise Systems are typically glossed as rejections of, or resistance to, 'the system'. However, we argue that these practices have far more complex and ambiguous implications for the place of knowledge in business practices.

Although 'work-arounds' were attempts to circumvent the Enterprise System, we suggest that these alternative practices *still* rested on a (situated) view of 'best practice' that we saw to be embodied in the rationale of the Enterprise System. Work-arounds functioned as a critique of the perceived inflexibility of a 'best practice template' (i.e. its 'best practice' was not good enough and was therefore in need of correction) and were typically glossed by our interlocutors as 'better' ways of pursuing organizational objectives.

In sum, the (essentially static) vocabulary of (technological and organizational) 'factors' and 'variables', which has tended to dominate studies of the success and failure of Enterprise Systems in organizations can only provide a very partial and incomplete account of what makes such a system succeed, or indeed work at all. Rather, in order to effectively understand the broader implications of implementing a specific application in a given locality, we need to recover and make visible the sheer amount of formal and informal, acknowledged and unacknowledged work, that has to be performed in order to make it 'work' and to keep it working against a noisome background of 'contingency and unreliability' (Constant 1999: 330). In our case studies, it was the ability to find *local solutions* that enabled these organizations to maintain the ideal of a global system. But importantly, these local solutions were part of the shifts in knowledge work that we have been witnessing and were not incidental to it.

What are some of their effects?

We finish our discussion with a consideration of the social and organizational effects of these shifting knowledge practices that rest on the informationalization of work, by looking at the question of how different communities of practice (Wenger 1998) and bodies of expertise have been required to align and (re)shape their knowledge(s) in relation to standardized packages like Enterprise Systems. What are the implications of the various struggles over knowledge and meaning that have developed around the (re)design, implementation and operation of such packages and which shape what a given system *is* or *does*? Enterprise Systems are typically viewed as belonging in a long succession of applications that have pursued an ever-increasing refinement in the ways in which business 'reality' can be represented and acted upon by organizational actors. However, if Enterprise Systems are to be seen as a chapter in an evolutionary story of progress, then implicit in this is the idea that some forms of 'knowing' and their practitioners are elevated while some others forms are demoted or 'left behind'. The ongoing redefinition and realignment of extant forms of 'knowledge' and 'expertise' is, we suggest, not without undertones of anxiety.

First, Enterprise Systems have meant that a lot of the old administrative and clerical work associated with personnel management (the calculation of wages and salaries for example) can now be done through online information systems management software. This has already facilitated the development of outsourcing and specialized service centres that operate like telephone call centres and has extended the fragmentation of previously integrated management functions like personnel. In BigRed Plc we discovered that there were plans to move to a greater employee-centred and self-service based use of information systems. In this case the employees themselves could directly update and input data on sickness and absence records, for example, into the online information network. On the one hand, this held the potential to eliminate time-consuming clerical activity from the work of personnel and in principle free them up to concentrate on the development of a more strategic role in organization. On the other hand, it appeared to challenge at least *some* of the activities that personnel practitioners had previously been able to claim formed part of the knowledge base that made them a distinctive and coherent, managerial profession.

In BigRed, as in other Enterprise System user organizations, we found that various professional groups and communities of practice responded to the challenges like those faced by personnel practitioners, by laying claim to the role of the interpreter of this newly acquired data stressing their ability to effect a transformation of data into usable business knowledge. Accountants were a powerful group in this respect. Much of the functional work of accounting had been usurped by the Enterprise System technology, so they had been required to find new ways of legitimating their professional status in the organizational context. Traditionally, the interpretation of accounting data has been the preserve of accounting professionals, guarded and monopolized to protect their areas of expertise and jurisdiction. Accounting departments had thus long acted as 'obligatory points of passage' between organizational stakeholders (including senior management) and financial data. In the age of Enterprise Systems this labour of interpretation is no longer 'black boxed' within the idiosyncrasies of their traditional managerial function and expertise. Instead managers can now use business analysis software tools to access such data. As a result, accounting practitioners are increasingly redefining their expertise and developing new types of professional competence and new claims to organizational knowledge, including but not restricted to, new forms of analysis, information assurance, and various forms of scenario creation and simulation made possible through the new systems. As one senior accountant put it: '[w]e want people who are more on the interpretation...a wider business knowledge, who are providing the support to various areas of the business, providing advice based on the numbers that have been produced.' While the Enterprise System had arguably led to a 'honing of data' to produce 'one correct data source', the transformation of this data into usable (meaningful) knowledge became a much more pressing political issue—one which senior accountants, for instance, were eager to appropriate for their profession. At the same time, the centrality of Enterprise Systems to accounting had made it 'essential' for new recruits to have WizSys experience as a part of this newly emerging form of professional expertise.

By interrogating the way in which people (re-)negotiated the descriptive categories and role definitions that determined professional standing, we gain an insight into how organizational members are (re)defining the nature of their knowledge(s) and therefore their place in wider organizational and marketplace conditions (see Knox et al. 2007). In this case, the implications of ICT for the changing value of accounting knowledge, and the discursive resources available to members for dealing with the consequences of such categorization, tell us something about the ways in which the experience of membership was related to, amongst other things, business expertise and its effects. This provides support for the view that computer-mediated organization remains a highly political and contested terrain made up of multiple stakeholders and interest groups who use claims to knowledge as resources in the course of wider organization power struggles (Knights and Murray 1994).

Conclusions

It would be too simplistic to see the 'effects' of Enterprise Systems on the various forms of knowledge and expertise that currently inhabit organizations (merely) in terms of increase and decrease, expansion and contraction—of who is in, for example, and who is out. Rather, we suggest, something more important is going on. We argue that the mediations of Enterprise Systems point towards a transformed (politically as well as intellectually) basis for claims to 'expert knowledge' in contemporary business settings. We have seen this in various dimensions that we have covered in this chapter—in the relationship between consultants and employees, in the ways in which Enterprise System vendors make themselves viable spokespersons for blueprints of organization, and in the responses of professional groupings to the informationalizing demands of Enterprise Systems. Ultimately all of these examples bring us back to the question of the ways in which reliable 'business knowledge' can be produced from mere 'data' (Davenport 1997; Abbott 2000; Galliers and Newell 2000). For most of our interlocutors, the proof that such 'knowledge' had indeed been produced was by virtue of 'its' ability to generate business value (Knox et al. 2007), to function as a *resource*. In short, 'knowledge work' consisted in transforming 'data' to 'information' to 'knowledge' and ultimately to 'business value' (Davenport 2000: 225). Against this backdrop, much of the 'knowledge work' we observed performed in relation to ICTs in our case-study organizations appeared to take place in the spaces 'in-between': in-between the 'screenworld' and the 'real world'; the global and the local; 'the system' and 'the business'; 'data' and 'knowledge'; 'meaning' and 'value'. This was the work deemed necessary by organizational actors to keep the two from drifting apart from one another. In other words, the work necessary to ensure that representation and object represented, the 'virtual' (e.g. representations of business practices process) and the real (actual practices and processes) remained in alignment. In this sense the process of 'alignment' should not be seen as a one-off operation, carried out when the system is implemented, but rather, an ongoing practical accomplishment that is the outcome not only of easy alignments but also of problems, barriers, and work-arounds.

The performance of 'knowledge work' and 'business knowledge' in relation to Enterprise Systems is increasingly conceived in terms of the ability to *reconnect* the representations and calculations generated by the system to the contingencies and exigencies of situated organizational practice. While Enterprise Systems have multiple effects, not least the relocation of knowledge away from those working within the lived complexity—the 'mangle' as Pickering (1995) calls it—of organizational practice, to the screens of managers and consultants (who work with objectified abstractions and overviews), they seem to also initiate moves in the opposite direction. As we have endeavoured to show, management practitioners know that their systems are both fallible and incomplete. They are acutely aware of the contingent and indirect relationship between abstract representations and calculations and transformations. They know, most importantly, that their claims to expertise rests on their ability to perform the reconnections between the systems' outputs and other more contingent, more 'upstream' practices, situations, and possibilities. In our case-study organizations, management expertise is performed less and less in relation to the practices of abstraction and objectification that have for some time been the objects of critical scrutiny in organization studies and beyond. Rather, we have shown how management 'expertise' that is responsive to and constitutive of an apparent informationalization of work is increasingly constituted through practices that *relocate* abstract 'knowledge' and make it 'evident' by the transformative effects it is able to achieve: namely the generation of 'business value'. Enactments of management knowledge and expertise in relation to Enterprise Systems require, we suggest, the effective negotiation of diverse levels of situated practice and thus—ironically—re-entangles management practitioners in the same uncertainties and the 'mangle' of situated practice from which information systems had once promised to deliver them while simultaneously reproducing the ideals of knowledge from which such systems derive their allure.

References

Abbott, Julie (2000). *Data Data Everywhere and Not a Byte of Use?* IBM Global Business Intelligence Solutions, EMEA.

Berger, P., and Luckmann, T. (1967). *The Social Construction of Reality: A Treatise in the Sociology of Knowledge.* Harmondsworth: Penguin.

Constant, E. (1999). 'Reliable Knowledge and Unreliable Stuff: On the Practical Role of Rational Beliefs'. *Technology and Culture,* 40: 324–57.

Davenport, T. (2000). *Mission Critical: Realising the Promise of Enterprise Systems.* Cambridge, Mass.: Harvard Business School Press.

—— (1997). *Information Ecology.* Oxford: Oxford University Press.

Douglas, M., and Isherwood, B. (1980). *The World of Goods: Towards an Anthropology of Consumption.* Harmondsworth: Penguin.

Fitzgerald, B. (2005). '$17 Billion Expected Future Growth in Enterprise Applications Market'. *AMR Research,* 12 October. Available at <http://www.amrresearch.com>

Galliers, R., and Newell, S. (2000). 'Back to the Future: From Knowledge Management to Data Management'. LSE Working Paper, available at <http://is.lse.ac.uk/Support/ECIS2001/pdf/059_Galliers.pdf>

Gattiker, T., and Goodhue, D. (2005). 'What Happens After ERP Implementation: Understanding the Impact of Interdependence and Differentiation on Plant-Level Outcomes'. *MIS Quarterly,* 29/3: 559–85.

HBS (2000). 'Mission Critical: Realising the Promise of Enterprise Systems'. Harvard Business School *Working Knowledge,* 1 February. Available at: <http://hbswk.hbs.edu/archive/1287.html>

Knights, D., and Murray, F. (1994). *Managers Divided: Organization Politics and IT Management.* Chichester, UK: Wiley.

Knorr-Cetina, K., and Bruegger, U. (2002). 'Traders' Engagement with Markets: A Postsocial Relationship'. *Theory, Culture and Society,* 19/5–6: 161–85.

Knox, H., O'Doherty, D., Vurdubakis, T., and Westrup, C. (2007). 'Transformative Capacity, Information Technology, and the Making of Business "Experts" '. *Sociological Review,* 55/1: 22–41.

Kumar, K., and Van Hillegersberg, J. (2000). 'ERP Experiences and Revolution'. *Communications of the ACM,* 43/4: 23–6.

Lévi-Strauss, C. (1962). *Totemism.* Chicago: University of Chicago Press.

MacKenzie, D. (1992). 'Economic and Sociological Explanation of Technical Change', in R. Coombs et al. (eds.), *Technological Change and Company Strategy.* London: Academic Press.

Mohamed, M. (2002). 'Points of the Triangle'. *Intelligent Enterprise Magazine,* 22 August.

Newell, S., Robertson, M., Scarbrough, H., and Swan, J. (2002). *Managing Knowledge Work.* London: Palgrave.

Newman, M., and Westrup, C. (2005). 'Making ERPs Work: Accountants and the Introduction of ERP Systems'. *European Journal of Information Systems,* 14/3: 258–72.

Pickering, Andrew (1995). *The Mangle of Practice: Time, Agency and Science.* Chicago: University of Chicago Press.

Pollock, N. (2005). 'When Is a Work-Around? Conflict and Negotiation in Computer Systems Development'. *Science, Technology and Human Values,* 30/4: 1–19.

Ross, J., and Vitale, M. (2000). 'The ERP Revolution: Surviving Versus Thriving'. *Information Systems Frontiers,* 2/2: 233–41.

Silverman, D. (1993). *Interpreting Qualitative Data: Methods for Analysing Talk, Text and Interaction.* London: Sage.

Tsoukas, H. (2005). *Complex Knowledge.* Oxford: Oxford University Press.

Wenger, E. (1998). *Communities of Practice: Learning, Meaning and Identity.* Cambridge: Cambridge University Press.

Williams, R. (2000). ' "All That Is Solid Melts into Air": Historians of Technology and the Information Revolution'. *Technology and Culture,* 41: 641–68.

—— and Procter, R. (2003). 'Fitting Standard Software Packages to Non-Standard Organizations: The "Biography" of an Enterprise-Wide System'. *Technology Analysis and Strategic Management,* 15/3: 317–32.

Part IV

Making Knowledge an Asset

14

Intellectual Property Activity by Service Sector and Manufacturing Firms in the United Kingdom, 1996–2000

Christine Greenhalgh and Mark Rogers

Introduction

The services sector now contributes the major share of output and employment in advanced countries and also makes a growing contribution to the balance of payments via earnings on invisibles. The old view of services exhibiting slow productivity growth in contrast to high-productivity manufacturing has been substantially modified and the new view recognizes the existence of dynamic high-technology innovation within both manufacturing and services (Miles 2000). Thus, financial services have been identified as an important source of productivity growth and as a conduit for innovation (Greenhalgh and Gregory 2000, 2001) and the rapidly developing communications sector is acknowledged as an integral part of the 'new economy' (Wadhwani 2001).

Nevertheless, most studies of innovation have been focused entirely on manufacturing firms engaged in supplying tangible goods (for a survey of mainly US studies, see Hall 2000; for recent work on the UK, see Bloom and Van Reenen 2002; Toivanen, Stoneman, and Bosworth 2002; Greenhalgh and Longland 2001, 2005). Very little was known about the role of intangible business assets in service sectors producing intangible products, such as finance and insurance, even though firms in these sectors are frequently engaged in product and process innovation and have strong interests in the marketing and protection of good reputations for their new brands. For this reason, our research project monitored the creation of intellectual property (IP) assets in services, as well as estimated the value of these assets to services firms, and compared these findings with those for manufacturing firms. In this chapter, we document the amount of intellectual property (IP) in the services sector and examine what kinds of firms and industries are most active in acquiring these intangible assets. Our studies of the value of IP assets are published elsewhere, but we make reference to these findings below.

Context for the research

Services have generally been neglected in studies of intellectual property acquisition, despite the major importance of this expanding sector of the economy and the growing acceptance of the view that intangible assets contribute to firm success within the global knowledge economy. Equally, studies of intellectual property have mainly focused on patents, despite the fact that trade marks are of greater importance for many sectors, especially services. One important exception is Jensen and Webster (2004), who briefly examine the aggregate trends in trade mark activity for Australia, the United Kingdom, and the United States from 1975 to 2002, before focusing on Australia. They demonstrate that in all three countries trade mark applications increased rapidly, by a factor of around 5 in the United Kingdom, 7 in Australia, and 10 in the United States over 25 years, peaking in the year 2000 and falling somewhat after the 'dotcom' bust. For Australia they also demonstrate that a dramatic rise in service marks was the major component of the rapid rise in marks, which accelerated during the 1990s but, as noted in an earlier study for Australia by Loundes and Rogers (2003), the rise occurred across many different industries and firm types, not just in telecommunications or Internet-related firms.

As documented below, we have created a substantial new database of UK service firms, drawing on a range of sources and matching information from these various sources for over 1,200 such tertiary-sector firms, deriving information to parallel our existing database for around 800 primary- and secondary-sector UK firms. We also investigate the relationship between a number of industry and firm characteristics and the propensity to acquire IP assets. All the analysis provides comparisons between services and manufacturing firms, and many of the descriptive statistics show results for twelve major industry sectors covering the whole economy.

We begin by providing a description of service sector IP, together with a comparison with manufacturing and other production firms. We focus at first on trade marks (including both goods and service marks), as these are the most widespread form of IP asset, covering both the historically important trade mark application route through the UK Patent Office and the new European Community trade mark route, which was introduced in 1996. We also document patents applied for via both the UK and European Patent Office routes, but necessarily these are less common forms of IP for service sector firms.

As trade marks have been a less frequent subject of study than patents, we first outline what role these intangible assets might play in the system of rewards to innovation. Economic analysis often distinguishes process from product innovation, but some analysts also distinguish new products that increase product variety (horizontal innovation) from those which offer significant increases in product quality (vertical innovation). Clearly, as novelty is a key condition for the award of a patent, we would expect firms to apply for patents whenever they have created significantly original processes or products, or sub-elements of such items, which fall in the range of items for which patents can be awarded. The patenting conditions require the advance to be novel, non-obvious, and capable of industrial application. This frequently limits patents to tangible products in the United Kingdom and Europe, where software and business methods have not been broadly accepted for patenting, unless there is an integral technical component. Thus, patents will be sought for novel process innovations and for superior products that depart radically from earlier ones.

In contrast with patents, trade mark applications are likely to be more strongly associated with the offer to the market of new product varieties that are not as strikingly novel as those awarded patents. The legal basis for a trade mark is construed without much reference to the economic concept of innovation. Trade marks define a distinctive mark, sign, or logo that identifies the source of origin of production and thus provides a signal of quality and reliability of supply to the customer. However, as firms engage constantly in product differentiation and advertising of distinctive brands with the aim of increasing customer loyalty to their products, this activity of non-price competition inevitably involves some degree of innovation, even if only incremental in degree. Firth (1995) argues that for both goods and services, 'trade marks and brand names provide important information as to the nature and origin of these products. Such information is essential to the functioning of a competitive market.' Both Firth (1995) and Cornish (1999) identify three ways that trade marks function: to guarantee commercial origin, to indicate quality, and to serve as a vehicle for advertising. However, Firth admits that only the origin function is universally recognized as the proper object of legal protection by registration of a trade or service mark, as the product quality and characteristics are not legally guaranteed. Nevertheless, new product varieties that increase horizontal diversification will usually provide significantly more choice to customers, thus reflecting a welfare-improving innovation.

The Gowers Review (HM Treasury 2006) reports on the proportions of enterprises rating different methods of protecting innovation as being of 'high' importance and finds that trade marks are second to confidentiality agreements and rank above patents. In the services sector, innovations prompting trade mark applications may include even the more novel vertical product innovations, in areas where patenting is not possible due to the nature of the service product, such as business methods. As a measure of the effective rate of innovation in services therefore, trade marks are likely to give a more accurate picture than patents. In manufacturing, even where patents are possible, trade marks will also be sought alongside these patents to protect brand names and support product identification and hence sustain customer loyalty. Evidence of correlation between patent and trade mark activity is given in Greenhalgh, Longland, and Bosworth (2003) for UK manufacturing and in Loundes and Rogers (2003) for Australian firms.

Some service industries, particularly the media and publishing sectors, rely heavily on copyright rather than patents or trade marks. As copyright does not have to be registered in the United Kingdom, we have no way of documenting the amount of copyright owned by firms in our sample. In a recent survey of the economics of copyright, Corrigan and Rogers (2005) make a plea for more empirical documentation of this important set of IP rights. As a subsection of our research, we attempted to trace the value of copyright through cases that were disputed in the courts, see Mazeh and Rogers (2006), but this exercise yielded a very small sample of information as many cases were settled out of court for undisclosed sums. In what follows we thus confine our analysis of IP to patents and trade marks.

Empirical study

The database

The IP database construction involved three major steps. First, we acquired and utilized firm ownership information from *Who Owns Whom* (Dun and

Bradstreet 2001) on the complex structures of parent firms to derive a list of relevant names for each firm under which intellectual property assets may have been registered. We then searched four sources of IP records using all the identified names, to determine the details of firms' annual acquisitions of intellectual property by counting trade marks and patents applied for via the United Kingdom and European IP offices by these firms and/or their subsidiaries. Finally, this IP information was aggregated to the parent-firm level to give the full numbers of IP assets of each type. For our economic analysis of IP, we matched the IP data with the company accounts of the parent group; the full reported company accounts for services firms were derived from *Company Analysis* (Thomson 2001) for the period to 2000.

The basic sample that we constructed covers 2,054 firms, for which we have some financial data drawn from their company accounts; these are classified into twelve major sectors using the SIC of their major product. Eight are service sectors comprising financial, real estate, wholesale, retail, hotel/catering, transport/communication, business, and other services, and covering 1,232 service firms; the four non-service sectors are agriculture, manufacturing, utilities, and construction, covering 822 firms, of which the majority are engaged in manufacturing, 640 firms.

Counts of the four IP assets (UK and EC trade marks and UK and EPO patents) were made starting from the common period of existence of these assets (i.e. 1996 when EC trade marks began to the year 2000), giving a maximum five-year span for each company that existed throughout this period, or less for companies that were created, or disappeared due to merger or bankruptcy. For each firm, many of which were large and complex in structure, we investigated the firm structure for the group reporting accounts at year 2000 and counted the IP assets sought by the parent firm and each of the subsidiary and associate companies. This was achieved by searching the four sets of annual IP records under all of the possible firm names owned by each parent group. (See the Appendix for more details of the data sources.)

Details of the number of companies per sector and their total activity in terms of value added, employment, and R&D in the year 2000 are given in the Appendix, Table 14.A1. The firms in this sample are mainly medium to large-sized and so these sample firms produce a large proportion of national output, sustaining a large number of jobs and contributing a large share of UK R&D activity into the bargain. For example, since total GDP in 2000 was about £950bn, the £304bn of value added generated from the firms in these data account for around 30% of national output.

In terms of UK R&D, the Office of National Statistics (ONS) estimates that £11.5bn was spent, whereas the firms in our data collectively reported

£12.3bn (this figure, which is derived from company account data, can be higher, since the ONS data exclude any R&D conducted overseas or by higher education or public agencies). In terms of intellectual property, our medium to large-sized firms are active in the acquisition of IP assets to bolster their market share and gain the rewards from innovation. The subsequent sections explore the extent and nature of this activity, but it is worthwhile comparing the overall scale of IP activity in the data here to the aggregate statistics.

Statistics from the Office for the Harmonization of the Internal Market website (OHIM), which issues Community trade marks, show that 43,010 applications were made in 1996 (the first year of their existence), with 5,705 from the United Kingdom. On average each application related to 2.46 trade mark classes, so the UK figure to compare with our data (where we count each class as an 'application' for a trade mark) is 14,034. In our data there are 5,309 Community trade mark class applications, which is 38% of the UK class applications, i.e. a substantially higher share than these firms' share of GDP noted above, suggesting an initial dominance by larger firms compared to small enterprises.

The total number of Community trade marks applied for, both as reported by OHIM and in our data, fell in 1997 and 1998. In 2000, the total UK applications to OHIM were 7,930 out of a total of 57,324, with a higher number of classes per application at an average rate of 2.81. The firms in our data accounted for 6,722 out of the estimated 22,283 trade mark classes for UK applications, which is around a 30% share, very similar to their GDP share, and suggesting a rise in the Community trade mark activity of smaller firms not covered by our database during the period 1996–2000.

In terms of UK trade mark class applications, the share attributed to firms in our data is substantially reduced. For example, in 1996 there were 34,109 applications for UK trade marks from domestic residents compared to a total of 7,164 in these data (21%). The growth of total UK trade marking has been rapid, with 60,979 applications made in 2000, and applications from the medium to large firms have largely kept up with this by rising to 12,450 (20% of total).

The numbers of patent publications are smaller than trade mark applications. The firms in our data had 747 UK patent publications in 2000 and 1,974 EPO publications. Comparative data on total publications are not commonly available, but the UK Patent Office granted 4,170 patents to domestic residents in 2000. For the EPO, there were 4,359 EPO applications in 2000, suggesting that large firms account for a substantial share of EPO publications. These statistics also show that the medium to large-sized firms in these data favour EPO patents over UK patents.

Summary of overall incidence and counts of IP activity

For the whole sample, the proportion of firms which made at least one UK trade mark application within any year (average for the five-year period) was 30% and the average number of UK trade marks per firm per year was 4.7. Activity via the new Community trade mark system was lower, with 18% of firms making at least one application in any year and the average number of marks per firm per year being 2.2. As expected, patenting activity was lower, with 9% of firms publishing a UK patent per year and 8% publishing an EPO patent, while the numbers of patents per firm per year were modest: 0.35 UK and 0.77 EPO patents. Behind all these averages, there was a very considerable range, with the highest numbers of trade marks and patents per year in a single firm being 487 UK trade marks, 624 EC trade marks, 58 UK patents, and 355 EPO patents, respectively.

These yearly figures conceal a considerable degree of rotation among firms, which do not necessarily seek IP assets in each and every year. As a result the percentages of firms seeking to acquire some IP within the whole five-year period are considerably higher than yearly rates. Details of these percentages by sector are given in Table 14.A2, which shows that in nine out of twelve sectors (the exceptions being agriculture, construction, and real estate) more than half of all the firms applied for a UK trade mark, and more than one-quarter for an EC trade mark, between 1996 and 2000. These applications for patents and trade marks can be seen against the reported R&D activities of the sample firms, which again showed very considerable variation in reporting rates and reported values, with around 18% of firms reporting R&D and the average annual value of this expenditure being £23 million in year 2000 prices, but with a range from about £1,000 to £2.5 billion.

In the four charts (Charts A, B, C, D), we display the percentage of firms in each of the twelve sectors that sought to obtain one or more of each type of IP asset in a given year of observation. (When comparing Chart A with Charts B, C, and D, note that the vertical scale on A is smaller than these latter so an equal height bar is larger in A.) Clearly, two non-service sectors, manufacturing and utilities, are the most active in respect of patents (Charts C and D) and are also very active in trade marks. Even so, the eight service sectors all show considerable percentages of firms applying for trade marks (Charts A and B) and in the case of UK trade marks (Chart A), retail firms are more frequently active than manufacturing firms, with more than 40% per annum of retail firms applying for trade marks, and the hotel and catering trade also showing a higher incidence of UK trade mark activity by the year 2000 than manufacturing.

301

Chart A: Percentage of firms applying for UK trade marks by sector and year

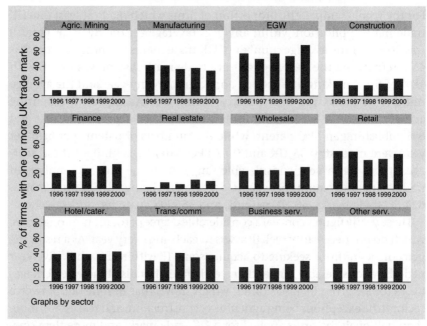

Graphs by sector

Chart B: Percentage of firms applying for EC trade marks by sector and year

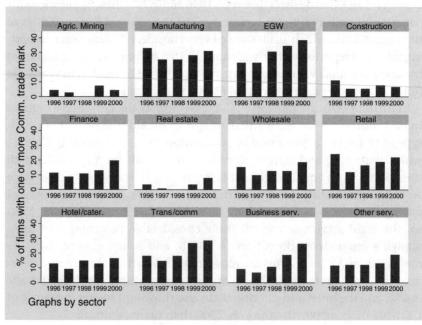

Graphs by sector

Chart C: Percentage of firms publishing UK patents by sector and year

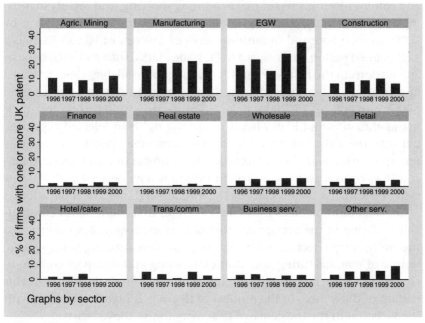

Chart D: Percentage of firms publishing EPO patents by sector and year

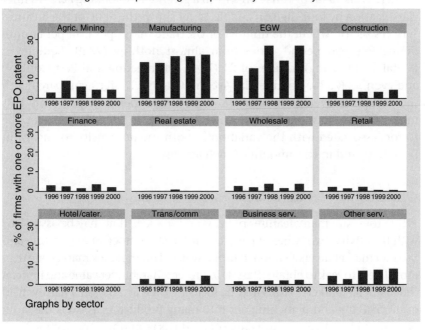

In the case of European Community trade marks (Chart B), the transport and communications sector makes a strong showing, and rapidly increasing rates of activity, reaching levels well above the all-firm average by 2000, are also observed in business services. Over most sectors there is a well-defined pattern with regard to EC trade marks, with an initial burst of applications in the first year this IP right became available, 1996, followed by a small drop, but then showing a rising trend in activity to reach even higher percentages by 2000. Before 1996 firms wishing to protect their marks abroad would have obtained separate rights in selected countries, but with the arrival of the EC trade mark came the opportunity to make one application and obtain protection in a number of countries simultaneously, so firms wishing to protect in 1995 may have delayed until the new system became available, causing the initially high rates of application.

Consideration of Table 14.A3 demonstrates that there is also considerable variation in the average number of IP assets acquired per firm across the twelve major sectors, with high rates of trade marking being characteristic of manufacturing and utilities, retailing and transport/communication, but also increasingly of transport and financial services. This pattern of differences in the number of IP assets is highly correlated with the variation in the incidence of IP activity in the above charts.

There is also a lot of variation within a given sector looking across a finer classification by four-digit SIC. Table 14.A4 shows the data for the Business Services sector, where the number of UK trade marks per firm per annum in the five-year period varies from almost nothing (7359, Equipment Rental and Leasing) to rates of 21 (7342, Disinfecting and Pest Control) and even 32 (7336, Commercial Art and Graphic Design) compared with the sector 73 average of two UK trade marks per firm per year. This indicates that it should be worthwhile trying to identify some of the factors associated with the variation in both the propensity to engage in IP activity and in the amount of such activity.

Characteristics of IP active firms

While there are many features of firms and markets that may be associated with IP activity, two issues of particular interest are stock market listing and product market diversification. If firms are listed on the stock market, are they more likely to seek to obtain IP assets to protect shareholder value and impress the financial markets? Firms may be focusing their activity on a narrow field or diversifying and branching out into many product areas, so is the latter type most likely to generate a range of products requiring IP protection?

Table 14.1. *Trade marking and stock market status of firms*

Company type	Observations	Services		Observations	Manufacturing	
		% observations with UK trade mark	% observations with EC trade mark		% observations with UK trade mark	% observations with EC trade mark
Unlisted company	2,431	18.8	7.7	1,184	32.8	21.6
Listed company	3,729	37.7	18.2	2,016	41.4	32.6
Pearson χ^2		143.9	135.3		23.4	44.4

Note: For both services and manufacturing sectors and for both UK and EC trade marks, the percentages of active firms by year are significantly higher for listed than for unlisted firms using the Pearson chi-squared test of association.

Tables 14.1 and 14.2 contain two-way classifications of the firm by year observations of trade mark activity, according to whether or not the firms were listed on the UK stock market and according to the degree of product market diversification within the companies, together with the appropriate statistical tests of significance of the differences in these probabilities between the types of firms. For both UK and EC trade marks and for both manufacturing and services firms, both stock market status and high diversification are significantly positively associated with being trade mark active. The above results suggest the need for further investigation into these characteristics in a multivariate framework, which can include other characteristics, notably firm size, and in which we analyse the incidence of patents as well as trade marks.

Table 14.2. *Trade marking and product market diversification of firms*

Company type	Observations	Services		Observations	Manufacturing	
		% observations with UK trade mark	% observations with EC trade mark		% observations with UK trade mark	% observations with EC trade mark
Not highly diversified	3,670	22.2	10.6	1,070	30.1	21.9
Highly diversified	2,490	34.7	19.2	2,130	42.3	31.9
Pearson χ^2		117.9	92.1		44.6	35.3

Notes
1. Highly diversified means that the firm is active in four or more four-digit SICs.
2. For both services and manufacturing sectors and for both UK and EC trade marks, the percentages of active firms by year are significantly higher for the highly diversified than for other firms using the Pearson chi-squared test of association.

The role of firm size in IP activity

There is interest in whether large or small firms are more likely to acquire IP assets, and in addition how the intensity of IP use changes with firm size (see the review by Cohen 1995). The economy will benefit from beneficial spillovers in the diffusion of domestic innovations, so the competition authorities may decide to allow firms to grow large in relation to market size if this produces higher rates of innovation, even when it generates distortions arising from market concentration. In an earlier analysis for manufacturing (Greenhalgh and Longland 2001), we found that the rise in the number of UK and EPO patents and UK trade marks with increasing firm size was either less than proportionate or roughly so. This suggested that two smaller firms would jointly obtain as many or more IP assets as one larger firm of twice their size. In a related study of the same data, Greenhalgh and Longland (2005) found that IP intensity was significant for raising total factor productivity in these firms.

In Tables 14.3 to 14.6 we analyse both IP participation (whether a firm is active in acquiring IP assets in the observed year) and IP intensity (i.e. the extent of this IP activity in relation to firm size, where size is measured by employment). Tables 14.3 (services) and 14.4 (manufacturing) show the analysis of IP participation, whereas Tables 14.5 (services) and 14.6 (manufacturing) are for IP intensity. Given that larger firms may also be more likely to be listed and highly diversified, these multivariate regressions thus investigate the role of firm size, stock market listed status and product market diversification when all factors are varying simultaneously. In this analysis we also include a time trend and a set of dummy variables to control for persistent differences by industry group.

In general (Tables 14.3 and 14.4), the strongest predictor of participation in IP activity in any given year for all four types of IP and both services and manufacturing is firm size. Even so, for services firms, the other firm characteristics are also independently significant. In contrast, for manufacturing firms, neither stock market listing nor product market diversification has a separate impact once we have controlled for firm size. This reflects stronger correlation between these three variables in manufacturing than in services, as the stock market listing and product diversification factors were significantly associated with trade mark activity in manufacturing in the two-way analysis of variance reported above in Tables 14.1 and 14.2.

To summarize the results for services from Table 14.3, IP participation is increasing with firm size for all four IP types, with the largest marginal

Table 14.3. *Probit estimates of the propensity to be IP active in services*

	UK trade mark	EC trade mark	UK patent	EPO patent
Firm size	0.256***	0.218***	0.261***	0.157***
(by employment)	0.012	0.013	0.023	0.023
Marginal effect	0.087	0.046	0.011	0.008
Listed	0.065	0.157**	0.303**	0.198
company	0.059	0.171	0.144	0.139
Marginal effect		0.032	0.011	
Highly	0.121***	0.146**	0.236**	0.225**
diversified	0.046	0.052	0.091	0.097
Marginal effect	0.041	0.031	0.010	0.011
Trend	0.024	0.107***	0.018	0.012
	0.016	0.018	0.030	0.032
Marginal effect		0.023		
Number of observations	4,477	4,432	3,842	3,297
Industry dummies $\chi^2(39)$	189.03	172.27	108.84	106.11

Notes to Tables 14.3 to 14.6

1. Firm size is measured by the natural log of employment in all four tables.

2. Standard errors are given below coefficients and the number of asterisks on the coefficient rises with the level of its statistical significance on a two tail test, * = 10%, ** = 5%, *** = 1%.

3. All the estimated equations contain a full set of dummy variables based on US SIC 2-digit industry. Tests of the joint significance of these industry differences are reported in the last row of each table.

Notes to Tables 14.3 and 14.4

1. The dependent variable is a 0,1 dummy variable, where 1 indicates the firm is active in that year in seeking to acquire the type of IP asset.

2. As coefficients for Probit estimates are not easy to interpret quantitatively, the computed marginal effects for those variables that are statistically significant are given below the relevant coefficient and standard error. For firm size and trend this gives the marginal rate of increase, whereas for the two zero-one characteristics (listed, diversified) the marginal effect is the discrete change in probability of obtaining IP associated with having the characteristic.

effects being for UK and EC trade marks. Listed firms of any given size are more likely to be active in seeking EC trade marks and UK patents, but not in UK trade marks or EPO patents. Highly diversified firms are more likely to be active in seeking all four types of IP with the biggest marginal effects being observed for both types of trade marks. We also find a significant positive trend in participation for newly available European Community trade marks, but there are no trends for the other three IP types. Finally there are significant persistent differences across the two-digit industries in the propensity to be IP active for all four IP types, as indicated by the final row test statistics.

Turning to manufacturing firms, Table 14.4 again shows a higher probability of IP activity in larger firms for all four IP types, with rather similar marginal effects being observed for all types of IP. However, for this group of firms, whether the firm is listed or diversified makes no difference once we have controlled for firm size. The trends for manufacturing are negative for UK trade marks, zero for EC trade marks and UK patents, but positive for EPO patents. As for services, there are persistent differences across

Table 14.4. *Probit estimates of the propensity to be IP active in manufacturing*

	UK trade mark	EC trade mark	UK patent	EPO patent
Firm size	0.258***	0.266***	0.377***	0.325***
(by employment)	0.017	0.017	0.021	0.021
Marginal effect	0.100	0.092	0.094	0.078
Listed	−0.058	−0.022	−0.119	0.028
company	0.082	0.087	0.102	0.104
Highly	−0.037	0.027	−0.136	−0.028
diversified	0.067	0.071	0.082	0.084
Trend	−0.043**	0.007	0.033	−0.073***
	0.021	0.021	0.024	0.024
Marginal effect	−0.017			0.017
Number of observations	2,374	2,374	2,358	2,374
Industry dummies $\chi^2(19)$	124.49	155.16	227.95	343.82

two-digit industries. In other respects, the profile differs quite a lot from services but, in comparing these two major sectors, we should not be surprised to find that they are both increasing their activity in seeking IP assets through European registries, with this increase being in respect of trade marks for services and patents for manufacturing.

Tables 14.5 and 14.6 show that, once the firm is an active IP participant, then the intensity of IP falls with firm size across both services and manufacturing and for all four IP measures. The intensity of IP is generally flat with the other three variables (except for UK trade mark intensity being lower if a listed firm in services) and in addition, for most IP types, there are no significant persistent differences by industry (again with the exception of UK trade mark intensity for services). These results show that there is generally a similarity of IP intensity at any given firm size, regardless of stock market listing, product diversification, industry, and year. The constancy of IP intensity across these other variables is similar to that in Table 14.4 for the propensity to acquire IP in manufacturing, but stands in contrast with the variable propensity to acquire IP in services shown in Table 14.3. For both services and manufacturing, the fall in IP intensity with firm size is consistent with the notion that, for IP active firms, a critical number of IP assets needs to be acquired to achieve a useful portfolio of intangible assets.

The financial services sector

Within the services sector, our database is large enough to examine these phenomena for specific sectors. In Greenhalgh and Rogers (2006b), we

Table 14.5. *Robust regressions of the intensity of IP activity in services*

	UK trade mark	EC trade mark	UK patent	EPO patent
Firm size	-0.044^{***}	-0.172^{***}	-0.0003^{***}	-0.001^{***}
(by employment)	0.009	0.008	0.0001	
Listed	-0.084^{**}	0.017	-0.0003	-0.001
company	0.043	0.013	0.0004	0.002
Highly	0.020	0.020	0.0001	-0.0001
diversified	0.018	0.016	0.0002	0.0005
Trend	0.006	-0.001	0.0002	-0.0001
	0.004	0.004	0.0001	0.0002
Number of observations	1,435	1,435	1,435	1,435
Industry dummies F (39,1391)	170.68	1.36	0.92	0.73

Notes to Tables 14.5 and 14.6
1. The dependent variable is the number of IP assets of a given type per employee.
2. Robust regressions were conducted using procedures within STATA 8.0 that reduce or eliminate the influence of outlying observations.

document the extent of intellectual property assets held by financial services firms (specifically finance, insurance, and real estate) and we compare these to the patterns of such intangible assets held by manufacturing firms and utilities providers. We demonstrate that the strong growth and development of the financial services sector in the United Kingdom has been accompanied by a rise in the acquisition of intangible assets in the form of intellectual property rights held by firms in this sector. These findings were reported by City and Financial Publishing (2005), who commented that 'there is no doubt that intellectual property will be of growing importance to financial institutions'.

The main type of IP asset acquired was trade marks, with only a few venture capital companies reporting R&D expenditure or acquiring patents. This pattern is consistent with the development of new varieties of financial services products, using new process technology bought-in from

Table 14.6. *Robust regressions of the intensity of IP activity in manufacturing*

	UK trade mark	EC trade mark	UK patent	EPO patent
Firm size	-0.044^{*}	-0.004^{***}	-0.002^{*}	-0.001^{***}
(by employment)	0.025	0.001	0.001	0.0004
Listed	-0.022	-0.006	-0.002	0.001
company	0.036	0.004	0.002	0.001
Highly	0.118		0.002	
diversified	0.092	0.003	0.004	0.001
Trend	-0.0002	0.001		0.0005^{**}
	0.004	0.001	0.0003	0.0002
Number of observations	978	978	978	978
Industry dummies F (19, 954)	0.74	2.81	0.85	2.38

the manufacturing sector. Even so, the incidence of new trade marks during 1996–2000 for financial service firms was still zero in over half of these firms; this is well below the rates in the manufacturing and utilities sectors. Although large firms account for much of the observed trade mark activity, smaller firms again make more trade mark applications per employee. We found no impact of stock market listed status or the extent of product diversification of the firm on the propensity to acquire trade marks for financial services firms, although these characteristics were significant across the whole sample of services firms.

The value of IP assets to firms

In another paper using these data, Greenhalgh and Rogers (2006c), we examine how far differences in firm performance are related to their intangible assets in order to gain some measures of the value of trade marks to firms. First, we analyse Tobin's q, which is the ratio of the firm's stock market value to the book value of its tangible assets. We expect Tobin's q to rise for firms acquiring valuable intangible assets, such as trade marks and patents, as the stock market uses the new information to revalue the firm to reflect its higher expected future profitability due to its innovative activity. We examine the impact on firms' market values from undertaking any trade mark activity and we also explore the effects of increasing trade mark intensity (measured as the ratio of the number of trade marks to assets or employment) among those that do.

Stock market values are positively associated with trade mark activity by all firms. We find larger differences between firms with and without trade marks for services than for manufacturing firms, for whom patents also contribute to market value. We also find bigger differences in Tobin's q when the services firm is applying for Community marks, rather than just applying for UK marks—for details see Table 14.7, which contains results drawn from estimates in Greenhalgh and Rogers (2006c). Looking at the intensity of trade mark activity, we found that increasing the intensity of Community trade marks matters for both manufacturing and services, although at a decreasing rate through the data period of 1996 to 2000. In particular, the rapid fall in the UK stock market in 2000 appeared to negate the benefits of extra trade marks for innovative services firms. However, in our study focusing on financial sector firms (Greenhalgh and Rogers 2006a), we also find that higher trade mark intensity is associated with higher market values. Furthermore, for these financial sector firms, the market's valuation of trade marking increased in the late 1990s.

Table 14.7. *Predicted difference in stock market value between trade mark active and inactive firms*

Activity in	EC trade marks only	UK trade marks only	Both types of trade marks
All firms	37%	25%	49%
Manufacturing firms	(7%)	(12%)	23%
Services firms	68%	32%	65%

Note: These estimates are from an analysis of Tobin's *q* using data for all listed firms in the sample. The control variables were book value of tangible and intangible assets, R&D, patent activity if any, product diversification, sales in EU or US, sales growth, and debt ratio, plus two-digit industry and year dummies. Parentheses around a figure indicate that the difference was not statistically significant at the 10% level. For full results, see Greenhalgh and Rogers (2006c).

We next investigate the relationship between trade mark activity and productivity; once again patenting and R&D activity are controlled for where appropriate. Previous analysis of firm-level productivity in the service sector is sparse, since the existing production function approach was developed for manufacturing firms. The idea here is that by increasing the quality and differentiation of products, the intangible trade mark assets are associated with the firm producing goods and services of higher average unit value.

Our analysis indicates that trade mark data can be successfully used to explain differences in productivity levels in both manufacturing and service sectors. Using the distinction between trade markers and non-trade markers in regression analysis, Table 14.8 shows that trade mark active firms achieve higher productivity (typically trade markers have around 10% higher value added, although this varies across sectors and type of trade mark activity). Further, the intensity of UK or Community trade marks has a positive coefficient in a (cross-sectional) production function regression and raises the explanatory power of the regression by around 5% in service sector regressions. In contrast, the accounting (book) value of intangibles, which is recorded in company accounts and generally

Table 14.8. *Predicted difference in productivity between trade mark active and inactive firms*

Activity in	EC trade marks only	UK trade marks only	Both types of trade marks
All firms	9%	11%	32%
Manufacturing firms	11%	(0%)	16%
Services firms	(6%)	19%	47%

Note: These results are from estimates of value added production functions for all firms in the sample. The control variables were capital stock, employment, R&D, patent activity if any, sales in EU or US, plus two-digit industry and year dummies. Parentheses around a figure indicate that the difference was not statistically significant at the 10% level. For full results, see Greenhalgh and Rogers (2006c).

reflects assets such as goodwill acquired on takeover, adds virtually no explanatory power.

Conclusions

This chapter provides some illumination of the neglected topic of the use of the intellectual property system by the services sector, which now employs the major share of workers in the United Kingdom and other advanced economies. By tracing applications for trade marks and the publication of patents by large companies, and by all the subsidiaries partly or wholly owned by these parent firms, we have documented the acquisition by firms of a variety of intellectual property rights designed to protect their innovations. In so doing, we have provided a novel picture of the extent to which these companies were bringing to market large numbers of new goods and services and new processes in the period 1996–2000. While the number of IP assets (patents and trade marks) sought through the UK Patent Office remained fairly steady across all firms, trends in registering trade marks in Europe were positive for service sector firms, while manufacturing firms showed an increase in their propensity to seek European patents.

Analysis of the variation across firms in their propensity to acquire IP has identified several firm characteristics that are positively correlated with IP acquisition, including larger firm size, stock market listed status, and high product market diversification. Even so, the intensity of IP activity per employee was found to be negatively associated with firm size, suggesting the need for a minimum portfolio of each type of IP asset per firm.

In our analyses of the value of these intangible assets, firm performance is assessed by what value the stock market ascribes to its future profitability, and by its current productivity performance. Both of these approaches show that the innovative activity reflected in applications for new trade marks and patents has a positive impact on performance in both services and manufacturing firms, although with some differences in magnitudes. This raises an important issue for public policy concerning how to support innovative activity in firms not heavily engaged in conventional R&D, who do not qualify to receive the R&D tax credit, but who nevertheless offer a significant range of important innovations to the market. These innovations create new profitable opportunities for firms using these products and offer benefits to final consumers by improving the range and quality of products.

Acknowledgements

The authors acknowledge the financial support of the ESRC, award RES 334-25-0002, within the Evolution of Business Knowledge Research Programme. This research project was titled 'The Measurement and Valuation of Intangible Assets in the Service Sector'. We are grateful to St Peter's College, Oxford, for accommodation and administrative support for this research. The database was constructed during this and previous research projects by Mark Longland in collaboration with the authors.

During the course of this research, the authors were invited to visit the Melbourne Institute of Applied Economic and Social Research and the Intellectual Property Research Institute of Australia on two occasions, where they were able to present working papers. The authors are grateful to the seminar participants and members of these Institutes, especially to Elizabeth Webster, for helpful comments on the work in progress.

References

Bloom, N., and Van Reenen, J. (2002). 'Patents, Real Options and Firm Performance'. *Economic Journal*, 112: C97–116.

City and Financial Publishing (2005). 'Intellectual Property and Technology Issues'. *Compliance Officer Bulletin*, Issue 26, May.

Cohen, W. (1995). 'Empirical Studies of Innovative Activity', in P. Stoneman (ed.), *Handbook of the Economics of Innovation and Technological Change*. Oxford: Blackwell.

Cornish, W. (1999). *Intellectual Property: Patents, Copyright, Trade Marks and Allied Rights*, 4th edn. London: Sweet and Maxwell.

Corrigan, R., and Rogers, M. (2005). 'The Economics of Copyright'. *World Economics: The Journal of Current Economic Analysis and Policy*, 6/3: 53–174.

Firth, A. (1995). *Trade Marks: The New Law*. Bristol: Jordan Publishing.

Greenhalgh, C., and Gregory, M. (2000). 'Labour Productivity and Product Quality: Their Growth and Inter-Industry Transmission in the UK 1979–90', in R. Barrell, G. Mason, and M. O'Mahony (eds.), *Productivity, Innovation and Economic Performance*. Cambridge: Cambridge University Press/NIESR.

—— —— (2001). 'Structural Change and the Emergence of the New Service Economy'. *Oxford Bulletin of Economics and Statistics*, Vol. 63, Special Issue.

Greenhalgh, C., and Longland, M. (2001). 'Intellectual Property in UK Firms: Creating Intangible Assets and Distributing the Benefits via Wages and Jobs'. *Oxford Bulletin of Economics and Statistics*, Vol. 63, Supplement, pp. 671–96.

—— —— (2005). 'Running to Stand Still? The Value of R&D, Patents and Trade Marks in Innovating Manufacturing Firms'. *International Journal of the Economics of Business*. 12/3 (November): 307–28.

Greenhalgh, C. A., and Rogers, M. (2006a). 'Market Value of UK Intellectual Property: Manufacturing, Utility and Financial Services Firms', in D. Bosworth and E. Webster (eds.), *The Management of Intellectual Property*. Cheltenham: Edward Elgar.

—— —— (2006b). 'Use of Intellectual Property by the UK Financial Services Sector', in D. Bosworth and E. Webster (eds.), *The Management of Intellectual Property*. Cheltenham: Edward Elgar.

—— —— (2006c). 'Trade Marks and Performance in UK Firms: Evidence of Schumpeterian Competition through Innovation', paper presented to the EC DIME Conference on Intellectual Property Rights for Business and Society, Birkbeck College, London. An updated version of this paper is available as Working Paper 300, January 2007, from <http://www.economics.ox.ac.uk/index.php/papers>

Greenhalgh, C., Longland, M., and Bosworth, D. (2003). 'Trends and Distribution of Intellectual Property: UK and European Patents and UK Trade and Service Marks 1986–2000', a report for the UK Patent Office, available from the first author, St Peter's College, Oxford.

Hall, B. (2000). 'Innovation and Market Value', in R. Barrell, G. Mason, and M. O'Mahony (eds.), *Productivity, Innovation and Economic Performance*. Cambridge: Cambridge University Press/NIESR.

HM Treasury (2006). *Gowers Review of Intellectual Property*. Norwich: Stationery Office.

Jensen, P., and Webster, E. (2004). 'Patterns of Trademarking Activity in Australia'. Intellectual Property Research Institute of Australia, Working Paper No. 03/04.

Loundes, J., and Rogers, M. (2003). 'The Rise of Trade Marking in Australia in the 1990s'. Melbourne Institute of Applied Economics and Social Research, Working Paper No. 8/03.

Mazeh, Y., and Rogers, M. (2006). 'The Economic Significance and Extent of Copyright Cases: An Analysis of Large UK Firms'. *Intellectual Property Quarterly*, 2006/4 (December): 404–20.

Miles, I. (2000). 'Services Innovation: Coming of Age in the Knowledge-Based Economy'. *International Journal of Innovation Management*, 4/4 (December): 371–89.

Toivanen, O., Stoneman, P., and Bosworth, D. (2002). 'Innovation and the Market Value of UK Firms'. *Oxford Bulletin of Economics and Statistics*, 64/1 (February): 39–61.

Wadhwani, S. (2001). 'The "New Economy": Myths and Realities'. *Bank of England Quarterly Bulletin* (Summer): 233–47.

Appendix

Data construction

The method of data construction was first to derive the financial accounts for over 2,000 firms from Thomson (2001). The next step involved extracting details of the structure of each company from Dun and Bradstreet International (2001) including the parent, its subsidiaries and associates, in order to get a full list of the names under which IP assets may have been sought for each firm. Using these ownership structures, records of each of the four types of intellectual property assets were then scanned for relevant name matches, beginning with computer scanning using both the full length names, including such items as PLC or Ltd., and the truncated names without these designations. Before matches were accepted, additional judgements were made concerning particular matches where the recorded names were similar, but not exactly identical. Because each IP application takes place over a considerable period of time, passing through various stages in the progression to the final acquisition of the IP asset, a decision was necessary concerning what to count and at what stage in the process. The approach we took for patents was to consider that the firm was IP active when they reached the publication stage in a patent application. For applications via both the UK and European Patent Offices, this is typically about eighteen months after the earliest global filing has occurred and it is the date at which the content of the patent specification becomes known to competitors. In counting EPO patents, which can be applied for covering many or few countries, we counted patent publications for which the United Kingdom was one of the designated states.

With trade marks there is some protection for firms through common law protection from so-called 'passing off', so registration of each name under which the firm is trading is not absolutely necessary to achieve some degree of ownership of the name. Even so, many firms take the step of formally applying for a trade mark to assert more clearly their ownership of brand names. It is easier in law to demonstrate infringement of a registered trade mark than to establish that a customer was misled by a product in an act of passing off. Unlike patents where the protection usually relates to a single class of patent such as chemistry or physics, trade mark applications can involve filing for protection in multiple classes, choosing among a large number of thirty-four goods and eight service products. To reflect the spread of products for which protection of the trade mark was being sought, we counted each class as a separate trade mark where the application was made to cover multiple classes.

Data sources

Bureau van Dijk (2003). *Fame,* online data.

Dun & Bradstreet International (2001). *Who Owns Whom D&B Linkages,* 2001/4 CD-ROM.

European Patent Office (2002). *ESPACE Bulletin,* Vol. 2002/002 (July), Feb. 1978–July 2002 CD-ROM.

Marquesa Search Systems Ltd. (2002). *Marquesa—Community Trade Marks (B),* CD-ROM October.

—— (2002). *Marquesa—UK Trade Marks (A),* CD-ROM March.

Patent Office (1997). *ESPACE ACCESS-EUROPE.* Vol. 1997/001 (December).

—— (2002). *ESPACE ACCESS-EUROPE.* Vol. 2002 (September).

Thomson (2001). *Company Analysis,* online data.

Table 14.A1. *The database of firms by sector*

Sector	Description	Number of firms	US SIC	Value Added 2000 (£million total for firms)	Employment 2000 ('000s)	R&D 2000 (£million total for firms)
1	Agriculture and mining	67	1–14, 17–19	14,621	372	107
2	Manufacturing	640	20–39	141,302	2,727	10,808
3	Utilities	26	49	11,158	132	90
4	Construction	89	15, 16	6,034	164	8
5	Finance	191	60–64, 66, 67	53,275	848	8
6	Real estate	112	65	3,137	43	0
7	Wholesale trade	181	50, 51	6,519	330	47
8	Retailing	132	52–57, 59	24,380	1,297	29
9	Hotels and catering	54	58, 70	5,163	445	0
10	Transport and communications	115	40–48	22,266	761	439
11	Business services	259	73	11,150	342	657
12	Other services	188	72, 74–99	5,134	208	122
All	All industries	2,054	1–99	304,139	7,669	12,315

Table 14.A2. *Proportion of firms making an application for IP within five years by sector*

Sector	Description	Number of firms	UK trade mark	EC trade mark	UK patent	EPO patent
1	Agriculture/mining	67	0.19	0.12	0.21	0.12
2	Manufacturing	640	0.67	0.55	0.40	0.35
3	Utilities	26	0.85	0.62	0.50	0.42
4	Construction	89	0.39	0.22	0.22	0.09
5	Finance	191	0.52	0.26	0.05	0.06
6	Real estate	112	0.22	0.12	0.03	0.01
7	Wholesale	181	0.52	0.33	0.12	0.07
8	Retail	132	0.75	0.40	0.08	0.05
9	Hotel/catering	54	0.65	0.35	0.06	0.00
10	Transport/communication	115	0.57	0.43	0.10	0.05
11	Business services	259	0.57	0.43	0.08	0.06
12	Other services	188	0.56	0.37	0.10	0.12

Table 14.A3. *Numbers of new IP assets sought by sector 1996–2000*

Sector	Description	Number of firms	UK trade mark	EC trade mark	UK patent	EPO patent
1	Agriculture/mining	67	235	97	169	44
2	Manufacturing	640	19,931	11,395	2,700	6,467
3	Utilities	26	2,272	461	79	59
4	Construction	89	616	231	92	42
5	Finance	191	4,216	1,675	85	243
6	Real estate	112	530	171	6	1
7	Wholesale	181	1,717	958	74	83
8	Retail	132	7,619	2,263	38	29
9	Hotel/catering	54	1,262	427	5	0
10	Transport/communication	115	4,617	2,028	62	740
11	Business services	259	2,583	1,681	61	33
12	Other services	188	2,779	1,246	222	128

Table 14.A4. *Business services: IP assets over the period 1996–2000 by 4-digit industry*

Industry	Description	Number of firms	UK trade mark	EC trade mark	UK patent	EPO patent
7300	4-digit code unknown	7	5	4	1	3
7311	Advertising agencies	9	306	209	3	1
7312	Outdoor advertising	1	3	0	0	0
7313	Media advertising reps.	2	7	6	0	0
7319	Advertising n.e.c.	4	39	6	0	0
7331	Direct mail advertising	1	0	0	0	0
7335	Commercial photography	3	4	6	0	1
7336	Commercial art graphic design	1	162	31	1	0
7342	Disinfecting and pest control	1	105	45	4	4
7349	Building cleaning and maintenance	4	22	0	0	0
7353	Heavy construction equipment rental	3	36	3	0	1
7359	Equipment rental and leasing	5	3	0	0	0
7361	Employment agencies	19	102	26	1	0
7370	Computer/data processing	17	65	49	0	0
7371	Computer programming	42	480	312	5	3
7372	Prepackaged software	40	464	350	6	3
7373	CI systems design	23	146	93	1	1
7374	Processing and data preparation	6	32	10	0	0
7375	Information retrieval	26	199	203	1	0
7376	Computer facilities management	3	3	1	0	0
7378	Computer maintenance	2	8	9	0	0
7379	Computer-related n.e.c.	15	49	93	1	0
7381	Detective, guard, etc.	1	25	6	0	0
7382	Security systems	5	140	38	25	6
7383	News syndicates	2	133	157	2	8
7389	Business services n.e.c.	17	45	24	10	2

15

Facilitating Innovation through the Measurement and Management of Intangibles

Chris Hendry, Georges Selim, David Citron, Clive Holtham, James Brown, Jo Holden, Nigel Courtney, and Fatma Oehlcke

Introduction

It is widely accepted today that growth in the economy is driven primarily by the ability of companies to exploit their intangible assets, meaning their non-physical and non-financial resources. Teece (1998) attributes this shift to increased liberalization and the efficiency of product markets, which have eliminated many traditional advantages that contribute to and focus on cost leadership. Because physical assets, such as advanced technology, can be readily traded and modern communications and transportation have reduced the advantages of such assets as location, firms are forced to create advantage from their 'difficult to imitate intangible assets' (Barney 1991)—that is, from their people, how they are organized, and how they work together. Human capital, or more broadly, 'intellectual capital' (Edvinsson and Malone 1997; Fincham and Roslender 2003), is thus of special importance; it is 'the foundation on which all intangible assets are created' (Hurvitz, Lines, Montgomery, and Schmidt 2002; Lev 2001).

A crucial driver of wealth creation and company performance is the ability to innovate—bringing new products and services successfully to market. Indeed, Lev (2004) identifies innovation as the key factor that accounts for differential company performance in stock returns. The identification and measurement of intellectual capital assets that create innovation and value should therefore be of direct interest to managers charged with creating value and to those concerned with valuing companies' wealth-generating potential.

This chapter is thus concerned with innovation and with how this is reflected in accounting practice that provides this valuation. Both, however, are problematic.

Context for the research

While there is an extensive literature on innovation, much of it fails to say how innovation is carried out inside firms and what determines basic differences in firm innovativeness (Brown and Eisenhardt 1995). To fix management (and the financial market's) attention on those intangible assets that drive innovation requires a robust model of innovation that incorporates these assets in a meaningful way. At the same time, much of the literature focuses on new product development only in the manufacturing sector. Given the size of the service sector in developed economies, new service development should be of concern for competition in many industries (Menor, Tatikonda, and Sampson 2002). We therefore need to go beyond theories constructed for the manufacturing sector and highlight areas of difference or, indeed, where generic models might apply. The way intangible assets are constituted as a resource for innovation is likely to differ between sectors. The growth of the service sector is a good instance of the need for evolution in business knowledge, in order that our models keep pace with changes in the real world.

At the same time, while intangibles have grown in importance, conventional accounting technology remains ill-equipped to account properly for them (Butler, Cameron, and Miles 2000), and company disclosure of the relevant drivers of wealth creation is often deficient. The result has been a long-term weakening in the association between accounting numbers and share prices (Lev and Zarowin 1999), as Figure 15.1 shows.

This gap implies that stock markets are interested in such assets, have ways of getting at (what they presume is) relevant information, and reflect this in their market valuation. Thus, analysts invest considerable resources in gaining information about intangibles that do not appear in financial statements in order to arrive at valuations that reflect future earnings potential (Barth, Kasznik, and Nichols 2001). There is also evidence of firms with higher levels of intangibles providing voluntary supplemental disclosures and conducting investor relations programmes to inform the

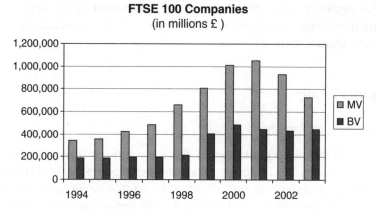

FTSE 100 Companies
(in millions £)

Fig. 15.1. The gap between book value (BV) and market value (MV)

market better (Tasker 1998; Gelb 2002) to overcome the defects in their accounting reports.

Accounting for intangibles, nevertheless, presents significant difficulties, and there are good reasons for maintaining prudential accounting, given such problems as control over the derived benefits and the absence of markets for trading in them (Lev 2001). While some observers have proposed ways of adapting the accounting model (Lev and Zarowin 1999), others have preferred to create an alternative, parallel system of internal company reporting that does not rely on financial measures, but uses non-financial indices and reports (Meritum 2002; Sveiby 1997; Jensen and Roberts 2001), including greater use of narrative reporting (Mouritsen, Larsen, and Bukh 2001; Fincham and Roslender 2003). As a DTI (2001: 35) study noted, 'Attempting to place a financial value on specific intangibles was seen [by companies] as unreliable, potentially misleading and dangerous.'

In terms of the language employed in this book, accounting is a 'meaning system' designed to reflect value in firms. As intangibles have grown in importance as a source of value, this meaning system has become detached from what it is supposed to represent. This, then, is a second instance of the need for evolution in business knowledge.

The problem we address in this work is thus compounded by inadequate models of what goes on in firms and inadequate models of valuation to represent this. This is the dual nature of the 'intangibles problem', and an illustration of one of the key themes driving the research programme and this book—the need for business knowledge to evolve to take account of the dynamic interaction between meanings that actors derive from business activities and the tools, concepts, and representations they apply to those activities.

Empirical study

Project aims and methods

The aim of the project has been to develop a fuller picture of the 'intangible' processes underlying innovation and to generate ideas for the better measurement of these, in the belief that better measurement will increase the attention managers give to the drivers of innovation and will lead to more transparent and accurate valuation of companies. The focus is on innovation, rather than the full range of 'intangible assets' (including such items as brands), first, because this is obviously central to wealth creation, but second, because progress in this difficult area is more likely to come from achieving small wins initially on a narrower front. The absence of a robust model even of what drives innovation is indicative of the problem—that without a sound empirical basis, simply adducing performance from 'intellectual capital' or intangible assets will lack conviction.

The project had four objectives:

1. To identify and describe key innovation processes of varying degrees of intangibility.
2. To identify company practices towards measuring and reporting intangibles.
3. To review the treatment of such intangibles by the accounting and auditing professions, and identify alternative and supplementary methods for measuring and reporting them.
4. To engage a wide range of interest groups concerned with accounting and auditing standards, preparing accounts, using accounts, and in other ways with the general quality of corporate disclosure, in order to develop and adopt improved methods for measuring intangibles.

Previous UK work on improving the accounting treatment of intangibles has invariably ended in bemoaning the intransigence of vested interests in supporting change (Vance 2001). The fourth objective was therefore explicitly designed to address the political character of change, by investigating the positions of key groups on the issue, raising the level of debate, and mobilizing forces for change. In the course of the project, the government's proposals for an enhanced Operating and Financial Review (OFR) assumed increasing significance in the political arena. Consequently, we saw the research components of the project influencing the way the OFR might evolve.

These four objectives resulted in four sets of activities:

1. Analysis of two large surveys in manufacturing (437 firms) and services (260 firms) to develop a robust model of the organizational drivers of innovation and the relationships between these.

2. Analysis of the annual reports of 150 companies on how they report on these 'intangibles for innovation'.

3. Case studies of how these intangible innovation processes are reflected in company performance management systems in order to understand the potential for improved measurement.

4. Interviews and focus groups with investors, fund managers, venture capitalists, accountants, auditors, and regulators to test their views on the potential for better forms of measurement and reporting of innovation.

We adopt Edvinsson and Malone's (1997) and the IFAC (1998) characterization of three forms of intellectual capital, and use this interchangeably with the term 'intangible assets':

Human capital is 'the knowledge that employees take with them when they go home or leave a firm' (e.g. creativity, know-how, experience, skills, teamworking, motivation, loyalty, training, and education).

Structural capital is 'the knowledge that stays with the firm' (e.g. routines, procedures, systems, culture, databases, information technology, intellectual property rights).

Relational capital is 'all resources linked to external relationships with customers, suppliers, and R&D partners' (e.g. image and reputation, customer loyalty, customer satisfaction, links with suppliers, commercial bargaining power).

As the four activities indicate, the overall project is notable for the use of a wide range of different methods through each phase. This is worth commenting on because of the issues it raises for what we can know and how we can know it—something that is rather relevant to 'business knowledge'. The adequacy and appropriateness of research methods to investigate 'business knowledge' is a key issue because, whether we are talking about modelling real world activity (innovation) or a system of meaning for valuing this (accounting), both as researchers or practitioners we face the problem of our own meaning systems for investigating and reflecting these.

Each activity involves a dual methodological issue, based, first of all, in the *ontological* problem of what is real in terms of its existence, causes, and effects, and second in the *epistemological* problem of knowing and being able to express this reality. 'Knowing' and 'representing' reality in turn involves problems at two levels. The first-level problem concerns the limitations in practitioners' own systems of symbolic representation and meaning. If these are 'inadequate' (as all symbolic systems in some way are liable to be), the researcher faces a problem of the first order. Thus, we might expect some disagreement even among managers about what matters in securing effective innovation. If this were not so, there would be less of a problem for organizations to be effective innovators. The second order *epistemological* challenge is then for the researcher to discover and represent what is real to the actors themselves (whether their representations are accurate or not). This means in some way 'objectifying' the research 'subject'. Some styles of social research purport to cut out the middle man in this (viz. the actors themselves) and reach straight for the underlying reality (e.g. by testing our own hypotheses of what produces effective innovation). This is likely to be inappropriate, however, when what we are investigating are clearly social constructions (as in company reporting).

These are fundamental problems for social science. One value of this research is to exemplify the different forms these take, the different challenges, and how effective our solutions might be. For each research activity, therefore, we comment on the nature and extent of this dual problem and how effectively we think we resolved it.

Describing the innovation process in terms of intangible assets

The first objective and task of the research was to develop a robust model of the organizational drivers of innovation and the relationships between these, in terms of the three forms of intangible asset (human, structural, and relational). A comprehensive model of innovation validated through research, however, was surprisingly difficult to find. The most satisfactory framework in our estimation was that developed by Chiesa, Coughlan, and Voss (1996), who, from an extensive review of the academic and practitioner literature, identified four core and three enabling processes as the determinants of innovation performance. This was used to develop an audit document promoted by the DTI in 1993 (*Innovation Your Move: Self Assessment Guide and Workbook*).

Building on this work, the Confederation of British Industry, IBM Consulting, and London Business School developed a project (called 'PROBE') to apply a modified version of this model in a large-scale auditing exercise. PROBE enables a company to compare its performance with a database of leading manufacturers internationally. Collaborating companies undertake a two-day, externally facilitated audit exercise with cross-functional teams to agree on their response to a 97-item questionnaire on their manufacturing, design, innovation, and product development processes. After the organization has identified its strengths and weaknesses, teams work on an improvement plan to implement the findings. The process thus gathers perceptual data from company 'expert' practitioners and develops an agreed ('validated') view of how the company manages and performs in manufacturing, design, innovation, and product development. The first PROBE was specific to manufacturing in the United Kingdom, but subsequent versions were used in service companies and the public sector.

The existence of this dataset, built up over a number of years since 1994, was fortuitous for us and generously made available for analysis by Professor Chris Voss. The result is two datasets of unusual scale that expose the intangible factors involved in innovation and their relation to business performance, covering 437 manufacturing and 260 service organizations. From this, we developed a comprehensive model of innovation processes, their interdependencies and perceived impacts on innovation performance (Hendry, Brown, and Voss 2005).

Having reduced the questionnaire items to a set of reliable factors, the relationships between these were analysed using structural equation modelling (SEM). SEM is ideal for this kind of perceptual, opinion-based data, as it allows latent factors grounded in observed data to be identified, along with intermediate factors that can be either dependent or contribute to final outcomes. In effect, SEM taps into sets of tacit and explicit relationships and people's understanding of them, and allows these relationships to be visually modelled. Mapping these latent and intermediate factors onto the intangible assets framework of human capital, structural capital, and network/relational capital, 'best fit' models of the relationships between intangible innovation assets ('processes') and innovation performance were developed for both manufacturing and services. This highlights important similarities and differences (shown in Figure 15.2a and 15.2b, for simplicity without their statistical weighting).

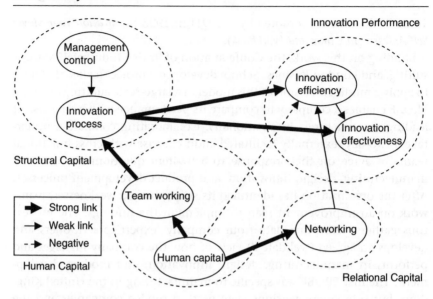

Fig. 15.2a. The dynamics of innovation in manufacturing firms

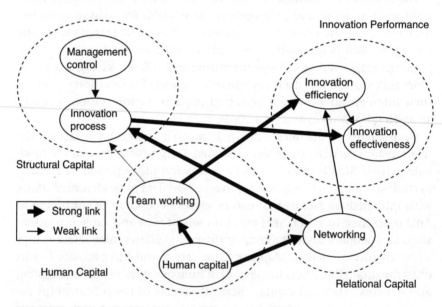

Fig. 15.2b. The dynamics of innovation in service firms

The first observation, which it is important not to overlook, is the interaction between the different intangible assets—or, as Reed, Lubatkin, and Srinivasan (2006) recently put it, each leverages the other. The key finding, which exemplifies this, is that 'human capital' (in manufacturing) has a negative and (in services) a non-significant impact on innovation performance, *unless* it is mediated through teamworking. In other words, creative, knowledgeable, high-quality people, though vitally important, in themselves are not enough—indeed, they can have a negative effect—unless their abilities are properly channelled through teams. In manufacturing, teamworking is moreover coordinated by formal processes (a structural variable), whereas in services the model shows teams directly impact on innovation performance. Innovation in services thus appears more loosely organized or organized in such a way as to engage wider contributions. This corresponds to the distinction in Clark and Fujimoto (1990) between 'lightweight teams' (teams that come together on a part-time basis for incremental innovation, which they associate in their sample especially with financial services) and 'heavyweight teams' (which have a full-time project focus).

These findings provide a robust justification for the frequent emphasis on teamworking in organizations and have implications for how innovation is measured and recognized. Conventional measures (typified in the DTI's Innovation Index) focus on R&D expenditure and patents and fail to reflect the drivers and effects of innovation in services. Our analysis provides a better way of viewing innovation in service firms and gets beneath the surface of such factors as R&D spending to identify the underlying processes that ensure this is used effectively.

How 'valid' is this as a representation of business knowledge? We suggest above that it is valid because of two things—first, it represents the views of 'expert' actors directly engaged in the processes we seek to describe, and second because of the way agreement is developed among them in each company. It thus enables accurate insights into a firm's practice, rather than seeking to test relationships proposed by an 'objective', 'expert' academic observer. We can therefore say we have a process of 'objectification' that works epistemologically. It shows the processes that experienced practitioners, in large numbers, observe to be valuable, in relation to defined performance outcomes, and faithfully reflects these views. Although we can never say that the 'experts' are perfectly right and fully understand all the key processes and relationships, it provides reliable evidence of a certain kind; it opens this up for testing by other systematic means; and certainly shows the state of business knowledge in the field.

The result is a model of innovation as a knowledge-creation process, comprising objects and the dynamic relations between these acted out over time, which is not dependent simply on what academic observers believe to be 'real'.

Company practices in measuring and reporting intangibles

As already observed, intangible assets are inadequately accounted for in traditional financial accounts. This gives rise to the large gap between firms' market value and the book value of their assets recorded in the accounts. Part of this gap is explained by the market attributing value to 'intangibles' like patents, proprietary software, and brands, which are the consequences of innovation, but are not always formally measured in the accounts. Our focus, in contrast, is on the organizational assets and processes ('intangible capital'), which underlie innovation and produce these. This distinction between outputs and means corresponds to a distinction at the core of the EBK Programme, between 'knowledge as stock' and 'knowledge as the flow' that creates this knowledge stock.

Interestingly, the system of financial accounting is much exercised by this distinction also. In one sense, financial accounting measures only 'stocks' (the assets of a business). But its interest in these lies in the economic benefits that 'flow' from such assets. This is made clear in accounting definitions of an asset: 'An asset is a resource controlled by the enterprise as a result of past events and from which future economic benefits are expected to flow to the enterprise' (International Accounting Standards Board, IASC Framework para. 49(a)). Similarly, the UK Accounting Standards Board 1999 Statement of Principles, chapter 5, defines an asset as: 'rights or other access to future economic benefits controlled by an entity as a result of past transactions or events'.

Where accounting standards depart from the 'business knowledge' perspective is in the restrictive criteria applied to what is classed as an asset. Most intangibles at some point fail one of these tests (viz. continuing use, economic benefit, separable, controllable, identifiable, apportioned value, and market value) (IFAC 1998; ASB 1999). As Lev (2001) notes, the concept of 'control' is a major stumbling block. The test of control from an accounting perspective is that an organization 'owns' it, such that it can dispose of the asset in a financial exchange. Only in a few cases is this true (as in the case of professional footballers). Most other types of 'intangible asset' do not pass this test, and most employees (the human asset or resource) can simply walk away.

The second research task therefore investigated the extent to which the shortcomings in measuring intangibles are compensated for in the narratives accompanying formal accounts in company annual reports—that is, whether such narratives pay sufficient and appropriate attention to the sources of innovation that will generate future value, in order for the market to factor these in. Or, to put it another way, 'what do companies want their investors to know about them?' Companies often rely on informal processes to amplify their reports and communicate non-financial aspects of their business to the stock market and their major shareholders (e.g. through investor relations meetings). However, if reporting is to mean anything, the important drivers of wealth in a business ought to be transparently and publicly available, and thus in published form.

For this, we analysed the 2003 annual reports of 150 companies, drawn from the 'All Share', 'AIM', and 'Fledgling' indexes, to give a range of company sizes, covering three manufacturing and three service sectors regarded as being 'more' and 'less' innovative (Citron et al. 2005). Focusing on the reports from one year allowed us to achieve wider company coverage, whereas viewing reports for fewer companies over, for example, a three-year period might well show little variance year-on-year and thus yield less rich data. Intellectual capital disclosures were quantified using content analysis software (Atlas.ti), employing a dictionary constructed around 760 relevant keyword combinations relating to human, relational, and structural capital. These keywords were derived from a range of sources, including Edvinsson and the PROBE questionnaire's definitions of people-related innovation processes. The resulting 'disclosures' were classified according to the three forms of capital.

Relational capital accounts for 60% of all intellectual capital disclosures, while only 14% cover human capital matters. This presents a very different picture from the innovation model previously outlined, in which structural capital plays a stronger role than either in manufacturing, and relational capital though important is weakest in both manufacturing and services. One obvious explanation is that company reports focus on more immediate influences on performance, and thus stress current relationships with customers and suppliers. In other words, they seek to assure the markets that they have prospects for the coming year. The narrative in company reports naturally addresses different audiences, but the risk is that in emphasizing the necessary short-term factors of doing business, attention to the longer term drivers of innovation and wealth-creation suffers.

Is this true, though, of all firms? In particular, do firms that rely heavily on continued innovation also under-report to give a distorted view? We

329

therefore examined whether intangible-intensive firms, as measured across a variety of dimensions, make more intellectual capital disclosures. This showed that levels of disclosure are, indeed, positively associated with (1) R&D spending, (2) with services, (3) with a greater market-to-book ratio, and, to some extent, (4) with labour-intensity—all factors reflecting intangibles. This confirms what Tasker (1998) and Gelb (2002) observed—that firms with higher levels of intangibles try to make up for the shortcomings of conventional accounting by increasing narrative disclosure—either because they recognize what their future prospects depend on, or perhaps just as likely because they feel the need to justify such investment.

A further test is whether the market appears to value intellectual capital disclosures, as measured by correlations between levels of disclosure and the book-to-market value gap. We found that there is, indeed, a positive association with intellectual capital disclosures, and in particular with relational and structural capital. For human capital, however, the amount of disclosure does not statistically correlate with the gap between market and book value. This implies that much of what firms write about people in their annual reports has little bearing on perceived business performance. This is not to say people do not matter, but that firms either add much that is irrelevant to performance (thus diluting the statistical effect) or that they do not (in the eyes of the investment community) emphasize what matters.

These findings suggest there is an economic rationale for firms' current voluntary intellectual capital disclosures. They also suggest that future regulation of narrative disclosure through a revised 'Operating and Financial Review' (OFR) needs to be careful not to introduce distortions into the reporting process. As we discuss below, UK plans for a revised OFR were abruptly cancelled in January 2006. The planned new framework, which was at an advanced stage of preparation, included the requirement that firms identify 'key performance indicators' (KPIs) relevant to their industry and strategy by which they could be measured. Any pressure to standardize these would risk introducing such distortions—especially since reference to innovation was noticeably absent from suggested KPIs.

Again, we ask, how accurate is this picture we paint? The research 'subject'—how companies publicly value 'intangibles for innovation'—was derived from a set of objectified data (company annual reports), which could be content-analysed electronically using Atlas software, so does not involve distortions introduced by ourselves. The use of content analysis software requires decisions on word combinations and interpretations, and is therefore not without problems, but the epistemological problem is largely contained. However, as we note above, accounting is a socially constructed discipline with strict conventions on what is 'real', imposing prudential criteria ('principles') on what it allows to be 'counted'. Companies seek to 'repair' the shortcomings of financial accounts with 'narratives' about their activities and prospects through the Chairman's Statement and OFR. However, these narratives remain relatively unstructured and arbitrary as to what they include, and tend to vary year-on-year as to what they include: the focus is on 'telling a good story'. A 'true' representation of the innovation intangibles that really matter to companies is therefore, at the very least, uncertain from this public self-representation.

Innovation and the performance management system

Having established how those closest to the innovation process in firms see it working, the purpose of the third activity was to see how innovation is reflected in firms' performance management systems—on the assumption that if something is important, it is likely to be a focus of the reward system. If we are looking for improved ways of measuring innovation, we need to see how firms measure it internally before we can hope to construct externally valid, acceptable systems of reporting.

The question is 'how far are the factors and relationships identified in the innovation models above acknowledged by companies in practice and supported in their internal measurement and reporting?' Most companies engage in a very large amount of measurement and management reporting. If innovation is of front-line importance, we might expect to see this reflected in the goals of an organization and communicated, monitored, and controlled through its performance management system—the assumed core of an organization's control system.

Things apparently do not work in this way, however. Naively, we might expect to find innovation objectives defined at board level, so that a researcher could drill down to see how these are communicated and rewarded (paying special attention to where they are crystallized more precisely in product development and R&D). However, in our discussions with senior HR managers to develop access for case studies, it became clear that performance management systems do not generally work in such an orderly, hierarchical way. It was also difficult for them to identify innovation as a distinctive concern in their companies: other priorities (such as managing costs) were often uppermost, and 'innovativeness' was focused on other things. In other words, our assumptions about performance management were flawed.

Apart from the problem that managers in different functions or at different levels see things differently and might simply 'not know' (Lawrence and Lorsch 1967), the lack of control by objectives suggests that innovation is recognized as an uncertain process, not as something linear and orderly that can be easily controlled. There is thus a radical disjunction between objective setting as a prospective activity that can be assessed through feedback and the uncertainty of innovation. While innovation goals of a general nature (such as, 'X % of revenue from new products') can be defined, innovation activity is typically controlled through its processes—through 'stage-gates' (Ajamian and Koen 2002)—and through what Kerssens-van Drongelen and Bilderbeek (1999) call 'feed forward control' (i.e. ensuring that the right organizational conditions are in place). However, much innovation is also of an incremental nature, 'essentially a known, predictable and repeatable process' (Ajamian and Koen 2002), implying that objectives can be set.

Faced with these ambiguities, a looser focus is therefore required to capture the subtleties of management control, since innovation may be managed through other kinds of measurement system, which we would otherwise miss. We therefore asked how innovation works in the company (in terms of its importance, strategic drivers, context, and the structures and processes supporting it); second, how the performance management system works (what it targets, what it measures, how it rewards, and how far innovation features in this); and, third, what effect does measurement (or the lack of it) have on innovation performance, and the barriers to more effective metrics. All of this focused on examples of actual practice.

Our nine cases comprised two telecommunications service providers, two retailers, a design consultancy, a distribution firm, an insurance company, an upstream gas company, and a manufacturer of retail branded goods. The services sector was thus heavily represented. However, retailers typically involve themselves closely in many aspects of their suppliers' own activity, and this can have implications for how they think about, and organize for, innovation. This heterogeneity means that, while the data reveals patterns, it would be simplistic to attribute these to systematic differences between manufacturing and services. Notwithstanding this, the findings do echo the broad distinction in the PROBE data in the types of intangible emphasized by manufacturing and services firms and the role of teams.

The cases reveal two distinct views of innovation—a systematic product and brand development process versus one in which innovativeness is an informal process that encourages contributions from different parts of the company. The first is characterized by an emphasis on structural and relational capital factors—procedures, routines, and databases, on the one hand, and supplier and customer relationships, on the other—and a pattern of more intensive measurement applied to these (for example, in B&Q's 'supplier capability assessment' model). The second emphasizes human capital, through creativity, skills, and teamwork (often accompanied by structural change to break down internal barriers and a move away from over-detailed performance measurement).

Management control in the service companies tends to be looser, with more autonomy given to service development teams and openness to external influences. As a result, innovation measurement systems in service organizations are more fluid. Teamworking has far greater prominence and the active development of external networks, including customers and preferred suppliers, is an important part of the innovation process. This ensures that additional or fresh knowledge is brought in and can be selectively embedded into a product or service. However, this is far from being a 'free for all'. Formal controls that set targets and measure progress are important for keeping a business on track, while informal controls give people freedom to explore new ideas within guidelines set by the overall context of the business. Moreover, controls and measurements can be quite formal where new ideas already proven experimentally are evaluated with a view to becoming standard offerings, and control increases to hasten the standardization of new offerings. 'Customer satisfaction' is typically a strong component in this control process. Service companies thus deploy multiple systems of control and performance measurement.

Both manufacturing and services have formal processes for new product and service development, therefore, but with subtle differences. Manufacturing pays more attention to the complete process including design and fabrication, whereas in services the process is positioned towards involving customers and suppliers and integrating teamwork into the innovation culture. This distinction nevertheless is becoming blurred as manufacturing companies increasingly include services as part of their offerings, and as service companies seek to standardize ideas that have been proven with customers in an experimental stage. The extent to which service firms go down this route, we suggest, will depend on the nature of the service offering—whether it is concerned with physical, information, or human-centred services (Miles 2001; Brown, Courtney, and Hendry 2006). The manufacturing approach to control also reflects the risks associated with larger up-front capital investments.

Innovation is a critical process within a company and as such is subject to management control. Modelling this from survey data presents a snapshot of the process, in which activities are condensed. Case studies, however, unpack this and reveal the subtleties of control, and why and how under different conditions this is differently applied. This part of the study, moreover, highlights the need to take a broad view of innovation—that it is not just about developing new products and services but also about improving organizational and process efficiencies—both of which create value (Munshi et al. 2005). The latter are typically more amenable to metrics and control, but typically lie outside the formal performance management system.

Towards improved methods for measuring intangibles with key interest groups

In this final part of the project, we interviewed twenty-seven people representing key interest groups: (1) the preparers of reports (finance directors, investor relations managers), (2) auditors and the professional accounting bodies that approve these, (3) users (analysts and fund managers), and (4) 'innovation promoters'. These interviews thus complement the analysis of companies reporting ('disclosure') by asking how the financial community and professions view the reporting of innovation. We asked how they rated 'innovative capacity' as a driver of profit, what information provided a measure or 'indicator' of this, how this information was obtained and communicated, how it was used, and how communication could be improved.

In this phase of the work, we confront the politics of communicating on company performance, which previous researchers have identified as a major issue (Vance 2001; Fincham and Roslender 2003). This was reflected in the difficulty even of getting willing interviewees to participate. There are likely to be a number of reasons for this, but all point to the difficulty of promoting attention to innovation in reporting. Second, there was a prevailing cynicism about the value of company reports. Any revised 'Operating and Financial Review' will have an uphill struggle to overcome this, although it may enable a fresh start. Third, there was a general sense of interviewees having difficulty in staying focused on the subject of innovation. Their remarks were constantly coloured by other preoccupations with company reports.

While this sometimes reflects a proper 'holistic' view, in which innovation is but one consideration in assessing performance, at other times it suggests a certain 'stuck-ness' in the present model of financial reporting. Or put more sympathetically, high-status individuals, used to addressing issues of wealth, governance, and power, have difficulty staying focused on the subject of innovation because of their wider concerns about company reports and what they should say. Wider systems of meaning thus determine their focus of attention.

In some ways, this community comes closest to the problems and concerns of the researchers themselves in determining what is the state of business knowledge. That is, they act as 'reflexive researchers', concerned with the problem of eliciting and communicating what is 'real' of value inside companies. Thus, the nature, quality, and reliability of information is of primary concern, involving issues of trust and communication—the need to ground the assessment of performance potential in reliable, hard, solid data, in numbers, 'factuals' and 'real information', and going beyond the PR presentation of such data with 'soft' data from face-to-face meetings, where the evidence can be checked and interrogated and the competence of senior management can be directly assessed. This highlights an essential paradox in company reporting. Investors value 'intangible' things that enable them to get behind the reported 'facts' and give them confidence in a firm's ability to implement its strategy. But these intangibles cannot be adequately expressed in written form, and if companies tried to write them into the OFR, their readers would not trust them anyway!

The second issue highlighted is the emphasis on strategy and risk. These provide the context for innovation and suggest how the treatment of innovation could be effectively anchored in the OFR. That is, innovation needs to be driven by a clear strategy, which has a short- and a long-term horizon showing where returns are capable of being generated in a business. In this respect, the attitude to risk is interesting, not merely as something to be quantified, moderated, and managed 'down', but as something to rise and respond to. Avoiding risk altogether will not generate the desired returns. This justifies innovation and provides a hook for reporting it.

The final pair of themes touches directly on intangibles, in people (human capital) and culture (structural capital). Unsurprisingly, the investment community focuses on the role of senior management and leadership, in the ability to drive strategy and an inspiring culture. While this is a limited perspective on organizational performance and capability, it reflects the need for parsimony in reporting, where if 'key performance indicators' are to mean anything and be useful, they need to be few in number. Notably, though, among other factors highlighted, teamwork and an empowering culture are seen as important. In other words, there is convergence from three sources in the study on teamworking as a core intangible asset in innovation.

Conclusion

Through 2003 to 2005, proposals by the DTI to impose a statutory revised OFR gained increasing shape and momentum (Woodward and Selim 2006). This emphasized the need for firms to take a 'forward-looking view' and encouraged the development of industry and company-relevant key performance indicators (KPIs). This was due to be implemented on 1 April, 2006, three months after the project ended. While the overall shape of this was set down following the usual processes of government green and white papers and extensive consultation, it did suggest a valuable role for new research to influence the details as it evolved and bedded down. The decision by the Chancellor, Gordon Brown, to cancel the introduction of the new-style OFR in November 2005 changed the whole political scene—illustrating apart from anything else the powerful force exerted by government on the realities of 'business knowledge' as a system of meaning defined by regulation (or its absence).

From another point of view, this event revives the prospects for influencing reporting so that it pays greater attention to intangibles in innovation. New EU regulations (although lacking the two key features of the UK proposal) have come into force, and many companies (such as BP) that had done considerable work in preparing for the UK change, and were keen supporters, are implementing revised reporting practices anyway. A less constrained agenda may give more scope to shape reporting to reflect innovation intangibles more fully than the original proposal did. The government also seems to be edging back towards reform. The proposed focus on strategy and risk remains pivotal. The challenge will be to link teamworking to these in creative ways.

References

Ajamian, G. M., and Koen, P. A. (2002). 'Technology Stage-Gate™: A Structured Process for Managing High-Risk New Technology Projects', in P. Belliveau et al. (eds.), *The PDMA ToolBook 1 for New Product Development*. New York: John Wiley & Sons.

ASB (1999). *Statement of Principles for Financial Reporting*. London: Accounting Standards Board.

Barney, J. (1991). 'Firm Resources and Sustained Competitive Advantage'. *Journal of Management*, 17/1: 99–120.

Barth, M. E., Kasznik, R., and Nichols, M. F. (2001). 'Analyst Coverage and Intangible Assets'. *Journal of Accounting Research*, 39/1: 1–34.

Brown, J. E., Courtney, N., and Hendry, C. (2006). *Innovation and the Performance Management System*. London: City University Working Paper.

Brown, S. L., and Eisenhardt, K. M. (1995). 'Product Development: Past Research, Present Findings, and Future Directions'. *Academy of Management Review*, 20/2: 343–78.

Butler, J., Cameron, H., and Miles, I. (2000). *Grasping the Nettle: Final Report of a Feasibility Study Concerning a Programme of Research into the Measurement and Valuation of Intangible Assets*. Manchester: CRIC/PREST.

Chiesa, V., Coughlan, P., and Voss, C. A. (1996). 'Development of a Technical Innovation Audit'. *Journal of Product Innovation Management*, 13/2: 105–36.

Citron, D., Selim, G., Holden, J., and Oehlcke, F. (2005). 'Do Firms' Voluntary Intellectual Capital Disclosures Provide Information about their Intangible Assets?', Cass Business School, working paper.

Clark, K. B., and Fujimoto, T. (1991). *Product Development Performance*. Boston: Harvard Business School Press.

DTI (2001). *Creating Value from Your Intangible Assets*. London: Department of Trade and Industry.

Edvinsson, L., and Malone, M. (1997). *Intellectual Capital: Realizing Your Company's True Value by Finding Its Hidden Brainpower*. New York: Harper.

Edwards, T., et al. (2005). *Pathways to Value: How UK Firms Can Create More Value Using Innovation Strategically*. London: Advanced Institute of Management Research.

Fincham, R., and Roslender, R. (2003). *The Management of Intellectual Capital and Its Implications for Business Reporting*. Edinburgh: Institute of Chartered Accountants of Scotland.

Gelb, D. (2002). 'Intangible Assets and Firms' Disclosures: An Empirical Investigation'. *Journal of Business Finance and Accounting*, 29/3–4: 457–76.

Hendry, C., Brown, J. E., and Voss, C. (2005). *Probing the Intangible Drivers of Innovation Performance and their Representation in Performance Measurement Systems*. 21st European Group for Organizational Studies (EGOS), Freie Universität Berlin.

Hurwitz, J., Lines, S., Montgomery, W., and Schmidt, J. (2002). 'The Linkage between Management Practices, Intangibles Performance and Stock Returns'. *Journal of Intellectual Capital*, 3/1: 51–61.

IFAC (International Federation of Accountants) (1998). *The Measurement and Management of Intellectual Capital: An Introduction*. New York: IFAC.

Jensen, H., and Roberts, H. (2001). *Intellectual Capital: Managing and Reporting.* Nordic Industrial Fund.

Kerssens-van Drongelen, I., and Bilderbeek, J. (1999). 'R&D Performance Measurement: More than Choosing a Set of Metrics'. *R&D Management,* 29/1: 35–46.

Lawrence, P. R., and Lorsch, J. W. (1967). *Organization and Environment: Managing Differentiation and Integration.* Boston: Harvard Business School Press.

Lev, B. (2001). *Intangibles: Management, Measurement, and Reporting.* Washington, DC: Brookings Institution Press.

—— (2004). 'Sharpening the Intangibles Edge'. *Harvard Business Review,* June: 109–16.

—— and Zarowin, P. (1999). *The Boundaries of Financial Reporting and How to Extend Them.* Paris: Organisation for Economic Co-Operation and Development.

Menor, L. J., Tatikonda, M. V., and Sampson, S. E. (2002). 'New Service Development: Areas for Exploitation and Exploration'. *Journal of Operations Management,* 20/2: 135–57.

Meritum (2002). *Project Meritum: Guidelines for Managing and Reporting Intangibles.* Madrid.

Miles, I. (2001). *Services Innovation: A Reconfiguration of Innovation Studies.* Discussion Paper Series, Manchester: University of Manchester.

Mouritsen, J., Larsen, H. T., and Bukh, P. N. D. (2001). 'Valuing the Future: Intellectual Capital Supplements at Skandia'. *Accounting, Auditing and Accountability Journal,* 14/4: 399–422.

Munshi, N., Oke, A., Puranam, P., Stafylarakis, M., Towells, S., Moeslein, K., and Neely, A. (2005). *Leadership for Innovation.* London: Advanced Institute of Management (AIM).

Reed, K. K., Lubatkin, M., and Srinivasan, N. (2006). 'Proposing and Testing an Intellectual Capital-Based View of the Firm'. *Journal of Management Studies,* 43/4: 867–93.

Sveiby, K. E. (1997). *The New Organizational Wealth: Managing and Measuring Knowledge-Based Assets.* San Francisco: Barrett-Kohler.

Tasker, S. (1998). 'Bridging the Information Gap: Quarterly Conference Calls as a Medium for Voluntary Disclosure'. *Review of Accounting Studies,* 3/1–2: 137–67.

Teece, D. J. (1998). 'Capturing Value from Knowledge Assets: The New Economy, Markets for Know-How, and Intangible Assets'. *California Management Review,* 40/3: 55–79.

Vance, C. (2001). *Valuing Intangibles.* London: The Institute of Chartered Accountants in England and Wales.

Woodward, S., and Selim, G. (2006). 'An Investigation into the Development of the Operating and Financial Review in the UK'. Cass Business School, working paper.

16

The Uses of History as Corporate Knowledge

Michael Rowlinson, Peter Clark, Agnes Delahaye-Dado,
Charles Booth, and Stephen Procter

Introduction

An organization's knowledge of its own history is not usually considered as a form of business knowledge, so our project set out to examine the ways in which companies manage and represent their histories. Our contribution conceptualizes, examines, and compares the uses of history as a form of knowledge by academics and by corporations. Although we do focus upon comparisons between the United Kingdom and the United States, we have examined the case of the German firm, Bertelsmann. We have made comparisons between the histories shaped by academics in their role as organic intellectuals and those histories shaped by corporate sponsors. There are important differences.

With regard to academic contributions to the uses of history, we have examined how academics publishing corporate histories have sought to extend and replace the metric of calendrical dating as a time-frame by processual metrics. There was a 'history break' in the business schools from the mid-1960s onward. The break was accompanied by the almost complete absence of counterfactual narratives in business school knowledge. We have addressed this issue. The consequence of the history break has been that history has only very rarely been used to construct counterfactuals. One reason that counterfactuals are criticized is their tendency to make exaggerated transformations. We have therefore sought to highlight past situations that could not have been very different. We refer to these as superfactuals (Clark et al. 2007). For example, it is highly unlikely that

Henry Ford could have built his productive, financial, and market empire if he started out from the Birmingham region of England (Clark 2000, 2006). Analysing pathways that were not possible considerably develops existing path-dependency models for theoretical relevance and practical utility. For example, it becomes possible to examine whether British sectoral pathways into the future can be made more robust by importing innovations from comparable American sectors.

We have compared academic accounts of corporate histories published as books with the books published by corporations. The corporate-authored histories in book form have increasingly used outsourced specialist suppliers. This spectrum is well illustrated by the multiple differences between the academic history of the Rothschild Bank by Ferguson (2000) and the corporate-funded *Insideout: Microsoft—In Our Own Words* (2000). The corporate uses of history have been transformed by the web as a source of consumer knowledge. We report on a sample of how large UK and US corporations used history on the web in one year, 2002.

There is a tendency to conflate history and memory as in Weick's contention that every manager is a historian, and 'any decision maker is only as good as his or her memory' (1995: 71). We also noted that historians concerned with heritage have elaborated a distinction between history and memory. However, according to Lowenthal (1985), memory, and by implication also organizational memory, is *not* a repository of knowledge about past events, but consists of recollections that express feelings about past events. The distinction between memory and history forms a key backdrop for our research. Our interest in memory and representations of the past distinguishes us from business historians, who are preoccupied with reconstructing the past per se. Equally, our concern for history and historiography, especially in relation to documents, separates us from qualitative management and organization researchers who favour only ethnographic methods to study the social construction of organizational history.

We have organized the context for the research, the empirical study, and the discussion in six sections:

- Commodifying corporate histories
- Charting the metrics of history and process
- Counterfactuals and superfactuals
- Web-based histories in 2002: UK and US samples
- Corporate history books
- Episodic memory, social memory, and organizational mnemonics

Our contribution confirms the interdependence of different kinds of knowledge for academics and corporations. Moreover, while there are common, genre-like elements in corporate histories on the web, there are also differences between UK and US corporations. The role of history in the American national cultural repertoire is distinctive (Clark 2005; Clark and Todeva 2006). We contend that understanding national predispositions in the use of history is consequential and revealing.

Commodifying corporate history

An unexpected finding is the *commodification* of history by corporations through the outsourced employment of full-service consultancies. These consultancies occupied a strong though not particularly visible face in the American market place.

This means that the make or buy decision applies to the provision of history as to other services that companies may produce in-house or contract out. Firms face a decision as to whether to establish in-house archive programs, place records with an external research institution, such as a university, or to use commercial archive and commemorative consultancies. There are several well-established consulting firms in the United States that are concerned with the production of corporate history (Carson and Carson 2003), most notably The History Factory, 'Making History—Today', and History Associates Incorporated (HAI), 'The Best Company in History'. The History Factory describes itself as 'a heritage management firm that helps organizations discover, preserve and leverage their history to meet today's business challenges'. It seems likely that consultants will professionalize the discourse and formalize the genre of corporate history. Coffee table books will increasingly replace academic tomes for commemorative purposes.

However, companies facing historical controversies will still turn to academic historians, as shown by companies facing scrutiny for their relations with the Nazis. We refer to the case of Bertelsmann later.

Charting the metrics of history and process

This part of our programme examined how academics address the uses of history in case studies of major corporate events. We charted the use of calendrical dating in a small number of studies that claimed to be longitudinal and compared these with the approach of Chandler. Before presenting these, it is necessary to comment upon the 'history break' of the 1960s and to note the claims of a 'history turn' more recently (e.g. Clark and Rowlinson 2004).

In the immediate post-1945 period the core of business school knowledge construction was in transition. There was an uneasy period in which the particularistic knowledge from specific corporate cases coexisted with the emerging generic knowledge designed to be useful across many contexts. An array of research programmes appeared in which the organization as a unit of analysis was consciously abstracted from its context (e.g. Perrow 1967). The most obvious exception to this powerful ascendant research programme was Crozier (1964) for his claim that the specifics of French history and culture overpowered and shaped the abstractions of the new theory of organizational design. Crozier's claim, which combined history and nation, was contested by Perrow (1967). At the time Weick (1969) had published his manifesto for organizing, attention to 'place' had been replaced by the notion of space and attention to history had been totally removed. Weick observed (1969: 64–5) that the temporal metric replacing the calendrical chronology associated with historians had not yet been formulated. He suggested the evolutionary notion of time implicit in D. T. Campbell (1965). Few, apart from Aldrich (1979, 1999) took up that challenge.

There was a clear and intentional 'history break' in the early 1960s when much of knowledge construction was relocated within frameworks that were posited to be relatively enduring. Hence, both the Aston Programme (Pugh and Hickson 1976) and Tannenbaum's (1974) attitudinal survey research on the control graph claimed that their findings endured for a period of several years. Consequently, the problem of time-and-process was heavily bracketed (Pugh and Hickson 1976: 1). The main approaches to process were preoccupied with multi-stage typologies and models. Rogers's (1962) theory of how to construct and diffuse adoptable innovations became one of the best known examples of a sophisticated multi-state model containing a sequence of states starting with a pre-innovation situation and extending beyond attempts at innovation into the ultimate outcomes.

Chandler (1962) became the most visible bearer of the label of business school historian. His early studies used calendrical metrics, for example, to show how major American corporations experimented with novel structural features in the face of new problems of trading across different geographical zones and with diverse product portfolios (see Figure 16.1). Later studies used a linear teleology. Our purpose is not to restate the critiques of Chandlerian teleology.

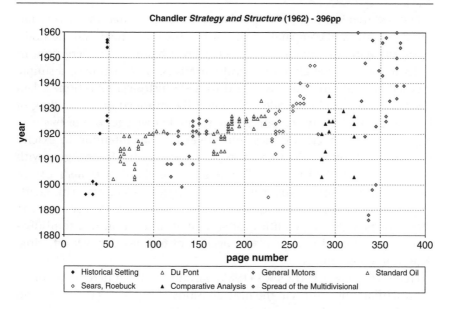

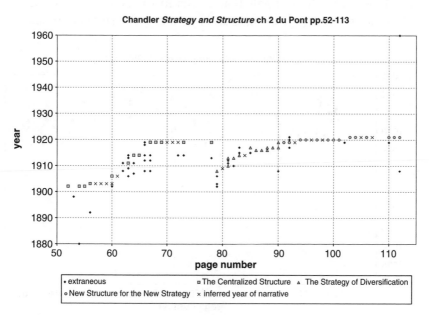

Fig. 16.1. Chandler's (1962) use of calendrical metrics to show how major American corporations experimented with novel structural features in the face of new problems of trading across different geographical zones and with diverse product portfolios

Source: Chandler 1962: 396.

Source: Chandler 1962: 52–113.

Our research has examined the claims for longitudinal studies through the systematic and comparative charting of the use of historical methods, especially dating chronologies by Pettigrew, Chandler, and Ferguson. In order to chart and analyse historical narratives, we constructed a simple methodological procedure as an aid to meta-historical reflection. Taken together these would provide a theoretically informed understanding of how corporate history can contribute to the knowledge-base of business organizations. Underlying these objectives was our intention to extend the 'historic turn' we identified in organization studies by engaging with the philosophy of history. In Figure 16.1, we chart Chandler's use of calendrical time against the pages in his *Strategy and Structure*. This charting explicates Chandler's bold attempt to combine and extract a generic model of process temporalities for structural innovation (i.e. multidivisional form) from the time–place specifics of four leading, yet differing, American corporations.

Figure 16.2 charts Pettigrew's (1985) narrative of the different outcomes of structural innovations in the nine divisions of ICI during the 1970s and early 1980s. The chart reveals that events in the period 1974–1982 are linked back to events occurring in and just after 1926. This pattern reflects

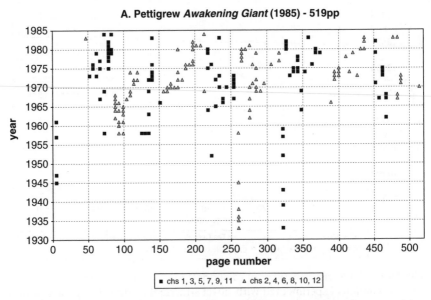

Fig. 16.2. Pettigrew's (1985) narrative of the different outcomes of structural innovations in the nine divisions of ICI during the 1970s and early 1980s

Source: Pettigrew 1985: 519.

Pettigrew's commitment to the proposition that contemporary organizational structures and processes are birth marked. Pettigrew takes 1926 as the birth of ICI because 1926 was the calendrical date when the British state completed its initiation of a national chemical industry from a variety of British and German entities. However, this often cited proposition is only thinly explicated. In contrast, the study of innovation design in Rover from 1896 to 1982 combines the use of calendrical time with processual metrics (Whipp and Clark 1986). The major metric is the periodization of the firm in terms of changes in its problem-solving approach to product and process design. Another metric is the evolution of consumer selection criteria. Intriguingly, the year is a key metric that contains marked seasonal variations coupled to the role of yearly international shows and then the reality of the balance sheet. Rover constantly faced the problem of building sufficient reserves from which to accomplish the next period of new car design.

We do not show the use of calendrical time by JoAnne Martin (1992) in her account of corporate culture because the chart would be blank. Moreover, although Martin implicitly uses many proto-metrical markers of temporality in her analysis of cultural processes these are not theorized. There is only a weak analytically structured narrative.

Our contention is that the underplaying of calendrical dating is difficult to defend. Equally, the absence of analytic metrics for processes is extremely limiting. The evolution of business knowledge requires their combined usage, especially in studies of innovation and of radical innovation design (Clark and Rowlinson 2004; Abernathy 1978). The processual metrics could be shown in lines parallel to the time axis in Figures 16.1 and 16.2.

Counterfactuals and superfactuals

Counterfactuals or alternate histories are narratives that raise the question 'What if?' That is, counterfactuals focus on a past event and ask what would have happened if that event had been different in some way. It is almost impossible to find examples of counterfactuals in the array of journals published through the Academy of Management.

Counterfactual narratives are commonly used by historians and political scientists to advance understanding of causal events and processes, through highlighting 'points of indeterminacy' at particular historical junctures; to test theoretical or empirical generalizations by applying them to specific historical situations; and to highlight gaps or contradictions in belief systems by creating thought experiments that challenge the 'certainties' generated by those belief systems (Tetlock and Belkin 1996). We therefore arranged to produce a stimulating and relevant collection of counterfactual narratives of business history in order to facilitate thinking about alternative pasts and futures.

Superfactuals aim to show pathways that are impossible (Clark et al. 2007). Our claim is that time–place events are historically specific. The structural repertoires of firms and nations contain the finite and specific capacities to undertake particular actions (Clark 2000). By implication some strategic directions are impossible for the combination of corporate and contextual agency. We mentioned the impossibility of Henry Ford establishing a global auto firm by starting from the English West Midlands. Equally, we argue that Benetton could not have become a global firm by starting from the English East Midlands even though that region was the major area of knitwear and—for a period—the home base of suppliers to Marks & Spencer (Clark et al. 2007). To demonstrate this case, we reimagined the history of the English knitwear industry from 1962 onward so that its decline evident by the mid-1980s was avoided. The superfactual introduced massive transformations at multiple levels. For example, the intervention of corporate agents (e.g. Hanson) who broke open the pre-existing cognitive pillars and released an alternative ecology of firms. Although the imagining illustrates a fruitful exercise in using knowledge of varied kinds, this is not a possible alternative history of the sector. Superfactuals are designed to challenge the established doctrine of business school teaching and research, which is still pro-innovation (see Knights and Swan et al., in this volume).

Counterfactual narratives are closely connected to the construction of multiple research-based scenarios. History can significantly contribute to explicating impossible pathways and this clarifies one element in the claim that history matters (Clark 2006; Maielli 2006).

Web-based histories in 2002: UK and US samples

To complement our other routes of investigation, we sought to understand how corporations were presenting their histories on the web. We had noticed that web-based histories are readily altered and re-envisioned to take account of current events (e.g. being Green) and to avoid future criticisms. We therefore surveyed a sample of UK and US firms from the year of 2002.

Our survey took the thirty-six British companies in the 2004 Fortune Global 500 ranked by revenue, plus the joint British and Dutch companies Unilever and the Royal Dutch/Shell Group. In order to incorporate a more comparative dimension than originally proposed, forty-six US companies from the Global 500 were selected, matched with British companies by industry. Several large US companies were included for which there is no British equivalent, such as Microsoft, as well as Bertelsmann and News Corp. as matches for Time Warner (see Table 16.1). Web pages and annual reports were examined for each of the eighty-six companies, as well as entries in directories, such as the *International Directory of Company Histories*, which has entries for almost all large companies and lists published histories. For the survey of web pages conducted in January 2005, historical content was successfully downloaded from eighty company web pages.

The survey recorded the following information from the web pages:

- The number of clicks from the home page to history pages
- Title of section containing history
- Number of pages in history section
- Divisions within history section, e.g. by chronology, subsidiaries, theme, activities, brands, etc.
- Whether there were pdf files for downloading
- Timeline: animated, moving, etc.
- Extent of written text
- Links to museums or historical visitor attractions
- Orientation, e.g. educational or entertainment
- Links to company archives and location of archives
- Nature of any illustrations, e.g. people, products, events in national history
- List of published histories
- Founding dates for the company or subsidiaries
- Mention of commemorative events

Also, the historical content of annual reports was coded using NVivo and analysed for counts of selected historical terms, such as founder, heritage, tradition, history, and story. From the *International Directory* and the Annual Reports, the following information was compiled for each company: dates of most recent name change; dates of merger, de-merger, or buyout in relation to the company's name; date of incorporation; dated roots of the company; dates of commemoration; official historical publications; corporate museums and archives.

Table 16.1. *Companies in survey*

US companies ranked by revenue	British companies matched with US companies
Wal-Mart Stores	Tesco
Exxon Mobil	BP
General Motors	—
Ford Motor	—
General Electric	—
ChevronTexaco	Royal Dutch/Shell Group (Britain/Netherlands)
ConocoPhillips	—
Citigroup	Royal Bank of Scotland
IBM	—
American International Group	—
Hewlett-Packard	—
McKesson	—
U.S. Postal Service	Royal Mail Holdings
Verizon Communications	Vodafone
Home Depot	Kingfisher
Altria Group	British American Tobacco
Boeing	BAE Systems
AmerisourceBergen	Alliance Unichem
Bank of America Corp.	HSBC Holdings
Pfizer	GlaxoSmithKline
J.P. Morgan Chase & Co.	HBOS
Time Warner	News Corp. (Australia)
	Bertelsmann (Germany)
Johnson & Johnson	AstraZeneca
MetLife	Aviva
—	Standard Life Assurance
Safeway	J. Sainsbury
AT&T	BT
Microsoft	—
Allstate	Royal & Sun Alliance
Wells Fargo	Barclays
Lowe's	Kingfisher
Prudential Financial	Prudential
TIAA-CREF	Legal & General Group
Wachovia Corp.	Lloyds TSB Group
Duke Energy	Centrica
Alcoa	Corus Group
Coca-Cola	Diageo
3M	Wolseley
Cendant	Hilton Group
AMR	British Airways
McDonald's	Compass Group
Halliburton	—
Exelon	National Grid Transco
May Department Stores	Marks & Spencer
TJX	GUS
MBNA	Abbey National
AFLAC	Old Mutual
—	Unilever (Britain/ Netherlands)
—	Anglo American

A number of companies, either from the survey or already known to us, were selected for case studies, as interesting examples of the different ways in which history could be treated. For these companies a literature search was carried out, focusing on published company histories, both commissioned and critical accounts. Given the volume of publications involved, it was decided to apply the charting procedure set out in the proposal to a sample of twenty texts from the case studies.

From the survey of company web pages, annual reports, and directories, it is clear that nearly all companies produce historical accounts of themselves. Only five company web pages did not have historical content: Bank of America Corp., Time Warner, Cendent, News Corp., and TJX. Typically the historical content can be found within two or three clicks from the home page, often as a section within the 'About Us' pages. However, the quality of historical material is variable. Over fifty companies surveyed used a timeline to present history. Many of these timelines are technically sophisticated but difficult to navigate. They are clearly technologically driven. Our conclusion from the survey points to a consensus that there should be some reference to the history of a company in its web pages, but that web designers have yet to find a way to convey the *story* of a company's history, and not merely a chronological timeline. The survey indicates that a higher proportion of US companies report official publications or corporate museums, although over 90% of both US and UK companies provide information on archives (see Table 16.2).

Corporate history books

We examined twenty case studies published in the form of a book to explore the similarities and differences between those books constructed by academics in their roles as members of university institutions and those constructed by corporations and their suppliers. We have already referred to the commodification of history. We present three in this section and

Table 16.2. *Survey findings*

Companies by country	Commemoration	Official publication	Corporate museum (excluding virtual)	Archives
US companies (46)	26%	52%	30%	91%
UK companies (38)	30%	27%	11%	97%

then briefly discuss the question of whether these can be analysed as a dynamic genre (Frow 2005).

First, the Bertelsmann example represents the rarely mentioned dark side of history. German and non-German companies have increasingly been called to account for their conduct in Nazi Germany between 1933 and 1945. Revelations that Bertelsmann published anti-Semitic literature during the Nazi period came to light in 1998, when Bertelsmann was acquiring Random House. These revelations jarred with the company's image of corporate social responsibility and undermined the company legend, which alleged that it had an impeccable record and had even been shutdown for opposing the Nazis.

The company set up an Independent Historical Commission (IHC), led by Saul Friedländer, the renowned historian of Nazi anti-Semitism. Bertelsmann's Annual Report for 2002 made it clear that the company accepted the IHC's final report, *Bertelsmann in the Third Reich* (published by Bertelsmann in 2002), 'as the official corporate history'. This highlights a paradox, which is that in order to achieve credibility, companies such as Bertelsmann have to hire prominent historians who are inevitably identified with particular historiographical positions. Friedländer, for example, is identified with an 'intentionalist' interpretation of the Holocaust, whereas Mommsen, author of the official history of Volkswagen, is associated with a more controversial 'functionalist' interpretation that downplays the individual role of Hitler. In order to produce a convincing story, rather than a dry compilation of facts, commissioned historians have to include rhetorical elements that reflect their historiographical positions. By accepting the IHC report as 'the official corporate history', Bertelsmann could be construed as endorsing Friedländer's particular historiographical interpretation of the Holocaust and post-war German history.

Second, the monumental use of history is illustrated by the example of HSBC. Their use of history shows the wide spectrum of historical practices available to an organization. Since the 1980s, HSBC has moved its headquarters from Hong Kong to London and sought to consolidate its global strategy. In 1986 the chairman commissioned an economic historian, Frank King, to write *The History of The Hong Kong and Shanghai Banking Corporation*, published in four volumes by Cambridge University Press between 1987 and 1991. The research-based narrative thus gives the firm an official story validated by the academic credentials of its author, which the bank acquires metonymically. HSBC's past has also been inscribed in its physical space, through commissioning a History Wall for the entrance hall of its London headquarters. Composed of nearly 4,000 images from the Group's past, it 'combines the characteristics of a gallery, a library and a work of contemporary art'. HSBC's extensive use of history suggests the wide array of possibilities available to an organization seeking to utilize its history; from academic business history, through historical web pages, printed pamphlets, to public design work, the firm's past is materialized as heritage.

Third, the case of Microsoft is particularly interesting, especially for what it exemplifies in the American West Coast commodification of history. Numerous books were published about Bill Gates and Microsoft during the firm's first twenty-five years. Many were concerned with Gates's control over the organization, his ascent in business, and the legal quagmire in which the firm was caught throughout the 1990s—what was the secret of Microsoft's success? Given this attention, it is hardly surprising that the commemorative commissioned work, *Insideout: Microsoft—In Our Own Words* (2000), published for the firm's twenty-fifth anniversary, clearly states its revisionist intent:

Although several books have been written about our extraordinary history, there has never been a detailed account by the people who actually work here. So, over the past year, nearly 1,000 Microsoft employees around the world were interviewed and asked to tell the Microsoft story in their own words.

But *Insideout* does not give sources, the previous books alluded to are never named, it is published by Warner Books, hardly well known for historical works, it does not have an index, and the contents page is minimal. Almost all the text is composed of direct quotes from employees, who are listed alphabetically on the inside front and back covers. The book does not have a named author, but Kathleen Cain is credited with providing 'the book's editorial voice and commentary'. The Cain Creative website displays samples of their work, including *Insideout*, described as a 'coffee table book'. *Insideout* can be regarded as an example of corporate history of Microsoft, insofar as it commemorates an anniversary, although according to our charting procedure it is not a work of narrative history at all, and it has little in common with the dense, authoritative volumes produced by academic business historians.

The survey and case studies indicate that corporate history might be considered as a genre that encompasses a multiplicity of texts: published books—both commissioned and critical, academic tomes and glossy coffee table books—as well as web pages, annual reports, promotional pamphlets, and works of art. However, and so far, constructing a genre has proved awkward.

351

Episodic memory, social memory, and organizational mnemonics

Our research leads to the conclusion that the concept of organizational memory, as a branch of knowledge management, does not adequately explain the phenomenon of corporate history. This has broader implications for the evolution of business knowledge. As Nissley and Casey (2002) have pointed out, the dominant image of organizational memory is that of a 'static repository', which reflects a managerialist preoccupation with the 'utility' of information retrieved from organizational memory for 'organizational outcomes and performance' (Walsh and Ungson 1991). The 'storage metaphor' is borrowed from the literature on 'individual-level memory processes' and results in a naïve realist view of history, reflected in a preoccupation with the 'problem of inaccuracy', whereby 'a culture may carry an interpretation of why a decision was made but this received wisdom from the past may or may not be accurate' (Walsh and Ungson 1991: 68).

Organizational memory studies have operationalized the psychological concepts of procedural and declarative memory. Procedural memory stores motor and cognitive skills, e.g. for riding a bicycle, whereas declarative, or semantic memory, stores conceptual and factual knowledge. Procedural and semantic memory allow us to carry out activities without any subjective experience of remembering the required knowledge and skills. But organizational memory studies have neglected the psychological concept of episodic memory, which emphasizes the importance of the subjective experience of the rememberer, for whom the remembered past is essential for a sense of identity. Whether an experience is remembered depends very much on whether it is committed to memory in the form of a story, since 'Human beings are storytellers, and we tell stories about ourselves' (Schacter 2001: 31).

With few exceptions (e.g. Nissley and Casey 2002), organizational memory studies have also neglected social or collective memory, apart from ritual citations of Halbwachs (1992). Social memory studies (Olick 1999; Zerubavel 2003) are concerned with the social practices whereby the past is remembered and meaning is attached to it. Olick (1999: 335) draws upon Halbwachs to support a 'collectivist' approach to memory, which challenges 'the very idea of an individual memory. It is not just that we remember as members of groups, but that we constitute those groups and their members simultaneously in the act (thus re-member-ing)'. According to Zerubavel: 'Unlike psychology, sociology is particularly attentive to the social context within which we access the past, thereby reminding us that we actually remember much of what we do only as members of particular communities' (2003: 102). Zerubavel refers to these as 'mnemonic communities' (2003). There is scope for a new field of research, organizational mnemonics, studying organizations as mnemonic communities. Business history has also neglected the literature on history and memory, invented tradition, and the heritage debate. Besides, as Zerubavel (2003) points out, the study of collective memory is less about 'what actually happened in history' and more about 'how we *remember* it'. Zerubavel also notes that 'the social commemoration of "origins" is not confined in any way to nations or religious communities and is just as evident in the various anniversaries through which cities, colleges, and companies celebrate the historic moments when they were founded' (2003: 3). But social memory studies concentrate on ethnic groups and nations as mnemonic communities, neglecting business organizations.

One of our theoretical concerns has been to engage with the philosophy of history. Paul Ricoeur's monumental work, *Memory, History, Forgetting* (2004), appeared in English during the course of our project, and we are still reflecting on its significance. Ricoeur refers to 'the historical condition' of literate societies, in which 'we make history, and we make histories, because we are historical' (2004: 284). Given their influence in society, historical discourse concerning organizations seems unavoidable. By extension, we contend that organizations make history, and organizations make histories, because they are historical. This formulation avoids the managerial or functionalist insistence that in order to explain or justify history in organizations it is necessary to identify some managerial purpose that it serves.

We conclude that corporate history cannot be adequately explained, let alone promoted, in terms of knowledge management, as a store for procedural or declarative memory. Instead, it can be understood psychologically in terms of episodic memory and the importance of stories of the past for organization members' sense of identity. Sociologically, in terms of social memory studies, corporate history, consisting of regular commemorative events as well as texts such as web pages and commissioned histories, can be thought of as the social practices, organizational mnemonics, whereby organizations remember and constitute their identity. Our survey indicates that a higher proportion of US companies have commissioned histories and corporate museums. This could be interpreted to mean that they are better than British firms at managing their organizational memory in terms of remembering how to do things. But it is more likely to be because they pay more attention to managing their heritage as part of their corporate identity.

Conclusion

The call for a 'history turn' and 'history under cover' illustrates the spectrum in the use of history as corporate knowledge. The use of historical knowledge by corporations has become commodified, especially by leading American corporations. We argue for closing the gap between business school history and public history with a specifically historical orientation. Moreover, the historical content of corporate visitor attractions such as the HSBC wall of history reveals key features in the unfolding attention to history as a *necessary* form of corporate knowledge. Therefore, future research should develop the concept of organizational mnemonics. Storytelling and history have become key ingredients in the 'theatre of consumption' blending fact, fiction, faction, and fantasy by corporations seeking to neutralize detractors while enrolling appreciative support. Consequently, further research is required into the expanding role of consultants in creating corporate histories for public consumption. These consultants are increasingly providing the stories that corporate members utilize when talking to one another about their employers. The use of history in business schools should include much more attention to serious counterfactuals, which coherently connect initial conditions and outcomes. Superfactuals provide a strong challenge to the 'can do' tendency typical of business school knowledge.

Booth and Rowlinson (2006) argue for closing the gap between public history and business school history by responding to the 'history turn' with a specifically historically orientation. Thus, our future research priorities are to further examine the role of consultants in corporate history and to develop the concept of organizational mnemonics. Additionally, the historical content of corporate visitor attractions like the HSBC wall of history reveal key features of the unfolding attention to history as a necessary form of corporate knowledge. However, part of the challenge is to analytically narrate and explain how history has become a key ingredient in the 'theatre of consumption' blending fact, fiction, faction, and fantasy.

References

Abernathy, W. J. (1978). *The Productivity Dilemma: Roadblock to Innovation in the Automobile Industry*. Baltimore: Johns Hopkins University Press.

Aldrich, H. A. (1979). *Organizations and Environments*. Englewood, N.J.: Prentice Hall.

—— (1999). *Organizations Evolving*. London: Sage.

Booth, C., and Rowlinson, M. (2006). 'Management and Organizational History: Prospects'. *Management and Organizational History*, 1/1: 5–30.

—— Clark, P. A., Delahaye, A., Procter, S., and Rowlinson, M. (2005). 'La memoria social en las organizaciones. Los métodos que las organizaciones usan para recorder el pasado' [Social Memory in Organizations: Organizational Practices for Remembering the Past]. *Revista Empresa y Humanismo*, 9/2: 95–130.

—— —— —— —— —— (forthcoming). 'Scenarios, Counterfactuals and Alternate Histories: Three Types of Modal Narrative', submitted to *Futures*, under review.

Campbell, D. T. (1965). 'Variation and Selective Retention in Social-Cultural Evolution', in H. R. Barringer, G. I. Blanksten, and R. Mack (eds.), *Social Change in Developing Areas*. Cambridge, Mass.: Schenkman.

Carson, P. P., and Carson, K. D. (2003). 'An Exploration of the Importance of History to Managers: The Meaningful, Manipulative, and Memorable Uses of Milestones'. *Organizational Dynamics*, 32/3: 286–308.

Chandler, A. D. (1962). *Strategy and Structure*. Cambridge, Mass.: MIT Press.

Clark, P. A. (2000). *Organisations in Action: Competition between Contexts*. London: Routledge.

—— (2005). 'America's Market Polity of Knowledge and Ferguson's Struggling Colossus'. *Prometheus*, 17/1: 83–99.

—— (2006). 'Superfactuals, Structural Repertoires and Productive Units: Explaining the Evolution of the British Auto Industry'. *Competition and Change*, 10/4: 397–414.

—— and Rowlinson, M. (2004). 'The Treatment of History in Organization Studies: Toward an "Historic Turn"?' *Business History*, 46/3: 331–52.

—— and Todeva, E. (2006). 'Unmasking Americanization: De Grazia's Irresistible Market Empire Advancing through Twentieth Century Europe'. *Prometheus*, 24/1: 101–15.

—— Booth, C., Delahaye, A., Procter, S., and Rowlinson, M. (2007). 'Project Hindsight: Exploring Necessity and Possibility in Cycles of Structuration and Co-Evolution'. *Technology Analysis and Strategic Management*, 19/1: 1–15.

Crozier, M. (1964). *The Bureaucratic Phenomenon*. Chicago: University of Chicago Press.

Ferguson, N. (2000). *The House of Rothschild: The World's Banker, 1848–1998*. London: Penguin.

Frow, J. (2005). *Genre*. London: Routledge.

Halbwachs, M. (1992). *On Collective Memory*. Chicago: University of Chicago Press.

Lowenthal, D. (1985). *The Past is a Foreign Country*. Cambridge: Cambridge University Press.

Maielli, G. (2006). 'History under Cover'. *Competition and Change*, 10/4: 320–32.

Martin, J. (1992). *Cultures in Organizations: Three Perspectives*. Oxford: Oxford University Press.

Nissley, N., and Casey, A. (2002). 'The Politics of the Exhibition: Viewing Corporate Museums through the Paradigmatic Lens of Organizational Memory'. *British Journal of Management*, 13 (Special Issue).

Olick, J. K. (1999). 'Collective Memory: Two Cultures'. *Sociological Theory*, 17/3: 333–48.

Perrow, C. A. (1967). 'A Framework for the Comparative Analysis of Organizations'. *American Sociological Review*, 32: 194–208.

Pettigrew, A. M. (1985). *The Awakening Giant: Continuity and Change in ICI*. Oxford: Blackwell.

Pugh, D. S., and Hickson, D. J. (1976). *The Aston Program*. London: Saxon House.

Ricoeur, P. (2004). *Memory, History, Forgetting*. Chicago: University of Chicago Press.

Rogers, E. M. (2003 [1962]). *The Diffusion of Innovations*. New York: Free Press.

Schacter, D. L. (2001). *The Seven Sins of Memory: How the Mind Forgets and Remembers*. Boston: Houghton Mifflin.

Tannenbaum, A. S. (1974). *Hierarchy in Organizations: An International Comparison*. New York: Jossey Bass.

Tetlock, P. E., and Belkin, A. (1996). *Counterfactual Thought Experiments in World Politics: Logical, Methodological, and Psychological Perspectives*. Princeton: Princeton University Press.

Walsh, J. P., and Ungson, G. R. (1991). 'Organizational Memory'. *Academy of Management Review*, 16/1: 57–91.

Weick, K. E. (1969). *The Social Psychology of Organizing*. Reading, Mass.: Addison-Wesley.

—— (1995). *Sensemaking in Organizations*. London: Sage.

Whipp, R., and Clark, P. A. (1986). *Innovation and the Auto Industry: Product, Process and Work Organization*. London: Pinter.

Zerubavel, E. (2003). *Time Maps: Collective Memory and the Social Shape of the Past*. Chicago: University of Chicago Press.

17

Conclusions

It is risky to generalize too far about a series of studies that ranges so widely across different settings and topics. In surveying the contribution made by preceding chapters, though, it seems safe to claim that they demonstrate the extraordinarily multifaceted nature of knowledge and learning in a business context. Previous studies have rather emphasized the formation and application of particular forms of knowledge, be it through organizational learning, the scientific knowledge produced by R&D functions, or the specialist expertise of engineers and other professional groups. The much richer view that the preceding chapters give us is in many cases testimony to the methodological choices made by their authors. In a number of these chapters, the micro-level or multi-level approach adopted sees knowledge as essentially 'socially constructed' (Berger and Luckmann 1967); not so much an input to or output from firms, but rather emerging from the way people work together in different business contexts, both to develop shared understandings of their work and to create and absorb new ideas about it.

In addition to emphasizing the multifaceted qualities of knowledge and learning, the EBK studies highlight the interdependency between different forms of knowledge. For example, as several of the previous chapters have shown, the innovation process within an advanced industrial economy like the United Kingdom is not just about exploiting science and technology. Just as important is the management and organizational knowledge that creates the routines, systems, and strategies that sustain this process of innovation and the wider network of relationships that make it successful. Such interdependency is addressed by some writers through the concept of 'complementary assets' (Teece 1986). This highlights the benefits to be gained from inter-organizational collaboration. On the other hand, as the preceding chapters have shown, recognizing the interdependency between different forms of knowledge also helps to explain some of the important constraints on the development of business. Chapter 2, for instance, suggested that small firms often lack the organizational capabilities that would allow them to escape from a constant round of fire-fighting and reacting to events.

Highlighting this kind of interdependency may suggest a new perspective on the evolution of firms, which focuses more on the interplay between different forms of knowledge over time. This interplay has previously been debated in terms of the 'absorptive capacity' of the firm—that is, prior knowledge enabling the absorption of new knowledge within a particular field (Cohen and Levinthal 1990). However, as other writers have noted, different forms of knowledge may also compete, or come to substitute for each other over time, as the source of the firm's competitive advantage (e.g. Haas and Hansen 2005).

Although issues of strategy and competitive advantage have not been a central feature of many of the studies presented here, there is little doubt that the contribution of knowledge and learning to practice, and hence individual, group, and ultimately business performance, is a major concern. As several chapters have suggested implicitly, and Chapters 14 and 15 more explicitly, the question of the business value of knowledge is rarely completely absent from these studies. In some ways, the pervasiveness of this focus on business performance really demonstrates the power of the capitalist business enterprise as an engine for creating, sharing, and exploiting knowledge. The flexibility of the enterprise form certainly enables it to overcome established institutional boundaries between science, art, and business. It even allows the business enterprise to reach into new areas of social critique and comment, with domains such as corporate social responsibility and business history, as described in Chapters 12 and 16, being eventually translated into growth opportunities.

Implications for policy and practice

This recognition of the role of the firm in transforming multiple sources of knowledge into economic value is at the heart of policy makers' interest in the 'Knowledge Economy'. Under this banner, governments and business executives are aiming to extend the transformative power of business enterprise into new domains. In a UK Government White Paper in 1998, for example, the knowledge economy was defined as 'one in which the generation and exploitation of knowledge has come to play the predominant part in the creation of wealth. It is not simply about pushing back the frontiers of knowledge; it is also about the most effective use and exploitation of all types of knowledge in all manner of economic activity' (DTI Competitiveness White Paper 1998).

The Lambert Review, commissioned by the UK Government, sought to translate these ideas about the knowledge economy into practical policy (Lambert 2003). It outlined measures to improve 'knowledge transfer' between UK universities and business so as to enhance the UK's national competitiveness. As such, it reflected a much wider set of policy assumptions on the part not only of the UK government but of many other governments in Europe and worldwide. Key to these assumptions is the view that the greatest challenge for the knowledge economy lies in improving the production and transfer of knowledge. This leads, as with the Lambert Review, to an emphasis on R&D activity and mechanisms that improve the exploitation of science and technology.

Now, the studies of business knowledge presented here are not concerned, for the most part, with these wider macroeconomic debates. However, the focus that they have generally adopted—viewing knowledge and learning as an integral part of business life and not simply an output from R&D—is supported by alternative perspectives on the knowledge economy, which question the government's emphasis on science and technology. Leadbeater, for example, sees the knowledge economy label as 'not just a description of high tech industries . . . (but as) . . . a set of new sources of competitive advantage which can apply to all sectors, all companies and all regions, from agriculture, and retailing to software and biotechnology' (Leadbeater 2000: 5).

This alternative view of the knowledge economy is more appropriate to both the scope and findings of the work presented here. For one, the studies described here repeatedly question the concept of 'knowledge transfer' as a useful model for grasping the movement of knowledge across contexts. This is addressed directly in Chapter 11, for example, which questions the proposition that consultants transfer knowledge to firms. Similarly, Chapter 5 finds little evidence of the transfer of research-based knowledge from business schools to practitioners. Even the study of brokering in high-tech start-ups, outlined in Chapter 6, makes the argument that this brokering activity is intertwined with aspects of social structure in terms of the different networks that brokers are able to access. These studies are arguing, in part, that the sharing of knowledge between different communities is more complicated than a linear transfer model would suggest. Features of the relationship between those communities, such as the extent to which one can challenge the other, are important in guiding the scope and ultimate effect of their interactions. Equally, other studies underline the problem of knowledge interdependency; that sharing knowledge—as, for instance, between biotech firms and big pharmaceutical corporations in Chapter 8—depends on having supportive organizational capabilities in place.

More generally, the majority of studies question the knowledge transfer model indirectly. They do this, as noted in the Introduction, by highlighting the embeddedness of knowledge in organizational and institutional contexts. Thus, Chapter 4 suggests that organizational capabilities emerge out of the particular contexts in which firms are operating. Similarly, the study of the film industry in Chapter 7 found that the different institutional contexts of the United Kingdom and United States exerted a significant influence upon the development of film project. For example, the greater reputational impact of critical acclaim in the United Kingdom encouraged a very different approach to the selection of project members.

The implications of this kind of analysis for policy and practice seem to be twofold. First, they suggest that focusing narrowly on knowledge production and transfer is not only to gloss over important forms of knowledge (management and organizational knowledge particularly) but also ignores the problem of contextual embeddedness. The latter is key to explaining why knowledge does not flow readily even in a knowledge economy. The corollary to this, however, is that policy and practice needs to be more attuned to the processes that enable knowledge to be embedded and disembedded across contexts. Examples of these processes were highlighted in the Introduction and have been described in more detail in the succeeding chapters. They include not only the sharing of knowledge among groups but also the integration of knowledge between different groups, as well as different ways of representing knowledge. All of these processes are closely intertwined with the development of collaboration between groups, firms, and even across institutions. Importantly, these processes can be seen as operating at multiple levels of analysis. Thus, in the preceding chapters we read that the processes for representing knowledge range from the micro-level use of artefacts in the design process (Chapter 9), and in signalling trust between innovators and inventors (Chapter 10), to meta-representations of knowledge itself, as reflected in Chapters 14 and 15 and their accounts of intangible assets.

Second, this analysis suggests that social science can make an important contribution to wider debates on the knowledge economy by developing a better understanding of these processes. The need for such an understanding has already been highlighted by Manuel Castells, whose work suggests that it is crucial to grasp the changes associated with the knowledge economy as a shift in society and not simply in the economy alone (Castells 1996). Castells argues that the true test of a knowledge society is not the centrality of knowledge per se—knowledge, as he notes, has always been central to productive activity. What is distinctive about the knowledge society is rather what we are now able to do with knowledge.

Applying this insight to the business domain suggests that a narrow focus on the production and transfer of knowledge is misplaced because it fails to grasp those very processes and mechanisms that give firms their capacity to process knowledge—that is, to embed and disembed it across different contexts. In contrast, the research studies described in this book have sought to unpack these processes by focusing on the ways in which knowledge is shared, integrated, and represented. As such, they make a serious contribution to our understanding of the evolution of business knowledge. At the same time, they stand as an important corrective to some of the assumptions behind the rhetoric of the knowledge economy.

References

Berger, P., and Luckmann, T. (1967). *The Social Construction of Reality: A Treatise in the Sociology of Knowledge*. New York: Doubleday Anchor Books.

Castells, M. (1996). *The Rise of the Network Society*. Oxford: Blackwell.

Cohen, W. M., and Levinthal, D. A. (1990). 'Absorptive-Capacity—A New Perspective on Learning and Innovation'. *Administrative Science Quarterly*, 35/1: 128–52.

Haas, M. R., and Hansen, M. T. (2005). 'When Using Knowledge Can Hurt Performance: The Value of Organizational Capabilities in a Management Consulting Company'. *Strategic Management Journal*, 26/1: 1–24.

Lambert, R. (2003). *Lambert Review of Business–University Collaboration*. London: HMSO.

Leadbeater, C. (2000). *New Measures for the New Economy*. London: Centre for Business Performance.

Teece, D. J. (1986). 'Profiting from Technological Innovation—Implications for Integration, Collaboration, Licensing and Public-Policy'. *Research Policy*, 15/6: 285–305.

Index

Note: page numbers in *italic* indicate figures and tables.